D1133174

$15

The County Books Series

GENERAL EDITOR: BRIAN VESEY-FITZGERALD

BUCKINGHAMSHIRE

THE COUNTY BOOKS SERIES

A series comprising 57 volumes. It covers every county in England, and there will be five books on Scotland, two on Ireland, two on the Hebrides, and one each on Orkney, Shetland, Wales, the Isle of Man, and the Channel Islands.

THE FOLLOWING TWENTY VOLUMES
HAVE NOW BEEN PUBLISHED

PLEASE WRITE TO THE PUBLISHERS
FOR FULL DESCRIPTIVE PROSPECTUS

BUCKINGHAMSHIRE

by

ALISON UTTLEY

Illustrated and with a Map

London
Robert Hale Limited
18 Bedford Square W.C.1

First published 1950

PRINTED IN GREAT BRITAIN
BY WESTERN PRINTING SERVICES LTD., BRISTOL

CONTENTS

CONTENTS

ILLUSTRATIONS

ACKNOWLEDGMENTS

The illustrations above, numbered 10, 11, 34, 36, 37, 41, 42, 46, 47, 48 are reproduced from photographs by the Norman Foster Studio of Studham; 14, 15, 29, 32, 33, 35, 45 by Mr Reece Winstone, A.R.P.S., of Bristol; 2, 6, 9, 17, 26 by Mr Ronald Goodearl of High Wycombe; 3, 20, 43, 49 by Humphrey and Vera Joel of Radlett; 1, 19, 22 by Mr E. S. B. Elcome of Woking; 16 by Mr E. W. Tattersall of St Albans; 30 by 'The Times'; and 7 by 'The Furnishing World.'

The remaining seventeen illustrations are reproduced from photographs supplied by Mr Staniland Pugh of Amersham.

viii

FOREWORD

W H E N I was asked to write about Buckinghamshire I hesitated, for many have written on this county, people who have a deep knowledge of its geology, its archæology, and its history, and there is a whole literature of the Chilterns, and guide-books without end. It seemed to me that there would be nothing left to say after all the experts had explored the ground. Then, considering it further, I thought of the countrymen to whom I have talked, who speak freely because they know I understand their language, and they feel that I am not a stranger. Perhaps I could add to the store of information something that has been left unsaid, and this book is the result.

As I have wandered about, looking here and there at the homely little villages, peering into the hedgerows, standing at the gates, I have taken something for myself from this most lovely county, and so I present a kind of anthology. All the things I love are here, the tales I have heard, in field and hamlet, in workshop and barn, the things I have seen. For this county of Buckinghamshire is the epitome of England, and the way of living is that of country people, and I have fallen in love with its beauty and changelessness.

In this anthology are the small churches, which are still the centre of village life. Whether people go to chapel or nowhere at all, they feel that the church is their own possession, and rightly so. In the churchyard are the graves of their ancestors. It is their own acre. They expect the parson to visit them and to be a friend, who will share their sorrows and their joys. So I have found that the church is very important as part of village life, as it has always been.

There are the little cottages which are often like fairy-tales, and a few great houses, whose life is bound up with the village, the farms, the orchards and fields, but always I have chosen the small before the important, the cottage before the hall, the unknown people before the famous, the common flowers of the hedges and fields before the rare and curious orchis of the woods.

It is an individual choice, and I have gathered together the things that have delighted me on my journeys, and in my life in this adopted county of mine. For a countryman is at home in any county. There are likenesses on every hand—farm implements, the shapes of stacks, the fields, the cattle, and the talk of the country people.

So I have collected pictures, and once it was a piebald mare and her foal grazing by the pool of ice-blue water at Stoke Mandeville under a dazzling blue sky of winter; and next it was an old red brick barn, ivy-covered, with a little cupola on the roof, by the roadside; then it was a chalk pit with a coloured tapestry of flowers, blue and magenta milk-wort, yellow rock-rose, purple thyme, and tiny blue scabious. Sometimes it was a cottage with golden thatch, and windows peeping from straw brows, or a bunch of wheat ears on a rick of corn, a smooth round rick, built by an architect without pencil or compasses, or it may have been an old man slashing the hedge, weaving it into a work of art, or a herd of Friesian cattle, or a gipsy caravan with the dark-skinned women making their wooden flowers—all of these make up the pictures.

I have such a cargo of memories, I feel like an Elizabethan returning from an adventurous voyage, for life is warm if you enter into its harmony and if you accept the companionship it offers, but I have had to omit some of the little villages which I know well and love.

I am well aware that many of the cottages are inconvenient by modern standards, but so are many modern houses. The cottages lack water laid on from the main, and electricity, and the modern houses lack character and warmth. All my young days were spent in the country with none of the amenities, and we never missed them. Even when I returned home from London I was enchanted afresh by the soft glow of candlelight, the warmth of the open fires, the delight of a bath of hot rainwater, the sweetness of the taste of water from a spring.

There is an intense pride in the beauty of their county among Bucks people. Over and over again I have been told, "I've heard this is the prettiest county in England."

Again, there is a love and a feeling for simple things, the bit

of hand-made lace, a piece of wood-carving, some good thatching and hedging, a tool, a Windsor chair—for this is a county of
craftsmen. It is a happy county, with men who have a good way
of talking.

A thatcher remarked, "Lads nowadays is always wanting
summut fresh, they aren't content without they're driving a tractor. As for me, I'm as happy as all the birds in the air." A shepherd said he was as happy as the birds in the wood. An old
Bucks labourer I know says he has had a grand life.

I am especially indebted to certain country people who have
shared my enthusiasms. Among them I include Mr Jack Norris
of Beaconsfield, an old Bucks countryman, who tells me tales,
and makes wheat tassels and whistle pipes for me; the Rev. C.
Norman White of Ellesborough, who is deeply interested in
every aspect of the county in which he was born; Mr Stephen
Capp of Whitchurch, an old musician, self-taught, and a wheelwright; Mr E. Lambourne of North Marston, who knows his
countryside minutely; Mr Cheshire, who remembers many tales.
I would like to thank the Verneys of Claydon, who shared their
store of historical memories with me; Lady Carlile of Gayhurst;
Mr J. F. Roxburgh of Stowe School; Miss Palmer of Thornborough, who made lace for me with her nimble fingers; Mr
Goodchild of Naphill, a fine craftsman and a wise countryman;
and all the kind people who have shared this book.

I wish to thank Miss Beattie of the Aylesbury Library; Miss
Baker of the Bucks Archæological Society; Gwladys Llewellyn
who read the proofs; Katharine Sibbring, my secretary; Aileen
Wardle who explored some places with me. Lastly I thank my
son, John C. T. Uttley, who drove through winter's snows and
spring storms to the remote little villages which captured our
hearts with their quiet beauty.

INTRODUCTION

BUCKINGHAMSHIRE is this green strip of England, long and narrow, squeezed between more important neighbours, and nicknamed affectionately "Leafy Bucks" by the Londoner who discovers it only a score of miles away from his city. It embraces some of the loveliest, unspoilt country in England, for it has many secret and private charms which it only reveals to those who accept it and regard it with country eyes.

The origin of the name of the county is obscure. Some say it is derived from the Saxon *boc*, *buccen*, meaning beech trees, others that it comes from *buccen* meaning the wild buck, others again that it is the name of the Saxon tribe of Bucci who invaded England and wandered to this land. Antlered buck, flecked and shadowed by the beech trees around the green glades, or Saxon tribe walking the Icknield Way, the choice is an alluring one.

The county runs roughly north to south, and the Chiltern Hills cut it like a curving scimitar. They give it a character of its own, and preserve it from too rapid change. These chalk hills of about fifty-two miles long stretch from north-east to southwest, from Dunstable in Bedfordshire, reaching to the bluff of Ivinghoe, sweeping south through Wendover and Princes Risborough, bending towards the Thames and going through Berkshire to Wiltshire. They never rise higher than 850 feet, but the abruptness of their slopes on one side and the gentle fall on the other give the impression of much greater altitude. Especially is this noticeable where the Chilterns overlook the Plain of Aylesbury, that great vale of undulating pasture land, with elms growing tall in the field borders, with rich grass and cornland making a patchwork of golden and green fading to the deep blue of the horizon. Around Whaddon Chase the ground rises to the woods, and then it drops to the northern valleys of Ouse and Ousel.

These chalk hills are clothed in soft turf; they are sprinkled with downland flowers and wooded with beech trees. The scars on their sides, where the chalk peers through, are dazzling white, and the leaves of the whitebeams, rustling in the wind on the hills, carry on this flashing brightness. This colour contrast is characteristic of the Chilterns, and one finds oneself seeking for the pattern of white on green, and discovering it in a flock of sheep feeding on the uplands, or a hedge veiled in creamy tufts of old man's beard, a hawthorn in full blossom of may, or a narrow track worn in the slopes, climbing steeply like a pathway of summer snow.

It is this range of hills which keeps Buckinghamshire more remote than many counties. There are three gaps in the hills from the London side to the Vale of Aylesbury, and through these the traffic moves. One is that taken by the Roman road, Akeman Street, which goes through Aylesbury. Along this course runs the Grand Union Canal, that delightful waterway which moves quietly to appear in odd places like a familiar friend who greets you. This way is taken by the old London and North Western Railway.

The second gap runs through Wendover, between the spurs of the Chilterns, along the valley of the Misbourne, through Amersham and the Chalfonts to Uxbridge. This also carries a railway line, the old Great Central.

The third crosses the Chilterns between the hills of White-leaf and Bledlow Ridge, at Princes Risborough, and this is the main road that goes through the Wycombe Valley, turning at the fork of West Wycombe. This again is the track of a railway, a country railway which joins the villages from Aylesbury to High Wycombe, and then goes on through Beaconsfield to London.

Along these three ways moves the traffic of road and rail, but between the routes are many valleys cut into the hills. There is hidden away a life secluded and rich, undisturbed by mass-production, a simple way of living with which country people feel at home and at peace. There is nurtured the strength and courage which is carried to far countries in time of war.

Buckinghamshire has been a secluded county, unknown to the great majority, until recently, when the new railway was made, the invasion of townsmen seeking a country home began, and new interests were taken in country ways of living. Consequently it has kept much of its original beauty and simplicity in the small villages where agricultural pursuits are followed as in the old days. Methods may change but the central core of hard work is the same, whether men are driving a combine-harvester, or are reaping by hand the wet barley.

"I've been brought up to farming, my father before me, and I can't change to anything else," said a farmer, struggling with the weather and losses of crops, and I understood.

Industries are chiefly in the south, concentrated at High Wycombe and Slough, but there are large industries on the north-east borders. Slough is a model of an industrial town, with well-designed factories and their amenities, playing fields and social centre. To one who knows the industrial towns of northern England, this is a clean hive in a pleasant garden. Whether it has a character of its own, whether the people who live there are devoted to it as men and women love the dark towns of Lancashire, I do not know. Then there is High Wycombe, Chepping Wycombe until lately, an ancient and once beautiful market town which has grown to an immense size, with factories and mills spreading themselves, and little new houses running up the slopes into the adjacent valleys. This town has individuality which can instantly be felt as one enters it.

Wolverton with its great railway works and printing works is important in the north of the county; Fenny Stratford with its brush and timber factories, Newport Pagnell with its motor works, and Bletchley the big junction, are the chief manufacturing towns. Aylesbury, the capital of the county, has printing works and cheese and milk factories and ironworks. All these places are concentrated, and the country around them is still beautiful. Slough has Eton and Windsor near, High Wycombe has its woods crowning the hills. Wolverton has villages of charm, and Aylesbury has its own lovely Vale. For Buckinghamshire is at heart an agricultural county, and the industries are mainly those which have developed from the land. The furniture trade of High Wycombe originated in the beech woods. Aylesbury is the centre of the farming world.

This county is divided into South and North Bucks, with no arbitrary line of demarcation, but there is a distinct change as one goes from south to north. Country people say the north is the true Bucks, because there has been little influx from the towns, and the railways are less adequate, so the ways of the villages are simpler. My own impression of the difference is that South Bucks is more aware of itself and its show places, with many strangers living within its bounds, while North Bucks, roughly north of Aylesbury, is unselfconscious, proud of its heritage, but taking it for granted.

South Bucks is perhaps more picturesque, with its woods of lacy-boughed beech trees, its deep lanes with flower-filled banks, its charming cottages, and its little towns which are perfections of beauty. Amersham's High Street, Beaconsfield's wide road of Georgian houses, Denham's green loveliness, Marlow and the river, each place has distinction, but North Bucks has something else. There is a depth in its beauty, a strength in its thick-walled thatched cottages, a feeling of security and warmth of heart.

For North Bucks is a homely, pastoral countryside, with river scenery and wide fields and great farms. The Ouse loops round upon itself at Olney, it winds through the meadows close to Buckingham, and runs past Water Stratford with its ancient church. Cows in the deep grass of water-meadows, shallow waters with lily cups and yellow flags and dragon-flies, are part of this placid, quiet scene. The warm red brick houses of the south often give way to stone, but the thatch of these old dwellings, and the way the cottages seem to grow out of the earth itself, is a happy sight. The people who live there have always lived there, and although change is coming rapidly, it will take longer to reach the north.

There is, too, the smell of the places. Each county has its own distinctive aroma. The smell of France when one comes off the steamer and walks on the quay at Dieppe, the smell of Scotland as one goes over the border, and London as one arrives at Marylebone—all have their own peculiar delights. Derbyshire has the strong and pervading smell of limestone and wet rocks and rivers. Westmorland has the fragrance of bog myrtle, of the lakes and fells.

So Buckinghamshire smells sweetly of beech leaves and cherry wood. When I first came to live in the county I was deeply aware of the delicate scent of the air. I breathed in the odours and tried to disentangle the many woven fragrances. Everywhere I could smell the sweetness, and I think the main source is the beech woods, although flower scents are intermingled.

Inside, the cottages have that well-known country smell which has clung to them for generations, wood-smoke, dried herbs, lavender, and sweet stuffiness. In spring there is the scent of cherry blossom from the countless orchards and the wildings in the woods. In winter the odours seem to rise from the wet tree trunks of cherry, beech, and silver birch, ravishing the senses on certain days.

When I cross the invisible border to North Bucks, I am again aware of the smell. It is rich and strong, not delicate and alluring as in South Bucks, but more heart-stirring. It is the smell of farmhouses and firesides and cattle and good earth. It is the smell of parlours and geraniums and old furniture.

"Can you smell the goodness of North Bucks now?" asked a country friend, as he sniffed the air at East Claydon. "As soon as you get near North Marston you get this lovely smell. There's nothing so good on earth as this smell of cornland and cattle and farmhouses."

The colours of Buckinghamshire are golden, tawny, from the beech trees in autumn to the rosy old red brick cottages and farms. White belongs to the Chiltern Hills, the blackthorn, and cherry foaming in woods and orchards, but red madder, crimson, rose pink, are the colours of the houses, of brambles, of willow-herb, of bryony, of spindleberry and cherry leaves in October.

The distant woods, piled one above another, as seen from Penn, or from the Chiltern heights, are soft blue, like the violets under the hedge, and in winter the snow shadows are intensely blue, even in bright sunlight, and the snow when it lies on the ground of the cherry orchards is a lilac blue of such dazzling quality it seems magical as a fairy-tale.

By the roadsides in the grassy verges are yellow toad-flax, which country children call wild snapdragon, marjoram with rosy-purple blossoms, yellow mullein with its purple eye and flannel leaves, and the slender beautiful flowers of John-go-to-bed-at-noon. In a hedgerow I found red cowslips among the yellow ones.

Down a lane one August Bank Holiday I met a procession

shining gold and yellow, so that at first as I saw it glittering in the evening light, I thought it was a circus. Five great wagons, newly painted yellow and red, and five great horses, with decorated manes, ribbon-strung and laced, tails plaited and ribboned, horse-brasses sparkling and jingling, bells ringing, short straw tassels nodding, men smiling and waving their long curling whips as they went slowly home from a horse show.

None of them had won a prize, but they walked along the narrow leafy lane in the evening sunlight like gods, with flecks of gold dust and silver light dripping from the wet trees upon the harness and the shining flanks of the horses, and the yellow carts.

It is easy to escape from the noise and bustle of towns like High Wycombe and Aylesbury, and in a few minutes to enter a field or wood where time seems to stand still and the present to be eternal. The air is full of music of robins and wrens and the bell-noted tits, and the shadows that move among the tree trunks might be those of fauns and nymphs. There is always movement in woods, and the shapes that flit to and fro are transparent ones, they are reflections from the leaves and glittering raindrops, and the blue shades of holly.

In South Bucks the beech trees are the glory of the countryside. In spring the pale green veined leaves, downy with silver hairs, catch the sunlight in their transparency, and the ground is flecked with discs of gold among the shadows. In summer when the woods are quieter, except for the cooing of doves and the harsh sudden shriek of jays, the great beech trees stand expectantly waiting, waiting, and their shade forbids the flowers to grow.

Then comes autumn, with its jubilant colour, the gold and copper red of the leaves, and the swinging of the branches, and the fall of the beech-mast, with the sweet-tasting nuts. In winter the trees are at their best, for the earth is carpeted with the tawny-rose leaves, from which the tree trunks rise in silver-grey columns. Sunlight, unobstructed by foliage, drops on their long outstretched grey arms, on their noble bodies, with intricate shadows and flash of light through the lace-like twigs. Then one sees a blue mist in the woods, so blue that it sometimes looks like a haze of hyacinths growing there. On the tree trunks are emerald-green streaks, where rain has run. Snow bands the trunks in dazzling symmetrical wreaths. There is infinite variety and beauty which changes every day in a beech wood in winter, and in Buckinghamshire one can gaze to one's heart's content at this daily miracle of nature's craft.

It is a windy county, but I once imagined it would be stuffy and calm. The prevailing wind is south-west, and this strong wind sweeps across England with nothing to stop it. One winter when a gale raged for several days, and I expected my roof to be carried away, I found my windows flecked white with salt. It was rime carried across the whole breadth of the land from the sea. My little bay trees, brought carefully here from the northern garden, died and shrivelled up in the frost and cold winds, and I revised my ideas about the warm south. Though many new houses have been built and new towns have sprung up, they are often concealed in narrow deep valleys or hidden by woods, and less harm is done to the Buckinghamshire landscape. I remember when I first came to live in the county I was taken to a woodland path, Mill Wood on the edge of the Beaconsfield plateau, and shown the Wooburn and Loudwater valley with the paper works and screw works down below in the hollow. They follow the line of the winding vale, concealed from the next valley and topped by the beech woods.

"This is how factories should be built," I was told. "Even the tall chimneys are hidden, and the land around is unspoilt."

We walked among the silver birches and bluebells, the golden broom and the hollies of that upland wood, and we noticed narrow tracks leading down to the valley through the bracken, and then came children to play in this green land of flowers close to their small homes.

Only along the borders outside certain towns there is definite ugliness, which could easily be changed. When new houses are built on the crest of a hill, to stand like teeth against the sky, or when white flat-roofed dwellings are hung out on a wooded slope, to be streaked with damp in our wet climate, or when a factory of grim aspect, a relic of war days, is left in a green meadow, there is real harm done to our countryside.

These unsightly sores are happily rare in the county which has a sense of its own comeliness. The houses seldom fill the valleys to overflowing, except at High Wycombe. There the hills which top the valleys and the woods which sweep across them keep their own dominance.

Nature is so lavish in this rich little county she will cover up unsightly places, throwing wild marjoram, rose-bay willow herb, scabious, and wild thyme over the rubbish heaps and upon the grubbed-up earth, especially if it is a chalk cutting. But nature will not hide the great wooden hoardings, many of which disfigure the road from High Wycombe to Beaconsfield. They make a cacophony as they shriek out their wares to the passing cars.

Ancient roads and tracks cut across the county, and thousands of little footpaths, each marked by a finger-post, divide the land. These little green pathways, leading round the edges of cornfields, into thickets of furze, through jungles of woodland, seem to be the roads to fairylands, lost in a green world. The real broad roads are exciting enough for the imaginative, who can people them with travellers, cloaked and hooded—early Britons and Romans, Danes and Saxons—through the centuries. They are roads of great antiquity, used by man before history was written.

I shall never forget walking up the steep road near Ellesborough Church, and meeting a stranger who stopped me.

"Do you know what road you are now walking on? It is the Icknield Way," said he.

He spoke with a strong feeling for antiquity, a Bucks countryman who was well aware of his county's exciting history. Yes, I knew I was on the Icknield Way, the ancient trackway of prehistoric man, and we stayed and talked together and he told me many things about the countryside.

The Icknield Way runs from east to west, following the line of the Chilterns close to the summit, where it would be dry and safe from robbers. For there is an outlook over the valleys from the Way. The summits of the hills were dense thickets, and the valleys were swamps in prehistoric days. The old road ran along the edge of the chalk belt high on the hills, below the ridge line but above the level of the springs. This Way runs near Ivinghoe Beacon, and there a modern highway at Edlesborough has taken to itself the ancient track, choosing it as the better road. It switchbacks along, dividing the chalk uplands from the richer pasture ground, and at a low level there is another track, the Lower Icknield Way, which was probably an easier path for good-weather days. The Upper Icknield Way goes through Wendover Gap, around the curving hillside, and it swings up and down to dips and hills, with glorious trees by its side and pasture and cornland rolling away from below the road. It runs through Ellesborough, and round the bend by Kimble, where there is a headland about which it turns. Then it goes to Monks Risborough, when it starts uphill passing under Whiteleaf Cross, and down again, across to Bledlow Ridge.

This early British road was later used by the Romans and the portion that goes in the valley is now a modern road, as at Ellesborough and Monks Risborough. Before the Roman occupation the Way was used for movements from east to west, for carrying goods, for travelling, for traders and fighting men.

It curves round the land, this grassy track with bushes of the wayfaring tree, with whitebeam and traveller's-joy, with little purple bell-flower and yellow rock-rose and wild thyme by its side. Low trees of box and juniper grow near it on the slopes.

The Roman Road, Akeman Street, passes through Buckinghamshire at Waddesdon, the model village on the Rothschild estate, and it goes through Aylesbury to Aston Clinton, and soon after it leaves the county. At Aston Clinton a Roman amphora was found.

Watling Street runs through the north of Bucks, through Stony Stratford, Fenny Stratford, and Little Brickhill, where there was once the Roman station of Magiovintum. All traces of the road structure are lost under the turnpike, which is now a roaring highway.

Buckinghamshire has the Thames itself on the southern boundary, with several little rivers running into it. The Chess, a lovely stream with watercress beds, is one of these, and the Misbourne, a small river which appears and disappears like a water-kelpie, is another. Once I hunted in vain for its waters, and it seemed to have gone completely, through the digging of wells in its vicinity, but lately it has returned.

There is the Wye, which rises in West Wycombe, flows through High Wycombe, Loudwater, and Wooburn, and works very hard for its living among the numerous mills on its banks. The Thame, a beautiful river, waters the Vale of Aylesbury.

In the north of Bucks the famous river is the Ouse, slow-moving, flooding the land in winter, carrying water-lilies and swans on its surface in summer, as it passes through fields and under many low little bridges. The Ouzel and the Lovat also water the land in North Bucks.

There are many brooks in the county, so narrow that they are almost threads of water in summer, and the small bridges spanning them over the rushes and thick grasses that define their way reveal their presence. Also there are springs that come out of the earth, at the junction of clay and greensand, in that joyous way that always fills me with delight when I come across these sources of water. They are innumerable, and one can see them at Penn, at West Wycombe, at Shardeloes and Chesham, at Hartwell and Denham, and at Bledlow, and many other places. They run through the fields, they enter the ponds, and they water the country in an unspectacular manner with none of the bustle and sparkle of the springs I know so well. They are quiet little springs, from water which is caught in the clay and returned to earth, but two at least of these springs made local history. One is the famous spring of North Marston, brought from the earth by a miracle, so legend relates, and the other is the spring of Dorton, which was nearly made a fashionable spa.

The county has many musical bell-like names: Maids Moreton, Whiteleaf, Wendover, Wing; Ravenstone, Quarrenden, Quainton and Penn; Little Marlow, Little Missenden and Ivinghoe; Lacey Green, Lillingstone Lovell, Chenies, and Brill.

Buckinghamshire has been the refuge of those with independent views, the Lollards, the Quakers, and others. They made it their stronghold of faith. They retreated to the little narrow wooded valleys and farmhouses for prayer and strengthening. William Penn, Isaac Penington, who heard Fox preach and joined his society, George Fox himself who lived some time at

Newport Pagnell, Thomas Ellwood, the friend of Milton, are names one remembers, but there are many lesser men who suffered persecution for their faith. Keach, a Baptist minister, was born at Stoke Hammond, became a zealous preacher at Chesham and Winslow, was arrested and tried at Aylesbury. There is a little Keach's Meeting House at Winslow, which is one of the oldest dissenting chapels.

Even to this day this religious independence persists, and an old Bucks man told me of a large country house where he used to attend service in his youth with several other lads. The master of the house belonged to a sect called the Flying Roll. He never had his hair cut nor did he shave. His long hair was caught up in an elastic, so that it looked short. His sons and daughters belonged to the same sect. They were followers of Jesus Christ in a literal way as far as possible. The master preached in his drawing-room on Sunday afternoon and evening.

One Sunday this farm boy met a friend who said to him, "Where've you bin? Up to some mischief?"

"We've bin where you ought to have went," he replied, and he took this friend to the evening service.

They sat in the room and a daughter rang a little bell saying, "I declare this meeting open."

They had a prayer, a hymn accompanied on the piano, Bible reading, another hymn, a sermon from a text, and then questions. This girl could answer any questions they asked, and the farm lads put some posers. It was so good they went again and again. At the end of the service they had refreshments, and the family always shook hands with them and asked them to come again. When the lease of the house expired these good people left and were never heard of again.

Poets have lived in Buckinghamshire—Thomas Gray lived at Stoke Poges, Cowper at Olney, Milton came for a short retreat from the plague in London to live in the roadside cottage at Chalfont St Giles, and Edmund Waller lived at Beaconsfield.

In recent years G. K. Chesterton wrote the splendid *Ballad of the White Horse* at Beaconsfield, and Rupert Brooke wrote his Chiltern poems after walking on the hills. I would include among these poets a modern writer, J. H. B. Peel, whose sensitiveness to the beauty of his own county is very acute and true.

John Hampden's family lived at Great Hampden, "from time immemorial." John Hampden, who defied Charles I over Ship Money, was buried at Hampden Church after the battle of Chalgrove Field in which he was mortally wounded.

Edmund Verney's family lived at Claydon, and surely there never was a more interesting history told than that which we can read in the famous Verney Letters, with their picture of Buckinghamshire life during the Civil Wars.

At Beaconsfield lived Edmund Burke, the great orator and statesman.

At Hughenden lived Disraeli, and at Chequers near Ellesborough dwells each successive Prime Minister of Britain.

It is a county of statesmen, of poets, of zealots and martyrs, but perhaps it is more important because it is the home of countless unknown men, without fame, who have worked in the fields, and lived in the old farms with their gables and great barns, who have worked in corn mill and paper mill, and made furniture in their little shops thatched with leaves in the green beech woods, and driven their cattle to market along the Icknield Way.

The feeling of the county is unchanged. It is a countryside of woods and villages and small towns, not yet overtaken by the outstretched clutching fingers of London. How long it will be able to resist the encroachment one cannot say, but it will persist in its own tradition and its own individuality.

It is not a county of magnificence, of splendid castles and the seats of the wealthy. Stowe is the exception, and this residence of the Dukes of Buckingham is now a public school. There are some great houses which come to mind at once—Cliveden on the wooded slopes overhanging the Thames; West Wycombe Park, with its painted ceilings and cold brilliance; Claydon House, much changed and rebuilt, but retaining its ancient magic, the home of the Verney family; Gayhurst, perhaps the loveliest of them all, a perfect Elizabethan house of cream stone, set in its park like a jewel, with fish ponds and little box gardens.

These are some of the greater houses, but there are many other manor houses, such as Dinton, a sixteenth-century house, whose gables and groups of red chimneys rise above the churchyard; Chenies, a Tudor manor house, the home of the Russells, with its splendid chimney-stacks; Swanbourne, that charming little Elizabethan house built by Sir John Fortesque for one of his daughters, so tradition says; Long Crendon Manor, with its ancient gateway and its courtyard; beautiful ancient Creslow, the romantic farmhouse, hidden away down the fields among its barns; and sixteenth-century moated Doddershall.

Buckinghamshire is the county *par excellence* of innumerable lovely little cottages, gems of country craftsmen's work, tiny dwellings of infinite variety, with roofs of thatch embroidered in designs to suit the taste of the country thatcher, or with old crinkled red tiles, mossed green and lichened gold to the colour of shot silk, with dormer windows and peepholes, with gardens packed with flowers overflowing in their abundance to the roadside. As we go through the little villages of Buckinghamshire, we are aware of the beauty of England, which seems to be spread out for the delight and rest of a war-weary people. We may look through the park gates at the big house, and catch a glimpse of the splendour, and then we turn aside from the imposing structure to the village street where each cottage is a gem. The intense life of domesticity and hard work and bringing up children is there within this background. Elms spread their wide branches in the street, the village green has a pump in the middle, or there is a pond by its side. Perhaps a broken cross stands near, a reminder of the old days when preachers spoke from the steps where now children laugh and play.

The speech of the people, the slow step of a labourer, are different from the hard sharp walk and clipped talk of a townsman in the country. The Buckinghamshire landscape is above all simple and warm-hearted, and the scene is never abrupt or strange. Bluebells growing in carpets of azure in the wood clearings, cowslips gilding the railway banks, cattle, red and white in the little fields, a horse standing by a gate of the red-roofed farmhouse, the square towers of the small grey churches, the bands of children running home from school—all these make up the daily picture.

Once, when we drove slowly along one of the country roads, we interrupted a game of cricket that was taking place. Stumps

were set up in the highway, the batsman was at the wicket in
the middle of the road, the bowler was running down the pitch,
and the fielders were in the grass verges. They snatched up the
wickets and stood aside as we went slowly past, and we smiled
broadly at each other, knowing the delights of cricket on a
summer's evening. Men leaned on the fence watching, others
were fielding in the meadow, and a boy sat scoring on a gate.
The smooth road made the best pitch they could have and very
few people went past to spoil the game.

There are churches of which any county might be proud—
magnificent Stewkley, a complete example of a twelfth-century
church, rich with carving; Wing Church with its Saxon crypt;
Hillesden, a fifteenth-century church lost in its green fields, but
the most lovely of all to me; North Marston, with its wealth of
tradition; Edlesborough with its splendid roof of the fifteenth
century and its grotesque misereres; fifteenth-century Maids
Moreton, with fan vaulting in the porch and great stone birds
for gargoyles; and Langley Marish with its Kederminster pew
and painted library of 1630.

There are inns of distinction—the King's Head at Aylesbury, now taken over by the National Trust; the Bull's Head of
that town; the Red Lion at High Wycombe, connected with
Disraeli; the King's Head at Stony Stratford, with tragic
memories of the Princes in the Tower; the White Hart at
Buckingham, proudly carrying its hart with a crown—and
countless little inns, the Red Lion at Bradenham, whitewashed,
flower-hung; the Red Lion at Wendover; the Black Boy at
Oving, a sixteenth-century inn; the Crown at Penn; the
Ostrich at Colnbrook; the Bull at Stony Stratford; and the
little Crooked Billet, with the doggerel verse hanging under a
real crooked billet:

> Mary Uff sells good beer
> And that's enough.
> A mistake here,
> Sells wines and spirits as well as beer.

There are inglenook fireplaces and old beams across the
ceilings. Here country people meet and tell their tales of drovers

and gipsies and "the parson who always got drunk but he was a good man," and the drover who was "the cleanest man in Bucks because he washed his feet every night."

Nothing is typical, no Buckinghamshire village or town is like another, all are unique. The little streets of cottages of old red brick, faded to a rose colour, scented like roses, too, on a summer's day, the narrow alleys, the paved and cobbled ways by the church, ancient paths much used when carts and market women passed that way, and the churches themselves, all are distinctive and special. Shapes of fields, the hedgerows, the wide-margined roads, all these make up this county of small and lovely things.

CHAPTER I

NIGHTINGALES AND PENN
BY COUNTRY LANE

MOTORISTS hurry to Penn along the main road, but the ordinary traveller takes the winding unspoilt country lane which runs under the shadow of the Hogback Woods, now part of the National Trust. The woods are on a gentle rise, and there grow beeches, with hollies and silver birches, but chiefly the great beeches. A copse of silver birches and a grove of larches cover part of the hillside outside the Trust land, and I fear they may go. The colours of these little woods are exquisite in early spring, when the tender green of the larches shines out before the other trees, and the silver-birch wood is a mist of plum-coloured catkins, with the silver trunks like ballet girls among them. I always go to pick a few larch twigs when the tiny tassels are out, for the scent of them is one of the most evocative of all smells.

Nightingales sing day and night in a wild grove of tangled trees not far from this wood, trees linked together by ropes of traveller's-joy, and I stand under an ash tree close to the bird as it rapturously calls at midday, and hear another bird replying from the wood. Lovely as is the song it has not the wonder and beauty of the night song. There is not the expectant listening air in nature, and the first long-drawn note does not reach the same pitch of rapture when other birds are singing their utmost too.

The clear ravishing note which warns the woodland that the song is about to begin is for me more romantic even than the song that follows. The low pitch, the timbre, the warmth of it, tell the world to listen, and then the cascade of brilliant music flows in such a torrent it seems as if the bird knows that life is short, that love is brief, that spring-time and the month of May will soon be over.

There is a pause and another bird answers from afar, then a third takes up the song. They provoke, they challenge, and call with musical trills and murmurous jug-jug, another rich utterance, like water falling in a beck in Westmorland, and again comes that long low call which began the concert, the trill that is superb above all other cadences. The nightingale goes through his musical medley, each time varied and distinct. I have listened for hours, tracing the sequence of tunes, trying to catch the magic on paper.

Then comes a longer pause, when all nature seems to wait and listen, and we are aware that the nightingales are all listening too. It is so intense, that waiting time, that I think of tiny ears a-cock all through the woods. The stars twinkle, the moon stands still, the leaves rustle softly and even the great trees are hearkening to the silence. Far away, very faint, another bird is heard, but we, all of the visible and invisible ones, are waiting for our nightingale.

It starts on the same low pitch, spinning the note with rapid vibration, and the warm air of night is made rich with the beauty of it. The flow of music follows, the woods breathe again, and the moment of tension is broken.

I have listened to a nightingale singing through the night and I came to the conclusion that it never slept, unless it dozed in the short intervals between the concerts. I never slept either, but it was a memorable experience, and I am certain the same bird was singing, as I could distinguish certain small details of modulation repeated in the song, which were invented by the original bird. Birds have their individual expressions, and there is a thrush here which sings one cadence different from other thrushes. This I have noticed in Buckinghamshire several times. A thrush a few years ago had a most lovely short tune, but I only heard it that year, and I have not heard it since. There was a blackbird, too, with a distinct song which I always recognized.

One evening at dusk I stood in a lane near my house waiting for a nightingale to sing. I felt sure it was about to begin as there was a hush in the air and it was time for the nightingales to arrive. Then came that long, low rippling note that always makes my spine shiver as if I saw a ghost. I was startled by the sudden flap of wings, and a dark, heavy bird flew to the tree under which I stood. The nightingale was singing about twenty yards away in the dense bushes. The bird waited in the tree and I could see it staring across and obviously listening too. I am

2

quite sure that other birds listen to the nightingales, from various observations and the silence that greets the first notes. Walter de la Mare once said he had seen birds listening to a nightingale singing in the daytime, but at night it is difficult to see what is happening, and one has only one's own heightened senses.

This bird, which I recognized as a starling, sat with its head towards the nightingale, and though I was very close to it, it took no notice of me. The nightingale went through its repertoire, which seemed more beautiful than ever, and both starling and I listened with intentness. When the nightingale had finished, almost before the last note died away, the starling began. It omitted that long exultant trill which begins the song, and went on to the cadence. It was a remarkable imitation, and I could hardly believe my ears. Nor could the nightingale, I think. There were mistakes now and then, sometimes ludicrous travesties, but the song was a most astonishing feat of mimicry; the note was harsher, but often the starling's song was the nightingale's own. The order was different, and the bird now and then repeated a dazzling phrase as if proud of its performance. It was hurried, too, with never a pause, while the nightingale's song has many hesitations and delicious little waits, as if to lure one on.

At last, with a flourish, the bird finished and waited, and then the nightingale began again. That lovely song almost made me weep, but the starling interrupted and sang at the same time. So the two went on, the nightingale's pure music, with the sweet pauses, and the starling's own good song, which lacked the clarity, but was a startling imitation.

The past year, with land taken for building, the nightingales have been few, and I have missed my friends in the copses near the Penn lane.

Cowslips grow in this part of Bucks, and it is said by country people that nightingales sing where cowslips grow. This cannot be true of all parts of England, obviously, but it appears to be true in the south.

In the valley is Holtspur Bottom Farm, a good sturdy little red brick farmhouse, with three dormers in its roof, and ivy on its old walls. Its cowhouses and sheds stand in a row at right

3

angles to the house, and the great timbered barn is opposite, so that together they form three sides of a square, with the manure heap and paved yard in the middle, as in the old days. I watched a tractor draw an immense load of corn through the wide open double-doors of the barn, and the whole disappeared within as if it was the house of a giant. This barn has five bays, an oak-beamed roof, and weatherboarded sides.

This is a plain South Bucks farm, warm and inviting, with its rich red brick walls, and its golden-green roofs, shimmering like silk in the sunlight. In the field by the back door is a walnut tree, and more walnut trees, of great size, grew in the orchard across the lane until recently. A walnut tree is a part of farm life, and I always like to see these magnificent spreading branches and the big leaves. The timber merchants of High Wycombe also have an eye for the walnut trees for their chair-making. The walnut by the house is one of those family trees, and country people will know quite well what I mean. It is a tree that is really part of the household. A swing hangs from its branches, a heap of timber stands against its sides, a clothes-line is fastened to a bough, a hen-coop is sheltered under it. I always look out for the special tree in cottage garden and in farm orchard. Sometimes there is a wooden seat under it, where old men sit, or children play house. At Coleshill there is such a tree, called Waller's Oak, where the poet is said to have written some of his poems.

One snowy day I climbed the steep field behind the farm and saw a picture that might have been painted by Pieter Brueghel. The sudden rise of small white hills, the lively awareness of the bare woods behind them, the rose-colour of the small farm nestled cosily in the deep valley, with its stackyard and barns, and the slate-grey sky, were such as the Flemish artist loved to paint. Down the field flew little home-made toboggans, with children in red hoods, blue scarves, and brown jackets. It was a picture enclosed in a frame of brown leafless trees, flecked with snow and streaked with brilliant green splashes, a picture painted four hundred years ago, for it had the flatness and lack of modern perspective, and the ice-cold atmosphere of a Brueghel winter scene.

The lane in spring, when we find carpets of white violets

4

under the hedges, and wild arums, and blue patches of bird's-eye, is not more beautiful than it is on a winter's day. The tall overgrown hedge by the fields is layered neatly, and the result is a fence which is symmetrical in design and a pleasure to see. All along the border of the big cherry and apple orchards which stretch opposite the Hogback Woods, pitched high above the sunk lane, the hedge is "eddered" or "heathered." The tall upright stakes stand at even intervals about a foot apart, and the willow and hazel and ash saplings are twined between them like good basketwork. Robins hop there and sing a few notes in the cold wintry weather, and there are little rustles in the dead leaves on the banks where mice are busy. Hazel catkins hang stiffly from parts of the hedge where slim saplings spring from trees cut last year. Hazel and ash saplings make good switches, and there are many of these by the roadside, spraying like the forks of a fan. Later they will be used for "eddering" the other side of the lane.

A well-known layerer of hedges, Harry Perfect, who does very clean hedging, lives at Forty Green, the hamlet on the way to Penn. I have seen his work in a lane twisting and winding round by Lude Farm, and the hedge is something of which the county should be proud. The long sprays of nut trees are spread out and woven into a fence through which no animal could penetrate. It makes me think of the hedge round the Sleeping Beauty, although the beauties are fat white pigs grazing within the orchards. It is made in a design which is both decorative and useful, with the fans of grey living wood twined into a border to keep the cherry trees enclosed.

Forty Green is a little hamlet among orchards and woods. Sunny cottages are dotted about, one with a yew in its garden, another with flowers that magically bloom even in the snow, and a third where a pet lamb lives with the children. There is a sixteenth-century brick and timbered farm at the corner, a picturesque place, where I once saw a young god of antiquity driving a tractor. Parsonage Farm is a lovely fifteenth-century house near.

The little cottages are mostly modern, with no adornment of thatch or gable, but the country people living there say they prefer them to the old ones where they were born, because these are easy to keep clean, and have water laid on. There is no electricity or gas, and no bathroom, but the water is most important and makes life easier.

Beyond this hamlet are cherry orchards with great old rugged trees. Some of the women supplement their husbands' earnings on the land by gathering fruit in the summer. Then the orchards that surround Forty Green are busy with pickers. Long, broad-based ladders stand against the trees, and the women peer down through the smooth cherry leaves as they work and laugh and chatter. They get 6s. a basket, and a woman can easily make 18s. in an evening.

I heard the other side of the cherry-picking problem from the farmer who took me round to see his trees, some of them so heavily laden that the branches were breaking. Certain trees he left, for the fruit was too ripe before the pickers arrived, so they were a dead loss. With the controlled price of fruit so low, the high wages paid to the pickers and the carriage of the fruit added, his profits were very small indeed.

On this winter's day the cherry trees looked white and ghostly against the pale sky, and a flock of grey sheep and a grey mare stood waiting under their bare branches while the farmer forked hay from a cart to feed them. Some of the very ancient trees had been cut down and lay ready for the sawyer.

I went through the orchard along a track which leads to Penn village. The field-path soon leaves the wood and goes alongside it under the low hedge, and this part of the woodland always fires my imagination, so that I linger here for a long time.

There is nothing special to see in this Bucks wood, but the air is caught in the branches of the beech trees, and an ultramarine mist seems to fill the spaces between the tall straight trunks. The colour is exquisite in every season of the year, as if blue pansies and violets were hanging there, and I know of no other place where there is this curious effect.

On one side of the track is this heavenly wood with its colour, its birds, tomtits in summer, blue as the mist, but never a flower or fern. On the other side are ploughfields and pastures sloping steeply to the hidden road which curves round the foot of the

6

hill and rises to Penn. Last year's barley is giving way to grass this year, the farmer told me as he cut the hay from the stack by the side of the path. When the barley was reaped last year I watched a young boy make a little red flame in the stubble to heat his dinner, before he was allowed to take his place on the tractor. He was very proud of the honour, and he blew up his fire and heated his can of food while a man drove the tractor in the field below him. It was his first day with the reaper.

In the fields through which this pathway goes there is a bed of tansy, that golden herb with the pungent bitter smell. I always gather a bunch to carry with me—a country smelling-bottle. The cornfields here are decked on the edges with the flowers of chicory, flowers of dazzling blue, in such quantities that they are like a piece of sky on earth. Later the scarlet berries of the bryony hang in long necklaces in the hedges, as if they had been placed there for a decoration, and the red leaves of ivy twine round the tree stumps. There must be iron in the soil here, and in Holtspur Bottom Lane, which makes the ivy ruddy, and I always seek these leaves with the rosy shades. In the fields bee orchis grows, and in the woods there is green hellebore.

By this field-path I once saw a lovely sight which I shall always remember. There had been a heavy snow and the ground was glittering on a frosty morning soon after Christmas. Two little round holly trees grew by a gate, every leaf shining in the sun. Scarlet berries so closely covered these balls of trees that they looked like a decoration for a kissing-bunch. They were obviously proud of their beauty, and I stood for a long time looking at them, enjoying something they gave me, sharing their happiness. I could not touch them, for they were perfect, and it was their Day.

Forty Green is the proud possessor of an old inn called the Royal Standard of England. In the parlour, which has a curved wooden wall like the cabin of a ship, is the grate which came from Edmund Burke's house, and the round table with an inlaid star, upon which the innkeeper puts one's glass of sherry, is from Beaconsfield Church, a seventeenth-century piece of work.

This inn was called the Ship Inn three hundred years ago. It is tucked away in a rough little lane, among cherry orchards.

7

Sometimes I walk to Penn by the narrow lane among the cherry trees, instead of branching off at Forty Green to the woodland path. Except for the hamlet cottages, the lane seems empty, but there are many invisible denizens, as I found out one day when I walked with a village schoolgirl. The lane is said to be the old pack road from Penn to High Wycombe. It was the road taken by the children who went to Penn school. No motor-bus carried them; they had the inestimable boon of walking and observing and getting to know a country lane in all the seasons of the year, and the memory of it will stay with them for life. Now, unfortunately, the school is closed, like many village schools.

I walked with little Joy Allen along the narrow lane with its deep high banks on the sides, and red apples hanging temptingly over the well-plashed fence. It is a celandine, wild violet, cherry blossom lane in spring, a wild rose and wild strawberry lane in summer, a lane for traveller's-joy and bryony, for dogwood and spindleberries, for blackberries and hazel nuts in autumn, and in winter, when snow is deep, rich red and amber ivy on the sandy banks.

From these banks we could see bright eyes watching us from behind the leaves, peering from screens of feathery grasses or from under the ivy, or behind yellow deadnettle and shining stitchwort. Shirt-buttons the country children call the white flowers of the greater stitchwort, and each little flower head resembles a highly ornamented pearl button on a fine linen shirt. So we found nests of robins, of thrushes, of tits, and the child told me of the secret life she shares with these birds, looking out for them each morning and evening, enjoying their friendship. She is an observer of rare quality, and has the quiet, listening attitude, the retentive memory and experimental zest that make up a naturalist.

The village of Penn runs along the crest of the hill, 540 feet up, and there is a climb till the old village is reached. On the side of the road opposite the ancient church are two tiny cottages which give me more pleasure than many a famous house in a great park. Their enchanting names are Robin and Wren. These two little rosy-bricked timbered cottages are comfortable and happy places. They have great fireplaces, now bricked up, where little modern grates are fitted, and the outside chimneys remain, ivy-covered and strong, against the walls.

I first noticed these cottages when the Madonna lilies were in bloom, for a snow-white company stood close to the walls, growing in abundance under the kitchen windows.

Opposite the cottages is a field gate, where every climber stops and stands and stares, for there is a magnificent view across the country, and Windsor Castle can be seen on fine days. Perhaps every village has its own gate where there is a special view. I have come across many in Bucks, and there is usually a countryman leaning there, admiring, dreaming, ready to point out the features which seem invisible at first.

The house on the hill-top, The Knoll, was the home for a time of Princess Anne, who was sent there while Mary reigned with William of Orange. A delicate little belvedere is called Princess Anne's window. From it the Princess must have seen Windsor and the vast panorama below. This is now the home of Viscount Curzon of Penn.

The early fourteenth-century church stands in a commanding position. From the summit of its tower one can see fifteen counties, I am told, but I prefer to think of that view of the sky the watchers had recently. The Observer Corps have gazed out during the war years, scanning the starry sky for enemy planes, watching day and night against invaders. The church tower of Penn is a great look-out place, like a lighthouse in the green sea of Buckinghamshire.

There are fine yews in the churchyard, and some wooden grave heads on which I always see robins perched. They seem to prefer the warmth of the wood to the cold tombstones.

The church at Penn is beautiful in its simplicity, with its whitewashed walls, its painted hatchments, its stone porch. The pews have doors with latches, so that one feels secure, kneeling there.

I remember the first sermon I heard at Penn. It was a lovely spring day, the sky azure as a harebell, the air sweet as honey, scented with flowers. Butterflies and bees were about, a yellow brimstone fluttered by the church door, and arabis and daffodils bloomed in Wren and Robin cottages, and in the churchyard.

"As I came across to church this morning, I looked up at the sky and thought to myself, 'This is a day to thank God for,'" began the aged clergyman, and his sermon was a simple talk about eternal country things.

Again, I think of Christmas in this old church, and the wreaths of holly berries and fir, and the beautiful crib with its roof of straw at the west end under the tower, and the Holy Child in the manger, with ox and ass, and little village children staring amazed at the miracle. It seems an integral part of the country church with its whitewashed walls.

At Easter the church is decorated by the children with flowers they have picked. There is a bed of white violets in the deep moss-lined window of the porch, and wild cherry blossom from the woods hangs in tumultuous foam by the altar. Daffodils fill the leaden font, one of the few lead fonts in the country.

The roof is fifteenth-century and has six traceried queen-post trusses which stand on stone corbels, with shields and heads of bearded men and angels. The tower has a ring of five bells with some interesting inscriptions.

The treble, dated 1702, is inscribed:

> I as trebell do beegin,

and the second says:

> Feare God, honour the king.

The fourth has

> In Penn tour for too sing,

and the tenor says:

> Unto the church I doo you call
> Deth to the grave will summans all.

Over the woods and down the valleys chime these bells, the sound carried by the wind, sweeping from the high tower on the hill.

"The Doom," the famous wall painting, was discovered in 1938. Some oak boards covered with plaster were moved from the

10

wall above the chancel arch, and colour was noticed upon them. A medieval picture of the Last Judgment was found there, painted in bright colours. The original work was done in the fifteenth century, and it was repainted in the same rich colours, during the same century, with different scenes. There is Our Lord on a rainbow, with red-winged angels around him, blowing trumpets and carrying symbols of the Passion. Twelve apostles below, with the Virgin Mary, are standing on a green hill, with souls rising from their graves. It is a picture which was made for the enjoyment and instruction of those people of medieval days who had a lively and imaginative church to satisfy their needs. Now it hangs on the south wall, with a curtain to preserve it from the light.

There is a stone coffin in Penn Church, called the Saracen's Tomb, a thirteenth-century coffin with a raised cross on the lid.

The church living was granted by Edward VI to Sybil Hampden, who had been his governess, on her marriage to David Penn, the barber-surgeon to Henry VIII.

Sometimes one arrives hot and weary with climbing the long hill to Penn. In the window of the porch there is always a jug of clean water and a couple of glasses "for thirsty wayfarers," and we drink and are thankful.

The air at Penn seems to be coloured, for the land falls steeply away from the ridge, with cornfields in the foreground, with woods in the distance, and a violet-blue mist hangs over those far trees and hills. The atmosphere is charged with sweetness, and sun and light, with the open spaces there. At the village centre near the church is a broken elm tree, a meeting-place, and across the road is the Crown Inn, a red brick seventeenth-century inn, with large chimney places, narrow passages, and comfortable rooms.

There is some confusion about the name Penn. The Quaker, William Penn, was not a near member of the family of Penn who lived in the village, but there is no doubt that the founder of Pennsylvania had a strong affection for the place which bore his name, and he named his house in Pennsylvania "Pennsbury"— there is a Penbury Farm at Penn. Penn was buried at Jordans in the Quaker burial ground, but his grandsons were buried at

Penn. In the nave is a stone over the vault where the six sons of Thomas, the son of William Penn, lie.

The village of Penn Street, a mile or two away down in the hollow, has old cottages and a green with a pond and leaning willow tree. In this village there are timber works of Messrs Dancer and Hearne, where chairs are made. Local people are employed by this old-established firm.

The great Penn Woods stretch near, and in the park is Penn House, the home of Earl Howe, now a school. Pheasants fly across the road and woodpeckers laugh in this leafy place. The house stands on a low hill among the glory of its trees. In the garden is a seat where Handel composed part of the *Messiah*, and in the house his spinet was kept until recently.

The road through Penn follows the high ridge by a stream which rises in that hilly ground. There are a few charming old houses by the roadside, one of them being Watercroft. It has ironwork balconies and weathercock made by craftsmen brought from Chelsea to teach the little French boys who lived in the Penn district at the time of the French Revolution. Sir George Grove had this house and his friend, Arthur Sullivan, wrote "The Lost Chord" and the good tunes of "Onward, Christian Soldiers," and the *Mikado* in the little summer-house. The well in the garden used to be the only source of water in time of drought at Penn and it never runs dry.

The hamlet of Tyler's Green is close to Penn, on the same ridge of land. Here is a village green with a pond, and around it are grouped the houses and the village shop which sells everything from postage stamps to calico and Christmas cards. Most of the houses are eighteenth-century. Tiles used to be made here, as in Beaconsfield, from local clay, and the industry dates from the Middle Ages.

Near the pond once stood Tyler's Green House, a house in which Edmund Burke founded a school in 1796 for sixty French children who had lost their fathers in the French Revolution. These little boys wore uniform, and white cockades decked their hats, with "Vive le Roi" upon them. Burke took great interest in this school, and sent food to it from his farm at Beaconsfield. Later it had a Government grant of £600 a year from Mr Pitt, but in 1820 it was discontinued. Now the memory remains in the name of a field, French field. Documents relating to this benevolent school are in the Aylesbury Museum. Putnam Place, which is fifteenth century, is now a farm in the midst of the fields, with the old drive leading to Tyler's Green.

The fair at Penn is held each year on September 17th on Tyler's Green. Up the hills come the caravans and lorries laden with hobby-horses and swingboats and all the wonders of the world. They straggle round the green, they carry water from the pond for their washing, they set free their hens, they loose and water their horses and turn them out to graze. The women wash their clothes and hang them out to dry on lines between the caravans. All the business of domestic life begins while the men erect the swingboats, the shooting booths, the sideshows. Children come home from school and stand watching the showmen lift the painted wooden horses from the vans and carry them to the merry-go-round. They run with milk and food for the showmen, and the women start to cook the dinner.

Tyler's Green is a happy little place, the centre of village life. The bonfire is lighted there on Guy Fawkes' Night, and flower shows and circuses come to the green.

There is a tale told of Mr Grove, a yeoman farmer of Penn, who died in 1823. He belonged to an old family of farmers, and was called Yeoman Grove. He was known to George III, the Farmer King, who was free and easy with him. When they met in the street at Windsor on market days, Grove would grasp the King's hand and ask, "How does your Majesty do? How is the Queen? How are all the children?" in a hearty familiar way the King liked.

CHAPTER II

JORDANS AND THE CHALFONTS

BUCKINGHAMSHIRE is closely connected with the family of Penn, and the name of William Penn, the founder of the state of Pennsylvania, is bound up with Jordans. Pilgrims come from America to see Penn's simple grave in the little green burial ground near the Meeting House. It is easy to imagine the Quaker figure, in his wide-brimmed hat, walking along that leafy lane, visiting the farm which is now a hostel, wandering through the field-paths of the open country, or standing in the cathedrals of the beech woods. His spirit seems to haunt Jordans, one cannot forget him, and I have felt he is present with other Quakers, sitting in silence on the wooden seat of the chapel, talking at the door to his friends, speaking gravely with no laughter.

A famous Quaker used to visit my father and stay with the family on our country hillside before I was born. I heard about him in the tales told round the fireside, and I remember that early wonder of a child as my father spoke of him. He always said Yea and Nay, Thee and Thou, and he addressed everyone as "Friend." As my father, too, always said Thee and Thou, Yea and Nay, I was drawn to this Quaker, who wore a wide-brimmed hat, indoors and out, and took it off for nobody. He carried no firearms, even at a time of danger, they told me, and he wouldn't touch a gun in self-defence. They spoke of a Quaker in America, whom the Indians trusted because he was never armed—perhaps this was William Penn—and there were many tales of the wisdom and peace of the Quakers.

Although our Quaker was a wealthy man, who gave sovereigns to the servant boy and girl and paid well for everything, he lived more simply than anyone. Instead of attending church, he went to a Quakers' meeting, where all sat silent until the Spirit of God moved one of the company to prayer. So I was deeply interested in all this, and years later I went to the Meeting House at Jordans and stayed at the hostel.

14

The stone floors to the parlours, the kitchen-dining-room with its old fireplace and bread oven and copper for boiling water, the brass utensils, the hollow bench for salting bacon, the red brick floor to the kitchen, were like home to me, although they were a curiosity to the other guests. The gay little garden and pocket-handkerchief lawns were all familiar as if I had been there before.

There I heard the story of those early Quakers who lived in Buckinghamshire nearly three hundred years ago—Thomas Ellwood, Isaac Penington, and William Penn's wife, Gulielma.

Isaac Penington, the son of one of Charles I's judges, married Lady Springett, who had been widowed at twenty. Her little daughter, Gulielma Springett, who was to be the wife of William Penn, was the playfellow in London of Thomas Ellwood. When the Peningtons with Gulie came to live at Chalfont, the two friends met again. In his autobiography, Thomas Ellwood gives an amusing account of the meeting and the change in the family since they became Quakers.

He speaks of the difference, from a free, courtly, debonair sort of behaviour, to a strict gravity. Then he goes on, "We staid dinner, which was very handsome and lacked nothing to recommend it to me, but the want of Mirth and pleasant Discourse, which we could neither have with them, nor by reason of them with one another by ourselves."

This reminds me of an old Bucks gravedigger, who said to a parson friend of mine a short time ago, "Sir, I *must* have my Mirth."

It was a difficult position and Thomas Ellwood and his father went away disappointed. However, they met again, and even went to a Quakers' meeting. Thomas Ellwood changed so completely that he too became a Quaker. His father was angry, particularly because his son wore his big hat in his father's presence, and would not address him as "Sir." Young Ellwood was imprisoned for his zeal in London and at Wycombe and Aylesbury.

In London he had been Latin tutor to John Milton, and he read poetry with the blind poet. Then he became tutor to Isaac Penington's children and he must have found his lovely friend

15

Gulielma very attractive—but he remained a sedate young man and later married Mary Ellis.

Mary Penington and the children were ejected from their home when Isaac Penington was in Aylesbury gaol, and Thomas Ellwood looked after them. He took them first to Aylesbury, and then to a farm near Chalfont St Giles, Bottrell's Farm. Finally they went to Amersham, to Bury Farm.

William Penn met Gulielma here, and fell in love with her quiet beauty, and married her at King's Farm, Rickmansworth. Penn set sail for America in 1682, and returned in 1684. He died in 1718, and he was buried at Jordans with his two wives.

Those names, Thomas Ellwood, Isaac Penington, Gulielma Springett, William Penn, and John Milton, make a solemn melody in this part of Buckinghamshire. The memory of them is vivid and enduring.

The Jordans Hostel was Old Jordans Farm, originally built in 1625. At the time of the Commonwealth, William Russell was the farmer who lived there and farmed the surrounding land. He joined the Quakers, and suffered persecution with them. George Fox, the great Quaker, visited Jordans Farm in 1673 and 1677, and his presence must have influenced all there.

William Russell in 1671 sold a piece of the field called Well Close Hedgerow, down in the hollow near the farm, for the Quaker burial ground. Meetings were held at Jordans Farm at that time. When the good old farmer died, he was buried in this ground, and also his daughter Mary. Then Isaac Penington and his wife were buried at the Jordans burial ground. More land was bought, close to this tiny croft, and the Meeting House which is still used was built. The corner of the ground called Coarse Hurdles was part of the land and garden.

The little burial ground, with the small unadorned headstones under the trees, is a memorial for all time to those early Quakers. It is said that 134 Quakers were buried there between 1671 and 1724, but no mark was made until 1862 for their graves. From their plain little headstones to the elaborate alabaster monuments in some of the Buckinghamshire churches is as wide a difference as was their simple lives from those who lived at the Court.

16

Mayflower Barn at Jordans

The Meeting House at Jordans is a plain well-proportioned little building with shuttered windows. It stands near the side of the road in its well-kept garden with a background of trees. Even to look at it is a pleasure, and there is a feeling of peace and restfulness there, as if the old red bricks exuded the goodness and steadfastness they have absorbed in the centuries. All thoughts of the persecutions, the sorrow and partings that have taken place, are forgotten in that strength which is present. So, in the little whitewashed room with its plain benches and its gallery, one feels the influence of the long dead. Their immortality remains, their thoughts permeate the air. I could swear I see them sitting there, the women up in the gallery, bonneted, shawled, the men stern, solemn, filling the downstair room with their presence, every one of them with that peace which we seem unable to find.

Up the field, and through the orchard, a grassy track leads to the old farmhouse, a place which brings comfort and quiet to many. The rooms are small and beautiful, with plain old furniture, and cretonnes and flowers. Meals are taken in the old farm kitchen, where all the guests dine together at a long polished pear-wood table. Grace is said before meals, and after breakfast there is a short time given to reading aloud. Someone reads either a portion of the Bible or a poem or piece of prose. It is a custom of the place, one which gives pleasure, for the words ring true in that old room, and well-known, even hackneyed, passages take on a fresh meaning, as if one heard some vital news for the first time.

The guests scatter, to spend their days as they wish. I wrote a book in that quiet garden, down in a corner close to the lavender beds, once upon a time. I remember one windy day, when the apple blossom filled the orchard, I saw two young girls from the laundry of the house carrying clothes-baskets of white linen down the flowery paths to the orchard drying-ground. Their aprons fluttered, their blue frocks shook in the wind, their laughter came through the air, as they hung up the sheets to dry on the lines between the apple trees, and as the wind tossed the clothes against an azure sky I seemed to see an immortal picture. In my mind, as through the other end of a telescope, I

c 17

Quaker graveyard at Jordans

also saw a tiny oval with our own old orchard, and the maid-servant carrying a clothes-basket, her blue skirts blown, hair flying, cheeks scarlet, as she hung out the clothes between the trees with their apple blossom.

One night at the hostel—and again this was linked with the past—we sat round a great fire in the inglenook in one of the little parlours, and we told tales. Everybody who could remember anything interesting told a story. We heard tales of the Maoris in their cannibal times from a New Zealand farmer, and tales of America, and tales of robbers and ghosts and hauntings, tales of India from an Indian doctor, and tales of South Africa. So in my childhood we sat round the farmhouse fire and told tales of far away. So in the childhood of that ancient farmhouse they must have sat centuries ago and talked to one another—tragical tales too.

In 1670 a meeting at Jordans was broken up with great violence by Ralph Lacy, a cow-stealer, and Aris, a highwayman, who were informers. There are many tales of the difficulties and agonies of these early Quakers, and their imprisonments and their escapes. Coleshill, which was in Herts in those days, formed a means of escape as it was over the border.

In one of the parlours of Jordans is an open hearth and ingle-nook with a tiny window with the original glass panes at the back. A concealed chamber was found behind the left seat of the inglenook, where a person could hide during the many searches and persecutions of the seventeenth century.

The kitchen holds a treasured possession. It is the richly painted and lacquered little cabinet of many tiny drawers which belonged to Gulielma Springett.

Now there is a new treasure in the hostel, a model of the *Mayflower*, 1620, "devised by Alan Keen and made by Alfred Pepe from wood of the original ship given by the Society of Friends, 1941." With it is a book bound in blue morocco, one copy of which was given to Winston Churchill and another to Franklin D. Roosevelt.

"This book telling of the finding of the timbers of the Immortal *Mayflower* accompanies a replica of the ship fashioned of oak from the barn of Jordans, in Bucks, to commemorate the

18

Atlantic Charter between the Free people of Great Britain and the United States of America, A.D. 1941."

Across the green lawn of the farmhouse, which must once have been the yard where cattle came home for milking, and horses for bedding-down in their stables, where all the men worked and women went in their pattens through the mud, there stands the great barn called the Mayflower Barn. It is a noble building, high-roofed and oak-beamed, with five bays.

There is good evidence that it was constructed from the timbers of the *Mayflower*, the ship that carried the Pilgrim Fathers to America.

The *Mayflower* was brought back to England and broken up, and there is every reason to believe the timbers were carried to Jordans and built into this magnificent barn. The timbers are said to be salty from the sea waters. A portion of a beam has been removed and sent to America as a token.

Swallows fly in and out of the door and build their nests in the great roof. Sunshine filters through and patterns the wooden floor. There is a constant movement and flicker of wings. Sometimes concerts are given there, on the little platform under the rough-hewn timbers of the roof; quartets play the music of Bach, or dancers revive old country jigs, or children come to play. It is a good use for an old barn, which is no museum piece, but a place of recreation.

In the spring the wind shakes the leaves, turning the silver undersides, moving slowly round the garden so that first one bunch of daffodils shivers and then another. The hyacinths sway stiffly, and the candytuft waves its white heads. By the steps little blue grape hyacinths stand erect like toy soldiers in blue uniform. The doors of the great barn are wide open, and through them the birds fly, to perch on the beams.

There is a village of Jordans, built round a green, a small model village, with a family shop where everything is sold. The houses are pleasant, nobody is poor, nobody is lost or forgotten, and the whole village is like a pretty toy, set in a ring of trees, with the swing in the middle. It belongs to a registered company called Jordans Village Ltd. It is sheltered by a wood, which has been presented to the village. For some reason the wood seems to have lost its wildness and become a model like the village.

In a field behind Jordans Village I found my first bee orchis. As I wandered I could see them spiking up their delicate green stems with the lovely dark bees clinging to them. It was a revelation of Buckinghamshire. They seemed part of the beauty of the Meeting House and the old farmhouse, with its sunk garden and orchard. In the woods in March I picked bluebells, white violets, lady's smock. The sky was blue as the forget-me-not which grows in the borders of the garden, and against the sky were the shining tops of the elms, misty with purple blossoms. I lost my heart to Jordans that day.

Near the Meeting House is Stone Dean, which was built by Peter Prince, a Quaker tallow-chandler, in 1691. Quakers also lived at Dean Farm, across the way.

About two miles from Jordans, along a country road which passes through Three Households, is Chalfont St Giles. In this village Milton lived for a few years, and his cottage is little changed. There is a field path to Chalfont St Giles through orchards and woods, where jays screech and green woodpeckers laugh. It dips down past a beautiful old house with a well in its garden to the main street of the village. There are old cottages, and mossy tiled roofs, bending and curving with age, and tiny shops, packed to the dusty windows with everything, and a pond by the small village green. This pond dried up during the war owing to the disappearance of the river Misbourne. Now the water comes from a well.

Milton's cottage is on the street, with its front door opening to a tiny garden, with apple trees in the square of grass, and sweet williams and snapdragons, foxgloves and campanulas, growing in the border. The steep red roof and dormer window overlook the road, and the great outside chimney abuts there. It is a charming and picturesque dwelling, of which anyone might be proud, a gem set in its trees and flower garden. At the front of this brick and timber cottage grow a vine, a white rose, and a plum tree, emblems of food, drink, and beauty. Through the narrow wooden gate one can gaze at this enchanted spot.

The two downstair rooms, kitchen and parlour, are now made into a museum of Milton relics. The rooms are well arranged and cared for so that one feels that the old poet might come stumbling down the stairs and sit in the night by the good fire in the kitchen to warm his hands, his blindness gone, his strength renewed.

I bought a small book here, with Oliver Cromwell's rules for good soldiers. They were so modern that my son read them aloud to his soldiers, soon to fight in another and more terrible war than the Civil War.

Milton came to this cottage in 1665 to escape the Great Plague raging in London. There is a description of this evacuation from London by Thomas Ellwood, the Quaker.

"Some little time before I went to Aylesbury Prison, I was desired by my quondam Master Milton, to take an House for him in the Neighbourhood where I dwelt, that he might go out of the City for the safety of himself and his Family, the Pestilence then growing hot in London. I took a pretty box for him in Giles-Chalfont, a Mile from me, of which I gave him Notice, and intended to have waited on him, and seen him well settled in it, but was prevented by Imprisonment. But now being released and returned home, I soon made a Visit to him, to welcome him into the Country."

Ellwood goes on to say that Milton lent him a manuscript to read at his leisure. It was *Paradise Lost*. When Ellwood returned it to the poet and they had discussed it, he was asked how he liked it, and what he thought of it. Ellwood made a remark that was perhaps a gentle joke.

"Thou hast said much about Paradise Lost: but what hast thou to say of Paradise found?"

Later Milton showed his friend the second poem, *Paradise Regained*, and he told him the idea was put into his head by Ellwood, "which before I had not thought of."

Paradise Lost was sold for the sum of £5.

A row of great elms borders the street here, growing in the field beyond the wall. A little lower down, among the old cottages and odd little shops, is the gateway and swinging gate leading to the churchyard. It is very surprising to look through this lych-gate in the houses and see the church and churchyard within.

There is a pulley for a rope, and the gate centre-post swings on an axle. Over the lych-gate is a room belonging to the sixteenth-century cottage next door, and this spot, one thinks, must have been a very important place in the village life, for every wedding and funeral, all the churchgoers, all the alive and dead must pass through that portal, to be viewed from that upstair chamber window. Ghosts seem to look down on the village street, at the pageant of country life passing before them.

Even to step through that lych-gate with the church bells ringing for service is to walk into another century, motor-cars left behind and ancient things before us, where the church is hidden by the fronts of the houses.

The church of St Giles is built of flint, and part of it is twelfth-century. It is a church of frescoes, a picture gallery of the fourteenth century. There is the story of Salome, very clear and modern in its conception. A jester in yellow and white, one leg yellow and one white, is cutting off the head of John the Baptist, and Salome, with her hair in a fillet, her dress red, her shape willowy and seductive, waits with a bowl in her long fingertips. Another picture of Salome dancing shows the girl curved backward in a semicircle, her body smoothly arched like an acrobat, and a flat hat upon her head. On the table are dishes and pots, and she turns her cartwheels and somersaults beside it, as at a medieval fair. The head lies on a dish, ready. Another wall painting is "St Mary and St John," with "The Creation" near, and "The Temptation and Expulsion from Eden." Satan's neat feminine head on a snake's body wound through a tree turns to Eve, who holds out the fruit to Adam. There are pictures of St Catherine, and grim faces of monks. Altogether there is here as fine a collection of tales told to the ignorant as one can imagine.

In some of the Bucks churches, set in tiny villages among cornfields and farmhouses, one realizes acutely the relation of church and villager. The painted walls, with Salome dancing at Chalfont St Giles, St Francis feeding the birds at Little Kimble, St Christopher at Little Missenden, were the picture books of the times. The statues of alabaster and stone, women in ruffs and fashionable bonnets with roses on the sides, men in gold and black armour kneeling life-size, all were real to the onlookers, as they are to me. The stained glass in the windows, the angels high in the roofs, playing their musical instruments up there, the poppy-heads with faces on the pews, all made a delight and a terror for the child mind throughout many generations. Their imaginations were roused, their laughter rang out, and later when they were grown men and women they saw those satirical faces and compared them to the rich swaggerers, the hard-hearted, the unjust, and derived a little malicious pleasure from the likeness.

Murals were the village pictures, and this is not as remote a gallery as may be supposed. I remember in Edwardian days we had some murals painted on the walls of our village church. We all admired them intensely, and I used to gaze up at them with the deepest interest, forgetting dull sermons and long litanies in my contemplation. I was very proud of them, and so was my mother. I was astonished when strangers said they were garish with gold and the art was bad. What did we care for good or bad art? We saw angels with wings, and horses carrying Elijah up to heaven, and the Apostles standing round the walls. Perhaps some of the murals now being uncovered and venerated in village churches were pronounced bad art by the pundits of the fourteenth century, but the people loved them and enjoyed their picture gallery.

In the churchyard at Chalfont I saw three long stone graves. Two yews guard the gateway to the street, and adjoining the churchyard is an old brick and timbered building with cobwebbed windows. A strong smell of fish and chips came from it, flooding the graveyard, and a wireless playing loud jazz music sounded over the tombstones.

The church has three oak benches of the fifteenth century, with fleur-de-lis finials, and there is a thirteenth-century font with a lovely oak lid. The tower has a ring of six bells, whose chime is sweet as it comes over towards Jordans. One of these bells has the inscription:

> Tho' I am but small,
> I will be heard amongst you all.

The little river Misbourne which runs through the village, a blue stream with ducks upon it a short time ago, has now almost disappeared, and there is only a trickle in the field. The old Chalfont mill is on this river, and next to it is a seventeenth-century cottage with a painted ceiling of Britannia.

On the village green is an inn called Merlin's Cave, mentioned a hundred years ago. There is a tradition of a cave in the meadow behind it. A house has a grape-vine growing by the street with crops of small grapes.

The Pheasant Inn stands at the corner of the high road to Uxbridge, where the road dips down to Chalfont. In the house named The Stone, Cromwell stayed after the Battle of Aylesbury in 1642. It was then the seat of the Ratcliffes, but it has been rebuilt. Shots were fired and some bullets were found in the roof of the church.

Denham village, on the eastern borders of Buckinghamshire, has some picturesque old houses of the sixteenth and seventeenth centuries. The river Colne runs near it and flows through the grounds of Denham Place, where Lord Vansittart lives. This is a stately seventeenth-century house with a beautiful painted plaster frieze in one of the rooms, with little houses, bridges, and trees. Several other rooms have fine decorations. The stables and coach-house are late seventeenth-century, and a little clock turret stands on the tiled roof. Around the gardens is a high old red brick wall of the same date.

The Savoy, " Savvy," a timber-framed farmhouse, has a moat which is partly fed by the Colne. This house contains a hall which was built in the fourteenth century. In the sixteenth century the chimney stack was erected. There are murals (1606) of Biblical scenes in a room. It is a beautiful example of a medieval dwelling which has been added to during the centuries.

In great contrast to these fine old houses are the ultra-modern green buildings of Denham Studios which are in the neighbourhood. Here close to the woods one can see the façades of Regency houses or the Hall of the Pharaohs.

Between Denham and Beaconsfield is the large residential district of Gerrards Cross, which has a green and pond and a few charming old houses around it. Bulstrode Park, with its hills and woods, stretches along the outskirts of Gerrards Cross. There are many legends and stories about Bulstrode which once belonged to Judge Jeffreys. Dick Turpin is supposed to have robbed the Duke of Portland when he was walking across his own park. There is a very large earthwork with inner and outer ramparts and ditch in the grounds.

CHAPTER III

HIGH WYCOMBE

HIGH WYCOMBE, the second-largest town in Buckinghamshire, is an ancient market town. It fills a valley whose wooded slopes keep it from climbing too far, but it spreads along several subsidiary valleys, always growing, for it has hundreds of factories with their attendant houses and shops.

The main valley is watered by the little river Wye, a swift small river which rises at West Wycombe, flows down through this long congested way, and curves round by Loudwater, Wooburn, and Bourne End to join the Thames. In its journey it works paper mills and factories and for centuries it was the source of power for several water-mills on its banks.

The town has a proud past, for it is a place of great antiquity. Although it was not on a Roman high-road, it was on a road of some importance connecting the Thames and the ancient British trackway, the Icknield Way. In 1772 a Roman settlement of good size was unearthed at a meadow, Penn Mead, part of the Rye. There was a many-coloured tessellated pavement with a beast like a dog in the centre.

This pavement was copied for Lord Shelburne by Mr John Rowel of High Wycombe, and then reburied for safety. There it lies, a hidden treasure, under the grass. With the pavement were found several Roman coins of the time of Marcus Aurelius, Antoninus Pius, and Nerva.

There are two hill camps, one at Keep Hill, where gold coins were found, and another at Castle Hill, where large arrows were dug up. There is also an earthwork, a prehistoric ring, called Desborough Castle, familiarly known as "The Roundabout." This was probably the meeting-place of the Hundred Court, or folk-mote.

The county was originally divided into "hundreds," the hundred probably referring to the ancient assessment in hides, although it may have been families or warriors. Desborough Castle, this great mound and ditch, was the meeting-place of the Hundred of Desborough, for each hundred had its own court. At the time of the Domesday survey there were eighteen hundreds in Buckinghamshire. Later the eighteen were combined in groups of three. Stone, Risborough, and Aylesbury became the Aylesbury Hundred, but Burnham Hundred, Desborough Hundred, and Stoke Hundred were left out. These three hundreds belonged to the Crown in the thirteenth century, and their stewardship carried a small fee. They are the Chiltern Hundreds, and as this part of the country was infested with robbers, owing to the wild nature of the hills and woods, the Steward kept order. Highwaymen have gone, but the office of Steward of the Chiltern Hundreds remains and it is an office of profit under the Crown. A Member of Parliament who wishes to resign his seat applies for the stewardship, and by taking this paid office he loses his seat, for a Member cannot hold any office of profit under the Crown. Since 1742 this device of resignation has been used.

There are legends of a great battle at Deadman Dane Bottom on Wycombe Heath, where it is said a great slaughter of Danes took place. Human bones and a battle axe were found there. But there are more peaceful tales of miracles worked by St Wulfstan at High Wycombe, and tales of the worship of wells, pagan rites which were put down by St Hugh of Lincoln. This well worship often occurred at places with good springs of water, and even now there is well-dressing with garlands and flowers in some parts of England, where clear pure water rising from the earth is regarded with wonder and with thankfulness to God.

High Wycombe is a town which once had great beauty of fine old houses and broad main street and the surroundings of woods on the hills and river in the valley. The wide street was there in the thirteenth century, and the market-place was at its west end. Now the town is commercialized with hundreds of factories, with chimneys and hoardings and rows of new red houses. Such is its spirit and character that even now it is not utterly spoiled, and a wise Town Council could stop the ravishment of this once lovely place. The woods are there, the broad

27

High Street is there, and many of the old houses remain under a modern disguise.

It has been a market town for centuries, as the name Chepping Wycombe denotes. The Old English word Chepping comes from the Anglo-Saxon *cheapen*, to buy and sell. The right to hold a market was an important concession, which has been guarded. Market dues were enforced, about a shilling for a stall-holder, or for standing by the road with goods to sell. The market was granted to Chepping Wycombe in 1226. The day Friday was fixed in the Charter of Queen Mary. It is still a market town, and the little market house and the lower part of the Guildhall and the pavements are packed with booths on Fridays and Saturdays.

Markets are much smaller than they were in the days when farm produce was brought from all the villages for many miles around to be sold in the streets. Then people brought their goods, carrying them in market baskets on their arms, begging a lift from a farmer, or walking the miles on foot.

"My father used to bring his farm stuff from Lane End to High Wycombe every week," said a countrywoman to me. "He didn't drive, they couldn't spare the horse, so he walked with his baskets and walked home at night."

There are stalls in the streets and wares spread out on the pavement, much as they have always been, but the cattle market is held on Monday mornings. Cabbages and apples, plums and damsons, pots and pans, flowers and plants, are heaped on the wooden stalls. Apple trees lean up against the wall of the church-yard, and wooden rakes stand by the corners, under old houses. The people come from neighbouring villages, the buses are packed, and the narrow bottleneck in the main street by the Guildhall is filled with slow-moving traffic, jammed together. Perhaps it is as well that cattle and horses have been banished from the streets.

In December the market is a colourful sight, with the wooden stalls piled with white celery, and round balls of brussels sprouts, and watercress grown locally; Christmas trees dangle from the sloping roofs, and mistletoe hangs from a cord across the eaves of the stalls. There is a jeweller's stall, with Victorian lockets and bracelets, and clothes stalls, and ribbon stalls, as well as book stalls, at one of which I noticed expensive books on art and poetry which would never have been sold in the country markets I have known. Here they went as fast as novelettes.

In front of the old Falcon Inn, under the hanging sign of the fierce-eyed bird, is a stall with hyacinth, daffodil, and tulip bulbs for sale, and next door is a music stall with violins and ukuleles. It is indeed a good market, as everyone knows.

The air is misty blue, as blue as those hyacinths will be when they come out in the spring, the town lights are on and darkness is coming down from the woods. It is easy to imagine anything at High Wycombe if one peers down the passages between the shops, at the crooked walls and old roofs. The people who swarm the streets are those of every generation in the blue dusk of a market day. They are medieval, and they are modern.

There is an enjoyment in marketing on the pavements and under the arches of the Guildhall or by the little red brick market hall, the Shambles, and round the corner of the church.

The church tower of High Wycombe rises high against the blue sky. Fish wives are arguing, a potman is banging a kettle, not breaking his thick china as in the rich old days of plenty. An aged crone goes past, dressed in the costume of the 'nineties, with beaded mantle and trailing skirt, and a young woman in scarlet trousers laughs at her. High in the church the angels play their musical instruments, a hurdy-gurdy and a lute, and in the market the thin wail of their music comes, or perhaps it is only the wind singing.

The Red Lion stands proudly on high gazing over the heads of the people who surge to the stalls near him. The little octagonal market house has humble stalls of winkles and vinegar and the white-aproned fat women sell them. This house with its leaded roof and lantern and its open porticoes was designed by the Brothers Adam in 1761. Now the floor is littered with waste paper and cabbage leaves, thrown away by the stall-holders. It is better, however, that the building should be part of the everyday life of the town than a museum place, shut away.

This Christmas there is a large Christmas tree at the end of one stall, and children stop to stare at it as they pass. Outside the

market house is the tinware stall, with tin kettles and scarlet and
gold dustpans brought from Slough where they were made. The
dustpans are so gay I buy one and carry it away with me, with
mistletoe and chrysanthemums.

The Guildhall is decked with fairy lights and coloured garlands, and a tall decorated Christmas tree stands under the
slender arches at the head of the High Street.

This fine Guildhall, whose arches are raised on stone pillars,
was built in 1757 by Henry, Earl of Shelburne, to take the place
of a much earlier wooden Guildhall. The ancient Guildhall,
built in 1604, was a strong timber building "on twenty-two
large posts of hearty oak." Between the pillars a corn market
was held every Friday, when wheat, barley, and rye were sold
between twelve o'clock and one at the ringing of the market
bell. Oats, beans, and various seeds could be sold at any time.
There was a very large market for corn here for many flour men
and maltsters lived at Chepping Wycombe and there were a
number of water-mills within the parish and near it. When the
springs forming the river Wye are low, wheat is low-priced,
was the local saying.

The Shelburne Guildhall has a large upper room with a lovely
double archway at the entrance. This is the Court room, called
the Shelburne Room. It is a beautiful place, which might have
more care bestowed upon it, for it is a treasure belonging to the
town. From the long windows one can watch the narrow side
streets with their old houses and rich red roofs and timbering
and see little ancient inns. "Rough houses, I calls 'em," said the
caretaker grimly, as he spoke of war days when Bomber Command had its quarters in the town.

Next to the Shelburne Room is the Carrington Room, where a
large painting from the church hangs, and there are pictures of
some mayors of Wycombe on the walls.

A wooden cupola crowns the roof and at the summit a
beautiful weathervane swings, a golden centaur who shoots into
the wind above the surging motor-buses and lorries and cars
which are forced to slacken their pace as they curve round the
projecting old building.

The Guildhall is "right in the way," people complain, and

some reformers wish to move it. It would be a thousand pities to do this, for more than the Guildhall would be taken away. The spirit of the town would be harmed. Why save a minute at the cost of a lovely ancient possession which many towns would delight to have inherited from the past? Even now the Guildhall is often defaced by advertisements, the most sinister being one of a boxer fighting Death on the roads. So ugly a sign I have never seen before, and I was glad when, as a result of public opinion, it was removed.

At High Wycombe the men used to stand under the graceful stone arches of the Guildhall once a year, at the Hiring Fair at Michaelmas, to be interviewed by masters. In their caps or buttonholes they wore their badge of trade.

Carters and horsemen wore whipcord in their hatbands, cowmen had a wisp of hair, shepherds had a curl of white wool. Gangs of men who wanted work came to this fair and hired themselves out. The farmers and others wanting labour met them, talked to them, and engaged the man they liked. The bargain was sealed with a shilling which the master paid out with ceremony, for a shilling went a long way and would buy a great deal in those days. It was important to choose a decent and cleanly man to enter one's home, to be part of the life of the farmhouse.

Perhaps it was pleasanter to wait under the shelter, with the golden centaur shooting his arrow high above their heads, than to wait at the door of the Labour Exchange, as one sees them nowadays. At any rate, master and man met and talked matters over, and there was a bright shilling to spend, the earnest money called Fastening-penny in some parts.

Boys went there for hiring too, and a Buckinghamshire woman told me of the adventures of her father, nearly eighty years ago. He came, a little lad of ten years old, to High Wycombe from his home at Lane End to offer his services as a farm boy. He stood under the arches of the Guildhall at Michaelmas, and he was taken on by a farmer to look after the pigs. One day he drove some pigs to High Wycombe market from the farm at Booker End. A dense fog settled down and the child struggled along the lanes with his little pigs running here and

31

there in the darkness. He lost them all. Although he hunted and called for hours he could not find one pig. He dare not go back to the farm and he dare not go home. When at last he got his courage up to confess to the farmer he was sent away. The pigs were never found. They had been stolen by somebody in the fields where they had strayed. That was the end of his farm service, but when the boy became a man he managed to get a small farm for himself. His wife helped the family fortunes by making lace. She went to a lace school when she was eight, and very important she felt, no doubt, as she learned to handle the bobbins and to prick the pattern on the slips of thick paper.

Soaring above the town is the sixteenth-century tower of All Saints' Church. The church is in the centre, with buses rushing past its walls, and people walk through the graveyard as a short cut from one road to another. Men going to work with ladders and tool-bags stand a moment and read the inscriptions.

"Seventeen hundred and sixty-two. That's a long time ago," says one man in cap and apron, with his bag in his hand, to his mate, and the other agrees and on they wander, through their native art gallery of stone tombstones.

High Wycombe, the town of craftsmen, has some good work in those gravestones. There are delightful cherubs, smiling and debonair, and some grim skulls, all by the pathway; one tomb has a pick and shovel carved upon it, like those carried by the workmen, and another, which pleases me very much, is a young country wench with full skirts, carrying a basket in her hand. She is a graceful creature like Polly Peachum.

It is very busy around the church at High Wycombe, and buses roar past the doors, so that the dead are never lonely.

The church, the largest in the county, was originally cruciform with a central tower, but the old tower was taken down in the early sixteenth century and the present western tower was built. There is some thirteenth-century work in the church. The south doorway and fine porch still remain in their early beauty of carving.

The great tower is over a hundred feet above the street, shining white in the air. It has a ring of twelve bells and lately a tablet was put up commemorating the peal for victory.

32

Milton's Cottage, Chalfont St Giles

The most beautiful part of the church is the roof of the nave, which is painted with delicate blues, reds, blacks, greens, and whites as it has been for centuries. It rests on angels holding musical instruments, but so high is the roof one cannot see the detail.

There is a carved oak reredos painted in brilliant colour, in memory of the men who fell in the First Great War, and the carving was done by local craftsmen. High Wycombe is happy because it is the centre for the wood craftsmen, and there are many signs of their creative work. In the modern Town Hall there is an Oak Room, with beautiful and highly decorative carvings round the walls and over the doors, done by High Wycombe craftsmen in the slump after the war of 1914–18. There are some clever pieces of work—a basket of fruit, the head of a woman, a swan, the town's symbol, incorporated in the pediments of the doors. The row of windows has stained glass commemorating famous men of Buckinghamshire—John Hampden, Penn, Burke, and Disraeli.

One modern window in the church is specially interesting because it is dedicated to seventeen famous women. In the centre are the Saints, Margaret, Bridget, Winifred, Hilda, and Frideswide, with Margaret Beaufort, Margaret Roper, and Margaret Godolphin. Other women are Emily Brontë and Emily Davies, Elizabeth Fry and Florence Nightingale, Queen Victoria when young, Grace Darling, Christina Rossetti, Alice Marvel, and Mary Slessor (with a little black child).

On Victory night we saw the church tower flood-lit. Particularly beautiful was the tracery on the tower's summit, for under the pointing light it seemed to have a delicate edging of white stone lace. How exquisite is that stone carving! The flood-lighting brought out faint pink and rose in the stone. We crossed under its walls and gazed up, and many others were looking at their tower. Close to it was a little alley, a bit of dirty, medieval England with timbered walls nearly touching.

The street near was closed for dancing and there was a strange air of past days as if the present had receded and another century had rolled back again. Girls and men swayed in the thick mob of people in the centre of the street as they might have done in

D 33

Entrance to churchyard, Chalfont St Giles

Tudor times, near the white walls of the old Falcon Inn with
the Guildhall arches behind them. The little centaur on the
top of the lantern pointed his arrow, caught in a flood of white
light, and his grace and beauty swung high in the air, matching
the beauty of the church tower across the road. The wailing voice
of a crooner came beating up against the church, singing mourn-
fully of love, but the strong old tower and the dancing little centaur seemed to be symbols of Christianity and Paganism, both of
which were alien to that voice coming from the loud-speaker.

This town of surprises, of ugliness and beauty, of antiquity
and modernity, of countrymen and townsmen—this town has
so many aspects that one hardly knows what to expect. I have
seen High Wycombe when it looked bedraggled and dirty, an
industrial town in its worst mood, and I have been there when it
was a gay market town, full of colour and life. Sometimes it
sulks and sometimes it smiles, but always it is a place of strong
character. High Wycombe has many secrets, and it carries
memories of such a full and satisfying past that it can afford to
conceal its treasures, and to show only its ugly side, but of a
sudden it reveals a score of hidden pleasures. Every time I go
to High Wycombe I get a glimpse from bus or car of this concealed loveliness—a scroll of ironwork, an inn sign, a fine window or door, a cottage squeezed in a corner. It is easier to see
these when riding, for there is always the danger one may be
run over if one gazes at a dormer window or a crinkled red roof
in a narrow street packed with traffic.

High Wycombe's old houses along the High Street and in the
narrow side streets have been changed by the modern shop fronts
with large windows and signboards. They have been lost when
enormous cinemas were erected, but we have only to glance at
the roof line with the uneven gables and crooked old red roofs
and chimneys to see what was once there. If we peep down a side
alley there are many old timbered beams with tiny windows and
great chimneys with gardens and apple trees. They remind me
of old people shut away when visitors are coming, and they slyly
look out from their retreats.

I think many houses in High Wycombe have their secrets,
their scraps of beauty and antiquity hidden out of sight, but

enjoyed in private. They show their dull side to the passer-by, and keep their treasures behind the façade. The backs of the houses, the steep roofs in a jumble of gables and ends, the passages with timber crooks showing in the walls, the elegant fanlight over a door here, the string course over a window there, all reveal the eighteenth century and earlier. Sometimes there are dormer windows in a mossy roof with an altered shop window below.

Buildings have been pulled down for the convenience of the motorist, but the way through the town is sinuous, and the Guildhall stands there, an obstinate little place in spite of its elegant air, turning the buses round the corner.

In the High Street stands the Red Lion, a famous inn, which is built on the site of an even older hostelry mentioned in the early fourteenth century, for the original Red Lion was held by a family named Cok of 1312. The present Red Lion has stood in the broad High Street for centuries. In 1636 the inn is referred to as the "Lyon." It is an old posting inn which has an archway leading to stables in the courtyard. The great red lion stands majestically on the summit of the portico. From this same place Disraeli spoke at the Wycombe election of 1832, addressing with eloquence the crowds below, after Colonel Grey had made an ineffectual speech. In 1945 Winston Churchill spoke to even greater crowds. Naturally the landlady of the Red Lion is very proud of these historic speeches.

There is a curving staircase with beautiful ironwork in the banisters. Above the great side door at which the passengers from the coaches could alight under the shelter of the archway there is a fine and elaborate fanlight. We went into the rooms Disraeli used when he stayed at the inn. The bedroom window has the great red lion on the platform outside. This bedroom has the two little hobs in the high fireplace, which I was glad to see had been left. A portrait of the famous man used to hang here but guests objected to his stare, and it was removed.

Princess Victoria, with her mother, the Duchess of Kent, passed through High Wycombe, changing horses at the Red Lion in 1832.

Many modern changes have been made in this hotel, a great

neo-Georgian dining-room added and the old dining-room made into a bar.

A very old inn, the Catherine Wheel, which stood opposite the Red Lion, was burned down in 1780. This ancient inn was visited by Charles II with his Queen and the Duke and Duchess of York in 1663. They came from Oxford and stayed the night in High Wycombe. They left between five and six in the morning, and the King arrived in Whitehall before "nine of the clock." The Queen left at eight and dined at Uxbridge, and then went to Whitehall at eleven.

The Falcon is mentioned in the seventeenth century. The White Hart, the Wheatsheaf and the Angel were old inns.

The beautiful house called Loakes, the seat of Lord Shelburne, was visited by John Wesley and by Dr Johnson. This house was replaced in 1795 by Wycombe Abbey, which in 1896 became a famous school for girls, after having been the Royal Military College and Lord Carrington's house. During the late war it was taken over by the United States Army Air Corps, but it is now a school again.

High Wycombe has certain inestimable boons, and one of these is the Rye, about thirty-five acres of meadow land which belongs to the town. It stretches by the river Wye, with the road running by its side and the woods behind it, forming a lovely piece of green land. Here the common cattle were pastured in old days, and here the "law days" were held. Every settled inhabitant of the borough had the right of common grazing in the day-time for two cows and a bullock. "All the inhabitants of the borough have liberty to walk, and use sports and pastimes, running, leaping, wrestling, riding, backswords and others playes at their pleasures, without being trespassers." Now it is the playground and the recreation ground for the townspeople. It is unspoiled and perfect, a priceless possession for all time. It does not get that worn and jaded look of ordinary recreation grounds, it remains a broad meadow, green and sparkling.

The ancient meadow of King's Mead has had grazing rights for hundreds of years. These rights have been exercised from time immemorial. The Mead, which is a meadow in the Wycombe valley by the side of the river Wye, has rich pasturage and the land is well watered, but the neighbouring farms and hills are scorched in the heat of a dry summer.

Lammas rights are common rights for pasturage and for sharing the natural land. From April 1st to August 1st each year, King's Mead is closed, but after haymaking the land has always been common property and those who had Lammas rights could turn their cattle to graze there. Young stock, heifers gone dry, and horses were put in the meadow. One could often see about sixty animals feeding upon King's Mead. Lammas rights are invaluable to farmers, but it seems they can be taken away. The farmers of Wycombe Marsh, Loudwater, and other villages have lately appealed to Parliament against the taking of the Lammas rights on King's Mead.

Fairs were once held in Alan Bassett's fields, by the Rye, and on the land belonging to St John's hospital. The hospital of St John Baptist consists of a twelfth-century hall, ruined and roofless, and a detached wall, perhaps part of the chapel. In 1550 the old hospital became the grammar school, and when the new grammar school was made, in the nineteenth century, the ruins of St John's hospital were left. Now a large modern school has been built on the top of the hill, and the valley school is a technical school.

The medieval fairs brought fame and prosperity to the town, and one can imagine that the level ground by the river must have been good camping-ground for those old performers. Fairs and circuses are to this day a feature of High Wycombe. There must be a tradition of prosperity and gaiety in the town, for there always seems to be a fair or a circus coming or going at the corner of the Rye. In the rush of traffic there are often caravans and wild-beast shows moving slowly and clumsily forward, as there have been for centuries.

Celebrations are held on the Rye for great national events. On Victory night we stood on the little bridge, by the old water-mill, and watched the dancing flames of the bonfire. Around it was a frieze of faces, like a quickset hedge, partly in shadow and partly in light. They might have been people of two thousand years ago, congregated together for some kind of fire-worship. The rain stopped and the sky became green and blue and silvery in the darkness. Against it a band of great trees stood outlined, and beyond these the curving streams of fireworks flew into the sky, rockets with showers of silver stars, red and blue and green fireballs. There was a strange silence about those fireworks, rising from Wycombe Abbey, soaring above the beautiful trees and dropping down again in colours.

There have always been important mills at High Wycombe, whose swift little river has worked them. Six water-mills were mentioned in Domesday Book and one or two of these are still in use. Pann Mill stands on the river Wye at the little bridge in the midst of houses and it is one of High Wycombe's delightful surprises. We went through the open door of the white timbered mill where they were grinding cattle food. We talked to the owner, a genial man with plenty of good sense and country knowledge. A son of a farmer who had been a miller in Kent, he came to this mill which was almost derelict after the 1914 war and saved it from the hands of housebreakers. He put in new floors, new machinery, and transformed it to a fine mill worked by water power.

We went behind the mill house to look at the great water-wheel slowly turning with green mossed "sluices." The sound of the water slipping off it was like music. The surroundings have been made into a garden with a little bridge across the water and a rock garden bright with primroses and violets and daffodils. This lovely scene, hidden among the barns filled with sacks of grist, was a few yards from the roar of the traffic. The miller deplored the desire of people for the very white bread which can only be made by special processes using much machinery. His son, a young commando who had fought in Holland and had been a prisoner of war there, was with him. He, too, was going to be a miller, but he was critical of the ancient timbers, feeling the mill was rather old-fashioned in a world where only new things are valued.

There is another mill on the Rye which is said to have a long lineage. This is Bowden Mill. At Bassetsbury there was a water-mill which is not now working. The mill-wheel is there by the river in that hidden corner of the meadows.

Down a side road is the little bridge over the river which

38

leads to the ancient and beautiful house, Bassetsbury Manor. There is a record that Queen Elizabeth slept there on one of her travels from Oxford to Windsor by way of Bradenham and High Wycombe.

This old red brick manor house and mill by the side of the river Wye has been restored and made into a dwelling-house combined with a museum by Mr Walter Skull. It is a model for future museums, for each room is furnished in a period and used, so that there is a welcoming, homely feeling and none of the chill of a showroom.

We went into the hall where there stands a Black Boy, painted two hundred years ago, in scarlet and gold tunic. The Chippendale Room opens off the hall, and this dining-room, with its period chairs, its sideboard with Waterford glass and bowls of coloured fruit, its fine mirror with elaborately carved frame and exotic birds, is both a beautiful room and a true picture of the eighteenth century.

Each room is furnished in every detail according to its period, the most interesting of all being a bedroom of the time of Charles II. Even the musical instruments and the music on the stands and the books on the shelves are in keeping with the needlework pictures, the china and the furniture of each room.

Near the manor there is a field through which the river flows before it turns into the mill stream at the bridge. An old man told me that in his youth this field belonged to a racehorse trainer, and many mares and foals used to graze there. Every day the mares were driven through the water to entice the foals to follow to strengthen their legs and people stood watching the delightful scene. There was a farm at the corner then and a farm on the other side of the road, but no houses. Near the Nag's Head was a chair yard where chairs were made.

For me the greatest charm of Bassetsbury is the corner with the river and bridge, the river twisting round by the disused mill-wheel under a great chestnut tree. The meadows here are like a Dutch picture, with cattle and horses grazing, and an air of unreality, because it is so surprising to find such a place near a town. In 1848 Bassetsbury had its principal room as a storage

39

place for the gleaned corn of the cottagers, piled there beside a winnowing machine.

Down an opening nearer the town is a glimpse of more timbered barns and tucked away is a group of buildings, an old timbered house and its open sheds, whitewashed, with green windows and little yard with millstones set in the ground. This is the stonemason's yard and house. There is an old red brick high wall round a garden set with a little pond and twisted old apple trees. This was part of the old garden of Lord Carrington. At the bottom of the garden runs the river, with the woods beyond, and all this close to the main road.

I went to this monumental mason's to order a small tombstone for a Scottie. "I've heard it is the prettiest corner in Bucks," said the young son, proudly.

Buckinghamshire is full of "the prettiest corners," and High Wycombe still has a few, although they are hidden behind ugly façades.

The main road from Beaconsfield to High Wycombe is bordered with houses, miles of houses, where once there were fields and farms, but many have gardens from older dwellings. Through the gaps in the houses the woods look down, green and plumy with beech trees. High Wycombe valley must have been a paradise of beauty once, but it has been rudely spoiled and the spoiling continues. It is not only the bungalows that line the roads, or the ribbon development—for people must have houses, and they must have factories for work—but the hoardings and advertisements are a blot on this valley.

Nature is lavish and quite soon a garden grows to hide the rawness of a new house. Even the bare chalk cuttings and the road verges are bright with wild flowers and by the main road grow wild thyme and marjoram with their purple blossom and sweet scent, gold and white Our Lady's bedstraw, amber spikes of agrimony, and the yellow candles of mullein with its soft blanket leaves. All bloom freely on the banks, but above them are the hoardings—with giant advertisements which stare down in all their ugliness among the trees and houses, and at night they glitter with reflectors. In no place in Buckinghamshire have I seen such a display. These signs are a real disfigurement.

40

An old Pest House used to stand on the London Road opposite Bassetsbury Manor, about a mile from Wycombe. It was used for smallpox, but probably plague victims were taken to it earlier. The sites for these Pest Houses are known to old inhabitants, who still speak from their memories of traditions of plague stories.

In the centre of the town there used to be a square with trees and seats where the townsfolk sat and a fountain played. Recently it has been transformed and many of the older people have talked to me about it. The trees have gone, the fountain plays no more, and the grass has disappeared to give way to a paved bus station. Frogmore is one of the ugly corners of High Wycombe.

An old custom of High Wycombe is the weighing-in of the Mayor and Aldermen which takes place each year in May.

CHAPTER IV

HIGH WYCOMBE AND
WEST WYCOMBE

HIGH WYCOMBE has an excellent little museum, fresh and uncrowded, with well-spaced objects in the two rooms. In it are some memories of Hannah Ball, the founder of Sunday-schools, who was born at High Wycombe in 1734. She was one of a family of twelve and she must have been very happy in her relations with children, for she looked after other families besides her own sisters and brothers. She became acquainted with John Wesley, whose teaching she admired and followed, and there are letters from the great reformer to her in the museum. She kept a diary for many years, and this is preserved. There are entries for candles in the accounts, and the paper and pens used, and the number of children at the school with their names. All is set forth with extreme neatness and method.

In 1769 she started a Sunday-school for children at High Wycombe and this was eleven or twelve years before Robert Raikes founded his school at Gloucester. When I was very young I discovered a Robert Raikes medal in a drawer and it became a childhood treasure. It was about two inches in diameter, very thick and heavy, made of lead. There was an impression of Robert Raikes in broad-brimmed hat on one side, and an inscription about the founding of the first Sunday-school on the other. There was a small hole in the medal and a blue ribbon was threaded through it as if it were a jewel of great value handed down from other generations.

At these early Sunday-schools many children received their only education. Hannah Ball taught children to read and write and laid the foundation for future primary education.

Hannah Ball's Sunday-school is now a chair factory, but there is a memorial to her in the Wesleyan Chapel which she built from plans sent to her by John Wesley. She was buried at Stokenchurch in 1792.

As High Wycombe is the centre of the chair-making industry,

there are fine examples of chairs of different centuries in the museum. The king of them all is a chair of the time of Charles II with crowns carved on the high back and the original cane seating. There are slender graceful chairs, and sturdy strong chairs of oak, yew, beech, and ash, woods that are used in the factories of High Wycombe. The "Champion Chair" is there, an ornate Victorian chair which won the prize at the Exhibition of 1851, but it has none of the charm of the simpler designs of the wheel-back chairs.

There are beech bow-back chairs, and Windsor chairs made in Wycombe, with a plain seat cut out by the adze. I know the shape of these seats very well, for the chairs were in the farm kitchens of many north-country farmhouses, sat upon by generations of men and boys and never wearing out. I never saw a broken Windsor chair.

There is a corner of the museum devoted to the tools of the chairmaker, and these old implements are mounted on an oak background with a long oak bench beneath. Several adzes hang there, tools for shaping the seats of chairs. The up-and-down saw, with its wooden frame, is a remarkable tool, for the wood is worn hollow in two places by the hands of generations that have held it. For making the frame of the chair a draw-knife was used. The chair legs were turned on a pole-lathe. Holes were drilled with a brace and bit, by a man who wore a "brace-bib" to protect his chest. Enormous screwdrivers also fit into this "brace-bib." There are turning-tools, gouges of many shapes and kinds, the handles made by the woodworkers, the metal by the smith. There are spokeshaves and travishers, sometimes fifty different tools. The stick hooks, which were metal hooks, were used for shaping the sticks of the Windsor chairs. Now all these are replaced by machinery. The loveliest tool is a little hand-carved plane, with the date 1795 cut into the design by the man who made it and used it.

In memory of the lace-making trade of Buckinghamshire, there are examples of the Bucks pillow-lace and point-lace made in the county. The threadwinder, for winding the linen thread on the bobbins, is a most ingenious contrivance, which every lace-maker possessed. Perhaps her wood-carving husband made

43

it for her. It is made of warm brown wood with a little handle to turn the wheel which held the bone bobbin in its centre. The thread was wound from four uprights.

There are gay little bobbins with their brass ornaments and carvings on bone, and their bunches of blue and white beads on a wire. Like the wood-carvers, with their individual tools which they choose out and handle by touch alone, so the lace-maker had bobbins which she could use almost with her eyes shut by the feeling of the wood or bone.

Pictures of old Chepping Wycombe hang on the walls of this museum, water colours of great delicacy with the beautiful houses and the wide main street as it was a hundred years ago.

The museum and library are in one modern building, which is just the right size for pleasure and comfort. It has the homeliness of a private house which one seldom feels in a civic building.

The craftsmen of Buckinghamshire have left behind them sturdy memorials of their work, in chair-making at High Wycombe, in the sculpture of the stonemasons in many a village church, in the design and ornament of common objects. Now that the machine has taken over most of the handwork, there is not so much chance for individual taste to be shown, but somehow it comes out. We asked an old man who was thatching the ricks if he would make a straw "dolly" on the apex.

"I've no time for that nowadays," said he. "I'm all in a hurry. I used to make 'em, but not now."

A Buckinghamshire carpenter came to put a draining-board in my kitchen and when he had done I went to look at his work. There was a finish and skill about it.

"That man's a master carpenter. He's a craftsman," said the other carpenter. "He's the best man for miles around, for he's a real craftsman."

I thought of this when I saw the tools in the museum at High Wycombe. Each tool had its own individuality, its handle of different wood fashioned by the man who used it. The lace-bobbins were carved with the names of the owners, with mottoes and texts. The lace itself, although following well-known patterns, had many original designs incorporated.

Craftsmanship is still alive, and although in these hurrying days it cannot be exercised in the joy of self-expression, in the ornament on a corn rick or in a pattern of lace, it comes out in other ways. I think the "eddering" of hedges shows a true sense of craftsmanship, for it combines beauty and utility, when the weaving of the saplings is made in a pattern around the green fields.

I went to see the furniture factory of the old firm of Messrs Nichols and Janes at High Wycombe. We saw photographs of the work they had done for nearly a century. In the office there was a miniature set of wheel-back Windsor chairs, similar to those they had made for the Queen's doll's house. All the men employed before the war had been craftsmen, but now they were making Utility furniture. However, a few of the older men were employed on better furniture-making for export only, work in which originality and talent were needed. We were told of a sailor who recently came to Mr Janes, bringing with him a specimen of carving he had done on his ship. It was a bust of Shakespeare, carved with a penknife. He was given work as a wood-carver and he was training to be a real craftsman, for he wanted to use his hands and not to be a clerk in civil life.

We went up a flight of open steps to an upper workroom, and even as the door opened there was an air of well-being. The smell of wood, the shavings on the floor, the beautiful chair backs reared against a wall, the benches with the specially qualified men in their white aprons, gave the atmosphere of a place where men work for pleasure. Working in wood seems to have a kindly effect upon the workers, for I have often been struck by the fine expressions on the faces of the men and their deep interest as they do the work they obviously enjoy.

The young sailor was there, carving the sides of a wood-box with a design of grapes and leaves, smiling as he cut the wood. Another man, the chief wood-carver, was using a fine chisel on the elegant banister-splat of a chair. The Chippendale design of ribbons, curled and waving in a wheel, was coming out from the wood as if it had been hidden there and he was finding it. He told me he used two hundred kinds of chisels in his work. Bit by bit the wood was chipped out and the delicate scrolls of the ribbon and the leaves were brought forth.

45

Another man was making the legs and sides in one long, curving piece. The whole of a modern Chippendale chair was made in this room.

There were chair backs of Hepplewhite design with the three wheat ears just evolved from the background, waving as if they lived and grew, especially real in the pale straw colour of the unpolished wood. There were chair backs carved in such delicacy of detail they looked like lace. We saw many designs of great beauty. The wood they were using was walnut from the country around High Wycombe. The trees are bought as they stand, but there is a careful examination first, for the walnut trees above all others may appear to be in full vigour of leaf and fruit when they are decayed and hollow within.

We went into a timber yard, which was really an orchard with old red brick walls and apple and pear trees growing along the sides. The ground was stacked with timber which was seasoning. Trees lay there, sliced in inch-thick slices, with wedges between so that they kept the shape of the original trunks. There they would lie for years. At least ten years is needed for the correct dryness, which is only 12 per cent water content. At Princes Risborough the modern research station is working on this and kindred subjects.

There was one tree in particular that interested me, a mighty tree, cut so evenly that one could see its form and imagine it upright growing in an open wood. In another part of this orchard was a pile of red mahogany imported for the work, but I like best the English wood. There were trunks of yew with their bark like shreds of rags lying there, and a pile of cherry trees cut lengthwise in thin planks, and pear wood and apple, beech and elm. Many trees lay in this orchard behind the shops of High Wycombe, for High Wycombe is indeed a town of surprises. This garden and orchard and the apple trees left growing there were part of the grounds of Wycombe Abbey when it belonged to Lord Carrington.

We visited the Utility section of the factory which makes thousands of bedroom suites, exactly alike, as ordered by the Government. Yet these pieces of furniture are not really alike, for even in this the good workman does better work, and the high-class factory, with its excellent craftsmen, is compelled by an inner urge to do its best work under restrictions. So when the furniture is sprayed with the polish, the finishing off is done by hand. Now restrictions have been removed and there is more freedom of design.

At Messrs Birch's factory we saw furniture which they have been allowed to make recently, as a break from Utility with its straight lines.

We went to a workroom which was beautiful, in a special way, with chairs of white sycamore, which the men were making for a ship. I never knew how lovely is sycamore, and the touch of it is like silk. Four men stood at their wooden benches, smoothing the wood, and shaping it with spokeshaves and steel scrapers, like razor blades of a large size. Their tools hung above them on the wall, clean and bright, and well-used, with marks where hands had pressed in the wooden handles. It seemed unbelievable that such a surface could be produced by a tool. To me, it was the silkiness that comes from generations of wear when hands have rubbed it. The men told me they were glad to be doing this special work instead of the Utility furniture or the aeroplane work.

Even the bending of wood for the curved backs of chairs was done by machinery, and very fascinating this was. The pieces of wood, several at a time, were boiled for an hour and then lifted from the oven and put three or four alongside, in a metal frame, whilst a giant hand bent them to an arc. They were left in the frame, carried to a drying-room, till they were set.

We saw the kilns where the wood is seasoned. The timber is left out of doors for six months, and then brought to the kilns, where the drying is speeded up with hot circulating air and moisture.

It was interesting to see great machines in motion at Messrs Keen's factory doing the work that men have done by hand, and I found it enthralling to watch them. There is something hypnotic about a machine cutting through a tree, slicing as softly as if the wood were butter. I wondered what the men who worked these machines thought about. Their attention could not wander or their fingers would be sliced off. The loveliest machine, to me, was the band-saw, whose metal band moved so swiftly it seemed to be motionless. A thousand chairs are made there a week, for this firm, like all the others, makes Utility furniture. Separate pieces are made in different rooms and then they are assembled and sprayed.

A machine likes straight lines; so do the people. The machine takes the shortest cut between two points, and the resulting chair follows this straight-line fashion. So the thousand chairs have only three or four patterns and the men who make them must get tired of the uniformity, but they were very attractive chairs with their simple design.

Through the windows of the factory I could see the white chalk of the hills and the green woods. Chair-making is clean work and there is the sweet smell of wood always present. Even the sawdust, which is the factory refuse, is burned to run the engine which runs the machines.

I asked about wood-carving and I was told there was one old man left who was a famous wood-carver. He had been fifty years in the firm. He was working by himself in a high room and as we went up to visit him I felt that we were going to see the old lady who had her spinning-wheel at the top of the castle in the fairy-tale of the Sleeping Beauty. I was not disillusioned either. In that high room, at a bench, sat an old man with the delicate hands and the sensitive touch of an artist. He had a miniature chest of drawers on the bench before him, and he opened the two outer doors slowly as if revealing a treasure. Inside were several narrow drawers which he lifted out for my inspection. They were filled with exquisite tools, each one a piece of perfection, fine steel with the sharpest points and scoops, tools with many kinds of handles of different woods, so that when he was working he could pick up any by the feel of its handle.

I enjoyed talking to this grey-haired, bright-eyed man, whose work had gone all over the world. He showed me the cast of one of his carvings, the arms of Chepping Wycombe, a swan with feathers most minutely carved.

"They don't want any carving nowadays. They say the dust gets into the crevices," said he, sarcastically.

From the ceiling beam hung old patterns they had once used,

48

High Wycombe

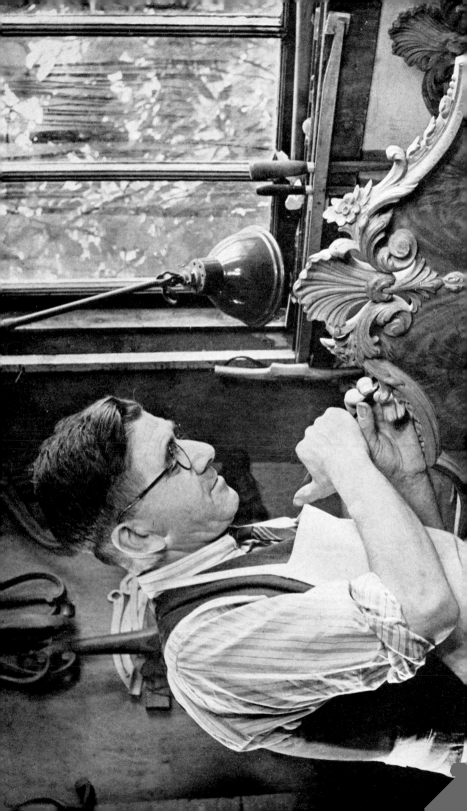

the splats of Windsor chairs, patterns of chair legs and curve-pieces. They hung there like the harness in a well-kept, neat stable.

In one of the long rooms were some chairs in blue and fawn leather that had come from the *Queen Elizabeth* that day for reconditioning, for the firm had made these chairs before the war.

There are hundreds of craftsmen in High Wycombe doing routine mechanical work, and some of these men spend their spare time at things which interest them personally. They work at their crafts and make furniture of great beauty. Sometimes several of them form an association and they do their special work outside their trade. Their routine work, which is mechanical labour at a machine, goes on perhaps forty-four hours a week, and at night they make their lovely things, working with affection for their tools and their creation. They use personal tools which they have made themselves, and the ironwork is made by the local blacksmith. There was one man working privately at home, carving a wedding-chest with a medieval design. He was bringing a whippet out of the wood, imbuing it with everything except life, breathing into it his creative power, with hair and movement and spirit of a dog. Lovely work seemed to flow from his hands as he stretched for one tool and then another, from two hundred tools spread out on a bench.

From these great factories which once turned out the most beautiful craftsmanship and which will soon return to their former glory, I hope, we went to the smallest workshop of all. We drove past Hughenden Park with its magnificent trees, to Naphill, a hamlet of old and new houses, to meet the man who is the last maker of Windsor chairs. Windsor chairs and very old heat-marked willow-pattern plates are an intimate and close part of country life.

We knocked at the door of the flint cottage which has a long, thatched workshop close to it, and as I waited my eyes were caught by the blue primroses growing in the stones between cottage and workshop this February day, and I forgot everything else, even the purpose of my visit. Mr Goodchild came out

E   49

A wood-carver at work at High Wycombe

with his dog, Candy, to show us the workshop, and again, as in that craftsman's room at the factory of Nichols and Janes, I was caught up with nostalgic joy. These workshops, with their sense of woods, their timbers, their spokes and many tools, bring back to me the memory of childhood, of the old carpenter's shops I visited with my father, and the wheelwright's shop and most of all my father's private workroom, called the Master's Chamber, up the flight of outside stone stairs, encrusted with ferns. There the tools were bright on the walls, the bench stood near the door, opening to a little platform where we gazed across the valley. On the walls hung chair backs, some inlaid with brass; pieces of furniture of a hundred years before lay in confusion on the floor waiting for my father to have the spare time to mend them, or waiting for the future.

This room had the same atmosphere and odour, but the thatched roof sagged and was held up by posts. A Windsor arm-chair with decorated banister-splat stood near, and behind it another of yew, with a seat of elm. Chair legs lay in a heap, waiting to be added to the chairs. These had been made by Mr Goodchild on the machine-lathe in the next room, but some of them had come from the bodger working outside in the woods at Great Hampden. The end of the long chamber was stacked with chair seats and the curved backbows and splats, together with a chair made up but not fastened together. There was a small Windsor chair with a back of interlacing arches, which is very beautiful, for it is like a church window framing a country view.

We went out to the orchard where the timbers were reared against a great cherry tree. On the grass was the large bath in which the wood was boiled before it was bent. There was an iron frame with holes regularly spaced over its surface and two iron stakes which could be moved to hold the wood as it was steamed and bent. I have helped in this steaming and bending of wood to make a smooth and lovely curve, and I was deeply interested in a piece of work that always seems so miraculous. Mr Goodchild told me that he used a wood frame until a relation, who was a shipping engineer, suggested the iron frame as being more durable. He had it made for him. So are inventions conceived.

We returned to the workshop to see how a chair seat was "adzed out." The handle of the adze, which had been used by Mr Goodchild's father, was indented in two places by the fingers of father and son. These smooth hollows in the handle worn by long use are the badges of family tradition. We used to point to steps that had been hollowed by feet of past generations, to handles of certain tools in the Master's Chamber, made thin in the spot where the hand always grasped them. In the museum of old tools at High Wycombe there is an adze, similarly marked, hollowed by the grasp of the long dead. I always feel that such tools are imbued with life, they are vital, aware, with something of the life of those others in them. Anyone with sensitiveness can feel it at once, running through their blood, as they hold such a tool.

The tools hung on the walls, the spokeshaves, the scrapers, the gouges, and others whose names I did not know, and on the floor was a litter of shavings which I always find ravishing. Is the attraction the same for a townsman? I wondered. Is a man brought up among bricks and mortar affected as one who has known these things from birth, and feels a nostalgia at the memories of childhood? The smell of wood shavings is as poignant to me as that of tea-roses or tansy, of honeysuckle or rue, or limestone rocks in the rain.

We went into the little room to see the wheel-lathe at work. Some years ago Mr Goodchild used the pole-lathe, and there was the hole in the roof where the pole projected, and the marks of the string on the bench. The pole-lathe made chair legs quicker than the wheel-lathe, I was surprised to hear. The simple pole-lathe, used in the woods by the bodger, could turn sixteen chair legs in an hour, whilst this more mechanical lathe, with its large wheel, made about eight.

In the cottage the chairs which had been made by Mr Goodchild are marvels of workmanship, with beautiful and varied splats. There are chairs of warm yew, so smooth they are like human flesh. Yew always has a humanity and warmth in its wood and it is imparted to chairs made from it. We saw a model wheel-back chair a few inches high, and the pictures that Stanley Anderson has made of this craftsman at work among his chairs.

The chairs are not stained, but they are polished to a glow with beeswax and linseed oil as in all country people's homes. "Linseed oil feeds the wood" we were told when we were young, and certainly these yew chairs look well-fed and living. Elm is used for chair seats, ash for the bows of Windsor chairs, oak, walnut, and yew for special chairs. Mr Goodchild experiments with different designs for his chair backs and we saw some beautiful and original chair splats. There was a yew bough, which is to be turned into a chair leg, for it has a natural curve. There were splats with a design of Prince of Wales feathers. One realizes the joy of making things to one's own liking, fashioned truly with a craftsman's eye to beauty.

Only a short time ago chair legs were turned with the pole-lathe by solitary men working in the Chiltern woods, each in his own little hut or "shop" of beech boughs. One could see men working in outhouses by their cottage doors, making chair legs. I saw some bodgers working in the woods at Great Hampden, with a pole-lathe through the roof of their huts and a great pile of turned chair legs stacked near. They cut the trees, sawed them up and turned them into chair legs out of doors in the depths of the woods.

Some furniture factories have their own sawmills and do everything. Others send their wood to the public mills to be sawn and then they turn the chairs. There used to be an industry of chair-caning at home. I know an old man who used to cane chairs or "rush" them. The cane was imported but the rushes came from Monkey Island, near Maidenhead, where he used to drive with horses and carts for loads. He described to me how to rush-seat a chair.

"You held the rush. You spat on your hand, and twisted the rush with the spittle and twisted it in at the left-hand front corner across to the right-hand, then back and round the chair."

In High Wycombe, under the shadow of one of the great furniture factories, there lives a craftsman of the highest skill and the most delicate feeling for wood, one who through the work of his hands brings happiness to thousands. Mr Hoing, the violin-maker, has made many fine violins which have gained him a reputation among musicians over the world. They are works of art with the pure traditional outline.

He fashions the entire instrument himself, choosing the wood from the best pieces at the factory, sometimes using the lowest layer from a wood that has been selected for veneers. The moulded back of the violin, which gives the chance for the display of beauty, is made from a handsome piece of grained wood, and the ribs are the same. He uses sycamore, chosen for its lovely grain. Each piece is, of course, different, as wood is a living thing, and trees have their own individuality. Occasionally he uses the richer wood of the maple, and we saw violins he had made, some of sycamore, others of maple, with delicate markings under the varnish.

The belly of the violin is made of pine, evenly grained. This wood is elastic and soft, the traditional wood for centuries of violin-making.

Mr Hoing cuts the back and front from pieces about five-eighths of an inch thick. Although the original pieces weigh about six pounds, the finished violin is only about fourteen ounces. There are about seventy parts in a violin, all to be made and joined. The scroll is an intricate work, finely modelled, made of maple or sycamore. The varnish, which is said to contribute to the tone, is made from a secret formula.

Violins hang round the walls of the sitting-room, with violas and other instruments he has made or collected. There is a copy of a Welsh harp, a crwth, made by himself, and a viola d'amore, and a narrow little "jig," which was used for street playing and dances, and then slipped into the pocket, a century and more ago.

The air of the little front room in the narrow street seemed to vibrate with music, the future music those violins would play in many lands. I could have written a fairy-tale under their influence, especially when I saw a miniature violin and bow Mr Hoing has made, two inches long, perfect in every detail. It is surely one of the smallest violins in the world and it waits for fingers of a Thumbelina to conjure its music.

This artist worked with Eric Gill, the famous sculptor, but he was originally a wood-carver. He showed me some work he has done which would have made his name renowned even if he had not touched violins and 'cellos. There are cameos in boxwood, the colour of old ivory, and a relief portrait of Sir Henry Wood in sycamore. There are graceful figures carved from single blocks of wood, and reliefs where the colour of the wood has been used for the natural colouring of the subject.

His latest work is coloured wood-carving, when each detail of a picture, in high relief, is in a different wood. He uses cream of natural sycamore for a Madonna's face, and rosewood for the warm tint of lips, the fine eyebrows of walnut, the scarf of another wood, with background and halo and frame of wood, all combining to make a picture of rare beauty. The wood itself seems to live again in the flesh of the face, and the texture of the cloths.

But violin-making is Mr Hoing's profession, and wood-carving has been set aside for the enthralling work of making musical instruments.

West Wycombe and High Wycombe are almost joined by houses, for the High Wycombe suburbs stretch out and the factories grow. On the south of the road are meadows and pastures with the river Wye flowing towards the town. Beech woods grow on the ridge and these woods are the glory of the whole district. The air is clean, for there is no black smoke as in the industrial north.

The busy road seems to run straight to the great round hill crowned with the church and mausoleum, but at the foot it divides most dramatically and one road swings to Oxford, the other to Aylesbury. On a patch of grass stands the eighteenth-century milestone and signpost, which was erected by Lord le Despencer in 1752. On its sides are the words

From the City 30 miles.
From the University 22 miles.
From the County Town 15 miles.

The road to the University (Oxford) goes through West Wycombe village, whose street of beautiful and ancient houses is narrow for the traffic which rushes along. It is dangerous to cross the road from the little grocer to the butcher's shop in West Wycombe. The traffic seems more ruthless and mechanical here and drivers appear to be automatons. There are no children on this road which sweeps close to the house doors and roars past the windows.

This village, which has been bought by the National Trust, has buildings of the fifteenth century and the nineteenth century cheek by jowl. There are bow windows and mullioned windows and transomed windows. Here is a Queen Anne house with a fine doorway and near is a Tudor house with overhanging upper story and moulded beams. Some cottages are the traditional wattle and daub. Wide timbered archways lead to miniature courtyards, with stables and cottages tucked away off the main street, and lilies and roses growing about them. There are gables of herring-bone brick on some of the houses. So here we have Renaissance, Queen Anne, Georgian, and Tudor work in a row. They are all different, and all beautiful. The reason for this beauty is not only the diversity of pattern and good craftsmanship, but the touch of time. There is no doubt that time is a beautifier as well as a destroyer. This is a great consolation to me. Humble shop and farmhouse and cottage can stand beside fine houses and there is a sense of continuity of design. They are all perfectly right. One feels this in many streets of Buckinghamshire, particularly in Amersham and Beaconsfield, with their broad High Streets with cottages and large houses next to one another, rich and poor, as neighbours.

One eighteenth-century house in West Wycombe main street is approached on either side by a flight of stone steps with a little rail, which reminds me of our brewer's house. Another has its great outside chimney built to the road, so that children can warm their hands, perhaps, on its sides. Another has little square windows and low red roof. A shop is entered by ascending steps to a room where a post holds up the ceiling.

Painted inn signs hang out: the Swan, the George and Dragon. The Swan has an old inglenook fireplace. The eighteenth-century George and Dragon has some pigeon-cotes. The sixteenth-century post office has wattle and daub, and the Plough Inn, dated 1743, has an open fireplace. The beautiful Black Boy Inn, which is seventeenth-century, is now an antique shop.

The most interesting house in the village is the Church Loft, dated 1417, which was a hostelry in medieval times, with cells for monks. All the pilgrims and travellers who went between Canterbury and the famous shrine of Walsingham or to London and Oxford, could use this resting-place. It has a projecting upper story, and its walls are timber-framed. There is a turret with a bell and clock on it. The wide gateway leads to Church Lane, with its charming little cottages climbing the steep road, and patches of garden a foot wide bordering the flowery cobbled pathway. One house has an angel's head over the doorway.

West Wycombe, with its quiet little houses, gives me the impression that time has stopped, and here is the land of the Sleeping Beauty. It is withdrawn and silent, amidst the ceaseless roar of traffic. It is beautiful as the scenery for a ballet, this little red-roofed village with its inns and open courtyards and oriel windows.

In the main street there is a farmyard with stables and barns, but no horse walks there, no haycart or tractor enters. It is a ghost of a farm, and I am always sad as I pass those old walls and see the row of shut doors and the cobwebbed windows and grassy cobbles.

The church stands high on a green hill whose slopes are dotted with groups of ancient black yews. This hillside, which belongs to the National Trust, is the playground for picnic parties, and little children at all times of the year coast down the steep banks on sledges and trays. They play cricket on the crooked sides. It is a colourful hill, with its bright green grass, its sombre yews—a good shelter during a rainstorm—and the happy company who are always there disporting themselves. The top of the hill is a strangely haunted and gloomy place, with the church and mausoleum. West Wycombe Church was built by Francis Dashwood Lord le Despencer in 1763 on the site of a far older church, and this again may have been successor of a very ancient place of worship, for here is an old British camp, with the earthwork and ditch clearly defined. This prehistoric camp has a double vallum and fosse, and the churchyard is defined by the inner vallum, the fence running along the ring. Through the little wicket gate one drops down into the deep ditch of that ancient fort. The position is remarkable, for the church is very high above the small village of West Wycombe, which appears as a cluster of rosy roofs nestling below. This British camp was built in a perfect place for strategy, for it commands the exit of three valleys converging to the valley of the Wye.

In several places in the county a spot sacred or important to prehistoric man has been chosen for the site of a Christian church. That was the wise policy of the Christian faith. At Cholesbury the church is built within the rampart of a clear oval of earthworks, much larger than this. Often there are tumuli near the churches, as at Kimble.

This modern church has had a strange career. Lord le Despencer, who was Chancellor of the Exchequer, founded the Hell Fire Club. His followers called themselves the Monks of St Francis. They included John Wilkes, Bubb Dodington, Paul Whitehead, Charles Churchill. They practised black magic at Medmenham Abbey and perhaps in the chalk cave of Church Hill. Modern guide-books whitewash the character of Lord le Despencer and call him merely eccentric, but the tradition of evil is strong among the country people. Evil can be felt, and this hilltop is a place of deep discomfort and unrest.

In 1774 Paul Whitehead died and left his heart to Lord le Despencer, who buried it in the great hexagonal mausoleum near the church with a procession of mockery, with French horns, pipes and drums. Later the heart was stolen. The cave, low on the hillside, with closed door and chained gate, is blocked up, but it penetrates a quarter of a mile into the hill. Some of the mysteries and orgies were performed in secret here, after the Club was disbanded in 1762. Inside the railings of the mausoleum one can see monumental urns, weathering and decaying.

The interior of the church on the day I first saw it was startling, and I could not believe it was a holy place. The flowers on the altar were dead—dead valerian, dead kexes, dead willow herb, forgotten wild flowers. The seats were thick with dust. Torn hassocks lay on the floor, like rag bags, and torn Prayer Books were tossed down.

The font, with its four doves feeding from a bowl like a washhand basin and another dove struggling to escape from the jaws of a serpent coiled round the stand, had no religious feeling.

On the ceiling in the chancel was a painting of the Last Supper, by Joseph Borgnis, and this partly mitigated the gloom. Chests of drawers and Chippendale arm-chairs take the place of conventional church furniture in this church.

A ladder leads to the copper ball which surmounts the tower. It is a room where ten people can sit, crowded very closely, and there the boon companions met, in some danger perhaps from falling on the open ladder.

The name Haveringdown, or Haveryngdoune, is used for the hill in old documents, and although some think this is an alternative name to West Wycombe, or even the name of a lost village, the word only occurs in documents relating to the church. Haveringdown woods sweep along the ridge to the top of Church Hill. The sides of the hill have groves of yews, some of the trees being very old. There are Great Pen and Little Pen Groves among them. Harebells grow there, and the clustered bell flowers and yellow rock rose, for it is a chalk hill with the lovely little flowers that grow in chalk districts.

There is a legend about West Wycombe Church which I have heard from several country people. They say that the building of the church started at the foot of the hill, near the village. One night the stones were removed and carried up the hill and laid out there in the great circle of the earthwork.

The labourers carried them all back and went on with the building. A short time afterwards the stones were all taken away by supernatural means and placed at the top of the hill. A second time the men brought them back to the valley, but again one night they were all removed and set in the British camp.

"It was the fairies who did it," said a countrywoman to me, "and it was no use fighting against those powers. So they built the church on top of the hill. It had to be built there, but it was always a queer place, they said. That's what my mother told me, and my grandmother told her. But I don't think there are any fairies. It must have been somebody wanted the church up there on the hill."

I was deeply interested to find a survival of belief in fairies of prehistoric origin, not the fanciful fairies of children's tales. They are pre-Christian and they are supposed to inhabit subterranean earth-houses, British camps, and Neolithic remains. The legend of fairies, or earth-spirits, moving stones away, or objecting forcibly to some proposal of mankind, is widespread, especially in Cornwall and in Ireland. I heard a tale recently of a carved gravestone moved from a field to a churchyard in Cornwall by a team of horses. At night it was back in the field, although it was too heavy for men to lift. Again it was removed and again it went back. Finally it was left in the field.

Certainly something seems to haunt this place on the hill-top and I felt disquieted in the church and in the graveyard.

There is a ghostly lane at Wheeler's End, near High Wycombe, I was told, haunted by fairies or earth-spirits; an unquiet road is near Hedsor, and another near Wooburn.

West Wycombe Park, the home of Sir John Dashwood, stands grandly on the opposite hill in beautiful surroundings. The house and grounds were given by the owner to the National Trust in 1944. It is an eighteenth-century mansion, built in the Palladian style with Doric columns. Sir Francis Dashwood, who died in 1724, built the house, and his son altered and enlarged it, perhaps with the advice of the Adam brothers. He employed the Italian artist Borgnis to paint the ceilings of several rooms. Even the ceilings of the colonnades are brilliantly decorated with colours which have retained their freshness. Over the west doorway is Diana in her chariot, and the east portico has a copy of Guido Reni's "Aurora" on its ceiling. Some of the frescoes have been harmed by wind and rain, but the weather has had little effect on the whole design. At the south front there is a magnificent double colonnade.

The Tapestry room, with painted ceiling, has tapestries from Tenier scenes of village life, and a delightful one depicts a load of corn coming from the granary, the farm men walking beside it. A labourer carries a pitchfork and another has a bottle of ale in his breeches pocket, which a small boy is filching. This is a change from the classical subjects which dominate the rooms. Some ceilings are painted in formal manner which accords with the building; one has a fine "Triumph of Bacchus and Ariadne,"

59

another "The Council of the Gods." The large music-room has an elaborate painted ceiling of "The Banquet of the Gods" —a table around which sit nymphs and gods, with figures circulating round the bacchanalian feast. The sky is a vivid Italian blue, and the painter, Borgnis, had to return to Italy to discover the paint for this exquisite blue, I was told.

A gay little ceiling in the small study was brilliantly repainted a short time ago by an artist of seventy, when the original work was flaking off. It has an English freshness in contrast to the heavy luxuriance of the Borgnis paintings.

There are semi-classical statues, and temples in the grounds, dark-stained and lugubrious. The charming Temple of Music across the water against a background of trees adds to the romantic atmosphere. Green lawns run down the slopes among groves of fine trees to the lake, which is thick with reeds and rushes. A small red brick bridge leads to an island. Water-fowl call as they swim among the lily-leaves, and there is a constant motion of wild life out there.

The present arrangements of the grounds and lakes were made by Repton. Yellow mimulus grows on the lake's edge, with water forget-me-nots. There are many yews by the fence and splendid trees grow singly or in thick groves.

The little river Wye, that hard-working busy little river, rises in Long Meadow, in the park, and starts its journey, flowing east through the meadows to High Wycombe and Loudwater and Bourne End, where it makes paper and grinds corn and does a thousand things in its short, hard life. The miller told me the river is losing its volume and its swiftness. The lake, which is overgrown now, was cleared out during the war to make sure of plenty of water if High Wycombe were bombed, but instead of increasing the supply the water has decreased. It may be the wells that are tapping the springs or the loss of rainwater caused by the new drainage systems.

Near West Wycombe is Myze Farm, a seventeenth-century farmhouse, and Ham Farm which was built in the time of Charles I. Good old red brick farms stand in each of the valleys, and the great farm below Church Hill always gives me much pleasure by its look of well-being—clustered buildings, red roofs, timbered barns, corn ricks, like a miniature town in the rich green valley.

At the far end of the village, near the gate leading to West Wycombe Park, there is a great old barn alongside the road and a large yard. There is much activity within this yard. Trees are sawn up with a mechanical saw, gates are made, hurdles and fences fashioned and doors for farm buildings made. This is the West Wycombe Park estate yard. There are fourteen large farms to be kept in good repair, gates mended, posts replaced, floors and walls to be looked after. The estate yard of a country place is a fascinating survival of the work chambers of craftsmen who keep order as they have done for centuries. In the estate yard one often finds men who have worked all their lives in the place, and their fathers before them. They know the traditions and the stories of the countryside.

The village of West Wycombe, beautiful and preserved in lavender, is still dominated in feeling by the spirit of Lord le Despencer. One feels he sardonically gazes from his curious modern church on the spur of the hill. One can imagine that he looks out from the large copper ball—where he so often sat with his friends—and stares cynically down that long straight road which he made towards High Wycombe.

Chapter V

BEACONSFIELD

THIS picturesque old town stretches along the cross-roads of two main thoroughfares, from London to High Wycombe and Oxford, and from Windsor to Aylesbury. These important highways meet at a small green roundabout, and the four roads have each their characteristic name of "End"—Wycombe End, Windsor End, London End, and Aylesbury End. Bordering these "Ends" are many old red brick creeper-clad houses, early seventeenth-century, Georgian and Queen Anne, together with old inns in a comfortable assembly. Behind the houses are gardens, with lawns and magnolia and cedar trees in red brick surrounding walls. There are timbered cottages and houses with lovely fanlights and dormer windows and some with wide door-ways which show they were once inns in the coaching days. Beaconsfield was an old coaching town at its heyday in the eighteenth century, and the two chief inns, the Royal Saracen's Head and the Royal White Hart, were the houses where the coaches stopped and changed horses.

The country was so well wooded and so wild that highway-men lurked ready. Some of these men are said to have lived at Beaconsfield for convenience, and one of them, Jack Shrimpton, was born at Penn. In those days the woods of Buckinghamshire sheltered many a robber. Jack Shrimpton knew the paths well, and attacked any horseman or coach travelling on the lonely roads from Oxford to London. Once near Stokenchurch he robbed a barrister of fifty guineas and his horse. Shortly after he happened by chance to meet the common hangman, who discussed with him the chances of his own hanging. He had a brother who kept an inn at Wooburn, and after dining with him one Sunday he robbed the coach on Gerrard's Cross Common, and took 150 guineas. At last he was caught, and executed, in 1713. His house still stands at Penn.

Claude Duval is another name remembered in local legend.

It is said that at the Crown Inn, Beaconsfield (now a house), Duval, who was a "gentleman bandit," joined a party, frightened them by a tale of robbers, and then robbed a farmer of a bag containing a hundred sovereigns. His name is connected with the King's Head at Holtspur, and the little wood below the inn is called Cut-throat Wood to this day.

"For why? Because they caught them there and did 'em in," said an old man.

There is a fine variety of painted inn signs hanging in the broad roads of Beaconsfield, but many have gone. The Bull, the Crown, and the King's Head are now private houses, but the King's Head in London End has the name over the door and a sundial on its front. There used to be the Prince of Wales, the Queen's Head, the Farriers' Arms, whose wide doorway may still be seen, the Elm Tree, the Alexander, the Plough, and the Chequers.

The Royal Saracen's Head, a black and white seventeenth-century inn, much restored, stands at the corner of the cross-roads, with its wide gateway to the courtyard where once the coaches drew up. It has the sign of the Saracen in gay turban. He swings with a background of flower-filled window-boxes, for this corner is bright with colour. The road is very wide and there is a broad pavement here. Great elms with seats round their trunks grow in the middle of the road in Windsor End.

The Royal White Hart, by Aylesbury End and little old Shepherd's Lane, is a comfortable-looking old red brick and timber inn, with gables and dormers and a roof with a fine chimney stack. The figure of a white hart stands proudly there, gazing towards Windsor. Once it used to stand on the ground at the corner to attract the coaches, as some of the old men can remember. This is an early seventeenth-century inn.

In Wycombe End stands the George Inn, with its window-boxes. It was built about 1600, but in the eighteenth century a new front was added which must have changed its appearance considerably. The interior remains much the same, with timbered walls, fireplaces with chimney corners, spiral stair, and crooked floors. There is the original oak staircase built round a newel. The George boasts that it had a living oak tree as the central post about which the staircase was built. Perhaps this newel is rooted in the ground, as the tradition says.

There is a legend that the highwayman, Claude Duval, stayed there and fought his way on the staircase, which has the cuts of a sword.

The oddly shaped little bar parlour, which reminds me of a farm kitchen with its wide fireplace, has a fine collection of horse-brasses and trappings, with martingales and copper-banded whips, and headbands hanging from the beams. There is a model of a coach made by the deft fingers of the present landlord who is a craftsman as good as any of the wood-carvers. It is always a pleasure to see the toys and models made by these craftsmen in their leisure time, and in many a house I have seen a treasured piece of work exquisitely fashioned.

There is a wide entry into the yard, through an archway with doors and roof, and a little stairway going to an upper room. I love these inn yards, with their stables and outhouses, their cobbled ways and plants in tubs, and all the charm of a country inn. I remember the sound of driving through them, the clatter of the mare's hooves on the stones, the slippery noise as she half-stumbled, the careful driving, "Wey! Whoa! Careful, Lass!" Then the mare was taken from the shafts, and led to the stable, with reins looped in a knot. I gave one last look at the trap with its shafts down as we entered the inn through the low dark doorway, and then all was confusion and strange with rich smells.

In Aylesbury End is the Old Hare, a little inn which had a rare sign of the hare running with eyes affrighted, legs scampering. This painting on a wood panel was displayed on the ancient roof, between dormer windows, not hung out as a sign. Unfortunately this has been replaced by one of poor design. There are three dormers in that crooked red roof, and a gable. This inn, which is one of the oldest in Beaconsfield, has a cosy parlour with oak beams and seats round the wall, very plain. There is a scrubbed long table, with stretchers marked by generations of feet, and cuts showing games played on it. There seem to be the marks of nine men's morris, and a kind of tiddleywinks. They have an old shove-ha'penny board too, but there are no frills or brasses. All is plain and simple in this village inn. Next door there was a

West Wycombe with fifteenth-century church loft

forge until a few years ago, as the place combined smithy and inn.

Little carts with ungroomed ponies stop at this door, and sometimes a gipsy caravan stays there, or a wagon with a team of heavy horses and a load of great oaks going to the furniture makers. It is a colourful spot, the kind of place that some of Thomas Hardy's men would have visited to wet their whistles.

The straight road called London End goes to the gates of Wilton Park and then swings aside. In former days it went through the park, and this was the old road to the Chalfonts. The lanes were closed in the eighteenth century by the owner of Wilton Park, who made the new road in exchange. This is a wide road, with margins where I have found growing the exquisite lavender-blue mountain cranes-bill and the tawny orange-golden hawk-weed, or Grim-the-Collier—two lovely strangers in clumps of colour, half-hidden in the grassy verges.

In London End is the Old Swan, a sixteenth-century inn with a yard in which stand little green tables. The White Horse Inn, near the Old Swan, has the marks of the structure of a windmill on its wall. A windmill stood there and ground corn for Beaconsfield fifty years ago. John King had this mill and the Beaconsfield men were grinders. A sail blew off in a storm and it was never used any more.

There are many tales told of coaching days fifty or sixty years ago. The coach left London at 11 a.m. and reached Beaconsfield at one o'clock and Oxford at 4 p.m., trotting all the way. They changed horses at the Saracen's Head. Four horses were waiting ready. They went from the Saracen's Head to Stokenchurch, but they stopped at High Wycombe at the Red Lion. Halfway along the Oxford Road, near High Wycombe, there was a milestone; on one side it said "27 miles to London," on the other "27 miles to Oxford." This was the halfway stone.

The old road to Stokenchurch went up a very steep hill and extra horses waited to help the coaches up the slope. Many old men remember this and speak of the waiting horses by the grassy corner near the inn. A new road was made called Dashwood Hill, but one can still travel by the old road. There was a third road even older which is now a grassy track with a gate across, and only the very old men speak of it.

F   65

"Time o' Dick Turpin," they say, when they talk of the oldest roads along which the highwayman passed.

The coach was scarlet and it was drawn by four horses. The coachman wore a livery of dark green with gold braid and a top hat. He carried a horn which he winded as he came to Beaconsfield.

A Beaconsfield carpenter on the Hall Barn estate told me the story of a terrible coach accident of a hundred years ago, a tale that has been told by the fireside over and over again. His grandfather, who was a prize-fighter, used to ride one of the coach horses in those days. There were six horses at that time to the coach and three riders, one man to two horses. The horses were fastened together in pairs. They changed horses at Beaconsfield where six fresh horses were waiting at the inn. The riders went with their own horses.

One night his grandfather was ill and could not ride. Another man took his place, one not so experienced on the road. There was a thick fog, so dense that they could not see, but the coach started off, down the steep hill at Wycombe End. At the foot of this hill at the side of the road there is a pond. Now it is partly drained and railed off, but there was nothing between it and the grassy verge of the highway in those days. By some mischance in the darkness the horses, dragging the coach after them, went into this pond, and all were drowned. The horses, being fastened together, could not get free, and every one was trapped.

It is said that the pond was so deep that it would bury a telegraph post. A cart and four horses was used to clean it out some time ago. It was seen to be like a deep basin in shape.

Several have spoken of this coach accident as the tale was told to them by parents and grandparents.

Beaconsfield is at its best perhaps on a day of snow when the old houses are wreathed in white garlands and the warm red brick glows under the frosty roofs, when fires shine through cottage windows and hooded people walk across the broad street to disappear in doorways or through the wide archways of the inns. Then the black and white Saracen's Head looks like an inn out of a legend, and the noble White Hart, standing high over its roof, snuffs the air and prepares to run swiftly away to Windsor Great Park. Beaconsfield has great beauty when the snow falls.

Or perhaps it is just as lovely in early spring, when the trees are just budding, and the four great elms in the centre of the road and all the other elms that grow in the town are rich purple with flowers. Then the sky is a delicate blue, and the tracery of the intricate twigs shows up in its bewildering pattern, and all the little and big houses open their eyes after their winter sleep.

Or is it best when the fair comes to the town? Then it wears bright scarves over its head and dances under the stars at night. For on May 10th the town has its annual fair, a reminder of the very ancient fairs that have come through the centuries, and there are colour and movement and gaiety.

Caravans and great covered vans wind slowly up the broad roads and the showmen set up their shows in London End, Wycombe End, and Windsor End. Hobby-horses and swingboats are erected in the roadway and stalls are set on the pavement edges. The caravans with the families of dogs and children creep close to the little red houses and put out their household gear, their stoves and stools, in the open. A woman fries fish and boils her kettle in front of the Old Hare, and the fuel is gas from a container.

Everything is going well, she says, except that she is short of fat for frying. Inside her little house on wheels one can see a stove and oven shining with chromium plate, and Staffordshire ornaments and blue glass, lace curtains and brass candlesticks. These show people travel through Buckinghamshire, going to Wendover, Amersham, Aylesbury, and the other towns before they go on to Hertfordshire and Oxfordshire.

Under the great elms near the church there is a sideshow of performing seals which flap upon a narrow stage, while the showman shouts and his wife rattles her tambourine and collects the pence. One merry-go-round has in the centre pictures of the world's leaders; Winston Churchill with his cigar, Anthony Eden looking debonair, Stalin, grim and white-faced, the King, Monty, Alexander, and Roosevelt—all are there, rather pale from the wet weather. They swing round to the jazz tunes and the prancing horses. Below them are the heroes of another war, Joffre, Kitchener, and Foch, paler still.

The swingboats fly upward, close to some old houses by the churchyard, so that the fliers can see through the bedroom windows. The largest merry-go-round stands on the grass where the air-raid shelters were. It sends out its grand, riotous music close to the gravestones and one can imagine the dead are listening and enjoying this day of days. Above all this magic and brilliance is the grey tower with its tiny pinnacles, a background for the fair. The Royal Saracen's Head, the Royal White Hart, and the George are hemmed in by the clamour, and the shooting booths and stalls and caravans are almost on their doorsteps.

At the cross-roads there is a small circle of grass and within this little haven of refuge two ponies walk round with children, while a white pony in a pony-trap takes babies for a drive down Shepherd's Lane. Wooden horses and horses of flesh and blood are all the same to the imaginative, and the children ride first on the real ponies, and then on the gold-maned ponies of the roundabouts.

The church, which stands in an important position in the centre of the town, was entirely rebuilt in 1869. It is made of flint with stone dressings and its fine tower, rising above the trees, can be seen from some distance as Beaconsfield is on high land. The broad roads, Windsor End and Wycombe End, run past it, but they are separated from it by a good width of church-yard. A row of little old brick and timber cottages have their backs on the graveyard and the villagers for generations there have seen the pageant of church doings from their kitchen windows. Sometimes a baby's perambulator stands among the gravestones, with flowers and grasses nodding at the sleeping infant. The mother can get on with her daily work and keep an eye on her child safe in God's Acre, under a blue sky. I am told it is very convenient to have the great face of the church clock so near, and it saves a clock on the mantelpiece.

The churchyard has gone wild, with musk mallow standing as high as the tombstones, and wild thyme covering a grave, and little changeling pansies, the heartsease, twinkling in blue and yellow, and tansy's gold buttons, and mullein's yellow spires.

The tomb of Edmund Waller, the poet, stands in its iron enclosure, forbidding with its skulls and spire, but the great walnut tree that hangs over the grave is a better memorial for the writer of lyrics. Near is an old tombstone with a carving of Death carrying an hour-glass in one hand and a curving scythe in another. The inscription is worn away, but the grotesque figure remains.

In this churchyard masses of roses hang from an old red brick wall, dropping their yellow and red petals on the footpath, scenting the air with a perfume sweeter than incense. I like the golden weathercock on the tower, and the great yew tree under which we leave our bicycles during the service.

Inside the church there is a fascinating seventeenth-century iron-bound chest. It has iron straps which frame small painted pictures; red and white roses are painted at the ends, and a ship with a flag and white sails lies in harbour near a tower with a red roof and tackle for lifting the cargo. Another ship is close to the shore under a tree.

The Old Rectory, which overlooks the churchyard, is a beautiful timbered house of the early sixteenth century. It was a cell of the Abbey of Burnham. It surrounds a small courtyard and inside there are panelled rooms and a fine fireplace and an oak staircase. It is a library, a dwelling-house, and a parish meeting-place now. It was well restored by the first Lord Burnham in 1901.

The present rectory is a large eighteenth-century house, but it has several rooms with lovely seventeenth-century panelling and old stables of the sixteenth century which back on to the churchyard. In the rectory grounds there grows a magnificent cedar, and one expects to see peacocks walking up the green paths in the half-wild tangled garden among the rose trees and lupins. There are small alcoves in the red brick walls, as at Chilton Manor House: their use unknown.

Edmund Burke lived at Beaconsfield in 1768 at a large house which was called Gregories, after its original owner, Gregory, who built the house in 1704. In the inns of the county one can see prints of this mansion hanging on the parlour walls. The house was renamed Butler's Court by Burke. It was burnt down in 1813 and never rebuilt. There are green mounds on the spot and a great fir tree grows there, which the old people point out. Some of these men can remember tales told to them by their grandparents of the famous man. When he drove out he came from his house down a drive which swept past Candlemas Pond, without coming through the town.

In recent times a new house called Butler's Court was built, but this has no connection with Burke. The house now called Gregories, where J. L. Garvin lived, was a farmhouse on the estate of Edmund Burke.

At the original Gregories, or Butler's Court, Edmund Burke lived the life of a countryman and a politician with many famous men visiting him and delighting in his company. Crabbe the poet, Dr Johnson, and Dr Burney came to Beaconsfield, as well as Fox and Grenville and Garrick.

Edmund Burke is one of the greatest men in the political life of this country. He had been returned to the House of Commons as member for Wendover, and in 1769 he bought an estate at Beaconsfield of 600 acres, costing £22,000, most of which was raised on mortgage. He became a great agriculturist at Beaconsfield, making orderly scientific experiments on draining and deep-ploughing, and he actually ploughed himself. The account of his draining of ten acres of boggy land is so interesting that I must quote it.

"Ten acres of land were so very wet that the crops produced by it were trifling. Mr Burke cut hollow drains across it, eighteen inches deep and three wide at bottom, some of them three feet deep varying with the fall of the land; they were filled with chalk-stones, and some bushes, the latter the cheapest; the drains answered extremely well for the land has since been quite dry."

One feels sure Edmund Burke stood by the labourers advising and helping. Land drainage has always interested me since I used to watch our hedger and ditcher, Tom Gratton, who came with his sharp soughing spade, pointed and bright, and his sackcloth cloak and his leather leggings to work at the soughs in our fields. Land was waterlogged with the overflowing springs and it was a highly technical job to drain away the water and make certain tracts dry.

We can imagine the great people coming out to Beaconsfield to meet Burke, being taken over his land to see the oxen, the cornfields, wheat, barley, and oats, clover and turnips—all of which are grown in surrounding fields to-day—to admire his six horses and fourteen cows and his stirks. His corn was ground in his own mill (there were several corn mills near Beaconsfield in those days, and even in living memory corn was ground at the windmill of Coleshill and at the mill at London End), and he fed the poor with the flour.

Dr Johnson's racy words about Burke are well known. "Burke, sir, is such a man that if you met him for the first time in the street where you were stopped by a drove of oxen, and you and he stepped aside to take shelter but for five minutes, he would talk to you in such a manner that when you parted you would say 'This is an extraordinary man.'"

This political genius died in 1797. It was proposed that he should be buried in Westminster Abbey, but he left instructions he was to be buried in Beaconsfield Church. There is a plaque of Edmund Burke on the church wall, which was put up in 1898. It has the words: "Edmund Burke, patriot, orator, statesman, who lived at Butler's Court, formerly Gregories, in this parish, 1769 to 1797."

His great estate of good farming land has been cut up into building plots, called Burkes Estate. The richly ornamented grate at which he warmed himself is in the parlour of a little old inn, the Royal Standard of England, at the hamlet of Forty Green, where in winter a fire blazes as hugely as any fire by which Burke sat.

Burke's name occurs everywhere in Beaconsfield—in Burkes Road, in houses, in fields and streets. The New Town has been built over his land. Trees have been left standing and the picturesque red brick houses are half-concealed in the verges of copses and woods. Cornfields, which had record crops even a few years ago, have been taken by the builder and more are disappearing. How many people give a thought to the great Edmund Burke, who once walked the fields where they have

71

their dwelling, who stirred England as Churchill has stirred the country?

Edmund Waller, the poet, 1606–87, who is buried in Beaconsfield churchyard, lived and died at the house, Hall Barn, which stands in its park on the edge of Beaconsfield. He was born at Coleshill, the hamlet on the hill three or four miles away. He was a cousin to John Hampden and a relation of Oliver Cromwell's. He went to school at Wycombe and then to Eton. He was a member for Amersham when he was only sixteen, and later he sat for other constituencies, including Wycombe.

He wrote many lyrics, some of which were set to music by Henry Lawes, but the poem by which he is remembered in this generation is the one beginning:

> Go, lovely rose,—
> Tell her that wastes her time and me,
> That now she knows
> When I resemble her to thee
> How sweet and fair she seems to be.

I think he wrote this at Beaconsfield in the garden of Hall Barn.

He was banished for some years for the plot, Waller's plot, against Parliament, but at last he was pardoned and he returned to his country house. He published "A Panegyric to My Lord Protector" in gratitude that his life was spared. At the Restoration he wrote another poem, "To the King upon His Majesty's Happy Return." When Charles II asked him to explain why this poem was inferior to that on Cromwell, he tactfully replied: "Sir, we poets never succeed so well in writing truth as in fiction," an answer whose quickness must have pleased Charles, with whom he was a favourite.

Hall Barn was rebuilt in classical style some years after Waller's death and this house remained in the Waller family until 1832. Later the first Lord Burnham bought it. The great yew hedge of immense thickness remains, and the artificial lake and gardens with statues and groves and obelisk.

The small houses too have had their famous people. At Wattleton Farm, a farmhouse which was on Edmund Burke's land, lived Mr John Rolfe, the son of Burke's farm bailiff. He was the infant model for the picture by Sir Joshua Reynolds of "The Infant Hercules in his Cradle, Strangling Two Serpents."

The great artist, Reynolds, was visiting Burke at Beaconsfield in 1788, and he spoke of a commission he had received from the Empress Catherine. He wished to paint a magnificent baby for the Infant Hercules. Burke told him that the wife of his manager of livestock had had a child of extraordinary beauty who would do as a model. They visited the farm bailiff's house and saw the little boy asleep in his cradle. Reynolds decided to paint him and when the child was six months old he became the model for the famous picture. When this child grew up the Duke of Buckingham said that he was the best farmer in the county of Bucks.

At the Beaconsfield boundary, on the road to Holtspur, a stone was set up in 1827 having this inscription:

"Boundary Stone of the Manor and Parish of Beaconsfield. The custom of tithing Corn in this Parish is (and has been so immemorially) by the Tenth Cock and the Eleventh Shock."

It was a triumphal stone, set up by the farmer John Rolfe of Wattleton Farm to commemorate his victory against the rector, John Gould, who brought an action against him and lost it in 1822. Unfortunately this stone has lately disappeared and it is thought to have been stolen. Another triumphal inscription is at Medmenham, by the Thames. This is indeed a county of "John Hampdens," fighting for freedom.

The three sons of John Rolfe lived down Wycombe End. William Rolfe lived at Wattleton Farm, now destroyed, John and Robert at Widgenton House on the opposite side of the road. The three brothers were all over six feet tall and all three were wonderful marksmen with the rifle. There was a little lawn where the Butler's Court lodge now stands, with a large peach tree, pear and plum trees and great walnut trees. Wattleton Farm stood there and at this farm horses which drew great four-wheeled wagons to London were stabled and changed. The walnut tree, the peach tree, the lawns, are remembered vividly by old men who once worked, or saw their fathers work, at this

73

lost farm. The handsome men and their splendid crops of corn are still talked about.

Beaconsfield Old Town has several picturesque little shops which have not been spoiled by the addition of plate-glass windows. There is one, a favourite of mine, that sells everything —a little old-fashioned place with two projecting windows and two steps up to the door, which is always open for light and air. Above the door under the "eyelid" which protects the customer from the rain, are the words: "Toys. Groceries." The writing of this old sign is in curved and flowing letters. In the windows are peg-tops painted green and whips painted red, marbles of many colours, and clothes-pegs. There are miniature tanks and notepaper, sweets and buttons. The ceiling is low and from it hang skipping-ropes and lanterns. The old gentleman has been there for seventy years and he stands behind the diminutive counter with an apron round his waist attending to the villagers. It is a Noah's Ark shop. The door at the back has a diamond-shaped glass set in it through which the grocer can glance into his kitchen.

"I've read that in the year 2000 all our little shops will have gone and there'll be nothing but chain stores," said the grocer sadly to me when I went in to buy biscuits. "They'll lose something, they will."

They will lose the personality and interest of the little shop, the kindness and the humanity. These small shops are homes, lived in and cared for. There are many of them in Buckinghamshire. Even the large towns have them. Little inns, little shops and little houses, and churches no bigger than barns—Bucks is a county of small and lovely things.

In Beaconsfield there are still a few crafts—weaving good country tweed on a hand loom, spinning sheep's wool on a spinning-wheel, hurdle-making, and a farrier's shop. There are three brothers who are clever craftsmen, blacksmiths, coach-builders, workers in wrought iron. Their workshop is the old blacksmith's forge, where once they shod horses. The long whitewashed building has rings in the wall where the horses were tied. At the far end is the open forge, with hand bellows and hood. The men are working in their leather aprons, but instead of shoeing horses they are turning out pieces of wrought iron. The red glow of the fire shines across the floor, through the heaps of articles waiting to be mended. It is a good place to visit on a winter's day with snow outside, as I have seen it. The door opens in two parts, like many of our north-country doors, and one can unlatch the top and gaze over without letting in the wind or disturbing the men.

One gate they have made was for the old post office at Beaconsfield, a grille was for the Roman Catholic church, a third beautiful bit of work was for the George Hotel stairway. The most intricate ironwork gates were for gardens, frames for the flowers within.

On the walls hung specimens of work these craftsmen had done: latches and hinges, mortised locks and handles of iron. I saw lanterns they had made, and brackets for wall candles. Much of it is very delicate work, and of course the nails are hand-made. They have branching candelabra, holding five or seven candles, and iron firebaskets. I have one of these, a strong, simply designed basket that holds my blazing logs.

It is always a pleasure to find a blacksmith's shop where horses are shod, and the tinkle of the hammer on anvil can be heard. Children of this generation miss a good deal through not standing at the door of the smithy watching the smith at work.

In September a competition was held at Stoke Mandeville for making horseshoes by youths working in blacksmiths' shops or by farriers themselves. They were required to fix a shoe, and then pass an oral examination on the anatomy and structure of the leg and foot of a horse. The winners were allowed to keep the shoes they made as souvenirs. The winner of the county prize received a leather apron, and the youngest got a farrier's knife. I saw a similar shoeing match at Aylesbury Show.

At Beachampton, a tiny village with a stream running through it, we found a memorial brass to a blacksmith in the church on the hill. The engraving of the smith shows a very wealthy-looking man, with long beard and a long coat.

"Here lyeth the body of William Bawdyn, of Bechampton,"

75

says the memorial, and there is a poem to him beginning most merrily,

Beholde I happie am indeed.

Farmers used to combine trades with their own farmwork to augment their income. A farm was often attached to an inn, the hanging sign of the inn swinging at the front door, the farm buildings at the back. This was a good combination and no dwelling-place was busier than inn-and-farm. The King's Head at Holtspur near Beaconsfield, with its sign of King Charles, was a farm until recently, and the well-known family of Pitcher, the farmers, lived there. Now the stables and timbered barns are made into dwellings and outhouses, and the rich variety of life has gone.

Widgenton Farm, which stood at the foot of the steep Wycombe End, made wattle hurdles and fences and besoms. Besoms were then sold at half a crown a dozen.

Several farms had blacksmith's shops adjoining when they were in a village.

Other farms in this neighbourhood combined brickworks with their farms. The best-known was Penlands, near Hedgerley, which made bricks until late years.

In Beaconsfield there was a chair-yard where Windsor chairs were made, down Wycombe End near the old post office. Caning of chairs was done in a small place near. Carts and vans were made by the coachmaker at Wycombe End. There was a saw-pit in this busy corner of the town worked by two men where the wood was cut.

All these little trades were home trades, where men were free. Then there were straw-plaiting and lace-making and bodging. In a little old red brick cottage by the churchyard beading was done, for in Bucks there was much employment in the home for beading, lace-making, and chair-caning.

There was much brick-making in the district, besides that at Penlands Farm. At Holtspur there were brickfields. "Bill Symonds and Dossett made bricks there." They dug the clay out of the earth, after taking the top soil off, and put it in the "pug," which was worked by a horse. Three hundred or four hundred bricks were moulded in a day. One day a week they burnt the bricks, building a fire and placing the bricks, arranged for the heat to pass through.

At Pot Kiln Lane, Jordans, in a lovely beech wood, are brickworks dated 1805 and thatched open storage house with great curved timbers. This place has had to give up, and now it stands quiet, with no workmen. The round brick-kiln is cold, and the busy works are silent, for there is no chance for the small man. The brick-earth, used for flower pots, is a natural mixture of clay and fine sand, found locally.

The district round Chalfont was famous for its potteries and little kilns, and the pots used to be carried in panniers on the backs of donkeys to Wycombe streets once on a time. Then brick-making increased, and the pot-making decreased.

There are several good farms around Beaconsfield, and the corn-land is very fertile with heavy crops. Hyde Farm, a seventeenth-century building on the site of the old Hyde Manor, has a central chimney stack and projecting wings. A long avenue of limes runs to the house. Overs Farm stands in the fields with beautiful elms behind it. One October day I walked here along Broad Lane, where spindleberries shone in the hedges, orange and pink, and dog-wood and rose briars lifted up their berries, and yellow butter-and-eggs lined the roadside. It is a bluebell lane in spring, a rose and honeysuckle lane in summer, a blackberry lane in autumn, and a lane for birds and wild life all through the year. The old red brick farmhouse is like the flowers around it. I sat in the farm kitchen, talking to the farmer's tall daughter, and I saw the doors with iron latches and the red brick floors. In the dairy were wooden benches where we had stone, and across the yard were the cowsheds.

The cows were being milked with the milking-machine, two cows in a stall, and chains fastening them. They seemed to like it, except one who absolutely refused to give her milk unless she was milked by hand. They were dairy Shorthorns, with a Jersey or two.

In a great barn I saw many sacks of clover seed, which they had just been reaping and threshing in the combine. I held some in my hand, myriads of minute dark seeds, soft as silk. All the country people are delighted to handle it, and they speak in awe of the price. Five pounds of clover will sow an acre. A sack holds about three hundredweight, and it is worth about £6.

Later I saw this harvester, the Minneapolis, at work in a field of clover, with only one man tending it, while the stream of seeds fell into the sacks and the clover stalks flew in a cloud at the back.

Sealey's Farm is partly sixteenth-century, an old red house, with flower garden under its windows, and panelling in two rooms. It is said that Sir Joshua Reynolds stayed here to paint. The date over a fireplace is 1572. The staircase has square newels and turned balusters. This is an up-to-date farm which possesses two combine harvesters, which I often watch in the cornfields. I went to see them in late August, after the heavy rain had spoiled so many crops. The roar of the machine came across the little woods from the cornfields, guiding me. As I climbed the slope of the field among the stubble, I half-expected to see a pair of great horses against the sky, although I knew it was impossible. For centuries there must have been horses on that skyline, and now there was the combine, a magnificent sight. The men were reaping the twenty-two-acre field of barley, and the barley was lying awry, a tangle of ears beaten down by wind and rain. The harvester made a good job of it, sweeping it up and carrying it through its marvellous mechanism, so that the man standing on the board with the open-mouthed sacks was kept busy. From this field they got one hundred and twelve bags of two hundred-weight each, and there seemed to be little waste. The stony rough ground here amazes me by its fertility.

Sitting on one of the sacks of barley was my old friend, the countryman. He had been there all day helping to tie the sacks, and admiring the great machine at work. I shared his infatua-tion for the harvester, and I felt too that I could have stayed for hours watching it at work, gathering the corn and threshing it and filling the bags.

The next day they were working after a heavy storm at another barley field. The men sat in a corner, drinking their tea and eating their sandwiches, for they began work at half-past seven and went on till half-past seven at night. One young man, golden-brown himself as the god of cornfields, told me of a new tractor with which he had harvested a hundred bags of wheat near Amersham. A crowd came to watch this latest model with its wide sweep. They were harvesting a thousand acres of corn for Sealey's Farm. I longed to take the combine harvesters to the cornfields of Mid Bucks where I had seen men struggling with their crops, fighting a lone battle against the storms.

On the verges of the cornfields I gathered a Bucks bunch of harvest flowers, in remembrance. There were scarlet poppies and long spikes of yellow mullein, with its soft leaves, and purple scabious and golden St John's wort, woundwort and willow herb. I found wild thyme on the chalk cutting in the field, and creamy traveller's-joy on the hedge, rose-coloured dogwood leaves, dropwort and wild snapdragon. It was a warm bright bunch of autumn's bounty.

I have found bee orchis growing at Beaconsfield, and the bird's-nest orchis on a hill. One year there were thousands of yellow and blue heart's-ease pansies, but the next year they had gone. Soapwort grows in the lane in handsome masses of pale pink flowers. It may not be truly wild, for it occurs near houses, although I have found it on the borders of fields some distance away.

The great corn-cockle, a splendid flower, grows very tall on the banks of a lane by a cornfield, and succory fringes the edges of the low cornfields in Holtspur Bottom in clouds of heavenly blue. Centaury, pink starred and white, grows in many places, and the wild gentian I have found here.

On the flower discs of the scabious which grows thickly in shades of lavender and mauve, the Six-spotted Burnet moth swings. Sometimes I have seen seven of these lovely insects on one flower head. The Chalk-hill Blue and Adonis Blue are to be found in the wild gardens of the chalk pits, where there is an abundance of small flowers. In the woods I found drifts of the rare lavender coral root, and lesser blue periwinkle. Wild golden-rod grows by the road near Beaconsfield.

Water is laid on in some of the fields to troughs, which are not the old beautiful troughs of a stone country, but galvanized iron. Near my Buckinghamshire home I see the farmer fill a milk churn with water from a tap in one field and wheel it in a little cart to fill a tub for his calves.

A weatherboarded granary at a farm near Beaconsfield is raised on stone staddles, but a small flight of wooden steps leads to the door. The oats stored there are safe from rats. A company of well-built little ricks at a farm near Hambleden are gaily perched on their staddles, and they look very happy and decorative and an advertisement for a good farm. Owing to the shortage of stone in Buckinghamshire, the staddles are brought from a distance. They are shapely stones for the making of staddles is an ancient craft.

The gates of the Buckinghamshire farms are well made and hung. They are painted white instead of the primrose-buff we used to have in our sandstone country, and white goes with the chalk hills. In Cornwall I used to see grey gates, matching the grey granite. The fastening of the gate always interests me, as it varies in different counties. The gate is usually fastened with bar and staple and the gate lifted to open. Many of the gates, including my own, are riding gates with hasps for the riding-crop to be inserted. I often come across a small gate which we used to call a "kissing gate," and the name is used here too. More gates are left open by careless people in this county than I had ever imagined. Perhaps the great number of field-paths, and the freedom allowed to the townsmen who walk here, is the cause. Many have to be padlocked and chained which would ordinarily be left latched.

Beaconsfield New Town sprang up when the railway was made in 1906. The well-designed red brick houses stand embowered in trees, and some of the woods have been left with gardens entering them. There were only three farms between Beaconsfield Old Town and the hamlet of Knotty Green, but now there are many small dwellings. The shops give the impression of the seaside, new and raw, not of a country town. The railway runs in a deep cutting, through a piece of land once called the Roundabout, where now the station is built. This was a gipsy encampment and common land, say the old men who remember it. This cutting, with its deep grass-covered sides, is so deep that trains run in a valley hidden between the houses.

80

The broad High Street, Beaconsfield

The soil was taken to build the great embankment at Holtspur Bottom, where the railway runs over a fascinating curved tunnel with the lane below.

Holtspur, now an assembly of new little houses, was called Holtspur Heath, and there the staghounds met. There was a toll bar at the corner of Broad Lane, and the garden boundaries can still be seen by the hedges on each side of the road. The next toll bar was the little round house which still remains near High Wycombe.

The steep descent from Holtspur to the Wycombe valley is a fine road, made over a hundred years ago. It is called White Hill, as it goes through the chalk of Cut-throat Wood. Before it was made the old highroad divided at Holtspur to form two ways, which joined again near Mother Red Cap Inn, in the valley. One road to the south, which was taken by carriages coming from London, is the narrow steep lane which goes past Glory Hill Farm. The northern road, for carriages going to London, has almost disappeared, but it can be traced in the hollow and the old inhabitants know it quite well.

In the New Town there is a miniature village which gives enchantment to thousands of children and grown people who come to visit it. Bekonscot is a landscape laid out with cottages and meadows and farms. Organ music comes softly from the tiny churches and lights shine from the stained-glass windows. A railway runs through the whole of this diminutive countryside and goods trains and passenger trains move electrically to the little stations. It has a lake and streams of running water with small bridges. There are cricket grounds with Tom Thumb cricketers in flannels, and an airport with planes and hotel. Horses and carts go along the tiny lanes, cattle graze in the fields, and a hunt is in full cry pursuing the fox over a hill.

This is all set in a most realistic manner in a large garden by the owner, who gives the money to charities.

Royal White Hart Hotel, Beaconsfield

Chapter VI

A BUCKS COUNTRYMAN

NOBODY knows the heart of his countryside, the tradition, the feelings of the places, so well as one who was born there. Jack Norris is a countryman with the vivid memory of his youth and childhood, and of all those who worked and played with him. He was born over eighty years ago in one of those comfortable little cottages by the main road at Wycombe End, Beaconsfield, and now he is a vigorous man whom nobody would call old. His sparkling blue eyes, his rosy cheeks, his air of well-being and content, his warm smile attracted me when I first met him at a stile crossing the fields.

"I used to go bird-starving here at three and sixpence a week when I was a little lad," said he.

Only a slight lameness speaks of the rheumatism that is the bane of country workers who have been wet through at their work year after year.

Like most countrymen he is deeply interested in all aspects of country life. He brings me whistle-pipes he has made from ash saplings, and wheat tassels for a horse's mane, and cuttings from the local paper about ploughing matches, and he proudly tells me of the ploughing match sixty years ago, at Stokenchurch, in which he won a prize. He puts his hat on the floor, and he sits in my room with his hands on his knees and laughter bubbling from him. He won't come near the fire, he is warm enough even on an icy day when the east wind is blowing. I think of countrymen throughout the length and breadth of England who have this same joy in life and this strength of character, with no grudging or bitterness or envy of others, but an intense and deep content. As he talks of those men and women of long ago, the squire, the washerwoman, the carter, the farmer, the bodger, the gipsy, all come to life.

Sometimes he brings a book he has read, or he tells me with a wealth of detail of a circus at High Wycombe, or a film about a sheep-dog, for he is up to date in his amusements, which he shares with his great-grandchild.

Arthur Bryant in his book, *The National Character*, quotes a reply of Disraeli, who lived at Hughenden, near High Wycombe. The statesman was asked by a contemptuous opponent in the House where were the freemen of Bucks to-day.

"Where you would expect to find them, of course—in the county of Buckinghamshire," said Disraeli quickly.

They are still there. I think of yeomen I have known, all of them Englishmen with a long tradition of farm life behind them —the men of Yorkshire with great whitewashed farms and the men of Westmorland with their grey low houses, and Cheshire farmers with timbered farms and Derbyshire men with their little stone farms embowered in elms, and the wiry farmers of Buckinghamshire, with the rose-coloured brick farms and buildings and thatched barns. I think of my friend here, with his blue eyes and knotted fingers, and wise old talk of chair-making and straw-plaiting and bird-starving and ploughing and reaping. All freemen of England.

Jack Norris went to school in the cottage which is now a craftsman's shop at Wycombe End. In this school there was a room for children to have their lessons, reading, writing, and arithmetic, but on Friday mornings they always had to unpick bonnets. The schoolma'am used to wear large and elaborate bonnets and she liked to alter the styles.

"A flower here, and a bit of ribbon there, and a piece of lace across the front," he explained, holding out an imaginary poke bonnet, which I could almost see in his brown hands. "We had to get a pin and unpick the lace, and take the cottons from the trimmings, and we mustn't make a hole or we got the stick."

So the little children were taught to be accurate and careful, and the schoolma'am talked to them as they worked.

"It takes ten men to make a pin," was one of her sayings, and she discoursed on pins, or lace, or the long silk ribbons which tied the bonnets under her chin.

"We tied a string to the sweetshop door, old Sally Moore's, and then we run away," said he, laughing at the childish pranks. He had twopence for his school money, but he used to spend a penny on a "show," and then he made a penny by feeding horses at the White Hart, the ancient timbered inn across the street.

His mother made lace on a pillow, and so did his elder sister. I have seen some of her beautiful lace kept for nearly a century.

"I've had many a good hiding for messing they bobbins about," he chuckles.

There were seventy bobbins on that lace pillow, each with its bunch of beads, called jingles, blue and crystal and white, dangling there. How tempting for a child to lift the lace cloth and touch them! He used to creep up to the lace pillow and try to make lace himself, and then the bobbin-threads were tangled hopelessly and he was caught.

His sister Ann went to a lace school at Wycombe End, up one of the alleys, and there she learned to make the lovely Buckinghamshire lace. When she was older she made the cane bottoms for chairs. She removed the "wisp," which was used for packing. She split the cane and resplit it with a sharp knife and wove it in the chair seat. The payment for caning a whole chair was 2½d, and for a long stool it was 6d.

I heard many tales of those Bucks days, and the life of these little children, with hard work and merriment, as they made lace, plaited straw, scared crows, and went to school.

"We all went out in the fields a-leasing. We got enough corn to keep a family for a year in flour. We took our food in a basket and all went off, children and everyone, for the whole day."

Little bunches called "dollies" were made by each child, ears tight together, tied round the neck with a cornstalk, and then laid on a cloth, all very neat, until a great bundle was ready for home. It must have been a joyful time, with the picnic and the dollies and all. Many women went, some with six or seven children, all eager to gather up the corn. The farmer threshed for the gleaners and kept the straw. There would be three bushels of wheat after threshing.

"Then you took it to the miller to be ground. The miller lived at Treadaway Mill, Loudwater. The 'toppings' and bran he kept for his trouble, and he gave you the flour to take away."

84

The bread his mother made from this flour was very sweet and good, and it never went mouldy or dry. It was like a nut for delicacy.

Three shocks were reared up in the middle of the field by the farmer as a sign that the field was not ready, and nobody might enter. They all waited at the gate. When the shocks were taken away they hurried in and began their leasing.

The threshing was, of course, done with the swingel and flail, which Jack Norris calls "swingel-and-frail." In the great barn at the farmhouse there was a winnowing door, or window. Sometimes there was a winnowing machine with a fan which turned and blew away the chaff. At Wattleton Farm, where the family of Routh lived, there was one of these machines.

The swingel was made of ash wood. This is the handle of the threshing tool. The flail, which actually did the beating, was made of blackthorn, a very hard wood, but it can be made of whitethorn, which is equally durable. They were hinged together with a piece of leather, and men of course made their own swingel and flail.

"Boil the stick to bend it. Bend it round with a leather lace," he explains, and he gives me a lesson on making this tool.

In that old Beaconsfield there were many local trades and crafts, typical of other country towns in the county. There was a chair-yard down Wycombe End. William Bowles had a hand-saw screwed up and he made chairs. The bodgers worked in the beech woods and with them went Jack Norris, for he enjoyed turning the legs of chairs in the green woods, working at that old craft.

One day when he came to see me, walking through the woods to my house, he said, "When I was coming up woodside I saw a little oak tree, slanting out of the ground, and I thought he would just do for a 'shop.' Peg him to the ground at two places, with two sticks tied cross-wise. Then put a string at his end. Fasten the string to the chair-peg. Turn the screws and use a spokeshave to shape the leg. That's how we used to do it, at Hogback woods."

The bodgers were the wood-turners, who worked outside among the trees, using a living tree bent forward to make their pole-lathe. A little hut, the bodger's shop, was built round a growing tree of suitable size. The hut was often roofed with boughs which they cut to make a green tent, although recent bodgers' shops I have seen in the Hampden woods had galvanized iron. The pole protruded through an opening in the side of the hut, over the simple lathe. The wood is split and cut and then shaved on the draw-shave horse, and turned on the pole-lathe from pieces about eighteen inches long. The bodgers often worked as haymakers and reapers in the summer, and they turned chair legs in spring. In winter they felled the trees, when the sap is down.

When the men went out to the woods they took only a bag of tools. They cut the little trees to make their house and lived there. They used a breastplate for holding the brace when making holes in the chair legs.

Another time he talked of the harvest, and he brought me tassels of wheat ears, five plaited in a delicate design of strength and firmness, so that it was like a little rope with the wheat ears spraying forth at the top. Oat tassels and barley tassels were also made, each a thing of beauty. The tassels were used for any ornament, for a horse's mane, for the tail, or for the hames on the harness.

"On the corn-ricks we put a corn dolly, or a rose and crown," said he. "I always made a rose and crown. It was three plaits with a bunch at the top. You made the plaits like an openwork crown, and stuck the ears of wheat through it, to be the rose on the crown. Then we put it on the top of the corn-rick."

The bundles for thatching were called yelms, or yellums. The straw bands were made with the wimble, as our old thatcher used to make them. A dozen straws made a band, twisted together. Pegs were made of hazel, but nowadays the thatcher uses a long needle to thread the twine across the straw.

Jack Norris's father and uncle worked at Penlands Farm, near Hedgerley, where until recent years there was a brick kiln. The bricks were stacked in thatched huts and taken to London. At this farm bricks, tiles, and drainpipes were made. This brick-making in small quantities in little kilns gave employment to

86

many of the men in country places, so that they could live in the villages and work near.

The clay from under the sand was dug out and stacked. Then it was put in the "pug," and a horse turned it for brick-making. Bricks were stacked criss-cross in a kiln of lime where chalk was burned, and the fumes slowly circulated through the interstices.

This brick-making in Buckinghamshire has been an industry since Tudor days. There is little stone for building, and bricks have been used, made from the local clay. In 1562, when rates of wages for workmen were fixed, five principal craftsmen were named—master carpenters, sawyers, bricklayers, tilers, and thatchers. Bricks and tiles were made at the time of the civil wars at Brill, and this brickfield is still there. Slough had important brickworks, and Burnham, Chalfont St Peter, Whitchurch, and Iver. Pottery was made at Brill with the potter's wheel, and the pots were fashioned between finger and thumb. There was a pottery at Coleshill, and Chalfont St Peter. This latter was called the Beaconsfield pottery, and the wares were carried to High Wycombe on donkeys and sold at the market.

The bricks made at Penlands Farm were carried to London, in great four-wheeled carts, which started at 1 a.m. from Penlands, near Beaconsfield, with Jack Norris's father and uncle in charge. They returned the next night. Sometimes a little boy went with them, wide awake through the starry night, travelling the roads to the great city with his uncle and father. That was a great adventure, to go through Uxbridge, to see London city at dawn, to ride on the load of bricks behind the great cart-horses. They went slowly for the load was very heavy, and the men walked or rode on the shafts.

Three great cart-horses took the load, two horses in front and one in the shafts of the broad-wheeled wagon. The iron tyres were six inches broad to go more easily on the bad roads. The names of the horses were Colonel, Diamond, and Dragon. The chestnut was called Colonel, and Jack Norris's father broke him in as a colt and had him till he died. The father died soon afterwards, and there seemed to be a link between their lives as often happens in countrymen who love their horses well.

Diamond was the second horse. The white horse, which was the shaft horse, was Dragon from Abingdon.

Ah! He knew where that horse came from seventy and more years ago! I heard how he was bought and brought back, bucking and rearing, and how he was treated and loved, the Dragon from Abingdon.

Horses are remembered with such poignancy, with such admiration and love by countrymen, that the animals might have been part of their own intimate family, as indeed they were.

The horses live again as they are brought back by memory's halter, and I see the gallant animals straining at great loads, pulling with all their strength, adding that extra effort which is born of character and will. So these three horses come back and the old man's eyes are dim as he speaks with deep affection of Dragon, Colonel, and Diamond, horses belonging to his father's master. One day he gave me a faded photograph of the wide wagon and the three horses, his most cherished possession.

He was coming home with his father from Penlands Farm after the journey to London with bricks one night in midwinter, about half-past ten, when he had a fright. The father and little son were walking through the pitch black woods, feeling their way among the trees, and they came to two tall trees which were a landmark against the sky in the darkness. No lanterns were carried, and the darkness was intense in the deep woods.

Two great eyes were staring down at him from beyond where there was a holly bush, two eyes "going wick-wack-wobbling."

"What's that, feyther?" he whispered.

"It's nobbut an old owl," said his father, but he clung to his father's coat tails as he passed and the owl set up an awful wailing and hooting at him. After that he wouldn't go home at night after the London journeys, but he slept, a small boy, in the stable with the horses.

When his father was working at the brick kiln the boy went bird-starving and got good wages. He got 3s 6d a week for scaring crows from the cornfields on the Oxford road, and he must have done his work well, for other boys only received half a crown a week. Then he was offered 4s a week for bird-starving at the other side of the road. That was a very high wage for a young boy. He had a clacker, three wooden pieces jointed together, and as he swung the handle the wood made a loud noise. Added to this he shouted and sang, so no crows came there.

A hundred years ago the wage for bird-starving was a penny a day, I heard in my childhood from old people. Little boys sat on walls with clackers, scaring the rooks and crows from the corn, and earning their first money.

His next work was hauling coal at Beaconsfield. Then he became a ploughboy at Wheatsheaf Farm. He had 6s 6d a week for these trades, but he had to keep himself out of the wage. He was very happy, and filled with content at that time, enjoying the hours off, and the bird-nesting, when they collected eggs, and sucked them or cooked them.

He used to turn up from the soil cast ox-shoes, from days when oxen had been used for the work. These shoes were fastened on like small boots, a bent piece up the front and nails curved up at the sides. Oxen were used by John Nash for ploughing in the neighbourhood. They stood for the night in the ox-yard, where there were stalls for them to sleep.

Sometimes the boys, filled with religious curiosity, went to Jordans Meeting House. There was no pulpit, no organ, no vicar, and the boys sat there waiting for something to happen.

"Perhaps somebody over there will jump up and speak," they thought, as they nudged each other.

At other times they went to a large house where there was a religious sect, and they sang hymns in the drawing-room, and had tea and cakes, a good meal, when the simple service was over.

There were bears in those days which were led through the villages for entertainment. Some were kept in the cellars of the Cross Keys, but the four largest bears were fastened with heavy chains to a great oak tree on Long Bottom, near Jordans. At the opposite side of the road were camped two or three families of Russians, with their horses and children and dogs, in tents.

Young Norris, who now worked at Wheatsheaf Farm on the Wilton Estate, was afraid they would get loose, and even the farmer said he would shoot them.

"I darena go past for fear I should meet they bears," said he.

89

One night Jack Norris was coming home from work in the dark, and a boy from the same farm came to him.

"Jack, I be afeared to go home past they bears. Come and go home with us, will ye?" he pleaded.

"Yes, I'll go along with ye," said Norris, glad of company, "but don't you make no noise or I won't go along with ye no more."

They stumbled along in the dark, and then the boy cried, "Hear those bears agrowling? I'm afeard. Stop a minute. I thinks I hears summut."

"It's nowt. Come along," said Norris, frightened himself, but trying to keep brave as his friend held back.

Then he heard a crackle behind him, and a wet tongue licked his hand and a deep growl came from his side. He yelled and ran, and the growling went alongside, deep panting and snorts.

"Summut wet touched me, and I heard 'un go 'Ugh! Ugh! Ugh!' " said the old man as he told the tale. "We run like torment."

He chased as he had never run before, back to the farm, and when he got to the gate he didn't stop to open it, but tumbled over it. The gate was shaken and rattled behind him and deep growls came roaring from it. He rushed into the house, more dead than alive, so frightened he could not speak. For a long time he was speechless with terror. Then the second boy came in, laughing at the trick he had played. Norris was upset for weeks, and he never came past the bears at night after this, but slept at the farm when the work was late.

The Star Inn, at the bottom of Wycombe End in those days, was the night house for wayfarers for London. Broad-wheeled wagons came there, four horses drawing them, laden with straw for straw-plaiting, paper from the paper mills, or hay from the farms for London. There was a great traffic of these large wagons, with their big wheels and splendid horses. The horses had weatherboards of leather under their collars for ornament, and all their array of brasses and bells highly polished. Two horses were in the double shafts of these carts and two were the trace horses. They took hay and straw from Wycombe and

Stokenchurch and Beaconsfield to Whitechapel. They brought back soot for the cornfields. They went off at night, the horses going all through the night, resting a little and returning the next night. It was a hard life and the horses were quickly worn out.

Many traders took their loads to London. "Fred Liner was one. He went from Stokenchurch to London, through Beaconsfield, on a Thursday every week. Just about now he'd be going through."

We sat by the fire, listening to the ghostly creaking wheels of that big wagon driven by Fred Liner seventy years ago, and the clatter of the horses' hooves.

"He'd take chickens and ducks and butter and eggs. He'd come back on a Saturday with a load of scraps of bread for his hens. He had three horses, two in shafts and one trace horse in chain-trace harness."

The loads of soot brought back by the wagons from London chimneys were used on the fields of wheat, and they made such marvellous results that one could see the difference in the corn where the soot had lain. The soot-manured corn grew tall and strong and rich.

In the field which is now a market garden by the Oxford road, there was lovely red-bearded wheat, five feet high, so tall and clean that a dealer bought it outright as it grew, carted it, cleaned off the "flash," and took the straw as it was to Luton for hat-making. The flash is the outer covering of the straw. The wheat-ails, in a case like this, were removed by a wheat-ailer, who used a multiple knife in the threshing barn, keeping the straw clean and bright.

This beautiful field of wheat, which always came up in a fine crop, was farmed by William Rolfe, "who knew how to farm."

He and his men sowed the grain by hand, broadcasting it, in that peculiar sweeping motion which is very ancient. They harrowed it, and they rolled it. Then, when the young wheat was coming up, they put loads of soot on it.

The succession of crops in those good days of farming was as follows. After the wheat, plough up in autumn, and sow oats. Next plough up and have roots. Then barley and spring oats.

Then grass. So the round of the land went on, the old succession of crops, by men brought up by Edmund Burke's farm bailiff.

Sometimes I have lessons from Jack Norris in country crafts. In layering hedges the hedge is first thinned. Then stakes are driven in, about eighteen inches apart. All the growing trees which have been cut near the roots are threaded through the stakes. The space is filled up to the top. Then the hedge is finished off by "heathering" or "eddering." For this willow, or briar (the rose-briar is meant) or sticks that had been cut out, are twisted and woven across the top to finish off the hedge.

"When you broadcast corn, you have a seed-cut, which is an oblong receptacle for the corn with a handle at one end. Put a strap through it and round your neck to hold it. Sow with your right hand and mark with your left foot. Throw up the corn to prevent the seed falling in circles. Go back the opposite way two and a half yards farther on; mark with a stick."

So round the room I go, sowing imaginary corn in a plough-field. I have learned chair-rushing, thatching, making tassels of wheat, straw-plaiting, using the pole-lathe to turn chair legs, gleaning, faggoting, and broadcasting corn from my old friend, and it is not his fault if I am not proficient.

I heard, too, about the old ice-houses, used before the time of refrigerators, built in the parks of the big houses. There was one in a wood near Beaconsfield and another in Wilton Park.

"When I was a boy doing plough at Wheatsheaf, we took ice off a pond in mid-winter, broke it with wooden mallets and carted it to the ice-holes at Wilton Park. We put straw under it and straw on top of it. Then we put the wooden cover to the hole over it and piled the soil on that. There was a ladder to go down to get it when it was wanted at Wilton Park in the summer."

This is the ancient method of keeping ice, which has been used since Elizabethan days.

"Going across that old park it used to blow pretty bleak. We wore sacks over our heads, and round our chins and ears, tucked in our jackets. When we had done, we got hot gin and beer and beefsteak pies from the House. It was Caledon George

Du Pre at that time. He was a grand old Squire was Caledon George Du Pre."

At harvest time each man carried a little wooden barrel to the field with his own beer in it. He drank by tipping up the barrel, much as I remember seeing the Basques drink from their wine-skins in the Pyrenees. These little barrels held two quarts, or a quart for each man.

At Wilton Park they had two-gallon jars with wicker around them and two handles for carrying.

There was a splendid Harvest Home, with great rejoicings and merrymakings. The farm men played the gardeners at cricket, in a match that brought much excitement and laughter. Then they went indoors to have supper. On the table was beef and dumplings and suet puddings. Polished copper jacks of harvest beer stood in the middle of the long trestle tables, and it was the coldest and best beer in the world. They drank from drinking-horns, and they toasted Caledon George Du Pre.

Bands of travelling harvesters came from Oxfordshire with scythes and bagging hooks bound with straw, carried on their shoulders, and sacks with tins of food. They went to Middlesex for haymaking, and then they walked back, working their way through Stokenchurch, West Wycombe, Wycombe Marsh, Beaconsfield, Gerrards Cross, and Uxbridge, harvesting at the farms that filled this agricultural countryside. They cut the corn with the bagging hooks and they sharpened their scythes and hooks with a stone rubber held upright, and kept when not in use in a piece of leather with holes in it tied round their waists.

One day I drove with him along the Bottom from Seer Green, the road where he walked as a boy from his farmhouse. He pointed out a certain field to me, by the road.

"That's where I learned to tell the time by the sun," said he. "Farmer learned me to tell the sun time when I was a little 'un."

Then he told me how the farmer set a stick upright in the field, to throw a shadow, and he planted another stick where the shadow fell. He took out his watch and showed the boy the clock time. Then with more sticks he divided the circle into the hours. Always afterwards the boy made his own clock in a part of the field where he worked, first checking it on some-body's watch.

In Beaconsfield there were several private boarding-schools, some for boys and some for girls. The girls went for their morning walk one way and the boys another, with half an hour between lest they should meet. On Sundays they sat on opposite sides of the church.

Jack Norris pointed out one of the large Georgian houses in London End that used to be a girls' school.

"I knowed the names of all the young ladies at that school," said he. Then he laughed and explained the reason.

His mother did the laundry for them, and he used to help with the ancient mangle. His special duty was the stockings of these young ladies of Victorian days. He had to sort them in their pairs and roll them. Hence he knew the names of those children long ago, as Hans Andersen knew the names of his mother's clients. The cottage was about the size of Hans Andersen's home at Odense, and the garden was a window-box. I like to think of that little boy matching stockings for young ladies, and taking them back in the laundry basket, of his straw-plaiting, and his mixing the lace bobbins, tangling them when his mother wasn't looking, of bird-scaring at 3s. 6d. a week, of ploughing and reaping and mowing.

"It was a good life and I had plenty of fun," he chuckles as as he recalls those days. The people of his generation lived with a deep simplicity, with an absence of hurry and fuss. They possessed the art of living.

CHAPTER VII

AMERSHAM AND CHESHAM

COLESHILL, a hamlet connected with the name of Waller who was born there, and Thomas Ellwood who retreated there, is on the spur of a hill between Beaconsfield and Amersham. There are fine views across the valleys from the Coleshill Common. The long winding road between woods used to be one of the most lonesome roads in Buckinghamshire, I was told by an old man who used to walk along it in the blackness of night.

"There was only the old owls up there shouting 'Who-o-o-o.'" It was a terrifying place sometimes, because some gipsies camped by the side of the lane in a large encampment and the boys used to take off their boots and walk barefoot along the road lest the gipsies should hear them. They were Russians and they had dancing bears fastened to the trees. The little boys were "tarrible 'fraid of those bars and those gipsies. The gipsies couldn't speak English, they only cried 'Dee-da-don, dee-da-don.'"

They had a great camp-fire burning, and the boys thought they would be cooked on it.

I drove along this road with this old man and we passed a fine farm with new buildings, a great barn, a well-built cowhouse and stables, and we all stared in satisfaction at the sight. Haystacks, tractor, carts, all were neat and clean.

"I remember that was only a bit of a farm, with only one horse and no cowhouses. Now it is a good place."

It was satisfying to hear of this improvement, but he made an adverse comment a few minutes later. We saw a rough field full of thistles and he looked at it sadly.

"This was a ploughed field once with good corn," said he. "There was a grand crop here, I remember, for it is good land."

The road divides at the Magpies Inn. The old Berkeley Hunt in their orange-tawny coats used to meet here. The old man used to go with them on foot when he was a boy for many a mile, together with other boys from the villages. When he came home his trousers were torn to shreds, his face and hands were covered with soil, and his mother gave him a good hiding. It was a grand life, he said!

This Magpies Inn is recalled by Ellwood the Quaker, who lived near. An old cottage—which is still there, half-concealed in the hedge—was mentioned by him in his well-known directions, in verse, for finding his house. In Ellwood's day Coleshill was in Hertfordshire, and no Buckinghamshire magistrate could arrest him at his farmhouse, Hunger Hill. He had only to walk a short distance over the border to escape back to Buckinghamshire from the Hertfordshire magistrate. Hunger Hill is now called Ongar Hill, but it still retains its old name among the villagers.

A Buckinghamshire woman told me a tale of Hunger Hill and its fields which she heard from her father in her childhood. It is one of those tales of humour in which country people delight, an ancient tale told and retold for generations.

A man went to a farm for food and they would not give him any. So he called it Hunger Hill. Then he went to a field to find something to eat and there was nothing there. So he lay down and slept and he called the place Poor Noll. Then he went to the next field and there was nothing there to eat. He called it Starveacre, and he lay down and died. Hunger Hill, Poor Noll, and Starveacre are well-known names in the district still.

On the summit of Coleshill is a windmill which was in use until recent years. Many people in Beaconsfield and surrounding villages have told me that they used to take corn there to be ground when they were young. The windmill belonged to Fred Ware. Barley, wheat, and oats were ground there. They took three sacks of corn up the long hill to Coleshill Common and returned with a load of their corn already ground, then back with another three sacks and home to the farm with more corn. There was a procession of corn going to and from this mill.

The Common hangs down the side of the hill, a place of wild flowers, where the country children play. I have had many a bunch of mixed flowers, of harebells and greater knapweed, of yellow mullein and agrimony, of woundwort and scabious, sent

The old Market Hall (1682), Amersham

to me from Coleshill Common, where there is such an abundance of beauty. There are great clumps of comfrey with its red and blue bells, and golden broom on the steep slope of this windy place. A small green platform on the grass is used by the little village boys for their cricket ground. This Common used to be called Donkey Common, the popular name for it, as many donkeys were put out to grass there.

"Harry Price had some, Hornel had some, Slade had some, and so had Will Norris. One donkey learned to open a gate by putting his nose through the bars and lifting the gate up."

Until quite recently lace was made by some of the old ladies who lived at Coleshill. There is a famous oak tree in the village which was the favourite of Edmund Waller. Near it is the ancient little house 'Stocks Place,' where the poet was born in 1606.

A steep hill, Gore's Hill, drops down to Amersham, and this is so precipitous it must have been a great strain on horses in the old days. At the foot of the hill is Bury Farm, where lived Gulielma Springett and her mother, Mary Penington, while Isaac Penington was in Aylesbury goal. It was Gulielma who became the wife of William Penn. On the walls of one of the barns of this farmhouse is an old notice asking drivers to loosen their bearing rein when going up the hill.

"An old ancient place that is," said our companion, gazing at the house with deep interest. But when, for the first time, he saw the modern flat-roofed white houses with overhanging slices on the green slopes of the new part of Amersham, he cried out in astonishment:

"Ooh, dear-a-dear! They are comical houses!"

I once asked a countrywoman what she thought about these ultra-modern houses which are near some of the most beautiful old houses in Buckinghamshire. "We don't think about them at all," she replied quietly. "We just don't look at them."

Amersham was the scene of religious persecution, for some of the people were Lollards. Richard Turner, Walter Young, and John Horwood were burned here in 1414. In 1506 William Tilsworth was burned at Amersham, and his daughter Joan Clark was made to set fire to the pile. Thomas Chase of Amers-

Tudor chimney stacks at Chenies Manor House

ham was carried to Wooburn, and he is said to have been strangled in the Little Ease at the bishop's house. Country people say he was buried on the hill near Wooburn and the place is still haunted by the grief and terror of those times. At the Reformation many were burned at the stake. There is a hill outside Amersham where the burnings for conscience' sake took place, and a monument stands there. It is a country tradition that the corn grew very sparsely on this terrible spot, and though a disbeliever dug down and found that flints were underneath upon which corn will not grow, the tradition remained.

There are many country tales and legends of the earth being affected by some happenings. I think deep sorrow and bitterness hang about a place for centuries, and can be felt by a receptive mind. There are ghosts of places as well as of houses, but nowhere could look more peaceful and serene than the old market town of Amersham, with its wide street and jumble of curving gabled roofs. I always enjoy the roofs of a town more than the house fronts, for they alone are unchanged, they carry their private decorations of moss and lichens, they wave and bow, with crooked chimneys and overhanging eaves, while down below perhaps a new brick front has been built, and the glass windows of a modern shop have been added.

The old name of Amersham was Agmundesham, and this name is still used by some old country people.

Leyland the traveller came to Amersham in 1540, and he speaks of it as "a right praty market towne on Fryday, of one strete well buildyd with tymbar." It is much the same to-day, a right pretty place with a beautiful street, but there is no Friday market. There is, or was until recent years, a cattle market every Whit-Monday. On September 19th and 20th there is a fair when the wide main street is filled with merry-go-rounds and booths.

The broad street of Amersham is as satisfying in its design and beauty as any place in Buckinghamshire. Fine old red brick houses of many periods, timbered, shuttered, and gabled cottages, old hotels, timbered, with hanging signs, courtyards opening into the road, with vistas of flowers round cobbled yards, charming old cottages of wattle and daub, make a good sight to

98

see. There is a warm colouring of russet and rose, grey and green, and there is a feeling of happiness in the place. The irregular line of gables against the sky has great variety. From the west end of the churchyard there is one of the loveliest foreground views of Amersham, a motley collection of red roofs and gables, a score or so, at various angles, clustered together.

In the most prominent position in the middle of the road stands the old Market Hall, which was built by Sir William Drake of Shardeloes in 1682. It is a red brick building with stone facings, two stories high, the lower part on open arcades. One of these was enclosed to make a lock-up. Above the Market Hall is the room which was the meeting room of the town. Its roof has an octagonal wooden bell-turret and clock and weather-cock. Inside the turret is a bell inscribed "C.H. made me, 1682." C.H. was Christopher Hudson. The coat-of-arms of the Drakes is on the walls.

Six seventeenth-century almshouses, with a little cobbled courtyard, are in the main street. They are perhaps the most charming of all the pretty almshouses in Buckinghamshire, although the dwellings at Ravenstone and at Quainton run them close in beauty. These six little houses, with lace curtains at their little windows, and flowers on their sills, have six round flower beds in the cobbled yard. The whole is set within its walls like a picture in a frame. On Sunday morning one can see the old ladies going to church with their prayer books. Outside the doorway to the courtyard are pollard limes, and in one of these I noticed a deep "cupboard," very useful for playing house. The alms-houses were built by Sir William Drake in 1657, and there is a tablet on one of the gables with the Drake arms.

The wide openings to courtyards, which were perhaps old inn yards, are characteristic of Amersham. I went through one to see a cottage with green ferns growing in a little stream and hanging baskets of flowers. It reminded me of a Derbyshire dale by the river. In another courtyard was a great golden honey-suckle and in a third a vine.

The Crown Inn, a coaching inn which was built before 1620, has old ceiling-beams and some panelling. Like many of the houses it is gay with flowers in boxes and tubs. Near it is the picturesque King's Arms Hotel, which is sixteenth-century. The old gables are still left at the back. The Swan Inn has gable wings, and the date 1671 on a chimney. An inn with a fascinating sign is the Elephant and Castle, which has a gabled front and old brick chimney.

At Mill Stream House one can see the mill-stream running through the house. Little Shardeloes is another interesting house, with gables, built in the seventeenth century.

The old half-timbered sixteenth-century malthouses are still standing, but now they are made into a restaurant. In one of the rooms the plaster has been removed from the wall to show the wattle and daub construction. Many of these old buildings have beautiful chimney stacks, and the whole effect of the line of roofs and chimneys is of great diversity and beauty.

Amersham has some remarkable wall paintings which were rediscovered recently. This craft rose from the desire of the people for some decoration and beauty on their walls. In the churches there are mural paintings which have been found under coats of whitewash, but in these paintings in houses the subjects are secular and highly ornamented in rich colours. In some houses the ceilings and timbers were painted as well as the walls, but usually these have been destroyed. Amersham's paintings are varied and original.

One is in a shop in the High Street, next to the old grammar school. During redecoration in 1931 a picture was found of Hercules with girdle of laurel leaves and a club. This may have been one of a group called "The Nine Worthies." It is thought to be seventeenth-century. Another painting on a sloping ceiling in an attic is a bird with a Tudor rose and leaves and a man in seventeenth-century costume.

In the Crown Hotel coffee-room is a copy of a Tudor coat-of-arms, in black outline, with the quarterings of England and France, and lion and dragon supporters instead of lion and unicorn.

"God Save the Quene" shows it was the time of Elizabeth. It is said that this commemorated the visit of the Queen to Shardeloes. The original was burnt in a recent fire.

In another house, 61 High Street, perhaps once part of an inn, is Julius Cæsar, wearing a scarlet cloak and blue helmet with a feather, and carrying a banner with double-headed eagle. Duke Joshua, in sixteenth-century armour, with the sun, King David, with a harp, Hector of Troy, Charlemagne, and Godfrey de Bouillon, adorn the walls in panels. The missing Worthies are Alexander, Judas Maccabæus, and King Arthur.

The colours are exceptionally brilliant, and the decoration must once have been very rich indeed. The Worthies stand on hills with grasses growing, and trees in the backgrounds. The face of Duke Joshua is well portrayed, and all are full of vigour. They may have been painted in this sixteenth-century house for a pageant when Princess Elizabeth was at Ashridge.

Charlemagne had been whitewashed, and pots and pans stored in the cupboard around him, so that his limbs were rubbed away. Others have been covered with whitewash, plaster, and paper. There must be few places in England where so many old mural paintings remain, but Amersham is an exceptional town.

Amersham Church, in the centre of the town, has a fine fifteenth-century tower. The fourteenth-century roof of the nave, with its traceried spandrels, is supported on stone corbels of angels and grotesque figures. There are many monuments to the Drakes, rather overwhelming in their size and heaviness. There is a small gem on the chancel wall, a brass with the engraved portrait of little John Drake, who died when he was four years old in 1623. He has frills at his wrists and curls on his forehead, and he kneels on a cushion, a small stout child, with a puzzled, rather anxious face. The inscription reads:

> Had hee liv'd to bee a man,
> This inch had grown but to a span,
> Nowe is hee past all feare of paine,
> 'Twere sinn to wish him here againe.
> Vewe but the way by wch wee come
> Thowt say, hee's best that's first at home.

I like the country word, "thowt," meaning "thou wilt," the contracted form of which can be heard any day in country places.

A tale is told of Parson Drake, who used to read the service at Amersham on hunt mornings with his surplice over his pink hunting-coat and his horse waiting at the gate. I remember our vicar who took early service dressed in his golfing suit under his cassock, and his golf clubs lay in the porch ready.

At Amersham Church the great John Knox preached, and one can imagine the journeyings of folk for many miles to hear his rough, powerful voice. John Baxter also preached here.

The little river Misbourne flowed through Amersham and once turned the wheels of several mills. A brewery and malt-house near the church used the waters of the Misbourne, but where the water flowed there is only the channel filled with grass. The river has disappeared. A little bridge crosses it and weeds and flowers choke the bed. People say the river has gone since a deep well was dug at Great Missenden. The brewery is now gaily painted and Goya perfume is made there.

Shardeloes, the seat of the family of Tyrwhitt-Drake, stands high on the slope of the park about three-quarters of a mile from Amersham. Two white lodges guard the entrance gate, and there is a field-path through the park and fields to Missenden. The Amersham cricket ground, a smooth stretch of green with a pavilion, is in a perfect setting in a corner of this park with the hills and woods behind it. Beyond the cricket ground the foot-path leads through a field of oats, a narrow path among the corn which is five feet high. Then it winds by the side of the artificial lake which stretches in front of the house in the valley. There is only a trickle of water and the large expanse of the lake is filled with reeds and willow-herb, meadowsweet and yellow flags. Great bulrushes grow in the narrow stream which still runs there, but the main part of the water has gone and the villagers are concerned for the disappearance of this beauty spot. There used to be many water-fowl here and it is the haunt of birds; the lesser spotted woodpecker and the redshank are found in this marshy place.

The river Misbourne, very small now, runs under a bridge far too big for it into the lake, and at the bridge it forms a little pool where boys bathe.

"Did you know that all the ducks on Shardeloes pond are

Drakes?" asked a countryman, punning with Shakespearian humour on the name of the Lord of the Manor.

The great house of Shardeloes was rebuilt in the eighteenth century. Queen Elizabeth visited the original Shardeloes on one of her royal progresses to show herself to her Buckinghamshire people. William Tothill lived at Shardeloes then. He was the father of thirty-three children, and his tomb is in Amersham Church.

Shardeloes Park has many splendid trees. There is one sweet chestnut which has three full-grown thorn trees growing out of its trunk. A row of tall poplars fringes the park along the main road.

Amersham's neighbour is Chesham, a very busy little town, which is as lively and full of vigour as Amersham is quiet and sleepy. Chesham has old houses, little alleys and running waters, but it has not the serene beauty of Amersham. Many small factories and handicrafts flourish in this little market town.

The river Chess runs through the town and springs and streams join it so that one wonders at first how many little rivers there are, as water appears in alleys and corners. The river runs by the side of the main road, hidden behind a wall. A green lawn, with rose trees and seats where old men rest themselves, divides the road and the river, but if we look over the wall we can see watercress beds in the shallow waters and men with their barrows with high fronts standing in the stream wielding their forks or cutting knives. There is a little hut down there for the cress-men and a pile of baskets ready for packing the cress for London markets.

The main road has shops of many kinds, mingled with old houses, wide doorways to courtyards with glimpses of the woods and some old inns. The High House is an early seventeenth-century dwelling. The post office too is an interesting place built about 1625. It has the original chimney stack and little staircases with moulded handrails.

The Market Hall, which was rebuilt in 1856, is not as attractive as some of the market halls of the county because its sides are plastered with advertisements. A coat-of-arms is carved on one of the walls. The upper part is sometimes used for concerts and plays. The open part below was used once for the market, but at present seems to be a store place.

In Elizabethan days Chesham was a town of crafts and trades. There were tanners, shoemakers, curriers, among others. To-day there are tanners, shoemakers, basket-makers, toy-makers, brush-makers, and woodworkers. So one sees timber yards, with stacks of timber and great tree trunks, with horses and tackle working.

A countryman told me about the tanning of leather at High Wycombe and Chesham. Oak bark was stripped from cut trees by pushing irons under the bark. Four forked sticks were erected and the bark put across. This stripped bark was sent to High Wycombe and Chesham and Rickmansworth for the tanners. It was put into water with the skin to colour it. This was an important industry among the men in this district, for the trees went to the furniture trade, and the bark to the tanner. Now they use chemicals and oak bark is no longer stripped.

Chesham made boots with this leather. They cost 10s a pair and lasted eighteen months of very hard work in the fields and farmland. They were, of course, hand-stitched. "Nowadays," says my countryman, "a pair of heavy boots costs £2 and isn't so good and watertight."

In one place, by a running unbounded little stream which seemed to spring up out of the stones under our feet, was an open shed and a yard with tackle for lifting trees. Horses stood there, resting after bringing their great loads, and men were sawing the tree-trunks. Inside the sheds we watched many processes, and there was a delicious smell of timber. Fascinated, I watched a young man with a lathe which worked electrically, turning wooden spoons, shaping the bowls and handles,smoothing the handles from square-cut rods and finishing off the ends with little ornamental rings. I could hardly tear myself away. The machine worked evenly and the man held his rough spoon to be turned into shape. There seemed to be nothing mechanical about this process. The man's skill was needed almost as if the whole fashioning had been done by hand. The curve and the shape of each spoon depended on his art. He made drumsticks too and rolling-pins, all out of beechwood.

In another part of the building the rough shapes for the spoons were cut from blocks of wood. There was also the finishing and smoothing process. In these works wooden bowls are turned and wooden rims are made for sieves and riddles. They used to make wooden spades for children and butter-prints, but these are now discontinued.

In Chesham the shallow wooden bowls are still turned, although now they are used for fruit and for ornament. We used large wooden bowls about two feet in diameter for cream setting, and one, with a pattern of rings round its sides, was kept for washing the silver and the best old china. Each wooden bowl was different, for the wood texture varied and the depth was suited to its use. When the separator came the wooden bowls were not needed. Through the open doors of the back premises in Buckinghamshire farmhouses one can see the shining separator, ready for use, and certainly the farmer's wife is eased a little by this.

In Aylesbury market I saw a stall heaped with wooden spoons and rolling-pins of various sizes, which seemed familiar to me. They came from Mr Thomas's factory in Chesham, the dealer said, and he held them up and rattled them together. I was delighted to see my small wooden friends, smooth and golden, ready for stirring sauces and beating up cakes, so I bought three. The beech was grown in the Chiltern woods, the spoons were made in the market town of Chesham, and they were sold at the county town of Aylesbury.

From there we went to the saddler's shop to watch leather being stitched. A saddler's is a favourite shop of mine and I like to stand among bridles and reins and whips and collars for horse and dog, and all the leather-work one can see. I think it is a craft as good as any to make these things, each according to the fancy of the worker. There is a fine individuality about a saddler's work.

The saddlers often live in an old house, up a couple of steps, with the ceiling supported by a beam and perhaps a fireplace in a corner. I remember the small saddler's shop at Whitchurch, with the photographs of prize spaniels and the tales I heard of the Squire and his family and the merriment of shooting parties. I think too of the saddler's shop at Eton.

I saw some dog baskets at the Chesham saddler's which had been made by a blind man, so I went along the road to find him. In a wooden shed in a cottage flower-garden sat Mr Hall, the basket-maker, working on the floor with a basket between his outstretched legs. His assistant sat on the ground across the way under the window. One was doing the edge of a shopping-basket, a neat and pretty piece of work. The other was making a baker's large white bread basket. We watched the finishing touches of the shopping-basket, as the uprights were bent down into a kind of plait, folded deftly into the next uprights, and the ends cut off with shears. The worker was blind but it was impossible to guess this from his rapid movements. His hands moved swiftly, weaving the osiers and reaching for his tools without any hesitation. The assistant, who made the great baker's basket, was deaf and dumb.

Mr Hall told us that often men combine basket-making with farm work or with a poultry farm, or pig-keeping, but he being blind had to rely solely on the basket-work, which kept him very busy. From the ceiling hung many kinds of baskets the men had made, great oval baskets without handles for vegetables, little round baskets with blue and red edges for children, shopping-baskets of great variety, and big brown market baskets. I chose two original and gay baskets to take away with me.

There are two kinds of osiers used, brown and white, and they vary in resilience. The best osiers have "waves" in the stems which one can feel by running a finger down. These basket-makers have a wonderful sense of touch. The osiers have the tiny marks of buds on the stems, called cock's combs. Mr Hall ran his finger down the smooth osiers to show the marks almost invisible to us. These osiers all come from Somerset, for Bucks has not the marshy places to supply enough for the work.

The brown osiers are made by boiling them and then peeling the skin. The dye from the skin enters the wood and stains it. These are used for most of the basket-work, chiefly because people prefer the brown colour.

The white ones are made by putting the green osiers in mud and leaving for some weeks to soften. Then they are peeled and their body is pure white. These are used for clothes baskets, bread baskets and laundry baskets.

The next week these two men would be making cress baskets for the watercress gatherers. They have runs of different kinds of work, according to the season and demand.

As we talked the deaf and dumb man finished his bread basket and commenced another, using strong, tough pieces of wood for the foundation—a kind of spider's web which he wove around the main stem. So I saw a basket begun and I saw a basket finished with the handle neatly put in. This basket-making place was a happy, cheerful workroom, where I stayed for a long time watching the nimble fingers fly over the work. I ordered my dog basket and I brought the small Scottie in to be measured for his home by the touch of the blind man.

There is a blind basket-worker at Penn who does similar work, in his hut on Beacon Hill.

In another part of Chesham we came by chance across a blacksmith's shop where they no longer shoe horses but now make wrought ironwork. The smith, Mr Goodall, had made many beautiful gates and the ironwork for inn signs. He had made weathercocks and latches and candlesticks. The forge was working at one end of the shop, and the roof and sides of the barn were hung with a grand assortment of ironwork, of patterns and pieces, old and lovely, some of which are now forgotten entirely. He was matching an iron candelabra with five candlesticks and leaves and tendrils when we saw him.

In Bucks I have seen some very beautiful ironwork on inn signs, especially at Stony Stratford, where there is an elaborate piece of craftsmanship at the sign of the Bull. In most towns or villages of any size there is a worker in iron at a forge where the smith still shoes horses but he depends mainly upon his wrought iron.

An avenue of Dutch elms leads to the church, and in little Church Lane there are several seventeenth-century houses of great charm. On ehouse is fourteenth-century, with much of its original work. It is like a house in a fairy-tale.

The church on its hillside was sweet-smelling of lilies and roses when I entered, and in the chancel arch hung a great bouquet of roses, hundreds of flowers making an incense of their own and a glory in the little church. The church is thirteenth-century and its porch, of the fifteenth century, has a room over it. There are some scratch dials on the walls of this church. These little timepieces always interest me as they were the countryman's way of telling the time. The church has a central tower and it has a doorway embroidered with little ball flowers like opening buds. In the churchyard is a cross to the memory of Thomas Harding, who was burned at the stake near Chesham.

At Chesham there lived in the seventeenth century a strange man, Roger Crab, who was called the Mad Hatter. His skull had been cut in the civil war, and he retired to Chesham to sell hats, at which he made a fortune. He gave away his money and lived on three-farthings a week, in extreme simplicity, eating roots and grass and herbs.

The valley of the Chess is very fair, and the road and river run along it between steep wooded sides. The waters have formerly worked several flour mills, and it was sad to see some of these mills falling to pieces.

Lord's Mill, a seventeenth-century mill, white-timbered and good as ever, is now grinding grist. Once it was a flour mill, but the great combines have put it out of action. Everywhere I heard the same tale, the little man had been thrown out of business and now each one is struggling for existence.

"Lord's Mill is nearly as old as the church," said the dusty miller's man as he hooked a chain to the neck of a full sack. "There is no chance for flour nowadays, so we grind oats, barley, rye, anything for grist."

This mill has a water-wheel which is now enclosed and out of use. The river Chess goes under a little bridge where there is a ford at the mill, and as we stood looking at the clear water with pebbles at the bottom, glinting in the sunshine, two horses walked out of a farmyard and came down by themselves to drink. Lorries, cars, motor-buses, rushed along the road, and this little scene of mill and river and drinking horses was like something from another world.

Farther down the valley we came to a great beautiful mill called Boys Mill, with little lawns and gardens running to the water's edge. The miller's daughter lived in the old mill house and she told me of the days when her father had the mill working. After being a flour mill it became a paper mill for a time. Now it is only used for storing goods. There, among the reeds and willows, ran the silvery Chess which once worked so hard grinding England's wheat. In this valley there was a deserted farm with barns falling to pieces and roofs decayed.

The river Chess, between Chesham and Latimer, is clear as glass and cattle stand in the water under the trees by the little bridge which spans the river. Among the reeds on the water's edge we saw two herons fishing. It is a peaceful, unspoilt place.

On the slopes behind the woods we could see Latimer House. It was here that Charles I was brought prisoner, and Charles II took refuge here also.

Latimer village is like a pretty toy. There are little red cottages round a small village green, and every cottage has a flower garden brimming over with flowers. There is a symmetry about Latimer as if each house is proud of the village and is determined to look its very best. Two great elms, with seats around them, stand on the green, and there is a pump under a red roof, with a place for hanging buckets. Outside the little post office waits a pony and trap, and it seems quite in keeping with the rest of the village.

The old name for Latimer was Isenhampstead Latimer, but the former part of the name was dropped last century. Near Latimer is the village of Chenies, famous for the Russell tombs.

Chenies, too, is a little Early Victorian model village of cottages round a small green near the Chess. The church and Bedford Chapel and also the great Tudor manor house of the Russells stand by the village green, and through the gateway one can see the golden-red brickwork and groups of twisted trees. It is a sixteenth-century house, built probably about 1530 by John, Lord Russell, the first Earl of Bedford. The graveyard is separated from the little church and we went into it to see the back of the manor house. The great old red brick wall of the manor, with its steeply pitched roof and splendid chimney stacks, some of whose shafts are enriched by ornament, is as rich a sight as the front of the house.

The church has a gateway opening on to the green, for here, as in many Bucks villages, church, cottage, and manor house are very close together. This church of Chenies was rebuilt in the fifteenth century. Along one side of it, parallel to the nave but divided from it by windows, is the Bedford Chapel. This building is locked, but through the glass one can see one of the most splendid memorials of the country. It is very bright and gay with colour, flags hang along the walls, and the ancient tombs are coloured in scarlet, blue, and gold. The floor is black and white marble. On the walls are helmets, and statues of St Peter and St Andrew stand in the corners. These statues were carved in France in the sixteenth century and brought to England. It is said that the oldest tomb in the chapel is that of Sir John Chenies and his wife, who lived in the fourteenth century. The figures, in coloured alabaster, are in perfect condition, with delicately moulded hands and richly carved clothes. The women wear coronets on their hair, and the men are in armour. It is an amazing scene of brilliance and colour, with no thought of death or sadness, as if these great earls still wore their ermine robes and coronets in heaven.

Chapter VIII

GIPSIES AND HEDGERLEY

BUCKINGHAMSHIRE gave me my first real acquaintance with gipsies and commons and little mellow cottages with thatched roofs warm enough to comfort a chilly world. I knew moors with grouse and curlew, moors spangled with bilberry and cranberry, wide lands where cottongrass waves and the lovely grass of Parnassus nods in the emerald bogs, but I had never known a small common, a comfortable open place with gorse bushes and short grass, and perhaps a few geese or a goat feeding, near the surrounding houses. The moors can be lonely savage places, but the commons of Buckinghamshire are kindly at-home spots, where children can play without getting lost.

Farnham Common, Gerrards Cross Common, and Stoke Poges Common are good open spaces, with silver birches and gorse and plumy gold broom, with little nut trees, and a pond here and there. Ibstone Common, high up on the hill above Turville, has a warning:

"Notice is hereby given that all persons who shall be found dragging or taking away any timber, turf, mould, gravel, clay, sand, stones, furze, heath or any other material—will be prosecuted."

Littleworth Common is one of the smaller friendly commons near Dropmore and Burnham Beeches. The woods near are bounded only by a ditch and low ridge, moss-covered, with trees growing upon it. This makes a freedom about the scene, and one can step away from the traffic into the cool green shade with no fence or barrier between. Sometimes there is a cornfield by the woods, or a cottage and garden, or even a deep pool.

The common is a reminder of Surrey, with many silver birches, and wide clumps of purple heather, with harebells and mountain scabious, devil's bit and St John's wort, growing in the sandy soil. There is no trace here of chalk and the flowers that grow on the Chilterns. Little boys shake the crab-apple

III

trees and pick the wild honeysuckle, and cars come to the edges of the land with their picnicking families.

The country roads wind among flowery patches in South Bucks, and the trees by the roads are mixed. Oak and elm, ash and thorn, spindle and wayfaring trees as well as beech grow in the woods. In the ditch which divides the road from the woodland grows skull-cap, with its bright blue flower, the scarlet beads of cuckoo-pint, bitter-sweet, curls of traveller's-joy, and the golden-yellow butter-and-eggs. Honeysuckle twines round the branches of the bushes and raises its crowns to the sky, and bryony slings its dark purple leaves there, ready for the time when the coral berries will add colour to the spindle berries, the holly, and the wayfaring tree. Musk mallow grows low by the verge, and mullein and agrimony.

"There's a lot of diddicoys about," says the roadman who is cutting the grass verge with a sickle.

"Yes, I've seen some down here," I reply.

"They're a regular nuisance, and there's a lot of nonsense talked about them nowadays," he continues fiercely for such a mild little man. "I have to go and clear up after them. If those as said the nonsense had to clean up the old rags the diddicoys leave, they'd change their talk. The camp down here has moved on, for they've been summoned. Fifteen shillings each they had to pay. They can only stay twenty-four hours in one place and they'd been here for a long time, for months, and they wouldn't go."

I had seen few gipsies when I came to live in Buckinghamshire, for although a woman carrying baskets of tinware called occasionally and had tea and currant loaf on the doorstep, gipsies found the journeys too far. In Buckinghamshire they have their homes, and they abound in the country places. One sees them travelling the roads, three or four carts with covered hoods like the covered wagons of the settlers, drawn by piebald ponies. They go through High Wycombe to the woods. Sometimes there are yellow and scarlet caravans, moving slowly, with faces looking over the doors and feathers nodding.

I came across an encampment one day, a village of tents and caravans with fires burning and food cooking, all in a wood

Lupton's Tower, Eton College

near Hedsor, with a by-road near. The children rushed at me, shouting "Give us a penny, lady," the dogs barked, babies plucked their mothers' long skirts, and the women eyed me with sidelong glances, for I had no purse. The gipsy women seem to keep to their old fashions, to the picturesque full petticoats, and gay bodices and shawls, black hair braided, big hats, fine brooches.

Farther on the road I met more gipsies, with their children. They were returning from the shops of High Wycombe laden with packets of tea, sugar, and loaves of white bread. They had sold the brilliant magenta and green and yellow chrysanthemums they had made out of wood shavings, dyed and curled to flowery shapes, and they had bought food.

Snow began to fall, the north wind was blowing, and I cycled with difficulty. The gipsies crouched under the lee of a hedge, some of them scrabbled up sticks with great speed, clutching with brown hands, laughing and chattering. Then one opened a newspaper, lighted a fire, and a blaze shot up. The bonfire blazed by the road, they warmed their outstretched hands and the children shouted and danced. I cycled slowly, enjoying the warmth that came over the road to me. Only the vile weather prevented me from joining the party. I turned round, and they had gone, leaving black ashes and half-burned sticks behind. They were trudging away along the road, the women with their baskets on their arms, the children carrying the last bright chrysanthemums, the remnant of their stock. They had some miles to walk before they would reach the shelter in the wood where a good fire and the cooking-pot awaited them.

The Penn country is a sanctuary for gipsies. They have their regular rounds, as I soon found when I came to live here. I was agreeably disturbed one evening by shouting voices, the clatter of horses and the grinding of cart wheels. Alas! Cart wheels are not as common as they used to be, and I love the shrill squeal of heavy trundling wheels, and the crack of a whip and the sound of a cavalcade of horses. There they were, going along the lane, a stream of brightly painted caravans, gold and yellow, glittering with brasswork, dark faces peering out, children and dogs running alongside, the elder boys looking after the horses, the children hunting in the hedges. They stopped a short distance away, for

I   113

The Cock Pit, Eton

their usual camping ground was reached and they had come home.

It was a three-cornered grass patch, with hawthorns and violets and sometimes a mushroom or two. Here the caravans stayed and the families dispersed. In a minute the woods echoed with children's shouts, the crackle of branches, the noise of the axe. In five minutes they had cut and broken enough wood to light a large fire, which flared up sending blue smoke high among the hawthorns, setting fire to a bush.

The clatter of galloping horses made me run to shut my gate. A dozen horses, piebald, brown, and white came careering past with shouting boys at their heels. They were turned back, snorting and whinnying, and then they began to eat the grass by the road, the thick grass that grew there uncut. What a feast it must have been for them! Soon there was quiet except for the eager cropping of the horses. A boy guarded them, but they were content among the rich plenty.

At the fire the supper was cooked and a big lad of sixteen with two little dark-eyed pretty sisters and a baby came to my back door to ask for drinking water. They filled their bucket and went off, but they returned again and again until I was tired of drawing it for them. They were called Rose, Bathsheba, Nelson, and Daniel. They brought brushes they had made, shoe brushes, nail brushes, and scrubbing-brushes.

Their sojourn was short, for my neighbours disliked the gipsies and complained to the police. The sympathetic policeman came to speak to them, very kindly, and allowed them to stay one night before they moved on. The great fire rose higher, songs and laughter came from the pitch, the horses grunted and shuffled and rolled, and the stars looked down on a scene that was as old as the Chiltern hills and the Icknield Way.

The next morning they came for more water, and then with a mighty creaking and cracking, a shouting and heaving, the caravans moved away.

They came back later, always for one night, before they were moved. The war was on, and their red flame had to be put out early. One of their camping grounds near was taken by the Home Guard. There was not room for all the caravans in the patch by the hawthorns and they have not returned.

They leave their track behind them—broken young trees, burnt sticks, charred paper, rags and boots, litter which spoils the woods and lanes. They are careless as children, but I cannot resist waving to them as they peer from their caravan windows, and their bright grins and waving paws reply. However, I see them on the roads, lugging their baskets of wooden flowers, or carrying baskets full of pussy-willow which they have ruthlessly ripped and torn from the trees near, or, alas! bearing baskets heaped with the lovely purple wild orchis and bee orchis, stripped from the fields, or cowslips torn from the banks, so that now the flowers are scarce. They stand in the town only a mile away from the fields where the flowers grew and hold them out for sale.

Buckinghamshire is their countryside, they know every lane, every hedgerow, every farm, they know where the best nuts grow, where firewood can be found and water, and where flowers bloom for their bunches. They have the secrets, and who are we to scold them and tidy them up? They curse and they bless, and I prefer their blessing, for I always feel it is a visible thing, and I envy them their nights under the stars in the beech woods.

They camp under the trees on the green verge of the broad road to Slough, that fine highway with grassy borders and parallel footpaths, bordered again by the beech woods and corn-land. There, with a pageant of buses and cars, army lorries and tractors, wagons loaded with gigantic forest trees, and little flat carts and fast-trotting ponies, they live by the roadside. Usually there are three or four caravans, with brass lamps and lace curtains, and women looking from the steps. A fire burns by the road, sticks crackle, and a pot simmers with something from the woods inside it. Rabbits scuttle in the fields close by, hedgehogs rustle the leaves, wood pigeons fly overhead, and a covey of partridges rises from the stubble. Sometimes a pheasant flaps across the road to the next wood. There is plenty for the pot.

A line of washing hangs out, dangling from a rope stretched between the beech trees. Red, blue, and black garments flutter there, and somebody stoops over the fire and throws on fresh boughs. The horses are cobbled on the wide grass verge. Children play and shout and stare from their home under the trees, and all the time the traffic flows past, unheeding this backwater of civilization, this centre of stubborn individualism.

The women are working, making clothes-pegs for other people's washing lines, carving the flowers and colouring them with violent dyes ready for sale, sorting out their old clothes, washing their rags in a tin basin, and some are on the road selling the goods they have made.

One evening we came through Great Hampden woods to look for the bodgers who work there in the winter and spring. We passed through the park gates and drove along among the cattle in as charming a piece of country as one could see. The bodgers must have gone home, for the blue evening mist was settling down on the leafless trees, and the distances were ultramarine. Suddenly we saw a tongue of fire, and then flames, and blue spiring smoke among the trees, close to the roadside, in a corner of the woods.

"It's the bodgers," said we, but we were wrong. The man who tended the fire was no respectable bodger, but a wild young gipsy, with tossing black hair and flashing teeth. He grinned at us from the flames. He had a cart wheel, and he was putting the iron tyre on it. The little yellow cart stood near, with its remaining wheel, and the small piebald pony grazed in the wood. Here was a craftsman who could turn his hand to anything.

Farther on, down the lane, we met his companions, two women with baskets on their arms and bright shawls on their heads. They would spend the night by the fire in that lonely corner far from houses, secure and free from being moved on. They would make clothes-pegs and brushes and scrubbers, which they would sell in the villages later on. They were using their hands at old crafts as surely as were the bodgers with their simple pole lathes.

By the road in the green verges, under the hedges and in corners of ploughfields, grows a herb which is a favourite of mine. It is mugwort, the wild wormwood, beloved of country people. It is tall and graceful, and the green of its finely cut leaves is delicate and misty grey. The tiny flowers are almost invisible, the herb grows unnoticed. I think the gipsies gather it and use it for their herbal teas. There is an ancient use for it which they may try. It is said that if a walker puts mugwort in his shoes in the morning he may walk forty miles before noon and not tire. I have put a slip in my shoe, but I have wearied long before that. It is noticeable, though, that often one finds the ashes of a gipsy fire near a clump of the aromatic herb.

The quiet tree-lined road to Hedgerley village is bordered with cornfields and meadows and woodland. Great oaks stand in the hedge, some of them of perfect shape, beautiful in their proportions, and one of these, perhaps three hundred years old, with widely spreading branches, carried a midsummer foliage of crimson leaves. I always watch these oaks with deep interest and admiration, as if they were characters out of history.

The wild untrimmed hedgerows of this lane have blue streamers of purple-tufted vetch, shading to ultramarine and azure, and honeysuckle, golden and cream, waves its crowns above the top branches of the nut trees. On the verge of the narrow road tall yarrow grows, the best I know, white and rosy-pink, with the rich heady scent which fills the air, so that I stay and breathe it in.

Here is a gipsy caravan, and there a travelling man who looks like the Ancient Mariner, and then a cottage with circular saw and stacks of firewood, and logs heaped up ready for the little painted cart to take them to the villages. Wapses is the name of the place. It is a country word I have always known, and the farm lads used it for wasps. I wonder idly as I walk past if it is a joke for the wasps' nests there.

Hedgerley lies in a hollow at the foot of the steep hill, nestling there like a bird on its nest. It is a village of quiet charm, to which I return with content, although I am told it is overrun by trippers on Sundays, when field-gates are left open and the peace is destroyed.

On the right is a gabled sixteenth-century house with timber framing and original chimneys, a house that seems to hold many secrets. Now it is made into three cottages.

"We think nothing of it," said a countryman when I inquired about my favourite house, so I was left dumb.

The church, which is perched on a hill above the cottages as a guardian spirit, was rebuilt entirely in 1852 on a new foundation owing to the subsidence of the clay. For me, it is very ancient and romantic, owing to the manner I first entered it. It was a dark rainy night, with thunder and lightning, when we went through the gate up the steep path under the sycamore trees, stumbling to the lantern in the church door. In the blackness the church seemed to be medieval, and when I entered and sat down among the packed congregation in the little nave in the dim light, the feeling of antiquity was enhanced. Down the narrow aisle swept richly clad people of the Middle Ages, scarlet robes flying, deep blue cloaks caught in the wind, black priests' garments dark in the night. The play of *Everyman* was acted there, so vividly, so movingly, that I was lost in time. Death came to stand in the little chancel, his deep voice ringing down the ages. Pride, Vainglory, Riches, came to the altar. Everyman himself was there. So for me Hedgerley Church is very old, it sheds its restoration, and remains as it has been for centuries. I was aware as never before of the power of a play in the setting of shadow and candlelight, in a small village church.

The limestone font from the earlier church has figures carved on its sides, with little mobile faces, with streaming hair and wry mouths, like the actors in *Everyman*. One is putting out his tongue in a grimace, and another is a cynic with big ears and hair like a flame round his head. At Bierton Church I saw a tiny carved head with the same wildness and individuality. There are many strangely vivid faces in church carvings.

A scrap of red velvet, from a cloak given by Charles I for an altar cloth, is framed on the wall.

Hanging high, too high for scrutiny, on the vestry wall is a seventeenth-century painting of the Ten Commandments with amusing illustrations in clear bright colours. Three modern corbels outside the church are lively portraits of village people a hundred years ago.

At the end of the village is the little inn called the Brick Mould. There the brickmakers supped their ale when bricks were made in the neighbourhood at Penlands Farm.

The inn is a well-proportioned little place, plain and good as a small red brick, with a tiny bar and a jolly countrywoman behind it. On the shelf are pewter pots and a lustre jug. In the corner sits an aged man, brown as a dead leaf, wrinkled as a nut, drinking solemnly by himself.

"What I should like is a drink of very cold water," I say, for it is a blazing hot morning. "Not tap water, but icy water from a spring."

"Then I wish I'd known early, I'd have got you a drop from our well," says the old man. "We lets down a bucket and gets the water from deep down. It's pure water, cold as ice. We've got tap water laid on, but I wouldn't have the well took away. The landlord wanted to fill it up, but I said, 'No. Hitler maybe'll have a go at the water main and then where should we be?'"

"And did he?" I ask.

"Yes, he dropped one not far away, took off my roof, and let the plaster fall on me. And he dropped another and it just missed."

And then he and the landlady talk of their bombs in the little village.

To this inn come the dwellers in a few small cottages on the hillside. They pay very small rents, and the villagers tease them and call them the folk from the Treacle Mine.

"The Treacle Miners will be coming down to-night," says the old man.

"What is a Treacle Miner?" I ask innocently.

"Those who get something for nothing," he replies.

We watched the little village school being dismantled across the way, as men carried desks and forms into a removal van. The village school, which had been in use for a hundred years, was now given up. We helped to get the piano on board the van, and stood while they closed and locked the school door.

"Yes. I went to school there, seventy years ago," says the old man at the Brick Mould. "They've no use for anything old nowadays. They must have change."

Up the hill, past the inn we went, to Mount Pleasant Farm, which was pleasant enough with its garden of Madonna lilies, roses and a walnut tree, its old buildings and trees. It is a seventeenth-century farm, brick and timber. An old chimney with a square shaft is there, but it is built in and a range for cooking has been inserted.

"I'm going to have the range taken out and use the old fireplace again," said the farmer's wife. "I cook with oil, and it would be nice to see the fireplace as it used to be."

Burnham Beeches and the adjacent woods stretch across the country with lanes connecting them to many small villages. These woods are not quite real to me, for sometimes houses are built within the shade of the beech trees, and motor-cars are parked in dells. I dislike meeting a car in a wood, squatting in the leaves like a grey elephant. The roads through Burnham Beeches are tarred, and tidy, and only in winter can one get the feeling of the place.

The magnificent trees are astonishing and rather frightening with their grotesque shapes and their sinister faces. They are the trees surely that Arthur Rackham knew when he made his fairy-tale drawings, and I can see many a goblin figure, many a leering face with sharp eyes watching, so that I walk circumspectly among them, never alone with them, half-expecting to hear voices and strange whisperings in an ancient tongue.

I step softly there, among the dead leaves, stopping now and then to stare enchanted at some monster of an ancient tree, as if I saw a Rip Van Winkle, in high hat, bearded to the ground.

Witches must live there, and perhaps the branches of one of these beeches lean down and twine themselves around a young pretty girl, catching her to its heart, and taking fresh life from her to help it to its own immortality.

I walk through them, lost in their magical quality, listening to the never-ending sounds and whispers, keeping a quick eye upon their movements, and suddenly I hear music: not the ethereal music of trees, but the splash of a band.

The most surprising thing, and somehow the most natural thing in this world of enchanted trees, happens. There is a fair with merry-go-rounds up the slope by the orchard in the clearing. Wooden hobby-horses with scarlet nostrils and waving tails are galloping round to the tune of "The Lambeth Walk." Swing-boats are flying high, children are laughing. It is a joyous sight, and I feel no incongruity in the scene, for the ancient trees are laughing at the sight.

CHAPTER IX

SLOUGH AND ETON
STOKE POGES AND DORNEY

THESE Buckinghamshire roads have broad margins, so wide in places they are like strips of fields by the main road. They are often planted with trees, and a footpath goes along them. Sometimes the width arises from the advent of a new road when the old is near. Then the old way wanders under the hedge and the fine modern road cuts straight through. A good example of this is near Whitchurch, and in the whole county it is my favourite piece of highway. Threaded with green meadow grass, a stream, and winding lane which curves round by the hedgeside over a little red brick bridge, it is a beautiful broad road.

The main road to Slough is particularly fine as it leaves Beaconsfield and the margins widen out and the footpaths appear in the grass. Sometimes a horse and cart is there, to gather the crop. Sometimes gipsies have their horses cobbled in the broad verges. A tramp saunters along with a rose in his hat. There is a leisurely feeling about these roads with their racing traffic and quiet borders.

The road dips suddenly down a cutting whose banks are bright in summer with rhododendrons and golden broom. Once the bus on which I was travelling stopped on the slope, and we waited, wondering what was the matter. The conductress got down and began to gather the flowers, just as they say trains once stopped while the engine driver gathered mushrooms in the fields. When her arms were filled with crimson and purple rhododendrons, she returned, divided her spoils between driver and herself, hung up a branch to decorate the bus and then we started off again.

At the top of the rise is the Yew Tree Inn, all alone in the wide green margin, with its cut yew and a bird atop. Every child points to this tree and laughs with joy over it as the bus sweeps past. I think it will be remembered a hundred years hence when wars and ruins have been forgotten.

Here is the lane to Penlands Farm, once the busy centre for brick-making, where the country people worked. Hedgerley and Burnham Beeches are near, down side lanes, and a branching road takes one to the Egypt Woods, perhaps named after the gipsies who live around here. I prefer to visit these places by the country lanes which wind in and out of woods and fields.

The main road runs beside the great woods, golden in autumn, through Farnham Royal with its gay little Green Man Inn, and its pump with red-tiled roof and its wide common, to the great town of Slough, the industrial centre which is overwhelming in its importance and size. It seems quite out of place in Bucks, the county of little old villages, but the giant has come to stay and it grows larger every year.

Slough was the home of the great astronomer, William Herschel. He was born in Hanover, but he came to England as a musician. He was devoted to astronomy, and he made his own telescopes. When he discovered the planet Uranus he was famous throughout the world. He was appointed Court Astronomer, and he settled at Datchet, on the Thames, the pretty Buckinghamshire village where Falstaff was ducked and stowed away in the linen basket. Then he moved to Slough, a quiet country village among orchards, in 1786. In his garden he set up his giant telescope, nearly forty feet long. It was one of the wonders of the world in the time of George III. In an old book of my grandfather's dated 1820, this "Doctor Herschel's Grand Telescope" is described as one of the Hundred Wonders, a telescope which magnified six thousand times.

With his sister Caroline, William Herschel mapped out the heavens and catalogued the known stars and nebulæ. He discovered the existence of double stars and dark stars, and the direction in which the whole solar system is moving. His researches are stupendous in their implications and their magnitude. His son, John Herschel, was born at Slough and worked with his father until he left for the Cape.

The house where the three astronomers lived is a large red

house by the side of the main road, windows looking down on the fleets of motor-buses and the swirl of traffic. The quietest scientific spot, where it was necessary to have no earth tremor, is now in a tumult of noise and jangle. The bus stop is opposite the door of the gardener's cottage, and one can see the hut at the end of the long garden where the giant telescope once stood before it was dismantled. There is something very moving about this house, Observatory House, and the genius that filled it, and I always think of the patient watchers of the sky as I pass this garden behind its walls in the town of Slough. That was the beginning of the scientific history of Slough, and nowadays there are inventions being made and research work carried on. I think particularly of the invention department of a great engineering works I visited, like a laboratory in the physics department of a university. There was the wonderful hydraulic beam detector, prepared for installation on a ship. I think William Herschel would have gone to see this and delighted in it if he could have moved forward in time.

This beam detector consists simply of two parallel beams of light, one of which shows a deflection if smoke appears in its path. Smoke in a building denotes fire, and these beams are fire detectors, especially important for shipping.

Many men worked on the inventions, for naturally there are many devices to be tried out. I felt I was in the presence of an engineering genius as Mr B. showed me this new marvel. Research men were working, making their own apparatus, as in a research laboratory, and carrying out their own experiments.

The modern industrial town of Slough is the outcome of a successful experiment to start industries in good conditions. The Second Industrial Revolution has already begun, whether we like it or not, and the bleak dark houses and grim factories of the First Industrial Revolution are succeeded by light airy factories such as those which have been built at Slough. They are the forerunners of new towns that will spring up as the industrialization of England moves on. They centralize work and keep the country clean.

Slough had already developed considerably in the last century, and a few factories had sprung up in a country district that was mainly agricultural. After the war of 1914–18 a vast dump of motor vehicles and army gear was left here, and the place became a byword for a rubbish heap. A new company was formed, called the Slough Trading Estate, to combat the disorder and to start a new enterprise.

The factory buildings are clean and well designed, they are fresh-looking and original, so that it is pleasant to see them. Some have long windows in perpendicular lines, and rounded walls of dark red brick. They are decorative and well spaced, and the air is free from smoke.

When I first came to live in Buckinghamshire I was taken to see Slough, much against my inclination, but my guide said I ought to see one of the wonders of the district, a spacious fine group of beautiful factories. I stared in astonishment, remembering mills in the north. These long bright buildings, with their many windows, their gardens, their canteens, were like a Wellsian city of the future. There were no tall chimneys, no ugly advertisements, only plain lettering with the names of the firms. I was impressed and I wondered what happened behind the green doors and glass walls.

Now I have visited some of the factories. They are well lighted, with green shaded hanging lamps, and warmed by heaters; they are bright with cream walls and delicate green paint. There is no smoke or grime, for the steam and electricity in the works come from the electric plant on the estate.

The list of manufacturing firms at Slough is so various there seems to be everything. Margarine, plastics, motor-cars, tooth brushes, press tools and jigs, asbestos, biscuits, milk-bottle discs, chimney pots, cosmetics, and many engineering works are there, concentrated in one huge centre.

The estate offices have flower beds before their windows, hollyhocks and snapdragons against the walls. These flower garden strips run along the front of many factories, but some firms neglect their chances and do nothing for their own garden, while others bring colour with their massed flowers, not only to their own works but to the street.

The Aspro factory has long beds of snapdragons and lobelia

stretching below its buildings for some distance. The interior of this factory is as gay as the exterior, with green and white rooms, polished machines, and pretty girls. The mixing, compressing, breaking up, and further compressing are done in the machines tended by only a few men, as packing takes most of the time for this product. Girls in white overalls were filling the little boxes, others were sealing the tablets in airtight strips of waxed paper by machine.

There was an excellent canteen, with small tables in a cheerful bright room, and we got a glimpse of the kitchens where the cooks in tall white caps worked with spotless pans. This canteen provides meals for others besides their own staff, and there were tempting smells of food. The concert room had a stage, and there were rest rooms. At the back I saw a flower garden for these girls to walk in, and hard tennis courts for their pleasure, while some distance away were sports grounds.

Music was relayed at certain hours, for it has been known for many years that music lightens work. In the harvest field singing helps labour. In the cowhouse and ploughfield the whistling boy is the happiest. Now in the factories music aids the worker to greater efficiency and content.

The most decorative and gay little factory is that of Eau de Cologne 4711. The scent of it came through the door, across the little green lawn, even before we entered. Girls sat in their rooms, filling little boxes, smoothing powder into cases, pouring shaving cream by machinery into tubes and sealing them. They wore white overalls and white caps covered their hair. They smiled as if they enjoyed living among scents.

In another room were the vats of shaving cream, cauldrons of thick fragrant paste, and great bins of powders of many shades. The air was delicately scented, and we sniffed each room with appreciation. Men were mixing the powders, but girls were pasting the red and gold labels on bottles and pots for export only, and others were sticking the cellulose covers over the tops and screwing on the lids.

Perhaps the most romantic room in this place of scent and powder was that filled with cases ready for export. The names Rangoon, Trinidad, Cape Town, Bombay were painted on their sides, and we thought of those delicious smells going across the seas.

Down in the cellar, which was a little room like a wine cellar in an old French house, we had a glimpse of the hogsheads of perfumes maturing for some months. The whitewashed walls, the dark vats, the polished brass taps, all had an un-English elegance. It was a secret place, and we breathed the scent-laden air and came away with regret.

One of the best-looking buildings on the estate is that of High Duty Alloys Ltd. This factory, with its long slender windows, is of excellent design, and I always admire it as I pass. It is a palace for a Glass Princess, I think, but in reality it manufactures the higher-quality aluminium alloys, particularly for the aircraft industry. In front of some of these factories the workmen sit, eating their sandwiches, in the strips of garden at the dinner hour.

The beating heart of this great industrial centre is the power station, which I enjoyed as much as a threshing machine or a combine harvester. There is something very stimulating to the imagination in a power house. I saw the immense high-pressure boilers, which provide steam at 800° F., and I looked through smoked glass at the fiery furnace behind the small doors. Then I went to the upper part of the generating station, where there are two English electric turbo-generators and two Ljungström units. All these turbines exhaust to separate surface condensers with their own pumps.

Circulating water is handled by three mighty towers, a parabolic concrete tower and two wooden ones. These towers dominate the scene, but they are not ugly and the parabolic tower is a strangely beautiful giant, rearing its height above the crowds of buildings.

This chamber with its turbines gave me great pleasure, for I consider a turbine is as beautiful as a work of nature. The smoothness and power of these immense machines, each of which generates at a pressure of 6,600 volts, is something to wonder at.

There are ten miles of railway lines and sidings, and four locomotives for dealing with the trucks in this great industrial undertaking, which is so vastly different from anything else in the county.

Three blocks of buildings with long strip windows from roof to ground form the Social Centre, which entertains and educates and cares for the workers in the factories. These buildings resemble the factories, with iron girders across the roofs and bare windows and workshop lighting. I thought this was a mistake, for the work of the factories and the clatter of machines accord with iron girders, but games and lectures should have a different environment.

I saw the great concert room, with its platform and amenities for plays and orchestras and dances. There were many recreation rooms in this large place, where the citizens amuse themselves after the day's work is done. Large airy rooms were used for a gymnasium, boxing, drama, and even for a bamboo-pipe orchestra. There are folk-dancing teams which go to Aylesbury and High Wycombe. A swimming-bath, which was full of joyful noisy little boys, and a nursery school for eighty little children made a gay little corner of child life, with gardens for these young ones.

It is an extraordinary experience to pass from the vast industries of Slough in their modern buildings to the beautiful houses of Eton College, rising like a kingdom of spires and pinnacles among the trees. The playing fields with their fringes of elms are a green barrier dividing the newest from the oldest, and the segregation is complete. At once the atmosphere changes, and one is caught up by the magic of the river Thames with its boathouses under the towers of Windsor, the smooth lawns, the ancient walls of Eton. The centuries roll back and there seems to be a break with time, but this is only apparent, for there is a continuity between new and old, and Eton is modern as well as ancient, for it is timeless.

Several games of cricket are in progress, loiterers stand by the roadside, or step within the fence to watch, boys lie on the grass; it is a country scene. There is clapping from the onlookers, each intent on one particular match—errand boys, postmen, all stay for a few minutes.

The seventeenth-century red brick building of Upper School

stands back from the road, and through the gateway there is the cobbled School Yard, a large quadrangle where the boys assemble for Roll Call, or "Absence." In School Yard stands the beautiful bronze statue of Henry VI as a youth, very much alive and aware of the generations walking past him.

Eton was founded by Henry VI when the young King was eighteen, and the Charter of the Foundation was issued on October 11th in 1440, over five hundred years ago. This was half a century before the discovery of America, a sobering thought. This precious Charter with the King's signature, in bold strong characters, is in the Eton Library. Henry VI was born at Windsor, and Eton is very close to the castle. The church of Eton is dedicated to the Assumption of the Virgin Mary, and Henry had a devotion to this feast day. The full title of Eton College is "The King's College of Our Lady of Eton beside Windsor." On Lupton's Tower, in School Yard, there is a carving of the Assumption, and the Lilies of the Virgin are incorporated in the arms of the College.

There is a lovely custom at Eton in connection with this. Each year three white lilies are laid on the tomb of Henry VI at Windsor on the eve of Founder's Day, December 5th, and the choir sings the King's Prayer. On the eve of May 21st three lilies are laid on the spot in the Tower of London where Henry VI was killed.

An old description of Eton in Elizabethan days says: "In the precincts of Windsor, on the other side of the Thames, both whose banks are joined by a bridge of wood, is Eton, a well-built College, and famous school for polite letters, founded by Henry VI, where, besides a Master and eight Fellows and Chanters, sixty boys are maintained gratis. They are taught Grammar, and remain in the school till upon trial made of their genius and progress in study, they are sent to the University of Cambridge."

To-day there are seventy boys who are King's Scholars elected by competitive examinations. They live in College and have their own splendid Long Chamber, on the floor above Lower School. College Hall, their dining-room, has three fifteenth-century fireplaces, and there are long oak tables, as in

Stoke Poges Church

university dining-halls. There are fine pictures on the walls, and cut in rude letters in one of the wall-panels is the following proud little inscription:

> Queen Elisabetha
> ad nos gave
> October 10 two
> loves in a Mes.
> 1596.

The majority of the boys, who are fee-paying, are called Oppidans. They lodge and board in twenty-five houses in Eton, under tutors. They have a share in the government of their houses, and this feeling for the community is part of their education. The boys have more freedom in Eton than in many of the public schools, and this is one of the privileges. Each boy has a room to himself, a tiny place, but his own, from the beginning, and there he learns to use his freedom rightly.

Besides these, there are about twenty-five boys in the Choir School, elected for their voices.

Upper School, which dates from 1690, is built over a colonnade where there is a bronze frieze inscribed with the names of 1,154 Etonians who died in the war 1914–18. In the long room Dr Keate, headmaster of Eton from 1809 to 1834, had a division or class of 200 boys to keep in order. In those days there were 500 boys and only nine masters. Now there are 1,100 boys and ninety masters. This room has various desks of the masters, and three or four divisions or classes went on at once. Names are carved in the panels, many famous names among them cut in the wood.

Round the walls are busts of some Old Etonians—the poets Shelley and Gray; the statesmen Walpole, Chatham, Fox and Grey, Canning and Gladstone; Fielding the novelist, Howe the admiral, and Hallam the historian.

Lower School, which was built probably in the time of Henry VI, has been used as a classroom for five hundred years. It is the most fascinating room in the whole College, with its timbers and its stout oak pillars holding up Long Chamber above it, put there in 1625. Queen Elizabeth gave the timber which

The Thames at Bourne End

forms the stout pillars holding up the ceiling from the ships of the Armada. Her face looks down from each archway. There is a small organ, made by George III for his daughter, which was bought for the school after it had been through some vicissitudes. There is also the old whipping block, and the porter remarked dourly, "There was nothing between the birch rod and the bare skin in those days." The walls are very thick, and when German bombs fell on each side with great destruction this little old room was unharmed. The shutters of the small windows are carved so closely with names they seem to be chiselled in designs. Some of the names date to Elizabethan times, in this schoolroom which dates not later than 1500. There are three masters' desks, for three divisions were taken here at once. An oak rail with balusters, smooth as silk, is said to have come from a ship, rubbed by men leaning over.

Lupton's Tower, named after Roger Lupton, Provost, in School Yard, was built in the time of Henry VIII. It has a fine two-storied oriel window, and flanking this are the twin octagonal turrets which rise above the embattled parapet and are crowned with lanterns and cupolas. On one of these is the design of a pot of lilies. Over the oriel window is a beautiful clock. The royal arms and a painted carving of the Assumption are upon this noble tower.

The chapel, on the right of the Yard, was originally intended by its founder, Henry VI, to be twice its present length, but the Wars of the Roses stopped the building, and it remained as it is now. The King laid the foundation stone himself in 1441. Eton College Chapel is one of the finest examples of Perpendicular architecture. On the walls are some remarkable wall-paintings, which give the impression of tapestries, in pale blue-green colour. They were painted in 1479, illustrating miracles in the life of the Virgin. They are full of movement and vigour, and very clear and fresh. They came to light after being hidden for centuries when the College stalls were removed. The windows of the chapel were destroyed by bombs that fell near and swept away the seventeenth-century Saville House and Greek printing press, but at the west end there remains one small lovely window.

The singing in this chapel of many boys and the choir is extremely beautiful and moving, for the sound soars up to the high roof with a lyrical quality. Particularly I think of a winter's night, just before Christmas, and the clear young voice of one boy singing the Page's solo in "Good King Wenceslas," the fluting unearthly beauty of the notes. I think too of the swelling chorus of many hundreds of boys singing the "Adeste Fideles," with its triumph and glory.

The younger boys go to the Lower Chapel, and there I like to hear the sermons, and the ripples of laughter over the jokes, and the good singing in the descants, all very simple and happy. This chapel has modern tapestries on the walls and great silver candlesticks on the altar.

In the College Library there are many treasures of early printing, books of the Aldine Press and Caxton's Press, manuscripts and ancient deeds relating to the College and its lands. There is a copy of the first printed Bible, and four folios and some quartos of Shakespeare. There are manuscripts of Gray's poems and of the "Elegy," with his corrections. In an old document there is a picture of Henry VI and his Queen at a religious ceremony, kneeling in a chapel which was built at Eton before the Great Chapel. It is a delicately drawn scene at the head of the parchment, which relates to Eton. Beautiful books are here, some bound in rich velvet with silver clasps, others in elaborately tooled leather, all with clear black lettering, and some with miniatures.

Down the steps in the Cloisters, old doorways lead to ancient rooms and private stairways, and there is a pump, a real village pump, which has fresh drinking water.

The playing fields, the wall where the Wall Game is played in a sea of mud on St Andrew's Day, with boys plastered like dark figures in a frieze against it, the lovely Thames flooding its banks on a winter's day, the distant view of Windsor Castle, with silver towers against a pale ice-flecked sky, the pinnacles of the chapel, and a great willow tree bending over the water, these make a picture of poignant beauty which catches the heart.

The Brocas, bordering the Thames, is a gay scene on June

4th, when the Procession of Boats goes down the river, with the captains wearing flower-garlanded straw hats and the coxes in midshipmen's uniform of the time of George III. At night there are fireworks on Fellows Eyot, their brilliance reflected in the water, and another Procession of Boats. The towers of Windsor Castle are silver in the background, then dark against the night sky. The boys, singing the "Eton Boating Song," swarm across to the "Burning Bush" and the crowded street, and the long full day is over.

The narrow main street of Eton passes between little old houses and shops, many of them seventeenth-century, with crooked skyline, with roofs crinkled and steep, with round windows, and shutters, with courtyard and alley, and along the pavements go the Eton boys, careless, confident, gay or gloomy, just like all boys. There are the Eton shops, which cater chiefly for the boys, "sock" shop, tailors', barbers', bootmakers'. There is the famous Cock Pit, at the back of a low-beamed shop, where Byron joined in cock-fighting. It had a knuckle-bone floor. There is also the bookshop which I think is the nicest in the county. Even as one enters the door to the passage a great bowl of many-coloured flowers catches the light in the distance as if it were illuminated. To the left is the small room with mixed books, all the little old books one read in childhood, *Robinson Crusoe* and Henty, Rider Haggard and Stevenson. On the right are the treasures, the flower books, the bird books, the ancient books with stiff brown leaves and black printing, the poets, the books of sports, all the old and lovely books with pictures made in more leisured times than these. A charming old lady brings out her precious volumes which she knows most intimately, and the schoolboys flock in to find presents and to spend their money. I think this is an important part of education.

Here I bought Gerard's *Herball*, and Maund's *Botanic Gardens*, and many an old and beautiful picture book. It is part of Eton, with its crooked little winding staircase, and its cupboards in the walls, and its rooms opening one into another.

Near Eton is Stoke Poges, where the poet Gray was buried, and where probably he wrote his famous "Elegy." Every Eton boy receives a copy of Gray's poems on leaving the school.

Gray was a Londoner, but his mother was a Buckinghamshire woman, and he went to school at Eton, where two of his uncles were masters. After his father's death he lived with his mother and aunts during vacations at Stoke Poges. It is not certain that this is the churchyard immortalized in the poem, and the beautiful church of Upton near Eton and Slough has been suggested as the place in the poet's mind. At Upton the curfew of Windsor could be distinctly heard, whereas it would scarcely reach Stoke Poges, about five miles away.

> The curfew tolls the knell of parting day,
> The lowing herd winds slowly o'er the lea,
> The ploughman homeward plods his weary way,
> And leaves the world to darkness and to me.

This picture of quiet country life is perfect to a countryman's memory. The poem is the best known of all in the English language. Its popularity ever increases. Pilgrims come to the church in bus-loads, to visit the grave of Thomas Gray and his mother. It is an altar tomb, close to the church walls, and the pathetic words on it were written for his mother by the poet.

"The graceful tender mother of many children, one of whom alone had the misfortune to survive her."

She was buried in 1753 and in 1771 Gray was buried in the same grave.

There are two lychgates to the church, and the long pathway is bordered by rose trees, pink and red roses dropping their petals over the stones. At the side of this path is the grave of a little boy, with his favourite toys cut out in stone—a top, a ship, a train. This is the place of pilgrimage for small children who visit the church. The church is picturesque with many gables and roofs against a background of trees. Outside the churchyard in a field stands a vast and gloomy memorial to Gray built by Penn's grandson.

Close to the church is the Garden of Remembrance, a garden graveyard, with no stones, but lovely gardens to speak of the dead. The grounds are laid out with an avenue of blossoming trees, and under them in the spring are daffodils and narcissi, and many-coloured primulas. The avenue leads to a lake with a fountain and rose garden. The little private grave-gardens, each with a simple and short dedication, are gay with flowers, and every small garden fits into the scheme of colour of the whole with its meadows, its fine trees, its water, and its avenue.

There is a village of great charm near Eton, one of those secret little villages, hidden away, uncaught by the modern rush as if the swirling flow of the times had missed it by chance.

Dorney has beautiful little cottages, half-timbered with brick filling, and tiled roofs, and flowery gardens. There are farms and a Tudor manor house, a little church, a post office of delight, and an inn with the painted arms of the family of Palmers who have lived at the manor for generations.

Dorney Court and the church are down a tree-lined lane, where chestnuts make a green shade. The church is another of those small perfect churches which hide in the lanes of Buckinghamshire. The red brick tower is Tudor, old rose brick with stone facings, and narrow slit windows and turrets. There is something warm and welcoming about a tower like this, which seems to hold the sunshine of past years, and to distil it on a grey day, so that heat and comfort come from it to warm one's hands and one's heart. The roof with its red tiles, mossed over, has a sheen like shot silk.

The nave is Norman, and the font, very sturdy and ornamented stiffly, is Norman work. This little church has a music gallery supported on four posts at the west end, and a short flight of stairs and oak seats and oak balusters. There are candles to light it. The front has the inscription "Henry Felo, 1634." On the wall are wooden pegs for hats and cloaks. It is all diminutive, and in the small church the gallery is not far from the chancel. Underneath is a kind of extra room for the congregation, a cosy place with a low roof.

The musicians sat in these little galleries, which remain in some of the Bucks churches, in the days before organs were used in country places. Even now some of the people can remember the fiddle and flute and bassoon being played in a tiny church. Quainton Church had a key bugle, which is now in the Aylesbury museum. Hawridge Church once had a bassoon with the following inscription engraved on a brass plate on its side:

> I hear some men hate music but these shew
> in holy writ what else the angels do.
> Then those who do despise such sacred mirth
> are neither fit for heaven nor for earth.

The great box pew for the squire is in the church, as in olden days. It has seats around it, and dark memorials to the Palmers on the panels of the wall, and painted coat-of-arms. There is a little oak table, and a long iron candlestick with a stump of candle for "the family." I was intrigued by the shape of this candlestick, a plain long stick on round base, for these ancient things were given to the Irish labourers who came for the harvest in my childhood days. They were relics of another century, wrought by the blacksmith, and as the candle burned low we pushed it up with a little round trigger. This church is lighted by candles. There is a Bible of 1617, with the intensely black print of the time, laid wide open at Jeremiah.

Under the gallery is a small window with a picture of Charles I, sad and unhappy, with orb and sceptre. There is much old woodwork in the church, Tudor seats with poppy heads in the chancel and stalls and pulpit. It is all very simple, and the floor of red brick is fitting for the simplicity and beauty.

In the little north chapel there is a tomb of great interest, a Jacobean family tomb showing the children and parents, carved in alabaster, painted in colour, all kneeling and waiting in the silence. I felt as if I had suddenly invaded the privacy of these people. Sir William Garrard, a knight in armour, kneels with his wife in a black hood and cloak facing him, her hands folded together, her white ruff freshly starched, her hood showing its white lining.

Below are the children, fifteen of them, all fresh and individual, the boys at one side, the girls at the other. The girls have red flowers with yellow corollas in their bonnets, and flowers and leaves near. I enjoy this gaiety in the tomb, this colour and life. Their bodices have stiff white collars and their skirts are full.

The boys are plainer, but two wear armour. Some hold skulls under their arms to denote they died in infancy, but the figures are those of girls in their teens, as they would have been if they had lived. Some are married, but they are all painted with the glamour of youth and beauty. Mary, Anne, Elizabeth, Judith, Jane, Martha, Katherine, are some of this charming family.

The roof of this little chapel is painted sky blue and the barrel roof of the chancel is also blue. A thick oak screen with heavy little doorway so low that it hides nothing is set across the chancel arch to this chapel. This is a church after my own heart, I think, as I breathe the warmth and simple delight of it.

Across the road, in the field, is the little churchyard under the chestnuts, and opposite the porch is part of Dorney Court with stables and outbuildings.

The road from Dorney crosses Dorney Common, with its farms near: Court Farm, Pigeonhouse Farm, and Manor Farm. This wide common, which is grassland, is grazed by cattle and horses, and a stream runs across it. There is a fine barn, weather-timbered, and a thatched cart-shed built on posts, with open side, and deep thatch over a framework of timber. It sheltered a tractor and two four-wheeled wagons, and the end of it was shut off to house a family of pigs. It was all simple and less costly than bricks.

At Dorney is Huntercombe Manor, a gabled house with painted ceilings and staircase of 1650. It has a heavily timbered hall, now the dining-room, and a solar. Three rooms have circular panels painted by Verrio, with girls and cupids and clouds, all as fresh as if they were new. A walled garden is called the Crusader's Garden. The high walls of rose-pink brick surround this oblong garden, which was filled with lavender and mauve irises, with poppies and columbines, when I walked within. The flowers were overflowing the borders, so that the narrow paths were tracks in the mass of colour. Yellow roses, yellow poppies, grew by the walls. The beauty was enhanced by the wrought-iron gates and grilles. One fine gate is called the Seville gate, as tradition brings it from Spain in Stuart times. Other gates, of older work, have sprays of finely wrought iron leaves at the summits. There are windows of delicate ironwork in the walls through which one can get visions of the flowers within the garden from the Broad Walk.

George Evelyn extended this Broad Walk through the grounds, and he employed Grinling Gibbons to carve the overmantels in some of the rooms, and Verrio to paint the ceilings. His cousin, John Evelyn the diarist, visited the house in 1679, and praised it for its beautiful gardens and its "rooms floored dove-tail-wise without a nail, exactly close."

This small manor house is one of the most delightful in the county, for it has a feeling of security and homeliness. It has been altered during the centuries, but it still remains a living whole, never grand, or great, but a perfect little dwelling.

CHAPTER X

WOOBURN AND THAMES VALLEY

THE steep roads that drop from the plateau of Beaconsfield to
Wooburn in the valley are cuttings with high banks and many
flowers, with trees against the sky, and ivy and traveller's-joy
binding the flanks of the precipitous inclines. Windsor Hill, one
of these roads, is lightened with silver stitchwort, with stork's
bill, and blue bird's-eye, and lords-and-ladies in their seasons.
Here too I have found cow-wheat. Glory Hill is another dipping road, and Holtspur Hill is a third. The river Wye runs
round the curve of the hill, under small bridges at the foot of
each road. It was at one of these little bridges that the ghosts in
the film *Blithe Spirit* waited for the oncoming car, and one goes
slowly down lest another ghost should appear.

The little paper-making town of Wooburn lies in this valley,
with the hills rising from it, and the white face of a chalkpit
staring across. Old black and white cottages encircle the church
at Wooburn Town, and trim gardens by its walls make a little
retreat from the traffic. One of these cottages, which was
formerly an inn, the Royal Oak, has two painted Jacobean figures
attached to the walls. They are said to be the builder and the
architect who restored the church. They wear flat hats, jack
boots, and short coats. One carries a compass and rule, the other
a staff. A sixteenth-century barn stood behind this picturesque
old house until recently.

Wooburn Green is built round the large village green, with
modern red villas as well as little old cottages, with the Red
Lion and the seventeenth-century Red Cow Inn. Limes and
chestnuts border the grass, which is an acre and a half, a good-
sized open space for a small circus or fair in this valley. Wooburn
extends some distance, to Loudwater in one direction, to Bourne
End in the other, with houses all the way, and paper mills. At
Loudwater, which is an industrial suburb of High Wycombe,
there is Ford's blotting-paper mill; Marsh Mill is the paper mill
at Wycombe Marsh. At Wooburn there is Glory Mill, where

photographic paper is made. The name Glory is that of a family who lived here in the twelfth century, and Glory Hill Farm and Glory Hill carry the name. These paper mills are ugly, with their yards full of piles of paper, dark and ragged, rotting in the rain, and nothing can make them beautiful, but from these buildings come the fine notepapers, lining papers, tissue paper and all the many varieties of paper-making.

The river Wye twists round Wooburn House, which is moated, and runs through its park, and then under the road to form a smooth stream in a wayside garden.

The row of Lombardy poplars between the moat and the road was planted in 1777, but many trees have fallen.

The manor house at Wooburn was a favourite residence of the Bishops of Lincoln. Later it was the seat of the Whartons, and Philip Wharton entertained William III there. His grandson, who became Duke of Wharton, spent £100,000 on the house and grounds. This palace was pulled down in 1750, and one of its wings became the present Wooburn House. Only the fishponds and moat remain of its greatness. Now it is the offices of the Imperial War Graves Commission.

The church at Wooburn Town is twelfth-century, with many additions and restorations. The Bertie chapel has a fifteenth-century roof, painted in modern colours. An ancient chest stands in this chapel. The chancel screen, carved and brilliantly painted, was given in memory of Caledon George Du Pre, the squire of Wilton Park. It lights up the dark church with its colour.

A brass in the floor of the choir to the infant son of Philip, Lord Wharton, a friend of Cromwell's, has the tiny epitaph:

> Nine months wrought me in the womb,
> Nine months brought me to this tomb.
> Let an infant teach thee, man,
> Since this life is but a span,
> Use it so as thou may'st be
> Happy in the next with me.
>   Born June 2, 1641
>   Died March 15, 1642

At Wooburn there is a large paper mill which gives employment to many of the people in the villages. It is the Soho Mill, one of the oldest of all the paper mills along the valleys. We saw over this large mill, where coloured papers, notepapers, lining papers, and embossed papers are made. I always thought paper was made from rags, but here I saw bales of the fibrous esparto grass piled up in sheds like hay.

I was interested to discover that paper was made in England in the fourteenth century, and there are leaves of water-marked paper dated 1333, but little is known of the process before Tudor times. Brown paper appears in entries of 1570 and bundles were sold for two shillings. Blotting-paper was mentioned in 1465. "Blottyng papyr serveth to drye weete wryttynge, lest there be made blottis or blurris." It is strange that sand was used at the same time—perhaps it was our native economy.

At the Soho works the esparto and rags are broken up with caustic soda and then follow the processes of boiling and washing, bleaching and reducing to pulp. We saw the breaking-up machines, where the substances are changed, and the wonderful process by which the paper seems to get adhesion, becoming solid, clinging together like wet flannel, pressed and changed, coloured, and finally, as it goes through the great paper-making machine with the drying-cylinders, rolls of paper come out. We saw the processes of water-marking paper and embossing paper, and in a small laboratory we had a demonstration of hand-made paper making. Women were at the cutting machines, where the sheets fell off in the correct sizes, and others were packing the papers.

The river Wye which runs through the Soho works is no longer needed for paper-making, as its waters are not clean enough. Instead deep wells have been dug, and the river water is only used for rough washing. This river enters the Thames at Bourne End, a residential town near Wooburn.

The great house of Cliveden, which was rebuilt a second time in 1851, stands in a superb position high among the woods with a view of the winding Thames deep below. The original house was built by George Villiers, Duke of Buckingham, the favourite of Charles II. It was here that Buckingham brought the

Countess of Shrewsbury after the duel in which her husband was killed by the Duke. She is said to have held the Duke's horse, in the disguise of a page, while the duel was fought. Pepys tells this story in his diary on 17 January 1667/8.

At Cliveden lived Frederick, Prince of Wales, father of George III. The national air, "Rule, Britannia," by Arne, was first sung there in a masque performed in 1740. Lord Astor lives at Cliveden, but part of the grounds, which he gave to the Canadian Red Cross for hospitals, has been presented to the nation since the war.

There is an enclosed little garden of intimate charm I once visited, shut in by old red walls, a place of other days, filled with flowers and lavender. Down by the river, where the Thames flows smoothly between green lawns, is a Judas tree purple with flowers in summer. These two, the little garden and the tree, are my small vivid pictures of Cliveden—not the great white house with its long terrace and colonnade, but the small and lovely things about it.

Little Marlow lies off the main road, down by the Thames, in a small corner with Jacobean manor house, and church and a tiny green, hidden away from traffic. The lychgate has a double-swing gate worked by a pulley on a central post. In the churchyard a heavily laden plum tree hangs its branches of blue plums over the graves, and roses grow there and box bushes. There is a Norman arch between the chancel and a side chapel, and under this arch an altar tomb to Nicholas Ledewich. The brass of Nicholas has gone, but his wife Alice has a dog at her skirts, its tiny tail curled up, and its collar stitched bravely. I always enjoy seeing a tomb or brass to a dog in church, for who are we to deny them immortality? It was Nicholas who rebuilt the nave and aisles.

This is a sweet-smelling, country church. The font is Norman, a plain stone tub, good to see. There is a beautiful fifteenth-century roof to the chancel and south chapel, and old tie-beams on the nave roof. A helmet hangs on a wall. In a window is a little yellow-haired angel with humorous ugly face and big ears, a fifteenth-century picture in glass.

An old red brick wall surrounds this churchyard, chestnut

trees and yews shade it, with ferns growing in the paths, and box bushes close to the church tower.

On one of the grey tombs there is the carving of a bird, and there are the usual delightful cherubs which one can see throughout Bucks.

I am always fascinated by the carvings on tombstones, the grotesque little angels, the decorative fruit and flowers, and figures of cheerful death. In the churchyards of Bucks there are some good specimens of the country craftsman's work. In the churches are the elegant memorials of the great people, a magnificent Roubilliac at Gayhurst, alabaster figures and painted monuments at Mursley; the Tudor parson looking down from the chancel at Chesham; the impressive figure of Cornelius Wood with his cannon balls and cherubs blowing gold trumpets on the wall of St Leonards tiny church, but in the thick grass of the gardens outside the church walls are the headstones of the people. Cherubs, frowning or smiling, but never in the same mood, winged and feathered, wearing frills and bibs, hair curled according to the whim of the stonemason, wreathed and flowered, all are there. There are skulls and crossbones, hour-glasses and scythes, carved on some tombs, and the lettering is often beautiful, with compressions and adaptations to fit into the limited space.

Ivy climbs thickly over some of these tombs as at Maids Moreton, smothering them so that they are mounds in the grass, but usually they are lichened with little rosettes of green and gold, and they lean slanting backward and forward, like tired old men. The high-growing hemlock and wild carrot in the unmown grass threatens to drown the grey tombs in waves of white flowers. Sometimes, as at Little Marlow and at Stoke Poges and Chilton, the grass is cut like a lawn, and the stones appear to be dancing with joy among rose trees and yews, while the cherubs sing loudly and shake their tight curls in their stone garlands. There is a feeling of gaiety, as if they were part of an enchanted garden. It is only in a modern town churchyard, with its marble stones and restrained epitaphs, that I feel that death is treated too respectably.

Great Marlow has its High Street lined with good old houses, many of them now turned into shops, but still keeping their air of grace. There is the noise and bustle of a country town, and the all-pervading rich heady smell of a brewery comes floating up. I am immediately transported to a little old brewery by a mossed water-wheel, with dripping water, and the sound of rooks in the elms above my head as I sit very small, in bonnet and gloves and cloak, in the spring-cart, absorbing that aroma of hops.

The Thames is crossed here by a fine suspension bridge of 225 feet span. It was built by William Clark in 1831. It replaced a wooden bridge built in 1789, and that again replaced a bridge which was mentioned in 1294, and partly destroyed in the Civil War in 1644, when troops were quartered in the church by the Thames side. The river is very beautiful here, with swans on the waters and woods close to the town. Every year the swanhoppers, or swan-uppers, are sent to count and mark the swans. Swans have always frequented this part of the river, and there were grants made by the Crown for their custody in the fifteenth century. From the bridge one looks down to the broad and beautiful river, with boathouses and gardens, and the serene stretch of wide water.

The church of All Saints, standing close to the Thames, on the higher ground, has smooth lawns running to the water's edge. This church was rebuilt in 1832. Only a few of the ancient memorials are left, and we entered to seek that to Sir Miles Hobart, who died in the seventeenth century, for it was he who locked the door of the House of Commons in 1628 and put the key in his pocket during a debate. He lived at Harleyford Manor (now rebuilt—a red brick Palladian-style house), near Marlow. He was sent to the Tower until 1631. Soon after his release he was killed by the overturning of his coach down Holborn Hill.

Nowhere could we find this monument, and we appealed to a clergyman who entered the church.

"There may be a memorial to Julius Cæsar here, for all I know," said he with utter contempt. "It's a Victorian church, and it is filled with Victorian stuff."

This was untrue, and we at last found the monument in the porch, so high up that we had to climb a ladder to look at it. Sir Miles, wearing a ruff, looked out from between curtains, drawn aside by two figures. Four galloping horses rushed down a hill towards a river with a coach, one wheel of which was broken, and the coach window was open. We also discovered, high on the vestry wall, a painting by Coventry (1811) of the spotted negro boy. He was a child from the Caribbean seas who was exhibited in this country by John Richardson the showman. The boy is dressed in a yellow skirt, and he carries a bow and arrows, with a sheaf of arrows on his back, a decorative little person. He and the showman were both buried at Marlow.

Near the church is a house with a sundial on the wall, and across the road a small green with a fountain memorial statue to Charles Frohman the playwright, who went down in the *Lusitania*. Children play there, and men sit resting in this quiet spot.

In the main road is the Borlase School, founded in 1624 by Sir William Borlase as a free school for twenty-four boys. On the walls is the motto, "If any will not work neither shall he eat." A crowd of jolly boys came running through the door as we gazed up at the inscription.

Shelley's house, called Albion House, is near this school. It is a picturesque long, low white cottage, with creepers on the walls and arched windows. The inscription is perched on the roof, so high up I could not read it, with the traffic racing past. The poet lived in Marlow in 1817, with Mary Godwin, whom he had married. He signed a lease for twenty-one years and he stayed here for eleven months, but he worked hard and wrote *The Revolt of Islam*, and *Proposals for putting Reform to the Vote* by the Hermit of Marlow. Mary worked at *Frankenstein*. Shelley did much of his work on an island at Medmenham. Thomas Love Peacock was already living at Marlow, and Leigh Hunt used to visit the Shelleys and walk through the Buckinghamshire country with them. Byron also came to see them at Marlow.

On the opposite side of the road is Remnantz, an eighteenth-century house with stables and gardens and clock tower.

An old rhyme associated with Marlow is:

> Here is fish for catching,
> Corn for snatching,
> And wood for fatching.

144

This valley road from the Marlows to Medmenham and Hambleden is one of the loveliest in the county, with hills, woods, green verges, farms, and glimpses of the river. Medmenham lies in a hollow under the white chalk cliff, with brambles and traveller's-joy and flowers covering the face. It is a pretty little village, with an inn, the Dog and Badger, with church and cottages, farmhouse and abbey.

The yew hedge, which encircles part of the abbey grounds, runs alongside the highway for some distance, a dense heavy hedge, jewelled on an October day with scarlet wet berries.

I went under the great yew at the gate of the little church-yard, and stopped a moment to watch a man making a fire under the wall to heat a soldering iron. He was putting a lamp in the dark branches of the yew to guide the country people to church on winter nights.

The churchyard was kept as trim and neat as a garden, and the little church was full of peace in the golden sunlight of the autumn day.

It was harvest thanksgiving, and we stepped through the Norman door into the shadows, breathing the rich strong air, heavy with the scents of flowers and leaves, of fruit and roots. The goddess Ceres might have been there with all her wealth. The church was so beautiful I caught my breath in astonishment. It seemed to be waiting with its bountiful store, its colour and light. It was surely thanking God for the good harvest of that year, all by itself without any congregation.

The fifteenth-century chancel had no stone arch but a glorious oak structure, consisting of king-post tie-beams with struts and curved braces. At the sides were two sheaves of golden corn, one of wheat and one of oats. Tawny dahlias, purple and blue Michaelmas daisies, roses, sunflowers, made a shimmer of colour, and every one of the deep windows was piled with shining vegetables, arranged so well they had the beauty of flowers. However, the main part of the decoration came from apples of even size, cheek by jowl along the ledge that ran round the church. Green apples surrounded the pulpit; they were strung like big beads across the altar, down the choir stalls, round the carvings, and over the heads of the cherubs. They looked like embroidery stitched to the walls. The altar cloth

L   145

The Dog and Badger, Medmenham

was ancient stuff, embroidered with grapes and silver flowers. It too was part of the harvest festival. The light fell from the narrow windows upon the silver cloth and green fruit, giving it a translucent air. The very essence of earth's treasures was displayed in this little church close to the Thames.

Outside, leaning against the church wall, were three or four tombstones with small angels carved upon them. I like angels, and these were stiffly correct with their short wings, their pleated skirts, and masses of curls surrounding their surprised little faces. They had tiny feet and pointed little hands like those of a fairy. Perhaps they were really fairies, carved on a tombstone by a poet.

Down the lane with trees overhanging and grassy verges, by the churchyard wall, past the post office, past the manor house on one side and the grounds of Medmenham Abbey on the other, we found the Thames. At this spot there is a ferry, and on the bank there is a monument, which at first we took to be a memorial of a battle. The battle was a bloodless one; it was fought for the freedom of the ferry.

The ferryman's long hut was hung with an array of tools, and a bench stood under its walls. The ferryman was a carpenter and wheelwright, but now his work is gone, there is no trade, and he can only wait for a passenger to be taken across the water to the green meadows on the Berkshire side. This long shed is covered with oak shingles, weathered to a rich colour. Above the door is a notice:

Medmenham Ferry
Crossed by King Charles II
Circa 1678

In the summer I came to this enchanting spot, where I found great clumps of white comfrey growing on the banks, and water forget-me-nots and purple water mint. The most dazzling flower, which was new to me, was an orange balsam, perhaps the "American balsam." It grew close to the water's edge along the banks among the rushes, a beautiful tawny-gold flower with velvet petals. This is *Fulva impatiens.*

146

A fisherman stood in the water on the opposite bank, water hens darted about and a coot called. Weeping willows drooped to the water from the lawn of Medmenham Abbey, and the house with its mullioned windows and deep porch seemed to be the abode of peace. It was difficult to imagine any wild roystering there, but this was a home of Francis, Lord le Despencer and his fellow Franciscans. They dressed in white robes, and the Prior of the mock order wore a red bonnet.

Very little is known of the practices of the Hell Fire Club and the black magic performed by this secret society, for the records have been burned. It was a return to paganism, by men who were in revolt against the Christian ethic. It was a serious revival of an ancient cult of evil worship. They invoked the Devil and they are said to have succeeded in bringing him to their ceremonies, although perhaps an ape was introduced for him. Women and men were present in the chapel for the Black Mass. Over the entrance to Medmenham Abbey the words "Fay çe que voudras" are carved. Now the river sweeps the edge of the sloping green lawns, and the kingfisher darts across the water, and the Black Mass is forgotten.

There is a little sixteenth-century inn, with three dormer windows, called the Dog and Badger, across from the church. It has that air of comeliness and cosiness that many old polished utensils get from the hands that have held them. Next to the inn is the stable, with wooden mangers and stalls for horses, and a little barn. It is the kind of inn we should have known very well, the homely inn where we should have put up our pony and trap, and stayed for dinner and walked in the kitchen garden under the white chalk cutting. We should have talked about the corn and the price of a quarter, and the hay harvest and the labourers and the Government. It is that kind of inn. We should have had roast beef and apple pie and thick cream for dinner and before it got dark we should have looked to the lanterns and harnessed and gone off. It is that kind of inn.

Next to the churchyard, with a little private green entry to the church lawn, is a fifteenth-century house, Yew Tree Cottage, now divided into three. It is a fairy-tale house, such as I come across quite often in Buckinghamshire, a house with odd little windows, and gables and roofs and bits of garden and moss and crusted lichens.

Behind the cottages and inn at Medmenham there is a cutting in the hill, white chalk with ivy and old-man's-beard hanging over it in festoons. It is always a joy to see the bare earth, to realize it is there under the grass. The chalk faces exposed here and there on the Chiltern ridge are a reminder of the strength of the rocks, the eternity of the earth. In every part of England this rubbing away of the polite covering of trees and grass and the exposure of the rocks underneath gives me a peculiar pleasure. There are no naked rocks in Buckinghamshire that I have seen, no bones of the earth, no skeleton is shown in this green county, but the white chalk is a memorable sight, as beautiful as a great forest tree, with all its bare branches held up in the snow. Sometimes I think Buckinghamshire is too leafy, its popular title, "Leafy Bucks," is trite. When the leaves have fallen, and the structure of the great beech trees is shown, the mighty boughs, the tip-tilted ends, the uplifted twigs, the thin spiring crests, then Buckinghamshire is at its best.

High above the cross-roads on the steep hill stands a gabled farm, called Lodge Farm. Near, in the beech wood, are the mounds of the Norman castle of the Bolebecs, lost and gone. We climbed the steep road and steeper grass slope where orchis and mountain scabious grow, among the cattle and sheep, to see this farm, which has been taken over by the National Trust. Its walls are of flint, and its front has a narrow path and low wall to bound it. It stands proudly, a gabled farmhouse with a range of good buildings sheltered behind it, but the house faces the mighty winds. It is in a superb position, like a small castle there, with grand views across the valleys, but those who have lived in high windy places will realize the difficulties of its position with no sheltering woods. From it one can gaze across woods and fields, to the large farm of Westfield, down in the valley. An old farm labourer lives in the house with his wife, as caretaker, and the farm buildings and land are worked by another farmer in connection with his own land.

CHAPTER XI

HAMBLEDEN, FINGEST
AND TURVILLE

THE most beautiful place in the whole length of the long Thames valley is the white timbered water-mill at Hambleden. Hambleden Mill has old traditions and ancient lineage, for it stands at an important place on the river and also at the foot of a deep valley which penetrates into the heart of the Chilterns. Up this Hambleden valley went the Romans and later the Danes. There has been a mill in this place since the Norman Conquest. The rent of Hambleden Mill was worth £1 a year in 1086, and before 1235 the mill was granted to Keynsham Abbey, Somerset. Two water-mills were named in 1338, one of which is the mill now worked by Messrs Barnett at Hambleden.

We walked through a gap by some old cottages, part of the mill buildings, to this water-mill whose shining whiteness is reflected in the Thames. The willows and the little islands with tossing water rushing down the sluices, the mill garden with water running round it, all make an enchanting scene. We went along the narrow bridge over the water, glancing again at the white mill. It is a picturesque and beautiful sight with the wide waters in front of it and the turret with the weathervane on the summit of the building.

The river, which makes a deep and sudden bend at this point, can be crossed by a long slender footbridge which twists and turns on its way from Hambleden to the Berkshire bank. Near this bank is the lock and the lock-keeper's cottage. The cottage, with its little garden and lawn, seems to be on an island cut off from the world amidst this stretch of water. Leaning on the little bridge opposite the cottage was a comely woman who was the lock-keeper's wife. We joined her and loitered there, gazing at the water, watching the three swans which dabbled on the rippling steps of the sluice. The sound of the cascading water was

149

like that of Aira Force in Westmorland. It rang continuously in our ears.

"I can't sleep when I'm away from it. I miss the noise of falling water," she told us.

I asked about the flowers which grow in the shallows. One year, when the Thames was very low and no water flowed down these "steps," many flowers sprang up there. Seeds were carried by the waters and left to flower in that dry season. Even on that day there were water forget-me-nots and loose-strife and water mints growing on the stones with the water flowing over them.

The river has a canal cut in it here so that boats can go through the reaches by the locks without going through the waterfalls by the mill. In old days, I was told, they had to carry the boats at this point and of course no large boats could come up the river. The lock was clean and fresh as paint. It seemed as if it were loved and the lock-keeper's cottage was a charming toy with its garden and hedge and little gate, and its vision of old china through the open door. Everything was trim and well kept.

Another day I watched motor-launches going through the lock and the little families on board helped the lock-keeper at his work. It was fascinating to see the water slowly enter and the boat rise, and several people leaned against the wall to share the quiet entertainment.

I went to Hambleden once after a great storm. There was a spate of brown foaming water which rushed down the wide sluices with a roar that was deafening. It churned itself with terrifying force below us as we stood on the bridge. Giant balsam and feathery rushes waved their long streamers and tawny flowers in the wind. The swans in the river and the cygnets actually walked up the stones against the strong flow of water, planting each foot slowly and firmly, but when they reached the top they swam away waving their little tails in pride that they had arrived safely. It was obviously a feat of strength and endurance and each bird showed intense satisfaction on conquering the difficulty.

The white walls of Hambleden Mill were reflected in the river but the mirror surface was broken and brown on this stormy day. The yellow river was throwing itself under the bridge and sweeping down the weir, and on the islands the willows were silver in the wind.

Through the open door of the mill we could see the belting of the machines and the white dusty miller's men working there. One happy day we visited this mill and were taken over it. We saw the old bevelled gear with apple-wood teeth used long ago, but now almost a museum piece. The mill has been made up to date in recent years with water-turbine instead of the water-wheel and steel rollers instead of the old millstones. The mill stream runs past the mill, through the turbine and round the little field where the ducks and willows enjoy the scene.

We saw the many processes through which the wheat goes in its transformation from the grain to fine flour, and we watched the moving belts and the intricate, and at the same time simple, changes in the separation of semolina and bran.

First the wheat is passed through a wheat-cleaning separator, when all the scraps of string and straw are removed. Then it goes through the barley and cockle cylinders. This is a remarkable machine, fascinating in its work, for the wheat ears are swept into one part, and the barley, slightly smaller, falls through another sifter. The process is repeated in another machine for the removal of cockle seeds. I held a handful of the little black seeds of kilvers, as they call them here, really cleavers, I think, which were in the cockle sifter. The wheat then goes through emery-scourers to break up any dirt.

When the wheat is clean the milling proper begins. At this modern mill they use a four-break roller system by which the bran is separated from the semolina. The bran, of course, is the outside sheath of the wheat, made from the thin layer under the husk, called the "bees wing." I dipped my hand into the bran and tasted it. A most delicious food, thought I, and I envied the animals who would eat it.

We saw the old millstones, made of French burr, a stone imported from France. Before French burr was used Peak millstone came from Derbyshire, a hard grit-stone. The French burr is a metamorphic stone, harder than the millstone. These round millstones are cut by hand with a chisel into lines radiating from the centre. These grooves are called "furrows," and the spaces between them are called "lands," a metaphor from ploughing. An old Bucks labourer tells me that he used to cut these stones with a chisel-hammer when he was young. It is an art in itself. The "land" is in the shape of a harp, and "harp strings" or drills are often cut so finely that there are twenty of them to an inch. They are chipped out of the "land." So these old millstones are covered with a most delicate design of lines radiating between the spaces.

The milling proper consists of breaking up the semolina and rolling it and dressing it through a machine with a silk cover. In old days men called boulter-men used to go round the farms to dress the flour when fine white flour was wanted. Now it is all done in the same mill.

The germ is separated from the wheat in the break-up of the grain. We tasted a pinch of the germ which fell in a heap from the grain. It is a very sweet and delicious thing, this centre of the wheat. This germ goes to Vitamins Ltd. for the manufacture of Vitamin foods.

The flour is sifted through silk cylinders, and I saw pieces of the fine white silk. This is called scalper separation. Smooth rolls grind the semolina into flour, which is dressed on centrifugal dressers in which there is a combination of air action and sieving action. We went up flights of wooden stairs and down flights, and up flights again, following the course of the flour in its many journeys between the machines. It goes up hill and down, and a bucket carrier takes it along travelling bands.

Some of the timbers of the mill are extremely heavy and very ancient, and it was a joy to walk in this old building. The top room of the mill under the cupola is a romantic room with stout roof beams and curving timbers, and windows looking out over the Thames.

In the wall of the mill by the water's edge there is an upper door and pulley by which the sacks of flour were lowered to boats. Now most of the flour is taken away by lorry.

Close to the mill is the mill house, a pleasant-looking dwelling-place of old red brick with lawn and cedar tree. On the opposite side of the road is Yewden Manor House, which dates from the early seventeenth century. It was built by Scrope in 1604. Charles I was a fugitive here in 1646. At Hambleden there are some fine farms with the farmhouse and many good buildings, with haystacks and corn ricks clustered together like a picture of rich content. Here I have seen stone staddles used, as in the Cotswolds, to keep the corn safe from rats.

Behind Yewden in the fields the complete remains of a Roman farm were found. A model of this farm has been put in the little Archæological Museum at Hambleden, housed very appropriately near the place of the discovery. There are the granaries, with furnaces below the floors to dry the corn. It has been suggested that these warming floors were used for grain gathered unripe or in wet seasons. It could be dried in large quantities. They even found some of the ears of wheat left by those Roman farmers. It was very exciting to see these drying-rooms at a time nearly two thousand years later when such things are desperately needed after a wet season and the spoiled grain. Nowadays there are some drying-chambers in very big farms and the grain is saved, but many men lose their harvest in wet summers through being unable to dry their corn.

From the excavations the archæologists have traced out the house of the Roman master and the houses of the servants, with the barns and buildings. A large barn or walled yard contained underground flues or furnaces. Apparently the area covered was large, perhaps twelve acres, enclosed by a wall and containing several buildings. One was a small corridor house, intended perhaps for a farmer rather than a landowner. It had a tessellated floor in many colours. The layout of the house is a model for a well-designed present-day house.

This fascinating Yewden Museum held many things of common use from those old days when the Roman settlement was in the valley. There were skewers, which we might use in the kitchen, wedges, keys for the doors, ox-goads which showed they ploughed by oxen, a weight for a steelyard, similar to the ones we always used for weighing, spoons, hooks for hanging meat, linchpins for fastening gates, split rings for holding a bunch of keys, staples, all similar to those now in use in farmhouses. Among the tools were gimlets and gouges. The most amazing

153

thing was a lovely red earthen bowl with decorations which had been broken in those Roman days and had been riveted in several places. As the rivets decayed in the centuries under the ground, the bowl fell to pieces, but the Roman riveting marks remained. This riveting is the same method as we now use, the tiny strip of metal with two holes. The pottery used by these people was decorated with country designs, with herons and vine leaves and beech leaves and willow and sometimes a lion's head for a spout.

The village of Hambleden is nearly a mile from the river and main road, up the lovely valley which leads to Turville. Hambleden Church is so astonishing in its strength and beauty that it dominates the village and valley too. It is like a cathedral in miniature, and although it has been much restored and its tower has even been called unpleasing, it always gives me intense pleasure. On the church tower are four weathercocks of local ironwork, and when I first saw them each was pointing in a different direction, giving a lie to the wind. Then I noticed that the rooks used the vanes for their evening recreation. They fly down upon them and set them spinning, one after another. They seem to take a great joy over this game, like little village children on four aerial swings, so the tower of Hambleden Church at least pleases the rooks and me.

The interior of the church is gay with its bright colouring, for the roof of the chancel has been repainted in scarlet and gold and the carvings of the ancient sedilia are painted. Above the seats are the stone heads of a stern bishop and a gracious saint, as well as twining animals. The clear-cut faces have been left and the head-dresses picked out with scarlet and gold.

In the side chapel we saw a beautiful Murillo, a Virgin and Child. It had hung in a private house, and was given recently to the church, the vicar told us, and he turned on the lights to illuminate that rapt face.

We saw the ancient brasses on the walls, some of which belonged to the Shipwash family, 1457. Above them was their shield with a sheep struggling out of the waves of the washing-pen—a pun on "shipwash," the country pronunciation of sheepwash.

In a corner was the alabaster group of the D'Oyley family,

154

and there we stayed, looking at that intimate little scene, thinking of the people who once lived, for the faces are so lifelike, so exquisitely formed in miniature, that one listens for a murmur of prayer from the closed lips. In the centre the parents kneel facing one another, dressed in elaborate Stuart clothes, with lace collars, the mother rather stern, the father serene.

They are Sir Cope D'Oyley and Martha, his wife. Behind them kneel their ten children, two by two, the sons behind the father, the daughters behind the mother. The eldest daughter is a beautiful girl, but each face is full of character, and there is a family likeness between them all. One feels they are real portraits, carved by a clever artist. The children who died before their parents carry a skull under their arms. They kneel on tasselled cushions. Their dresses have little bows down the fronts, the men's suits adorned with bows and ribbons. There are faint signs of colour upon them, and some day perhaps the colour will be restored.

Alabaster is the perfect medium for these sculptured portraits, of which there are many in Buckinghamshire, for this stone holds life within it. At the home of my childhood alabaster was quarried and the country people always had a special feeling about it as if the veins in it held blood. It had the colour of human flesh, the pale transparency of health and the faint blush of life, so these alabaster figures seem to be alive.

Lady D'Oyley's brother was Francis Quarles, the poet, who was born in 1592. He was a Royalist and he defended Charles I with great ardour so that he was in danger of his life. His poems were so popular with the Puritans that his life was spared.

There is a homeliness of metaphor about his poetry which endeared him to the people. They could understand his comparisons with hawks held by the keeper, or streams that are kept apart till they meet in the Thames.

He wrote the famous epigram:

My soul, sit thou a patient looker-on,
Judge not the play before the play is done:
Her plot hath many changes; every day
Speaks a new scene; the last act crowns the play.

He wrote the epitaphs on the base of this tomb, and this is the poem to his sister Martha, Lady D'Oyley, who resembles him in feature:

> Wouldst thou, reader, draw to life,
> The perfect copy of a wife,
> Read on; and then redeem from shame
> That lost but honourable name,
> This was once in spirit a Jael,
> Rebecca in grace, in heart an Abigail;
> In works a Dorcas, to the church a Hanna,
> And to her spouse Susanna.
> Prudently simple, providently wary,
> To the world a Martha, to heaven a Mary.

Under the tower is a great bedhead, supposed to belong to Cardinal Wolsey's bed. It is most elaborately and wonderfully carved, with beasts and men, with flowers and fruits and emblems, in eight large panels. The Cardinal's arms are there, and the Cardinal's hat. In another panel are the arms of Bishop Fox under a mitre. The work is intricate and delicate. A tradition says that the bed came from the old Bishop's Palace at Fingest, a possession of the Bishops of Lincoln. This Palace has long disappeared. The churchyard is well kept, the grass smooth, under the great cedar trees.

The font at Hambleden Church is Norman work, carved with a simple design of panels with crosses and fleur-de-lis. It is said that Thomas Cantelupe, the friend of Simon de Montfort, was baptized here. The manor house near the church stands on the site of his birthplace. He was canonized.

The manor is a Jacobean house with six gables of dressed flint, and its lawn is surrounded by an old clipped yew hedge. A vast chestnut tree grows there, a giant with many trunks rising from one main trunk. Several of the trees in Hambleden are enormous, as if they had been there for centuries, growing in that sheltered fertile valley.

The pretty village has its cottages around a square, with the church at one side, and an inn, the Stag and Huntsmen, in the lane leading to Frieth. Chestnut trees and the village pump are

in the square, and I was told that the water from this well is very
sweet and pure. In winter it is difficult to get across the icy path
to draw the water, which some people prefer to the tap water.

There is a blacksmith's shop opposite a cottage with a grape-
vine growing up it. We watched the skilful young smith, who
had lately returned from the army. He was hammering out an
iron spearhead—but it was really a pointed iron for opening out
a road. At the door were gates he had made of good wrought
ironwork in a lovely design. This smith shod horses in the
open building next door which had rings for the halters. Several
were coming the next day from the farms to be shod he told us.

Up the long and beautiful valley of Hambleden are fields
and woods, and sometimes a hill seems to block the way with
its rounded shape. It is a valley of which one never tires, for
there are sights of bird and flowers, of cottage and farmland.
Once I found multitudes of the flowers of the lovely clustered
felwort growing by the side of a lane, making a mist of cloudy
blue on the hill, growing so thickly the grass could not be seen.

In the woods between Fingest and Stokenchurch the daphne
grows. My old gardener used to dig it up and sell it for a penny
a root when he was a boy, and pence were scarce. In those days
there were hundreds of plants. My woodman says it still grows
there, he found some a year or two ago, but I have never discovered its hiding place.

Fingest and Turville, two delightful villages, can be approached
in several ways, and there is always an element of surprise about
them. They seem to be watchful, keeping a secret, hiding something there, and we creep up softly not to disturb them, to try
to catch them unawares.

The first time I saw Fingest I came down a steep hill, and
suddenly I saw that church tower, which is so striking that even
the passing motorist stops for a moment and puts his head out
of the window to stare at it. The tall and ancient tower dominates
the little village not by its size but by its strangeness. It is a
square Norman tower, rising from the ground, and topped by
twin red gables, a fortress tower built in the early twelfth
century.

Inside, the proportions of the church are so good that they

157

fill the observer with satisfaction and a deep gratitude that such a small lovely church is here. The long narrow nave has a very high and ancient roof. The seats are low, which seems to add to the height of the church. There is no chancel arch, only a Norman arch by the tower, and it is believed that the whole nave was once the chancel and the room under the tower was part of the nave. It might well be so, it seems fitting, as one stands under the tower by the two bell ropes and looks down the narrow way to the altar.

In Fingest Church is a record of two eternal charities and the wording runs:

"This is to record that Thomas Picket gave by deed dated 1690 a cottage and about two acres of land at Cadmore End, the rent of which is to be distributed yearly on St Thomas's Day for ever to the poor of Fingest. Also that Mary Mole of Fingest gave by will dated 1761 three pounds a year for ever out of the estate called Vining, to be distributed to the Widows and other poor people of the parish of Fingest."

The narrow slit windows in walls four feet thick seem made for defence. One feels in this village of Fingest there have been strange and stirring times of which we know nothing. Yet the little church with its whitewashed walls is comforting and kind, a warm-heated shelter of God.

The large churchyard was overgrown with long grasses, and along the boundary wall were limes which guard this Norman fortress. There are two seventeenth-century oak wishing-gates in this wall. The small double windows of Norman workmanship in the tower face add to the strength of that high look-out. Those limes bowed and shook in the wind and rain, as if they and the tower were one company in league with one another. There was an eerie look about church and churchyard under the lowering sky, a secret understanding. Inside, the church was warm and lovely, with colour and care, but from across the road the exterior gave a different impression.

We stood by the closed door of the Chequers Inn, with its green shutters and gaily painted sign, and above us there was the notice so daunting to a traveller, "No Teas." We watched the swallows and martins hawk over the grass, flashing their breasts in the slanting rain, then gathering on the telegraph wires, preparing for their long journeys, speaking in high voices of their meeting-place.

Across the road an old timbered red brick cottage with a great chimney at its end, an inglenook chimney, stood in its flower garden with sunflowers nodding, and a farm labourer went through the door to his tea. The great farm down the road with farmyard and barns and stacks was resting in the rain, men in barns and house, or walking across with sacks on their shoulders. Cattle stood in the straw and horses looked over the stable doors. Near this farm the hedges had been brashed and layered in the neatest manner, with upright stakes only a foot apart, and the branches twined into them like a piece of green leafy weaving, done by cunning hands of some labourer. It was indeed a fine piece of work, something to be proud about, which made the field open to the view, but safely enclosed.

High on the hillside—for this village is surrounded by hills—the chalk shone white in the rain, and the sheep grazing there were snowy as the chalk. The whitebeams ruffled their wet leaves and upturned them in the wind. Sheep, chalk hills, and whitebeams, all were shining on the green hillside. It was an epitome of the Chilterns. To crown the scene, a windmill stood against the sky, staring down at the well-known and unchanged valley. Another day we climbed to the mill, but on this day we walked along the valley to visit Turville. In the hedge I found some blue toad-flax, a flower that was new to me, for although I knew very well the ivy-leaved variety, this azure flower on its long fine stem was a treasure. It seemed quite fitting that a strange flower should grow in that romantic and secret place.

So down the lane we went to Turville, perhaps the loveliest village in Buckinghamshire. The film company who made a picture there evidently thought so.

Village green, village church, the Bull and Butcher Inn, red-tiled cottages, birds and flowers, were all glittering in the rain.

At Turville there is a diversity in the cottages, timbered, flint and brickwork, thatched and tiled, which is very pleasing because it is all on a miniature scale. Some little houses by the green had

159

arched windows and vines. Big chimneys at the ends of some cottages showed there was an inglenook within, and a warm cosy room. These great chimney stacks are good places for children's games, they are "dens" for hide-and-seek, and "homes" for many a game of running.

The little cottages have triangular dormers in uneven roofs, and the russet tiling is lichened, while some have porches of shrubs, and some have little lawns, and the inn has a box tree cut in the shape of an umbrella with a seat under it.

At Turville there is a cottage with a vine growing up it, and again I was struck with the number of vines I have seen in the county, at Princes Risborough, Hambleden, Aylesbury, Chalfont St Giles, and other places.

We went into the flint-walled church through a wicket gate by the tiny green, and on the way I stopped, for in the church-yard is a cottage, with timbered walls and brick filling and flowers on its front. Later I met the old man who lived there, but on this day he was not sitting in his chair in the churchyard watching the few people. The west door of the church was open, and through it we saw one of these memorable sights, a harvest festival prepared and waiting.

Just inside the door stood a plain Norman font, like a great stone cup, the best shape of all. It was covered with fruit and flowers, a ring of red tomatoes, a ring of apples, a cluster of beetroot and marrows, and a large jampot filled with dahlias in the centre. At the base were striped onions from those cottage gardens, and rosy potatoes scrubbed clean, and green apples piled high. It was a country cottage decoration, with the utmost simplicity. The font looked like a cup of fruit prepared for Pomona's feast, and a sudden gleam of sunlight fell upon the coloured fruits, with the background of the altar, beyond the rood screen, and the stained glass in the east window.

A large stone coffin, big enough to hold a giant, lay under the tower, its stone lid with a cross carved upon it. It also was piled with fruit. This coffin, made from a single block of stone, is early thirteenth-century work. It was found under the floor of the nave in 1900. It then contained two skeletons, one of the thirteenth century, and a later one, with bullet mark, of the

Hambleden Mill

seventeenth, which gives rise to sinister conjectures and imaginings.

The lovely old church has examples of every period of architecture, from Norman to Perpendicular in its structure. The roof of oak is thirteenth or early fourteenth-century, with king-posts. The arches of the nave are twelfth-century, and so is the south doorway.

In the village I met an old man with round rosy cheeks like apples, a broken-toothed rugged old man. His forehead was covered with deep wrinkles, and it was the colour of old oak, but his red cheeks were surprisingly smooth. His chin was bristling with black hairs, and his teeth too were black. His clothes had the colour of earth and sun and grass in them, and he wore one of those leather belts with a brass clasp in the shape of a snake, so familiar to me from the labourers of my childhood days.

He carried a two-handled saw under his arm, and his shirt was open to a black hairy chest. He smiled and we passed the time of day. He was born at Ibstone, up the hill, but he had worked at Turville all his life. He had been a farm labourer, doing a bit of everything. His ploughing was straight and he took a pride in it. He could use a scythe with anyone, he boasted, and I knew it was true. He was a born countryman and craftsman. He used to start mowing at three o'clock in the morning at hay-making time, and work till dark to get the hay cut. His father before him had worked on a farm, and his father's father.

Once he, Albert, had had a team of horses to look after. His eyes shone with pride as he spoke, and I knew exactly how he felt. They were beautiful horses, a dapple bay called Darling, and a black called Darby. He polished their hames and the martingales and brasses, all made very grand to look at, and the horses knew all about it. He looked after them for five years. Then the master died, and life changed. He had poor horses to look after, and he was ashamed for he could do nothing with the appearance of these worn-out animals, and one fell dead in the field.

His wages dropped after the last war, lower and lower. He didn't say anything at first, but he was thinking! He heard of

M   161

Fingest Church

navvying at High Wycombe at £3 10s. a week, so he gave
up farm labouring and went mixing concrete at Wycombe.
Many countrymen went by bus each day. All kinds of men
from all parts were working there, Irish, Welsh, men from
Newcastle who had come south owing to the slump. The
Welsh they called Taffies, the Newcastle men they called
Geordies. The Irish and the Welsh hated each other and
wouldn't work together. He spoke of an Irishman, different
from the others. His wife had died and he left everything, his
good home, his furniture. He told his mother she could have
them all, and he went navvying because his heart was broken.
He was a grand man, trying to work himself to death.

We stood near an old cottage, whose little windows looked
down on us through the rose tree on its side, and he told me the
tale of that house. A young woman lived there who slept for
seven years. They called her the Sleeping Woman, and the house
was called Sleepy House. It could tell many a strange tale, said he.
There used to be many carriages drawn up on the small village
green, belonging to people who came to see the girl who was
sleeping. They tried experiments on her, but nothing wakened
her. Famous folk came, doctors from London, and she went on
sleeping.

"So they said," he added. He was evidently a sceptic. The
mother died from a fall downstairs, and soon afterwards the girl
awoke from the long sleep in which she had grown from a girl
to a woman. She lived a normal life afterwards and got married
and had children.

"She can't have been really asleep," said he, "because when
her mother died she woke up and got married and had twins."

He laughed and laughed at his country joke. He had worked
at the house, and the old mother had been very good to him,
always giving him a cup of tea. "Not like some people who
never gives nothing to their labourers." But he couldn't believe
the woman was asleep for seven years.

We stood on the green, near the gate of the churchyard, and
Bert pointed out the window in the gable end of the old brick-
and-timber house behind us. Although he was secretly amused at
his story I was caught up by the queer enchantment of the place.

162

Across the road was a little white house with yellow curtains watching us to see the kind of people we were. "That house belongs to Merton College," said Bert proudly. On the hillside was a cornfield, and at the crest of the hill the mill, whose sails once flew round in the winds and ground the village corn. By the roadside was a barn where the farmer threshed his corn with the "frail." Bert had gleaned with his mother, and he talked of those leasing days and the corn he carried up the hill to Ibstone Mill.

He used to glean, and the farmer of those days always left a shock of corn behind in each field, saying he'd leave it till the last. When he came for it, it was gone. It was a country joke, a charming convention to give it to the gleaners. Then he'd have half a sack of corn for his mother with all his gleaning. It would be threshed by swingel-and-frail yonder in the barn by the road-side, and he nodded his head to a timbered red barn. He carried it up the hill to the miller and it was ground. Oh, the bread it made! It never went mouldy, it kept fresh for a week, and tasted like ripe cob nuts.

He stood there by my side, blue eyes very bright, cheeks red as berries, hair wild, chin unshaven, his teeth blackened and broken with age, and I thought he was like one of our Irish labourers.

He told me of haymaking days, when bands of men went from farm to farm, going first to Middlesex and then to Buckingham-shire, as the harvest was later here. Some were Bucks men, but Irish and Lincolnshire men went with them. They slept in barns and took their own scythes with them, and their "rub-bers." This is the name given in Bucks to the hone, or whet-stone, which our Irishmen carried in their belts at the back in a socket.

Bert's ripe wit and jesting conversation was in the broadest dialect I have met in Buckinghamshire, and sometimes his words defeated me. I chatted to another old man at Turville and again I found a difficulty in understanding, for it was un-defiled Chaucerian English.

A countrywoman of High Wycombe talked to me about the Sleeping Woman of Turville. She had heard about her in childhood from her mother and father who lived at Lane End. She too was incredulous, for the fact that the woman roused herself from her long sleep when her mother died was too much for her common sense.

"The doctors examined the Sleeping Woman all over for pin pricks where some drug might have been injected to make her sleep, but they found nothing. Many folk came to see her. The green was filled with carriages and people all come to stare at her," said she.

"Then why do you think it wasn't a trance?" I asked.

"Because when her mother died she got up and got married and had children like an ordinary person," she said obstinately.

I pointed out that the shock of the mother's death could be communicated to her, and it might have shaken her out of her long sleep. I said that trances were known, there were authenticated cases.

"A queer thing happened to my mother," said she. "She had not long been married and she lived in a pretty cottage at the end of the village. One day a man came to the lane and stared very hard at the cottage. He leaned against the hedge and didn't go away, so my father went out to him and asked if he wanted anything.

" 'I want just one thing,' said he.

" 'What's that?' asked my father.

" 'I want to come into the house to look at it again. I was born here and I want to sit down in the same place.'

" 'Well, come along in, with pleasure,' said my father.

"He came in and sat down. Then he stared hard at a corner of the kitchen.

" 'That's where my father had a trance,' said he. 'He was three weeks gone, neither eating nor speaking, but sitting in that corner in a trance. Then he awoke and went about as usual.'

"When the man had gone away my mother couldn't forget his words. She kept imagining she saw the old man sitting in the corner, and the feeling was so strong she begged my father to leave the cottage. So they moved to High Wycombe and I was born there. That's the only reason they moved, for it was a lovely cottage, but my mother said she could never rest in that house again."

This village woman must have been very sensitive to places and their influence, for her daughter spoke of other strange happenings, when footsteps were heard in a lane many times and nobody was there. The ghostly steps followed those who walked, but there was never any visible object.

At Fingest a ghost once walked, according to tradition. Bishop Henry de Burghest stole a piece of land, and not until restitution was made was his ghost laid.

One day I went up the hill to see the windmill, Copston mill, which had ground the village corn, and where Bert walked with his gleanings to be made into flour. Turville lay below deep in the valley, its blue smoke all flying like blue flags from the little chimneys. The black sails of the mill were broken, pointing disconsolately to the sky. Then I saw the windmill had curtains at the windows. I was glad somebody lived there part of the year.

Along that lovely high ridge we went, on the crest, with valleys upon each side, so that one couldn't see enough of them, for beauty stretched on the right and on the left. We searched for the little church of Ibstone, down a narrow lane. It is perched on an eminence, and a large wood grows close to it, keeping it secluded and hidden. In the churchyard there is a centuries-old yew, and some old graves with fine carvings of angels' heads with little feathered wings, one angel with a couple of trumpets all ready to blow for the resurrection. A face with wide mouth laughs from above a window, a most human face, so that I half-expected to hear it speak.

There is no real tower to Ibstone Church, but a little wooden bellcote, like a cap. The wooden porch led to a plain doorway with some diaper carving on the jambs, and I entered the very small Norman church.

Brown jars of holly berries stood on the windowsills, and a crib lay by the plain Norman arch to the chancel. Everything was simple, except for bits of carving high up on the stones, and the beautiful pulpit, richly carved with fifteenth-century work, was half-lost in the holly and ivy that entwined it that winter's day.

No organ, no hangings, were there, and the pews were plain wood, with candles for lighting. Oil stoves stood in the church for warmth. The Norman font was tub-shape. Behind it was a little flight of stairs leading to a gallery which extended half across the church, so that the top seats were close to the timbered roof, and the bells hung temptingly near.

Outside in the lane again bluebells were already pushing their green points through the winter earth. The signs of spring were there, in wood and field and bank. We passed by the common, which belongs to Merton College, Oxford. Two years later I saw sheaves of corn where the gorse and broom had held the land. Near the common is an inn, which has a double sign. On one side is a fox slouching along, and on the reverse a fine fox dressed up in a blue coat going boldly over the country. I have seen two or three inn signs in the county which have different pictures showing two aspects of the same subject.

CHAPTER XII

MISSENDEN COUNTRY
AND WENDOVER

LITTLE MISSENDEN is one of my favourite villages in Buckinghamshire, a simple, unspoilt spot, with the river flowing through the fields near, and the hills covered with beech woods rising slightly on each side of the valley.

It is a most pleasing picture of which I never tire, this old church, with the graveyard and yew trees, the high wall ivy-covered and lichened, and the ancient little manor house with its windows overlooking the churchyard.

There they stand, communing together, the grey church, the manor house, and a farm with seven golden ricks, all close together. From the open door of the church comes the hymn "Holy, holy, holy, Lord God Almighty," which is fitting for such a place. This gracious and homely trilogy of farm, church, and manor house is typical of the lovely village.

The sun shines across the churchyard, lighting up the great fifteenth-century tower, and a hidden strength seems to come from it. Every time I visit this place I feel a deep content and quietness, as restlessness and hurry fade away, and only peace and happiness remain.

Two little traceried windows are in the comfortable welcoming porch with its upright timbers, thick as tree trunks, and cross-pieces. A jar of palm willow with golden hairy buds stands on the seat. It is a warm intimate little church, and I have always enjoyed visiting it, going through the heavy door with expectancy and excitement, to the small ancient building with its worn old red brick floor. It existed before 1120, and the north chapel was added in 1360. There are alcoves like little cupboards in many odd places, an "Aylesbury" font and round Norman arches—but the church says they are Saxon.

Two of the bells are said to have been given by King John. A strange old key, fifteen inches long, with four wards hangs on a wall, like Bluebeard's key, or the romantic key out of a fairy-tale. The church has many delights. There is a wall painting of St Christopher and the Christ Child. St Christopher has bare feet, standing in rippling water, where an eel and a pike are swimming. Many other murals in the church are fast disappearing, and it is difficult to distinguish them. A number of the Bucks churches have paintings on the walls, done in tempera, but covered with whitewash in later centuries. In some places the original pictures have been rediscovered, but the old colours soon fade. This is the case at Little Kimble and Little Hampden.

There is an interesting modern window, one of the few modern windows I have really enjoyed. It is like a picture-book of a simple faith which all can understand, and I turn the pages with affection. There is a golden gateway in the centre, leading to the slopes of the Holy Mountains, where lambs and wolves are side by side. Lions and lambs and little children, all the innocence of the way to Paradise are there. The paths lead to the gold towers and many mansions of Heaven. Kneeling on earth are four figures, Florence Nightingale, King Edward I, St Hugh of Lincoln, and Alfred the Great.

At the foot is Dunkirk, with blazing houses, guns, tanks, battleships, a raging sea with foundering ships, the air with burning planes. This window is the first memorial to Dunkirk.

On a wall is the notice of a charity:

"Mr William Line by will dated Sept. 16. 1775, left two Meadows and an orchard to provide one 3d Loaf each to six of the oldest Inhabitants attending Divine Service on Sunday morning. Also one 2d Loaf to the Clerk for delivering the same. Mrs Sarah Bates by Will date April 14. 1787 gave 100 Pounds 3 percent Consolidated Bank Annuities."

Underneath, on a chair, we found a loaf of new bread!

Overlooking the churchyard is the old manor house, tall, many-gabled with windows peeping from every corner, and a good collection of stables and outhouses. Dr Benjamin Bates, who was physician to Sir Francis Dashwood, lived there. He too was a member of the Hell Fire Club, a very respectable member, who seems to have been the ballast for the rest of the wild set.

The garden and terrace of this house were designed by Angelica Kaufmann, and there are Flaxman bas-reliefs in the house. To me it is a magical place, like a Rex Whistler drawing for Hans Andersen, and I return and gaze and dream and wonder.

The village is warm and mellow, rich in umbers, reds and golds of cottage and flowers and cornricks.

Bordering the fields that run by the river, there is a long stretch of beautiful "eddering," as neat and trim as any I have seen. It is not quite as decorative as the hedge layering I saw at Forty Green, around an orchard, or that I saw once at Fingest, where the craftsman must have been an artist, but it is still perfect. The top band of "eddering" is well woven and a delight to examine. A true fence this makes, such as only a true craftsman can weave. I remember hearing of such a fence, made so that even "an ouzel" could not penetrate it. The finish of this hedge had a kind of basketwork of hazel and briars along the top of the upright staves, binding them together.

Near Little Missenden is Great Missenden, which is not great at all, but a village in the valley with woods around it. The old houses spread down a narrow High Street, and inns with painted signs and courtyards with old stables and timber-framed buildings show it was a market town. The George Inn is fifteenth-century with later additions, and the gateway has original timbers and a room over it. Coaches must have driven through this great open doorway to the yard.

The Red Lion is an old inn with a new front. The Buckinghamshire Arms has been made into a bank, and this was sixteenth-century with a staircase of the seventeenth century and handrails and turned balusters. Stevenson stayed either at the Red Lion or at the Buckinghamshire Arms, probably the former.

We walked up a lane, past a group of cottages which seem to wear little green aprons of lawns, some with borders of red and mauve asters, others with yellow and orange snapdragons. The lane twists and turns among houses with mullioned windows and high-pitched red roofs, green with moss, silky sheened with lichens and stonecrops. Sometimes we saw leaded windows in a narrow cottage, and sometimes splendid chimneys and golden-red brick in a larger house. Across the fields of brown plough-land a covey of partridges rose. We went through the gate which bounds the church walk to keep the sheep which fed there from wandering. In the hedge a goldfinch sported its wings and sang a song, and we exclaimed, "That was worth coming for."

We went up the steps, through a wicket gate to the church-yard, which is on a hillside above the village. The grass was so tangled and thick I longed for a scythe to mow it. We stood by the fence gazing down the valley at the haymakers in the fields. Then we turned round to look in the overgrown churchyard for the path to the church door. We were amazed. Through the dark yews we saw a radiant picture, burning like a fire. The west door was wide open behind the yews, and we could see directly into the church to the window at the east end. It was so brightly illuminated that I exclaimed, "Surely this is a ruined church? There isn't a roof!"

The many-coloured window seemed to be painted on a rock. It was an optical illusion. The bright sunshine fell upon the east window, and the lead of the glass took on the appearance of a stone wall behind it, with the colours thrown upon it. We scrambled through the thicket of grass and shrubs and entered the west door in the tower. The other doors were open, and the church was filled with light, no dim religious light, but the glorious light of day which made everything fresh and alive. How seldom do we get the colour and full beauty of a church! I saw King's College Chapel, Cambridge, once with the west door wide to the air and light and brilliance in the great building such as I had not seen before.

Great Missenden Church is a fine place, with a timbered roof about 1340. The font is an octagonal basin, twelfth-century. Against the background of yews and the fields, through the open west door, it looked transparent, shining white.

I liked the small heads carved high on the arches, a sulky face, another squinting sideways with a sardonic air, a third with his mouth awry, a fourth with the face of a British workman who is "fed up"—eyes heavy, moustaches drooping, a fifth with his mouth open and an air of surprise as he peers across the aisle, a sixth a sleepy man, and the last a man who is laughing at the one who is asleep. Such humour there is, such mockery and spite and laughter in these carved figures!

The disappointment of Great Missenden is the river Misbourne, which rises in a meadow. We hunted in vain for it, but although we could feel there was a trickle somewhere it was invisible. Willows and rushes and all the gay companions of rivers were there, but no water was to be seen. Perhaps it was one of its disappearing days, for from the old accounts of the Misbourne this variable little river, blue as forget-me-not as it flows through the meadows at Little Missenden, appears and goes away according to the season.

The river runs through Little Missenden, watering the meadows, and one can gather bunches of marsh marigolds of great size on its banks. I remember seeing the wet land golden with the masses of flowers. In summer the tawny orange monkey-flower grows there. Sometimes the springs rise in the lake of Missenden Abbey, a house hidden from sight by great yew hedges, south of the village. Sometimes, and legend says this happens at a time of national disaster, they rise north of the village, and flow south.

The Misbourne runs through the garden at Little Missenden Manor House, and onward to the lake of Shardeloes, and from there to the fishponds of Chalfont Park.

Near Wendover is the Green Man Inn. Another inn with this name is at Farnham Royal. A Bucks countrywoman told me that her father spoke of the Green Man on May Day. He went round the villages dancing in a bower of green leaves about a hundred years ago. He was entirely covered in a framework of leaves, a Jack-in-Green.

Wendover is an unspoilt little town in spite of the bungalows that line one side of the road towards Aylesbury in an unbroken stretch of ribbon-building. One has to accept bungalows, and in time they will be hidden behind their bowers of gardens, for their roofs are low and they could easily be gently smothered in leaves.

Wendover is a delight to the eye and to the senses. It has something which is lacking in many more beautiful towns—a warm intimacy and colour. Perhaps it is because its streets are open and the houses are small. The cottages along the cobbled ways with lime trees growing there run down one steep street and turn a corner to another street, equally attractive.

Every cottage is a home, a place of comfort and fun and beauty, or so it seems on an October day when the sky is blue-silver and the leaves are golden, and beech leaves float down to be caught in outstretched hands for a wish, and children run and play. The timbers make clear geometrical patterns on the house fronts, squares and oblongs and triangles, as if they were part of a six-teenth-century game the builders played. The thatch is edged with a decoration of crosses. The windows are dormers, and sometimes one sees a tiny square window high on a gable end. Nothing is symmetrical and everything is a joy. The character of the villages and small towns lives in some detail of cottage and barn. It is indigenous to the countryside. Each little house is a work of imagination, with its carving, its doorway, its odd windows. The designs of the cottages are simple as those of old furniture, cottage furniture, not Chippendale. A scroll, a latcheting, a dripstone, a gable end, all make up the pattern. A street of them is like a bit of a patchwork quilt, once highly coloured, but now faded, irregular, pleasing, with birds and flowers and orchards. A five-petalled flower on a church font, a cherub flying on a gravestone, a pineapple of stone carved on the gate of the Big House, a fantastic lion on the inn sign, a coat of arms painted in the church, all add to the design and fantasy of a village.

The main London to Aylesbury road goes through the town, and meets the Icknield Way, which is here called Pound Street and High Street, a divided street with houses between on an island.

A little brick building, with a clock tower and a drinking-fountain, stands at the junction. Near this corner are shops which were once old houses, one of which has the projecting upper story of the Elizabethans. These shops are good and simple places, which have not had their character spoiled by the transi-tion to modern uses. The transformation has not the devastating quality of shops at High Wycombe. The large window does not overpower the small house. The lettering is quiet. One goes in to buy papers or groceries, and there is a village shop, two house-rooms made into one, a fireplace in a corner and a kitchen behind the door.

There are several inns, with painted hanging signs, and there are open courtyards where old inns once stood, with stables beyond. The Leg of Mutton, with its extra title of Railway Hotel, stands at the head of the town, and down the steep road swing the White Swan, the Two Brewers, and the Red Lion, while the picture of a playing-card hangs in the London road over the King and Queen Inn.

There is the smell of leaves, of chestnut trees and wet moss, for the roofs are bossed with stonecrop and moss grows in the crannies of house walls and barns. Up one house grows a vine, and on another wall is a pear tree, and on a cottage a white jasmine, and at a gable end a plum tree. The sunlight gleams on the red crinkled roofs, with their uneven tiles and jumbled chimneys. In the distance are the hills and woods, with white scars of the chalk showing in the green turf.

Dormer windows are high in some roofs and low in others, and sometimes a little red-roofed projection has been added to the front of a house, like another dormer window, with geraniums close to the glass and bell flower hanging there. The roofs are on many levels and the green films of lichens and moss are like a pattern of shot silk thrown over the red-brown tiles. Beams and plaster, or beams and brick—the shapes of the beams can be seen very distinctly in the cottage sides.

The White Swan has a tiny room high in the roof. There are little square windows peeping out of gable ends, like watching eyes. Round windows are in the corners, and from them one gets enchanting glimpses of huddled roofs like a medieval town.

At night, when darkness fell and stars came out, I saw a candle burning in the dormer of a cottage in the street, and a girl stood before her glass, brushing her long yellow hair, like a princess in a fairy-tale. Her movements, her unconscious artistry, under that thatched roof were something to remember. The sounds of Wendover are those of a village, the chime of a bell, the laughter of a girl, the whistle of a man.

The Red Lion Hotel, half-timber with brick nogging, is a beautiful inn. R.L.S. stayed here on his walk through the Chilterns, and he wrote about it. It has its old fireplace with chimney corners in the lounge, and a good stairway with moulded banisters gently rises to the room where Cromwell slept in 1642. It is easy to imagine Cromwell standing at the window looking down at the street below packed with his soldiers. Now the same street, scarcely changed, has groups of R.A.F. men from Halton Camp on the hill near.

Prince Rupert came to Wendover in 1643 and did much damage, and the town suffered later by raids from the garrisons at Boarstall, that strong and brave citadel near Brill. Oak beams curve across the walls of the room, and high up a little wall cupboard is pasted over. A narrow secret door in the painted wall opens surprisingly to a barnlike garret with open timbers and a steep stair that once led down to the cellars, but is now blocked up.

Underneath this garret was a room with traces of two wall paintings over the fireplace. One of them was erased by white-wash, and only a dim coloration remained. The other was a scene of a gabled red-roofed house with a garden and a river running under the walls. In the foreground the river flows and on its waters is a boat with a man fishing. Another fisherman curves his rod from the bank among green rushes. There is a background of mountains and blue sky. It was like a portion of a Breughel painting, with its double-arched frame, a rainbow in the sky. Nobody knew the history of this delicate work. I returned two years later and the second painting had been white-washed over like the first, so now there is nothing left of the charming and delightful scene.

I bought two candles for three-halfpence at Wendover to light my way along a narrow dark roof passage to my bedroom in a strange house, for there was no room in the inn. I had an attack of claustrophobia in the smallest room I have ever entered, and I spent the night looking out of the dormer window under the full moon. The seven stars of the Great Bear hung like lamps in a blue velvet sky, with the tail of the Bear over the seven cornricks in the farm by the side of the road. In the dark-

174

ness of the great hill seven lights shone out from the hospital; I could hear a horse whinny and owls were hooting. Every hour the clock in the little clock tower at the corner of the two roads rang out. It was illuminated and I could lean from my high dormer over the mossy roof and watch it. It was strangely comforting to see the lighted clock and to hear the sweet clear bell-like chime, which had none of the awful doom of a church clock striking the hour in the middle of the night. I quite enjoyed my wakeful night up in the air with stars and chimes.

This gay little Victorian clock-tower is like a toy. It has a small ivy-covered dark red brick room which was once the lock-up, but it can only have held one delinquent at a time. The steep four-sided roof is green with moss, and above it are a clock and an open lantern and a weathervane.

In the village street is Bosworth House, an old timbered dwelling, now divided into three—a cottage with a room over the open gateway, a post office, and a house. The post office is a fine place to buy stamps, for it has panelled walls and doors. Buckinghamshire abounds in charming post offices: the thatched little post office at Gayhurst with its flower garden, the beautiful old red house at Dorney, the little place at Latimer, the old cottage up a flight of steps at Whitchurch, and many others, thatched and latticed.

So at Wendover the red mail van swings under the old open archway that has a little room built over it, into the stabled courtyard of the old house. In the wall of the gateway is a fifteenth-century pillar piscina, with a broken rim, its use forgotten by all who pass by.

Bosworth House, early seventeenth-century, had a series of good wall paintings which were discovered when alterations were made. Their colours are fresh and bright, with rivers and woods and houses. Some of them have been removed to Aylesbury, and some to the South Kensington Museum. A chimney stack has three circular shafts, rising from the roof of this old house.

At Wendover in 1848 a treasure was found on a farm called Dutchlands. It was a handsome gold armlet, which was dug up from under the roots of an old tree. The woodland there had

always been wild, but at this date it was brought under culti-
vation, and the trees were grubbed up. The lovely fourfold
armlet, skilfully wreathed together, is unique in its workmanship.

There is a windmill in the town, but it has no sails now, and
it wears a black cap. Another mill, a water-mill, by the side of
the stream that runs through Wendover, has been made into a
pleasant green and white timbered house, and the wheel is still
there, boarded up. This little stream, with ducks swimming on
it, went past a deserted farm, with broken gates and doors
and overgrown yard, a sad spectacle which filled me with
sorrow. The church and manor house are a short distance
from the town, and I walked by the side of this little stream.
I asked its name, but the only answer I could get was "The
Pond."

The church has two great yews which drop their juicy red
berries over the pathway. It is a dark church, dark as the yews
and junipers in the churchyard. The bright sunshine outside
could not penetrate the gloom, and I could scarcely see the
brasses showing William Bradshawe with his family, each with
a name underneath. The grandchildren's names were there also,
and I deciphered, in the dim light, the names of those children
who played in Wendover in Tudor days, who climbed Coombe
Hill and gathered the herbs and flowers of the chalk countryside, little William, Elizabeth, Sybell, Alice, Brigid, Johan,
Agnes, and the rest. The word "dede" was written under those
who were dead when the brass was made.

I walked down the chancel to look at the carved heads on the
arches, faces puckish, grimacing, frowning, sleepy, sly, cynical.
What touches of human nature are displayed on the faces carved
in a church! No saints are there, only the common people, the
friends and enemies, rich and poor, beggar and lord, carved to
make an everlasting joke. One can imagine the ribald laughter
as people came in and conjectured about them, and recognized
them.

The capitals of the pillars are delightfully carved, with fruits
and flowers and animals, like a harvest festival in stone. I only
saw them when the caretaker who came in to scrub the floor

176

Turville village green

turned on the lights. She told me that the building of Wendover church was started down in the village, but the "witches" took away the stones every night and brought them to this spot a mile away. At last, tired with the struggle against witchcraft, the church was built where the witches had chosen.

It is the same legend that is told about West Wycombe, where the fairies took away the stones. Ibstone Church too has a legend of witches.

The church at Wendover was begun in a field close to the houses of the village, and this field is called "Witchall Meadow" to this day. In the fourteenth century the field was named "Wychewelle Croft," which supports the tradition.

Now a similar tale is told of Olney Church in North Bucks. The ancient church, which was probably Saxon, disappeared centuries ago, and about 1325 it was decided that a new church should be built on a different site from the original one. The position chosen was in a field, still called Lordship Close. The foundations were laid, but one morning when the builders went to work the stones had been moved to the original position. The workmen, fearful at this happening, nevertheless moved the stones to the field. Again in the darkness the stones were taken back to the original site of the church, and laid there as if by skilled builders, and carried with no noise. No human being could have done this so swiftly, so accurately, and the men feared the interference of supernatural forces, angels or devils. They gave way after consultation with priests and those in authority. They accepted the ruling of the invisible ones, and Olney Church was built.

After hearing the ghostly tales, and standing by the caretaker who was scrubbing the church path under the lychgate, I returned to the darkness. From under the church tower came a strange sound which mingled with the ticking clock above me in the tower. I started uneasily, for the muffled thud was as if someone were struggling to escape from a grave. The doors were shut and I could scarcely see my way. I went out, with quick glances behind me. In the churchyard, close to the tower wall, the gravedigger was digging up an elder tree whose roots had spread under the foundations. I was glad my ghost was laid.

N   177

Wendover was an ancient and very small borough. It sent two Members to Parliament even in the reign of Edward I. In the reign of Edward II this privilege ceased, and was not resumed until 1621 and 1624, when the town petitioned for its lost rights. John Hampden was the new Member. Wendover became one of the most corrupt constituencies in the kingdom. Drinking and bribery were the cost of votes, which anyone could buy. Some famous men were returned for Wendover—Richard Steele, Edmund Burke, George Canning. In 1832 Wendover lost both its Members.

Up the village street and along the Icknield Way, that famous old roadway, the land falls away to farms and cornland on one side, and on the other rises to the heights of Coombe Hill. There is a narrow white path up the great hill from Wendover, and the chalk is laid bare by the feet of the many who go along it. It is like an icy winter's road, for the chalk has a grey transparency with here and there snowy patches where a boot has scratched away the chalk surface and exposed a fresh layer. The ploughlands in the valley below (and there are many hundreds of acres of ploughland there) have grey soil, a silky grey, differing from the warmer-toned ploughland of the south, for here we are up on the Chiltern chalk.

In the soft springy turf that covers the hill are bushes of the glaucous juniper with blue-black berries, filmed with a bloom, and the colour is like the haze on the distant plain. Juniper trees resemble men—men walking, stooping, kneeling—and I was haunted by the feeling that dark figures were on the hillside, pre-Christian men, turned to trees, but capable of returning to human form when night fell. There were leafless sloes, with their oval bloomy berries clinging to their prickly branches like jewels, and whitebeams, half-naked, whose fallen leaves make a litter like the papers left by a picnic-party. There were clumps of gorse bushes, higher than myself, some in golden flower, and there were ash trees, dark green, with leaves perfect, for the ash which comes late into leaf keeps its foliage well.

In the grass as I climbed I found yellow rock roses, little short-stalked harebells and yellow mouse-ear. A magnificent stretch of country lay below, spread out in many colours, with

178

elms along the borders of the fields and along the roads, defining their shapes and paths.

The monument at the summit is dedicated to the men of Buckinghamshire who fought and died in the South African War. It stands there, facing all the winds that blow, carved with the names of the dead, and a golden ball crowns the tall obelisk. From far away it can be seen, and I have seen it from across the county, many miles away at Ashendon.

I read some of the names of the men, Tom and Dick and Frank, and I ponder their childhood. Perhaps they climbed these same hills and stood on this spot where now is a memorial to them, and they shouted and whooped and played leap-frog, those boys of long ago on Coombe Hill.

The ground falls six hundred feet or so from the monument, and all the land is spread out below. The Vale lies like a patchwork of brown and green, russet and grey. There are little villages, like toys hidden in the trees, and red farmhouses, and small haystacks in rows, and orchards and elm trees, exactly like the farmyard toys we used to play with. The tower of Aylesbury Church rises up, and below is the romantic-looking Ellesborough Church on its green hill. Away in the distance are the Quainton Hills, and hills towards Brill. Beacon Hill, a sudden steep hill near, looks very sharp and prominent. Out of sight is Cymbeline's Mount, that eminence of antiquity, which we long to visit.

I went along the main road from Wendover and turned at the old inn, Marquis of Granby, past a reservoir which lay with its waters behind the green hedges, to find Weston Turville, which has a very beautiful church. This twelfth-century church has a gate swinging about a central post with a pulley and rope which open and shut the gate, a country piece of work. The brick and timber porch had the remains of a poster stuck to it, with the Arms of England and a calling-up of the reserves. For a moment I wondered what war this could be, for it might have been the Spanish War, when Elizabeth called her men to arms. The flag of St Andrew was floating from the tower against a blue sky.

There are carved beams across the fifteenth-century roof, and the corbels are rich and grotesque—a woman with mouth awry, a jester, a devil with protruding eyes and pointed mouth, a woman with looped hair and sneering lips, bearded men with eyes closed, a sinister crew.

Over the altar in the plain glass is set a gem of fifteenth-century glass. It is a Virgin and Child with blue background, their crowns and hair of gold.

The pulpit has seventeenth-century carving of grapes and flowers and there is Tudor panelling on the altar and an ancient oak screen across one of the aisles. The Royal Arms of England are painted over the west end of the church.

There is some good furniture too—an oak seat with flowers and leaves, a chair with intricate carving on the back, and a panelled chest of the seventeenth century.

On a wall is a panel of wood whose words, heavily carved, are a puzzle to decipher:

FAITHN
OTEXER
CISEDSO
ONEWA
XETHSI
CKE
ANOD
OMINI
1578

"Faith Not Exercised Soone Waxeth Sicke. Ano Domini. 1578."

There are two tablets of bequests to the poor of Weston—the Widow Turpin's Gift, 1736, in which rents and profits of an estate are laid out in great loaves of good and wholesome bread, and the Pennant Trust, 1837.

CHAPTER XIII

BRADENHAM, BLEDLOW
AND THE KIMBLES

DIPPING down the wooded hillside among beech trees flecked with light, and sunlight barring the road with the shadows of the trees, we come to Bradenham, the little village that was the home of Isaac d'Israeli. A high old red brick wall bounds the left of the road, and this wall which curves round the church and the manor sometimes rises to a height of over ten feet where it is buttressed. The little flint church of St Botolph and the Manor House of Bradenham head the green, side by side, and along the edge of the road are the attractive little cottages.

We walk across the grass to enter the modern lychgate built in memory of the men who died in the First Great War, and the timbers of the gate make a true frame for the hills on the opposite side of this small valley so that one can but stand and gaze at the colours of the beech trees. There are tall fir trees growing by the ivied crooked wall and stiff Irish yews by the path of the neat, smooth churchyard. The windows of Bradenham House overlook the church, and the wide gates open to the village green.

The church tower is fifteenth-century, and against its walls grows a tree of pink roses. The earliest part of the church is the nave, which was built about 1100. We enter by the south door, which is early Norman, or it may even be Saxon. It has a round head, with a plain tympanum and heavily carved lintel and pillars. It is cut in a lozenge pattern. The door is concealed within a porch which keeps the weather from harming it. Inside the church a piece of sculpture is fitted within the tympanum space, and very attractive is this contrast between new and ancient work. It is the figure of St Botolph, with three flying swans, and a tiny model of the church before him with reeds and water.

In the vestry there is an enormous wall monument to Charles West which overpowers the small church, but at a corner is a cherub with such an engaging face and such a childish round cheek that I always feel that it lives. These little angels seem to have the warmth and reality of life to me as I cup their cheeks in my hand imagining that the marble is flesh and blood.

There is a modern rood loft with three painted figures raised up near the roof beams. The little church is happy and warm even on a cold day of midwinter, for it is cared for and obviously loved.

Isaac d'Israeli was buried at Bradenham. The father of Benjamin Disraeli was the author of *Curiosities of Literature*. He was an antiquary, held in great esteem as a writer, being a friend of Southey and Pye. Pye came to live at Stoke Poges and Isaac d'Israeli visited him from London and stayed in the Chilterns at Hyde House between Missenden and Chesham. In 1829 he gave up his London house and removed with his great library and his family to the solid old house at Bradenham.

I came across one of these "Curiosities" about which Isaac d'Israeli wrote, just lately. He tells of a Peter Bales, an Englishman, and a Clerk of the Chancery, who wrote out the Bible in full and enclosed it in "a walnut no bigger than a hen's egg."

"The nut holdeth the book. There are as many leaves in his little book as in the great Bible, and he hath written as much in one of his little leaves as a great leaf of the Bible."

D'Israeli goes on to tell of a contest between fine writers for a gold pen and how it was won by Peter Bales.

So the famous author came to live at Bradenham Manor, and with him came the son, who was to become even greater than his father. Benjamin Disraeli used the house as the model for Hurstley, in his novel *Endymion*.

Mrs Wyndham Lewis, who afterwards became the wife of Benjamin Disraeli, stayed at Bradenham Manor and her description is worth quoting:

"They reside near High Wycombe—a large family house, most of the rooms thirty or forty feet long, and plenty of servants, horses, dogs and a library full of the rarest books. But how shall I describe his father: the most lovable, perfect old gentleman I ever met with."

From the church one can see the line of the Chilterns, with its woods on the hills opposite, and a field of many acres below the woods. A cornfield is already reaped, and the corn stands in golden shocks. The fields dip to the main road to Aylesbury that passes along the bottom of the village green. There stands the colourful inn, the gay Red Lion, with baskets of flowers, whitewashed walls, green benches, and little garden, very inviting, in its corner. It has window-boxes in summer, and tubs of box in winter, and it is as neat as a toy placed by the roadside. Beyond it is a large farm with haystacks and cornricks, barns and cowhouses, all part of the village life.

The houses at Bradenham are close to the road that runs from the woods to the main road. Every cottage is pretty in its own particular way with windows, dormers, gardens. Here is an orchard, there a farmyard, and now Thrift Cottage, and now two or three little cottages with doors arched and windows latticed. They resemble daisies and primroses and buttercups growing by the grass, and the green and white inn is part and parcel of the picture. The little post office has a bandbox garden of flowers. These cottages of flint, with brick around the windows, seem as if they hold only happiness, but in one cottage I know there is an old farm labourer who has worked for over sixty years, up in the morning at four o'clock, out to the farms at Hughenden, and now he lies before the open door, looking out on the village green where he can never walk again. His great regret is that he cannot visit the church and go to the services there, nor can he share the life of farms and horses and cornfields.

When the cottage door is shut his view is cut off, for there is no window at the front of the room. Many of these little old cottages have to open their doors for extra light, and on cold days this is a great disadvantage. A little peephole window would make a great difference to the comfort of some of these old people imprisoned in their rooms. They have to carry their water, for none is laid on here.

Lord Beaconsfield said three things were necessary to a good cottage—an oven, a tank, and a porch. The tank is missing in some of these cottages.

Part of the green at Bradenham is enclosed to make a cricket ground for the men of the village, and children were playing their own games of cricket in the rougher grass close to this shaven portion. They were safe there from the traffic which rushes along the road at the bottom. It is a sensible green with plenty of room for a fair or a meeting, and big boulders along the edge keep the motorist from parking his car on the grass.

The green at Bradenham must once have been the scene of a great pageant, for Queen Elizabeth was entertained at the Manor in 1566, on one of her Progresses. At that visit she drove through the woods, down to High Wycombe and along the road to Bassetsbury Manor, where she stayed the night.

"Her Majesty and suite left Bradenham House on horse-back, passing through some of the loveliest bits of primeval forest at Walter's Ash, down Downley Common, through Tinker's Wood; down Hobbes' Lane to Wycombe, where she was greeted right royally and spent the night at Bassetbury House belonging to John Raunce."

Two miles away from Bradenham is Hughenden, where Disraeli came to live in 1845. He must have known the place well from his boyhood days. The original manor house was remodelled and a terrace made. There Disraeli lived his happy married life and he was buried at Hughenden Church. Until recently the house was kept the same and his study left as in his lifetime. An arm-chair, which was made for him at High Wycombe, and his school books, and many articles given to him by Queen Victoria, are still preserved in the room.

The house stands on the slope of the green hill, with the woods behind it and the parkland in front, with great trees. Several public footpaths lead through the grass.

One sunny autumn day of St Luke's summer we went up Bledlow Ridge. The woods were slowly turning gold, but the beeches were still green, although odd branches flung out yellow banners. The cherries were deep pink, the limes yellow, and the hornbeams old gold, each tree clearly defined. Far away on the opposite hillside in the wood overlooking Bradenham each tree was distinct, for the different colours—olive green, tawny, amber—of their rounded forms made a pattern like the worsted work of an old tapestry. Dark yews grow by the roadside on

Bledlow and I am reminded of a saying that yews are present where the Romans have been. On top of the Ridge we looked to the right and to the left at the fine views of the blazing pageant of autumn woods and the green fields with their white scars to remind us that the chalk was there, and sometimes a field of stubble, cut very short by the reaper, or a field of rusty clover left to form seed. The overgrown hedges by the roadside were filled with ash and oak, cherry and dogwood, they were jewelled with the scarlet ropes of bryony, with rose hips and sloes.

We saw a curious effect on Bledlow Ridge one afternoon later in the year, for the long low rays of the setting sun came from a blue frosty sky to project extraordinary shadows across the valley to the far woods on the opposite hill. The woods across the valley were bloomy purple in the sunlight, and along the whole stretch of the background of wood lay the irregular shadow of the hedgerow to the west at the Ridge top. The position of the sun was exactly right; the woods were the curtain spread out in the east, and the hedgerow, with its irregular trees, on the Ridge itself was the picture which was thrown across the valleys upon this backcloth. We could even distinguish certain trees near us whose shape was shadowed upon the screen many miles away. The fields in the foreground also caught this transfiguring light, and their green was brilliant and vivid as fresh paint. There was an air of unreality and extreme beauty about this scene. The land was luminous, and a lyric quality was in Bledlow Ridge.

We met an old woman coming along the Ridge, an old woman who seemed to come out of the past, for she wore her Sunday black bodice and full skirt and a white linen apron pleated round her waist. There was not a cottage in sight and she trotted along in the middle of the road on that high spine of hill. She smiled at me from under her black bonnet and I stopped to talk.

She was eighty-four, she told me, going on eighty-five.

She apologized because she was wearing her daughter's apron, and her daughter had died in the First World War, but her own aprons had worn out and so she wore her daughter's. Her hands were curled like little bowls and bent with rheumatism. She held them out and in them was the large door-key of her cottage.

"That's with doing heavy washing every week," she told

me, showing dark marks on the thin parchment flesh. "But the doctor says they'll get all right."

She told me she had made lace when she was young like all the other young women. Martha Wooster was her name, but she was no relation to all the other Woosters in Buckinghamshire. She was alone. Sons and daughters all gone away. She was proud of being alone. She was a sturdy, independent old woman, and I admired her for her fortitude. Her brown eyes shone and her mouth smiled sweetly. She must have been a pretty girl seventy years ago. I promised to go and see her in the cottage where she had lived for sixty years, but I could see no shadow of a house.

"Go down the hill, ma'am, and look in the hedge and you'll see a little green wicket gate. You have to look hard to find it. Go through it and you'll find my cottage, hidden away down there."

"Surely you don't live on this hill?" I asked. "There are no houses about here."

"Oh yes, ma'am, there's just my cottage and nobody ever sees it, because it's half-losted in the trees. I can read, but I can't write," she added, although I never thought of asking such inquisitive details of her education. "I can read well enough, but I can only write as nobody can read it."

I assured her that writing didn't matter at all. It was nice to be able to read a bit, but writing was overpraised. It was not at all necessary for good living.

Then we said good-bye and Martha, in her white apron, walked sedately down the hill, and we went higher along the hilltop to a hamlet with toy church and school, where no Marthas lived.

My thoughts fled back to her, to the snowy apron, to the life it represented, a life of hard work, of acceptance, of good humour and patience, the life of those who are the salt of the earth. Martha was exactly right for Bledlow Ridge. She was the strength of the stone. She was the Ridge itself.

We went down the curving road by Wain Hill and along the Lower Icknield Way, after cutting across the Upper Icknield Way. The yew trees accompanied the road, and fine elms and great solitary beeches grew in the hedge, with here and there a farm whose cornricks were newly thatched with bright, golden straw, and sometimes little clusters of these yellow ricks stood on the side of the Ridge.

Steeply down we went to Bledlow. The dictionary gives the definition of "Bledlaw" as Bledda's barrow, or grave, or Bledda's hill.

At Bledlow we stood watching the stream, the Lyde, in its chasm by the church. Transparent springs form this tiny river, which gushes out of the rocks and flows to pools in the glen, falling in cascades down to the valley. This hollow has been broadened artificially into beds that are used for growing water-cress. The stretches of cress were bright green down in that deep bowl, and the water was a silver trickle as it slipped through them and moved onward to the mill. We saw this again on a January day and the slopes of this dell were white with snow-drops growing among the dark, glittering ivy. Great hornbeams grow there on the sides of the chasm in groups, five from one enormous trunk, rearing their purpling branches as high as the church. The roots of these great trees had been washed from the soil by storms and they seemed to cling precariously to the banks. The great basin scooped out by the stream is covered with ivy in a green web such as the Elizabethans loved. Perhaps garlands of it were carried to deck the church on the rock above, together with holly and yew, and certainly the ivy binds the loose soil.

There is a narrow path down this valley and one can walk with the chasm on one side and the churchyard raised on its bank on the other. There is an old proverb about Bledlow:

> They that live and do abide
> Shall see the Church fall into the Lyde.

The church seems safe enough but one can imagine that if a storm broke the gigantic trees their fall would carry tons of earth to the vale, and the churchyard might be caught in the downpour.

In the graveyard a stone carving fascinated me, for there was an angel's head and a pair of wings askew, one up and one point-ing down, and above this petulant cherub was poised a crown, such as the King of England might wear. In one corner, by the outstretched wing, was an hour-glass, and at the opposite side a pick and spade, the emblems of toil. The inscription was faint, and the date erased by the weather.

We entered the church and stood for a few minutes by the door, gazing at the loveliness within. Sometimes the light catches the pillars and walls, shining from them as if they were sources of illumination. So this old grey church, perched on its rock above the tiny river Lyde, was caught by a web of light which revealed many beauties—the great round pillars with their flowers, the fine timbered roof with fifteenth-century beams, the narrow windows.

It is a thirteenth-century church, rebuilt from a Norman one. The low tower has a row of strange faces carved upon it, one with a very cynical leer. The fourteenth-century porch has thick walls and a sundial. Inside it there is a large holy-water stoup. The doorway has carved capitals, and a very beautiful doorway it is.

There is a wall painting of St Christopher carrying the Child. In other parts of the church there are fragments of ancient colour. A small lectern, with a finely carved old wooden eagle whose head is turned almost far enough to watch the reader, is a piece of fifteenth-century work. The north and south doors to the church have strap hinges, which always give me peculiar pleasure. The most primitive and ancient way of hanging a door is a strap hinge, and I saw many in farmhouses in my childhood.

The church has lamps and candles, and there is a fine candelabra with many candles in the chancel. This is not because there is no electricity in the neighbourhood, but the softer light of candles and lamps seems more suitable to the ancient place.

Against the chancel arch of 1260 is a rood whose figures are painted in blue and green, standing high up against the stone. The heavy chancel screen was moved to the back of the church and a new modern light screen has been placed in its stead. This is a brilliant piece of decorative work, painted in scarlet and black and white with a carved frieze of grapes. It gave me great pleasure, but I was told that many disapprove of it. Through the plain windows of the chancel one can see the hornbeams, the barns, and a cornrick at a farm. Fields and hedges are there, and I prefer this vision of the outside world to a stained-glass window. There are some bits of lovely old glass inset in one or two windows, but they do not obstruct the world of farm life and pasture.

The font is decorated with leaves in a design which has certain affinities with other fonts in Buckinghamshire, the "Aylesbury" type, and it may be the work of local craftsmen. The first time we came to see Bledlow Church there was a christening and the font was in use. The clergyman stood there with the baby and around him knelt a crowd of little children whose eyes were wide as they watched the ceremony. There were chrysanthemums and dahlias in the church and the corner where the ancient font stood was bathed in golden light.

Bledlow is a light church, and I wish more churches had this shower of daylight and sunshine and air entering in to make a place of beauty.

One cold day I thought I was alone in this church when I heard a little sound. I saw to my astonishment an old man with tousled silver hair and bright blue eyes squatting in the centre of the aisle. He wore a brown waistcoat, a threadbare coat and no collar, and he knelt there, bowed before the altar, with a bundle of sticks and some paper as if he were going to light a fire to the glory of God. For a wild moment I thought of Anatole France's story of the Juggler of Our Lady. Here was a man who was going to perform some old act of devotion, and it seemed perfectly fitting that he should. He was part of the antiquity of Bledlow Church. There he stayed, crouched on the ground near the Holy Rood, and I went across to speak to him. A little blazing fire in the middle of the aisle would have been fitting for that cold February evening, with the sun setting and the rooks going to their newly-made nests.

"Are you going to make a fire?" I asked.

He lifted his hoary head and smiled and drew the pieces of wood together, still keeping on his knees. His wrinkled face was full of humour, his eyes twinkled at me.

"Yes, I'm going to make a good fire to warm the old church," said he. "It's very cold up here in the chancel."

"Where will you make it?" I asked.

"Down below here. I goes down underneath here. I lights the fire under the aisle, and the heat comes up through the grating."

"That's a very good plan," said I.

"Aye, it's very good, except when the wind's in the south-west."

"It usually *is* in the south-west," said I.

"True. Well, when it's in the south-west the smoke comes up all over the church and fills it. But it's a good east wind to-night and the fire will burn well."

So we talked, and he stayed there kneeling on the floor with his sticks. I asked him about the change of screens. I told him I liked the modern painted screen.

"Some don't," he said grimly. "Some criticize it, and says we shouldn't have it, but it lets the light through and you can see the altar easily."

Then he hesitated a moment and gazed up at me with cunning eyes.

"I don't know what you are," said he slowly, "but we are what you call 'igh."

So that explained the gaiety of the old church. I said good-bye and left him starting to go down with his sticks and paper to the underworld.

In the tower room we read of a peal which was rung one Friday in 1921.

"Three hours and three minutes, a peal of doubles, 5,040 changes, being 3,600 of Grandsires and 1,440 of Bobs," and four of the ringers were Bledlow men.

It is always a pleasure to hear of these bellringers. The next day I met a vicar from the Chiltern Hills who is a friend of mine. He told me that he and some of his congregation were learning bellringing, and a real bellringer came to teach them. A woman passed us and he pointed her out as one of the learners going off for the practice.

Near the church there are several beautiful cottages with herringbone brickwork on their walls and thatched roofs. The Manor House Farm stands across the way, with a fine group of

dark red farm buildings and a seventeenth-century house in a
walled garden. The villagers were excited and happy because
the squire was coming back to live there. Down the road is the
Manor Farm, with long weatherboarded and thatched barns.
The Red Lion Inn is seventeenth-century. It has an original
chimney stack and cosy open fireplace.

Church, farms, and cottages are grouped together in a perfect whole. Behind is Bledlow Ridge, with its woods and its
juniper trees like little dark men standing about in the grass.
On the side of Wain Hill there is an ancient cross cut in the
chalk. Bledlow Cross is a Greek cross which measures about
seventy-five feet transversely with arms fifteen feet broad. Mr
John Clarke tells how his father accidentally found the cross by
walking over it. It was completely overgrown, but in centuries
before the shepherds scoured it.

We went on to see Radnage village and little church, which
has a magnificent roof of the fifteenth century. This is one of
the loveliest roofs on a small village church, and I stood in the
doorway looking at it with great pleasure. The low tower of the
church and the box hedges of the path and the little tub font of
Norman work all seemed part of the plainness of Radnage, with
its fields and paths and curving road by the farmhouse.

On the road to Aylesbury, the Chilterns, with whitebeams
blowing on their flanks among the darker green trees, show
patches of white chalk in cuttings. The whitebeams appear to
be powdered with snow as the wind catches them high up on
the hillside above the long valley.

Red-roofed farms with clusters of barns and stables, little old
cottages, some of them thatched, with peeping eyes of dormer
windows peering from the roofs, Friesian cows and calves, bay
mares and their foals, are there in the fields by the roadside. It is
a very lively way with fields of barley and fields of oats. The ridge
of Whiteleaf on one side and Bledlow Ridge on the other are
full of colour and beauty.

A pair of little thatched cottages by the side of the road look
like fairy-tale dwellings, for the small windows, their frames
painted brilliant blue, are inside the thatch and a blue door is
deep in the wall. The gardens are filled with a tangle of poppies

191

and roses, and everlasting peas grow up the house wall. I think that Ole Luk Oie must know those cottages.

Sometimes we go to Princes Risborough along the crest of the hills, travelling by a jolly little bus called Farmer's Bus. We travel through Lacey Green, where a windmill stands in a field.

On this ridge is the Pink and Lily Inn, which was the favourite inn of Rupert Brooke. It is a small, unpretentious place, with a lovely name. Next to the Pink and Lily is a field where haymaking is in full swing, men cocking the hay, others leading it, with old-fashioned thoroughness. From this ridge there are views for many miles across the Aylesbury plain, with coloured fields laid out and violet-blue distances. Cottages in this part of Buckinghamshire are thatched with embroidered edges, some with eye-shades over their little windows, but all have gay little gardens of flowers. Honeysuckle and bracken grow in the lanes.

Princes Risborough is a quiet little town with a curving street and many delightful little houses, some of them timbered, some of them thatched, some sixteenth-century timber-framed.

In the centre of the town is an old brick Market House which has open arcades. It is crowned with a wooden cupola and clock and bell. Near the Market House is a gabled building with herringbone brickwork. I always admire Vine House, a Tudor dwelling with a story projecting on timbers and a vine tree growing up its front.

The Manor House, which is early eighteenth-century, has a very beautiful seventeenth-century staircase of oak, with pierced scrollwork and large square newels with ball finials. This house now belongs to the National Trust.

Next to the Manor House is the Manor Farm, with fine old buildings, the stable door open and carthorses standing in the stalls, and harness hanging on wooden pegs round the walls. It was a very homely place to me, as the horses turned their heads at the sound of my voice. Lower down the road is the farmyard with pigs grunting in the straw and carts uptilted in the cartsheds next to modern farm equipment.

192

Harvesting in the Misbourne Valley

On the opposite side of the road is a lovely little old cottage called the Old Vicarage, a seventeenth-century cottage—but probably earlier. It has many corners and tiny windows and a large projecting chimney stack with wide fireplace inside. I thought Cinderella's godmother might have lived there. By the back door a tall pink hollyhock grew, nearly as tall as the cottage. I asked a little boy who stood near with a yellow kitten in his arms who lived there.

"Somebody new," he replied, "but Amy Johnson used to live there. This kitten lives in the farm. I am taking it back. It's been lost."

He slapped the great carthorse by the stable door and put the kitten down. Then away he ran to poke a stick in the hedge, to find the eggs of straying hens.

Princes Risborough possesses many country things and ways of living, and one picture that remains in my mind is a sixteenth-century house that looked like the backcloth of a Tudor scene, for it had a curious flatness in the low sunlight. It was warm and richly coloured, and faces were looking down from a crooked window as if they had always been there. An old man was driving a horse and cart through the town, and the cart was an old-fashioned one; the horse had ear-caps with scarlet, blue, and white bobbles dangling from them, and a thick piece of white netting on its flanks to keep off the flies. A herd of cows went slowly through the street with a Jersey cow walking timidly in the rear and the farmer cycling backwards and forwards and then waiting patiently for them to come along.

There was a reaping machine, driven by a girl in blue and pink, clattering along the road past the cattle. All seemed in keeping with the old town and its row of cottages. I noticed two old cottages with bulging timbered walls which had been made into shops and were hiding behind a modern front. They were like a countrywoman in town clothes.

There are the modern Black Prince Inn and the old George and Dragon Inn, with St George fighting a Dragon like a shaggy yellow dog. There are old houses, crooked roofs, and moss growing over them, making a sheen of yellow and green. It is a very quiet, sleepy place, dreaming perhaps of the great days

O 193

Wendover, the High Street

when the Black Prince had a palace there, for there is a tradition that a palace stood in the ground near the church. For centuries Princes Risborough belonged to the Princes of England.

For many years there was an ancient custom at Princes Risborough by which a bull and a boar were given on Christmas Day for the use of the parishioners. "They were distributed in large pieces, smoking hot from the copper at 5 o'clock in the morning for breakfast on Christmas Day." Four bushels of wheat and four bushels of malt were also made into bread and beer and given away. The custom was discontinued before 1847.

We walked to Monks Risborough, past the new Roman Catholic church which I mistook for a mosque but the gay interior resembles a white rose.

The main road runs along the Icknield Way here.

Monks Risborough belonged to the monks of Christ Church, at Canterbury, long before the Conquest and it was theirs until the Dissolution of the Monasteries. The church, which is mainly Perpendicular, is a warm, happy, living church, with flowers from the countryside in bowls. There is the feeling of the reality of a living God within its walls. The fine old door has original fourteenth-century hinges, like the hinges of field gates I have known, a pattern that has persisted in the countryside. There is an old lock of the fifteenth century with carved edges, and even the great iron nails that hold it are wrought like roses. The latch of the door is ornamented. This is a good piece of early craftsmanship by a medieval smith.

The font, "Aylesbury" type, of 1180 is fluted, with carvings in the interlaced ovals like beech leaves. On the sill of a long lancet window is the carved stone head of a woman wearing a coif on her banded hair. One window is filled with pieces of ancient glass, pale gold and amber.

The rood screen of 1500 is carved with flowers and leaves and it has the pictures of nine of the Apostles painted upon it. These figures were painted in the time of Charles I or II. They are bearded men in bright red and blue gowns, ermine capes, and ermine hats. Their cheeks are rosy, their eyes are bright, they are a happy family who look as if they were going to act in a miracle play in their best new clothes. In the floor many medieval tiles are inset.

The church has a grand old roof of timber of the fifteenth century. There are four bench-ends with poppy-head finials which are beautifully and amusingly carved. Three have little men standing back to back, grim-faced and noseless. The other is carved with two women's heads with embroidered neck-bands and elaborate head-dresses. They are fifteenth-century work. The tower, dated 1310, has six bells with "Hope in God," "Feare God," and "Honor God" inscribed.

In the tower there is an inscription which reads:

"On Saturday, 2nd June, 1923, a peal of Bob Minor was rung in this Church in 3 hours 16 minutes (5,040 changes)." Then come the names of the ringers and the bells, Treble, 2nd, 3rd, 4th, 5th, and Tenor.

Near the church is the Old Rectory, now a school. In its garden there is an oblong pond of lilies which is fed by a spring, and a stream from this pool runs out past a moated site. To the north of the church is a farmhouse in whose field stands a square pigeon-house with medieval walls.

On the hill above Monks Risborough is the village of White-leaf, which is situated along the Upper Icknield Way. It is a hamlet of pretty cottages, with thatched roofs and flower gardens, perhaps rather sophisticated, for many have been drawn to this lovely village in the beech woods. So one sees chintz curtains and artistic pottery in the windows of the seventeenth-century cottages.

We went up a narrow path in the woods, climbing until we came out to a natural lawn of short turf among the trees. In the grass grew harebells and rock-roses, and the little blue gentian, and the leaves of orchis were close to the ground. A gap between the trees framed a view of the vale, blue and chequered, far below. In front of us was the Risborough valley stretching across to Bledlow, with fields and villages. Behind were beech woods, magnificent woods curving down to a hollow and up to the hills, in a great bowl of trees. Juniper bushes, grey-green and low-growing, sloes, and whitebeam are plentiful on this Chiltern height, which is one of the most beautiful places in Buckinghamshire.

Near us, cut out on the turf, was the Cross of Whiteleaf. The green layer has been removed and this large cross on the chalk of the hillside is visible as a shining object from a great distance. It is eighty feet across both ways and the arms are about twenty feet wide. It stands on a triangular base which descends to the road below in a quarry, or perhaps it is a natural breaking away of the chalk here. The origin of the cross is obscure, and there are several theories, each of which has doughty advocates. The earliest record of the cross is 1738, when it was illustrated in a view from Wain Hill at Bledlow, and the Icknield Way is shown running up through Monks Risborough, after turning at Ellesborough and swinging past the cross. The writer, the Rev. Francis Wise, tells of the merrymaking each year at the scouring of the cross, but he gives no details of its origin. From this it is thought that the cross must have been there earlier or memories of countrymen would have related its beginnings. Some think there was a finger, an upright mark of great age, and the arms were added later. Nobody, neither Leland nor Camden nor Drayton, mentions the cross when speaking of the neighbourhood. Another theory is that it is connected with the village of Monks Risborough in the valley below. Monks Risborough was a manor granted to the monks of Canterbury and the monks may have carved this emblem on the hillside to show the symbol of Christianity to the countryside.

On the hill above the cross, but near to it, are two tumuli, crowned with beech trees.

Near Monks Risborough there is a portion of Grim's Dyke, that ditch and bank which runs through the southern part of the county. It is thought to be a prehistoric line of boundary which separated lands belonging to different tribes.

The ditch consists of a fosse and a rampart. It can be traced at Bradenham through the woods at Lacey Green, then, turning by Redland End, it goes through Hampden Park and onwards towards Great Missenden, where it crosses the valley and goes through Wendover towards Berkhampsted.

The Icknield Way bends round below the cross and goes

down the field as a lane with trees over it, smothering it with their interweaving branches. We went along the Icknield Way for some time, but when we came to a footpath crossing it we stopped and asked a woman the short cut to Princes Risborough.

"The Icknield Way is very stuffy," said she. "You go through the cornfield instead."

So we took her advice and walked down the footpath that led across a great field where golden wheat was growing deeper in colour, where blue scabious raised their pretty heads, and two red-backed shrikes swung on a wire, singing their shrill song. I talked to a man with a machine in the hayfield, for both corn and hay were being gathered at the same time, the corn with reaper and binder, and men putting the sheaves into shocks, the haymakers working with swathe-turner and side-rake combined. We spoke of harvests and labour, as two country people together.

The upper road, along the crest of the hill by Hailey Green between beech woods, with here and there a tiny thatched cottage alone in the world of trees, is, I think, quite the loveliest road in all Buckinghamshire on an autumn day when there is a touch of frost in the air and the woods are turning gold and red.

We went through the gates to see Hampden House and the church of Great Hampden which is close to it. There was a sound of bees in the church, and the murmur of wood doves, and a very sweet smell. The floor is made of old red bricks, like a kitchen, with some ancient coloured tiles inset. Five painted coats-of-arms hang on the walls, a gay row of hatchments, with heraldic beasts, stags and dogs, dragons and lions. A squint over four feet long goes through the pillars to the altar, and over it is the figure of a stout little man.

There are steep rough old ladders leading to the tower, and an ancient oak pillar with a finial rises by this rude stairway. A "Thank Him" made of wheat and straw with tassels of wheat and oats hung over the Jacobean pulpit. The church is the burial place of John Hampden, who was wounded at Chalgrove Field on 18 June 1643, and died at Thame six days later. There is an eighteenth-century memorial to him erected by his grandson, with a carved relief of the battle at the foot.

Hampden House, the home of John Hampden, is a magnificent pile of buildings which faces a green stretch of country with woods and the famous "ride" cut through them. In the house there were some relics of Hampden, but for me the most interesting thing was a painting of Queen Elizabeth in a jewelled dress, with an exquisite little portrait hanging from a chain at her waist.

The oldest part of this house is King John's Tower, built of stone, a small projecting wing of the fourteenth century. There is a beautiful main staircase of the seventeenth century which has square newels with urns and bunches of flowers and fruit.

Grim's Dyke runs near Great Hampden, and this piece of it is the best in the county, with rampart and ditch very well defined.

Little Hampden is a hamlet in the woods and the church is one of the smallest in the county. It stands on a rise with a cottage and flower garden next to it, and sometimes a baby lies in his perambulator in the churchyard.

Its walls are of flint rubble, and the medieval porch is timber-framed with plaster filling. This porch has an upper story, a priest's room, and the bell rope hangs down. The bell has been rung for twenty-five years by the countrywoman who tends the church so lovingly.

The church is very tiny, intimate, and friendly. One feels happy as soon as one enters from the lovely porch, for it is like a dwelling-house and it holds only about thirty people.

There are some faded wall paintings of the thirteenth century, and two of these are of St Christopher. A Saxon altar is in this little old church.

Below the church is a white farmhouse, the Old Manor Farm, with a yard full of cattle nosing in the straw, and from the doors a little green path leads into the woods. Church, cottage, and farmhouse are all close together with the beech woods around and cornfields by the churchyard.

Just recently the funeral was held here of the cowman at the farmstead. The little church was packed with countrymen who came to pay their last respects to him. Their gaiters were polished, they wore their blacks, and their faces had the fresh

bright complexions of those who live out of doors. The coffin
was brought from the farmhouse and laid on trestles in the yard,
while the cattle looked on to see their master carried to his last
resting-place. No motor hearse was there, but men bore the
coffin. They sang "Rock of Ages" and "Abide with Me" and
the Twenty-third Psalm. Such simplicity is very moving, it is
the true spirituality of the country people which is unchanged.

Great Kimble, a small village, is close to hills, and just across
the road is a chalk cutting in the face of the woods, with beech
trees around it. The tumulus near the churchyard in the field
was opened last century and Roman and British remains were
found within. Near is a great barn of the sixteenth century.

Opposite the church is the creeper-covered inn, the Bernard
Arms. It is fresh and bright as the clear air of Great Kimble. A
painted sign hangs out of the Bear and Ragged Staff, and on a
December day, just before Christmas, the inn was decorated with
holly and ivy in the traditional manner. We felt we ought to have
driven up in a coach and four to that wide-flung door and the
hospitable interior of the small homely inn. Great fires burning,
and holly over every lamp and picture, made a glitter on that
white frosty day of sunshine and cold weather. A high hedge of
box divides the garden from the road, a hedge one often sees in
this part of Buckinghamshire, where box grows to a considerable
size. The first box hedge I noticed was at Wendover, but there
are hedges at Radnage and many places in Mid Bucks.

Great Kimble and Little Kimble, its tiny neighbour, are said
to take their names from Cunobelinus, the British King, father
of Caractacus, famous in history. I like to think that Caractacus
perhaps walked these Chiltern hills, for in childish imagination
one has seen him, with cloak swung around him, facing his
captors with defiance in Rome. The tale of Cunobelinus was
the source of Shakespeare's *Cymbeline*.

It was at the village of Great Kimble that John Hampden
made his famous protest against the payment of Ship Money to
Charles I. The church stands by the roadside on a raised mound.

One notices at once in Great Kimble church the magnificent
font which stands in the centre of the aisle on raised steps, as if
it had been there first and the church built round it. Usually the

font is taken for granted, and the greatest treasures of carved stone are away at the back of the church, but at Great Kimble the majestic Norman bowl, with its carved base and band of foliage around it, is pre-eminent. The nave has a fifteenth-century roof, with king-posts and tracery in the spandrils.

On the north wall hangs a copy of the report of the parish meeting held on 9 January 1635, with the names of those who refused to pay the assessment of Ship Money. John Hampden's name heads the list; he was in the chair at the meeting. He was assessed at 31s. 6d. Other country names were William Yeoman, Jeffrey Goodchild, Widow Goodchild (who was assessed at 5s. 6d.)

The case of John Hampden was so famous, and his name so deeply bound up with Buckinghamshire, that I must recall the facts. The Petition of Rights had been passed and one of its provisions was "No freeman shall be obliged to give any gift, loan, benevolence or tax without common consent by Act of Parliament." When Charles tried to levy Ship Money he went outside Parliament, and the money was not intended for the Navy but for his own purposes. A ship of 450 tons was demanded from Buckinghamshire, and although Hampden's assessment was small, and he was a wealthy man, he refused to pay, as a protest against the legality of the King's action. He was sued, and the judgment went against him. In 1640 the judgment was cancelled, but the protest had been made.

The fine modern statue of John Hampden stands at the head of the market square in Aylesbury, reminding people of his action of defiance for freedom's sake.

In the west porch of Great Kimble Church hang the striped bell-ropes of six bells. One of these bells has "Gloria in Excelsis Deo" engraved upon it, dated 1588, and another of the same date has "Ave Maria Gratia Plena."

On a ledge I saw a lithograph by the artist Clare Leighton of the bellringers ringing a chime.

Over a doorway are a lion and unicorn, white as ivory. There is a tiny chapel, modernized with painted arches and roof, decorated with bright colours. Against a wall stands an old chest reputed to be thirteenth-century, with iron bands across the top and iron rings at the ends for lifting the heavy weight. The iron banding of this chest must be admired for its splendid simplicity and strength.

This church was built in the fourteenth century, replacing an earlier one, and, as so often happens in Buckinghamshire, the site is an old earthwork. Carved faces peer down from the tower, queer scowls and grins of animal and man, looking across the green graveyard to the hills.

A short distance from Great Kimble, round the sweep of the green hill in Chequers Park, is Cymbeline's Mount, a British earthwork, and the name carries on the traditions and legends.

"That's where King Cymbeline lived," say the country people, as if Cymbeline had had a castle there recently.

This Kimble country has a special atmosphere of its own, a memory and something else, so that one's heart is uplifted, and I, for one, desire to stop for ever, enchanted and caught by magic, by the pagan feelings that seem to linger for those who are able to pick them up. I felt this at Great Kimble long before I heard of Cymbeline's Mount, and indeed the site of British camps is often sinister and fearful, but Great Kimble itself is not haunted, except by kindly people.

The road through Kimble is the Upper Icknield Way. Little Kimble Church is half-hidden at the cross roads behind a couple of giant elms, but its jolly little bellcote with two green bells in a small turret hangs over the porch visible to all. A stream, the Bonny Brook, runs past, and darts under a tiny bridge. Rooks build in the elms and the sound of their cawing fills this small church. The red-tiled floor is homely, the church is warm and simple. It has a fourteenth-century door. Perhaps the wall paintings have brought joy to other generations, for there is a medieval picture gallery round the walls. The most interesting mural is St Francis preaching to the birds, which are perched on a tree listening to him. The saint is clearly painted and at least seven birds sit in the branches of the stiff tree, a robin at the top, a seagull near, and an owl with little ears near the foot. In a village among the woods with birds around it is an appropriate scene.

There is St Christopher, a favourite always in murals, for

he is the patron saint of travellers. The clearest picture is St George, carrying a lance, wearing a red cross on his coat and shield.

Under a mat lie six medieval tiles, very clear in their detail and modern in the treatment of the faces. It is thought to be the story of Tristan and Iseult. One tile shows a man giving a book with a hanging seal to a woman. Another has a king on his throne. A third is a queen holding a squirrel, and a fourth has a horse and rider. Around them are mermaids and devils.

There is some old glass in the windows, golden oak leaves and acorns, and the lions of England and the lilies of France.

CHAPTER XIV

ELLESBOROUGH AND
CYMBELINE'S MOUNT

THE road from Wendover to Ellesborough runs under the curve of Coombe Hill, on high ground, with a fine view over the plain. It is the Upper Icknield Way, and along this ancient road a modern road has been superimposed. This road is like a gentle switchback, going up and down as the new road follows the early British track. Between the road and the foot of the wooded hill are fields and ploughland. A boy drives a tractor and scatters fertilizer on the newly sown wheat in a smooth field of fifteen acres of the silky grey soil which is the Chiltern earth. The chalk, they say, is only a foot or two down below this fertile layer, but it is good land. Below the Icknield Way there is dark rich land. The ancient footway was made at the division between these two soils, climbing along the roots of the hills to Ellesborough, the Kimbles, by Whiteleaf, close to the cross, down the valleys and up to the slopes of Bledlow. In another field two men are using a new potato-digging machine, painted red and green, very smart and clean from the makers. This is the first time it has been used and the farm men are delighted with their toy. There is a meadow under the shadow of the great hill and a timbered cottage. Two little red-cheeked, red-shawled children, who look as if they had stepped out of a picture by Millais, are driving a flock of turkeys through a gap, with thin switches.

Down in the valley I noticed a beautiful old farmhouse, with great chimneys and an air about it of ancient grandeur. A group of golden ricks stood near, and many farm buildings. I couldn't take my eyes off it as I walked along the high-road, but it was away in the fields, among trees. A friendly postman, tramping the long road, was also enchanted by the golden glow of autumn on the valley, and he stopped.

"This is the Icknield Way," said he affably, as if he were

203

telling me it was Oxford Street. Then he pointed to the farm in the valley.

"That's a very ancient farm, called Wellwick," said he. "Have you ever heard tell of Judge Jeffreys?"

"Bloody Jeffreys?" I asked.

"That's the man. Well, he lived there. There's secret cupboards in that house behind the larder shelves. I've seen them when I've been taking letters and they showed 'em to me."

Wellwick is a tall rectangular farmhouse, of rose brick and flint, with handsome chimneys. It has the date 1616 on the chimneys, and the great doorway is arched, with a crest above it of the Brudenells. The barns, too, are seventeenth-century work, with open timber roofs. The tale of Jeffreys is perhaps a tradition, but the judge may have stayed there. Later I saw this lovely old house with cattle and rickyard and barns approached by a long rough lane. One of its fields is bordered with great elms on two sides, and this makes a striking landmark which one can see for many miles.

This road to Ellesborough, swinging with sudden dips and steep rises, is bordered with tawny beech trees whose long straight trunks are like pillars with top-knots of flaming hair, not the flowing branches of the ordinary beeches. These trees grow on a raised bank along the side of the road, and many of the fields in this part of the country have full-grown trees on grassy knolls instead of hedges.

There are many varieties of trees on this Icknield Way, and the colours in autumn are so vivid they seem to be on fire. Dogwood bushes, crimson-leaved, catching and holding the sun, rose-pink guelder, golden maple, spindle with pink narrow leaves and striking orange and pink fruits, whitebeams, dropping their leaves in a tangle of white paper, hornbeams, turning rusty gold, nut trees, cherries, all are there, with the giant elms and beeches towering above them.

The road turns a corner, following the contour of the hill, where the obelisk stands against the sky, and it runs down to the next valley, past Butler's Cross, past the Rose and Crown, a thatched inn, lovely as a rose itself, green and pink and white. There are a few old houses and some new cottages, but all have gardens, and all have fields rolling to their back doors. One can walk over Coombe Hill and drop down into the valley, but this Icknield Way is my favourite route on account of the trees which grow by its side.

I walked up the steep incline to Ellesborough Church, and I met the vicar coming down the hill.

"Do you know you are walking on the Icknield Way?" he asked. There is a strong feeling for the past linked with the present in Bucks, as old and new are bound together.

The Church of St Peter and St Paul stands on its hill defiant, strong, and living. There is something stark and grand about its outline against the sky. It compels by a latent vigour from the centuries of the past. I have seen this church from the Aylesbury road afar, when it looks like a stone ship riding a green sea, poised on a curving green wave in the distance. The houses are hidden, and the church seems alone in the hills. At first I thought it was a deserted church, left in the fields by a receding population, but it is a place of extraordinary life. From the top of Coombe Hill we have looked down on it, and from the far ridges of the Chilterns by Ashendon Hill we have seen it, and always it is splendidly growing on its own hill, part of the strength of the earth itself. It is said to have been haunted, and one can well imagine men coming back to that resting-place under the Chilterns. Beacon Hill is behind it, towering over it, and on a shoulder of Beacon Hill is Cymbeline's Mount.

The church is made of flint and stone, and the tower is battlemented. From the churchyard there is an immense stretch of the Vale of Aylesbury spread out to the dim distance.

I went to the church to see the marble effigy of Brigetta Croke, who died in 1638. She lies on her side, a graceful young woman, in all the splendour of Stuart dress, under an arched canopy of painted shields. Four black marble pillars bear up the roof of her dwelling-place on the church walls. Her dress is so delicately made that every detail is clear from bows to ribbons, from laces to the shoes on her feet. She wears a necklace and jewels, and round her slender neck is a lace frill. In one hand she holds a book, as if she had just been reading, and her curled head rests on the other hand. I like these casual positions, these wide-awake girls and men who seem to be watching the doings of the villagers with deep interest.

In the vestry windows are some pieces of old stained glass, with the symbols of the Trinity in one and the head of Christ crowned with thorns in another. A side window has some richly coloured fragments, glowing with brilliance—one, a man in a turban, carrying a sword.

I found a little old book on the windowsill of the vestry. It was the *Children's Poetry Book* of 1868, with coloured engravings by the Brothers Dalziel. In the quietness of the church, safe on its great mound, I read the "Ballad of the Blind Beggar's Daughter of Bethnal Green," and the "Tale of Llewellyn and His Dog." There was Cowper's poem, "The Poor Bobbin Weaver," with a picture of a lace-maker of Bucks. Cowper lived at Olney, and he must have seen many lace-makers sitting at their doors as they sat at Ellesborough and the villages all over the county.

> Yon cottager, who weaves at her own door
> Pillow and bobbins all her little store,
> Content though mean, and cheerful if not gay,
> Shuffling her threads about the livelong day,
> Just earns a scanty pittance, and at night,
> Lies down secure, her heart and pocket light.

I saw this church one day when it was decorated for the harvest festival. It was like a feast prepared, and every corner held a group of vegetables and fruit, arranged with the simplicity of a countryman and the beauty of an artist: scrubbed white potatoes, apples, sheaves of wheat and barley, giant marrows, and all the produce. I think everyone in the village had sent a good share of his garden. The church was scented with the earth, with flowers and soil, and roots and corn.

Close to the church down a green path which leads on to Beacon Hill and Cymbeline's Mount are the little eighteenth-century almshouses, tucked away under a hedge. They were founded by Dame Dodd's Charity in a will dated 2 March 1746.

Each pair of houses has a large common room as entrance hall, washhouse and meeting-place, and off this hall are the two rooms, a bed-sitting-room for each inmate. I went to see an old farm labourer who lives alone in one of these little houses. There was one good-sized room with a fire burning brightly. A large wooden bed with strong posts at its corners stood there, against a partition down the room which kept off the draughts and screened the bed, but allowed a view of the fire to the occupant at night. The bed looked very comfortable, for the old man had made it nicely and turned it down ready for night.

At the foot of the partition, near the fire, was his table, with a bottle of milk and loaf of bread, his cup and plate ready for tea. Behind it he kept his plants, cuttings, and seedlings in boxes, for he is a good gardener. The window had tall geraniums, and he told me to be sure to come in summer when his fuchsias and geraniums would be out.

For sixty years he had worked on the land, and now he did a few odd jobs, stoking the furnaces at the church, and he looked after his garden at the almshouses where he had fine crops and some fruit trees.

Then we talked of his work for farmers and the horses he had looked after. Horses are always remembered with pride and affection, his blue eyes sparkled as he spoke of them in his broad dialect which was difficult to follow. He stood there, a fine old man, one who has worked in Buckinghamshire all his life. Now he has his own little home, and he can be as tidy or untidy as he likes, and grow his cuttings near his bed and keep them warm with the fire which warms his own body.

I have been charmed by the almshouses in Buckinghamshire, and I have had the privilege of entering several at the request of the old people. There is a kindliness and warmth in these old charities by which cottages were provided for those who wished for their own little dwellings. I talked one day to a charming old lady who lives in one of these houses. She is a Londoner who has lost everything, and now spends her last days in the heart of the country. She wouldn't go back to London. She has found great happiness in the almshouse and many would envy her that little cottage with the hills around it.

I heard of another Buckinghamshire countryman who is deeply interested in the history of his county. A man of no high education, he has a remarkable knowledge of history because he still shares the life of generations long past. He feels they are his kin. He sent a message to a friend of mine a short time ago that he had found out the names of those who had died in the Black Death in his village. So the centuries roll back, and this medieval historian labours in the village and sends his mind back to delve in the past as he does his research work in the fields.

Up and down the county I have found men each seeking for the truth of his little plot of earth, each keenly interested in the history and archæology of his place.

Ellesborough Church is the parish church of Chequers, the country house of Britain's Prime Ministers. Chequers is hidden from the road, and the parkland of 560 acres stretches upwards to the hills, with many fine trees. The road to the house swings away near Kimble. On the hillside is the famous Cymbeline's Mount, an earthwork of great antiquity. The grassy slope at the corner is called Velvet Lawn, and a lovely little glade is Happy Valley. Now the land is ploughed and the grace has departed for a time.

The fifteenth-century manor house of Chequers was rebuilt by Sir William Hawtrey, and the initials, A.H. and W.H. with the date 1565, are entwined over one of the great fireplaces. There was confined Lady Mary Keys, the sister of Lady Jane Grey. Lady Mary Grey had been kept at court under the eye of Elizabeth, as her claim to the throne was remote but real. She secretly married Thomas Keys, and at once she was sent to Chequers in disgrace and her husband was sent to the Fleet Prison. He died, and the little widow died a few years later.

Cromwell relics are here, his clothes, jack boots, and sword.

All around this district there are legends and reminders in place names of the British King Cunobelinus, father of Caractacus, called Cymbeline by Shakespeare. Only tradition is responsible for the tales, but country memories are long and place names linger unchanged except for minor details through the centuries.

The ancient name for Kimble is Cynebel, and there are

208

numerous barrows around this place, close to the ancient Way of the Britons.

There is a hill near Kimble and Whiteleaf Cross which has always been called Soldiers' Mount, but nobody knew who were the soldiers or when they lived or died, until last century when excavations showed Roman coins of the reign of Constantine the Younger, A.D. 337, and Constantine the Great, A.D. 325. The Soldiers' Mount may have been an observation post of a Roman legion stationed there, overlooking the valleys.

For a long time I wished to see the famous Cymbeline's Mount, but for various reasons I could not do so. From the height of Coombe Hill I had looked down to a rounded hill, Beacon Hill, rising abruptly from the valley and I knew the earthwork was near. One day in July we went past the excellent Bernard Arms at Kimble, only stopping to glance into the thatched stables to see the horses, and to walk into a cottage to see an old lady who wanted to show me her smoky fire. We talked to this and that one in the little village, and visited the tumulus by the church, which always attracts me. Little Friesian calves grazed near it, and I gathered a bunch of dark-leaved, blue-eyed alkanet, growing tall and hairy by the side of the road. Campanula, the tall bell-flower, was there, and meadowsweet. I was nearly taken captive again by Great Kimble, for that corner is very delightful, but I dragged myself away to Ellesborough where a friend was waiting to take us up the Mount.

We walked along the Icknield Way and turned opposite the church of Ellesborough down a grassy lane past the almshouses, where the old labourer lives. This July day I saw his windows gay with tall scarlet and dark crimson geraniums, as he had promised. He was away harvesting, or I might never have arrived at Cymbeline's Mount.

We climbed the slope and circled round Beacon Hill, which rose like a sugar cone above us. In the grass on that Chiltern slope we found the pyramidal orchis growing, in lovely crimson spikes of blossom, and the small pyramidal bell-flower. The grass was starry with yellow rock-roses, and there were beds of wild thyme, which scented the air. It was a sweet place, with bees and butterflies and flowers, all living in that chalky upland.

P 209

"For these lands in Stoke Mandeville John Hampden was assessed"—Hampden Monument

The outer rampart of the Mount lay there, very clearly defined, and we climbed it and crossed the ditch to the steep inner fort. From its summit we could look through the trees to a ravine, one of those narrow gorges in the hill which run down abruptly. This place sheltered by the Beacon Hill, where there would be outposts, is safely hidden but in a commanding position.

Cymbeline's Mount is an awe-inspiring place; one can feel at once the presence of something invisible guarding the ancient Kimble's Castle. With Beacon Hill behind it and its own ramparts commanding the valley, it must have been a formidable camp. In this neighbourhood was fought a battle, according to persistent legend, between the British King Cunobelinus, or Cymbeline, and the Roman General Aulus Plautius, and one of the sons of Cunobelinus was slain, and the army defeated.

"Even the grasses seem to moan, as though they wanted to tell you something on Cymbeline's Mount," said a country-woman who lives near. "It's got a queer unearthly feeling. And have you noticed how the dead leaves rise up and turn in the air when there's no wind?"

The ghosts of those times haunt the place, even in broad daylight. My friend visits the Mount in all seasons and at all times, and he says that at night it is indeed eerie. Once when he was there in the darkness a shrill cry, a weird unearthly long-drawn wail, came out, which made his hair stand on end and sent shivers of ice down his spine. He knew quite well what it was—a vixen calling—but that made no difference, and away he went, very fast, down the hill. He had seen fox cubs playing in the sunshine on the hillside more than once, and he often watched a fox lope past the Mount.

It is a strangely lonely place, Cymbeline's Mount, birds not singing and flowers not blossoming. Rock-rose and harebells had deserted the rampart, only the wild thyme and little patches of the golden stonecrop grew on the chalk sides. Then, on the centre of the Mount I discovered a large bushy plant, like a tree. It was a giant deadly nightshade, the *Atropus belladonna*, whose outstretched green branches held lurid purple bells and the death-giving black berries. It was indeed a fitting place for this plant, which I had never seen before, although I recognized it at once

210

It is rare because it is usually destroyed on account of its deadly poison, and many people think the bittersweet or woody nightshade of the hedgerows and woods is the deadly nightshade.

In my youth I remember the horror of one day when a messenger came to tell us that some cattle we put out to grass in the parkland were dead after eating the deadly nightshade. Three stirks were slain, our own and a neighbour's. My father drove off hurriedly to see the place, and we waited sadly for his return.

The dwale or deadly nightshade is so handsome, its foot-long leaves so green, and the purple bells so splendidly triumphant and beautiful that I gathered some sprays and took them along with me. The next day I touched the flowers and shining berries, and examined them minutely as they stood stiff and bright in an earthenware pot. Shortly afterwards I swayed and became faint and ill, and I could not see all day. I never thought of the flowers, but later I read that even the artist who had painted deadly nightshade for illustration had been seized with dizziness and her eyes affected. I suppose I touched my eyes after holding the berries and wet stalks.

We left the romantic and haunting Cymbeline's Mount and climbed slowly upward, along a narrow chalk path called the Cradle, past the head of a lovely tree-filled ravine, a dense jungle of trees growing in the narrow defile, for water flows there in a thirsty land. On the bare slopes in the short grass grew a clump of tall brilliantly green flowers, the dyer's rocket or weld. The flowers were nearly three feet high and very striking, alone on the hillside.

We went into the box wood, among the twisted ancient trees with their smooth snaky trunks and their tiny dark green leaves. This wood is very remarkable. I felt as if I walked in an enchanted place, for the scent of the box was very strong and subtle. "Box and snowdrops and winter days," I thought, as I sniffed that aromatic air, kept under the thick mat of evergreen branches, heavy and odorous, which I had not smelled for many years. At once I saw in my mind a box tree under which I once sat with my dolls, and the vision was very clear in that dark box wood on the Chiltern heights. When anyone died we made wreaths of box and snowdrops in winter, of box and roses in summer, and sent the garlands to the mourners. This was no sad memory, for a wreath was a cheerful thing, a present to old labourers and farm men and village people.

Higher in the wood we climbed to the range of Beacon Hill. Through the long branches of box we got glimpses of hills far away, purple-blue in the distance, of fields spread out in a patchwork, and scarcely a house in all those miles of green land. The dark box, curling and twisting, made frames for its varied pictures, enhancing the beauty of that day of high cirrus clouds in a tender blue sky, of cold wind and bright sun, and a touch of the icy chill of frost crystals somewhere in that vast space above us.

As we came out from the trees of the beech and oak wood which lay along our path, I saw a dazzling sight on the bare hill across a little valley. Brilliant blue flowers grew there in a patch some yards across. They shone like blue glass, and the colour was so vivid I could not imagine what they could be. We went across the narrow dip and found the tall prickly spikes of viper's bugloss, spearheads two feet long growing on stalks of three feet, marvellous shaded blue and red snake flowers, more beautiful than any wild flower I have ever seen. There were several clumps of these, and as the sun shone upon them, bringing out the transparency of the delicate blue and purple-red petals, the long stamens, shaded rose with blue knobbed pistils, and all the green feathers between, we felt we were looking at the kingfisher among flowers.

The viper's bugloss is one of the most luminous of wild flowers, but here, on the lonely heights of the Chilterns, its blue-pink and violet-purple bells, in long pyramids of colour, were something to remember all one's life.

We found the scented musk-thistle and the biting stonecrop in full flower, clinging to the chalk where the grass was absent. Also we picked up a piece of worked flint with the marks of an ancient stone adze or knife upon it. We hunted in rabbit-holes to discover treasure, but we had not the luck of our companion, who once found a coin of Hadrian's reign in a rabbit-hole. When he rubbed it, it was clear and fresh as when it was new.

From the summit of Beacon Hill we could see Brill on its own hill, on the horizon, and Oving on its hill, and the Quainton Hills and Waddesdon faintly red among the trees, and we could distinguish Ivinghoe Beacon and the Pitstone Hills, familiar good places.

Then down the steep slope we went, by the short way, picking the crimson pyramidal orchis and the harebells, down past the field gate where the rich and heady smell of cattle came to us, to remind us all of childhood days when we took mugs for a drink of milk fresh from the cow, down further, past the little red almshouses with the geraniums glowing in the old man's window, and a dove calling, "Tak two coos, Taffy. Tak too coos, Taffy. Tak," as it flew out of the garden of the almshouses. A great field, made out of three or four fields whose hedges had been uprooted by a modern agriculturist, lay there under the hill, shimmering silky green with young corn; cloud shadows passed over it, and an aeroplane cast a shade like a bird as it flew over. This field always interests me, and I follow its growth through the months. There was a good crop of golden corn, swinging audibly, a wonderful sight and sound for seldom have I seen such a field. Then came the storms and although the corn was stooked it would not dry. Again a new method was used, and the corn was stooked on frames, as they do it in Scotland. I thought the field looked enchanting with its "stacks" of corn, like yellow houses. In another field, close to Chequers, at the entrance which is no longer used, corn was dried in the same manner.

Wild blue geraniums held up their bright blue pennies of flower to the sun on the lane's edge, and yellow bedstraw and silky lavender-shaded great plantain stood upright in the grasses.

We had tea at the Vicarage, and we talked of ghosts and strange happenings, of medieval Bucks people who live to-day, born out of their time, but bringing humour and gaiety and practical jokes to try to amuse a grim matter-of-fact world that has nearly forgotten how to laugh.

Then away we went home, along the green-lined roads, past the tumulus of Great Kimble, and the tinkling bellcote of Little Kimble, past Velvet Lawn, which no longer looks like velvet, past Princes Risborough with its little grape-vine-clad house, and Whiteleaf Cross on the hill, away we went home with our viper's bugloss and our deadly nightshade, and the bunch of orchis and wild geraniums and purple bell-flower—away we went home under the stars of a July sky.

I heard recently of a legend connected with Cymbeline's Mount. An Ellesborough man said that when he was a boy, about fifty years ago, the children used to run around Cymbeline's Mount seven times, because there was a tradition that the Devil would appear. An older man, also born in the district, used to run seven times round the smaller of the two tree circles on the top of Beacon Hill to summon up the Devil. Both men remembered that the old people spoke of these legends in their own childhood, so the tradition was passed on from one generation to another. This must be a relic of paganism or witchcraft, handed down and told again by those who had actually run the pagan race. It must have required some courage in the lonely haunted places, especially for imaginative children, and I remember hearing of a little boy who never managed the seventh round but scampered off home as fast as he could, thinking the Devil was behind him.

CHAPTER XV

AYLESBURY AND WADDESDON

AT once one feels warm and happy to be in a real market town, alive and thriving, retaining its individuality, its humour, and its gaiety through the centuries; individuality because each little house is distinct, with crooked roof or projecting eave or peeping window in the town's centre; humour because when I first saw it there were two great lions lying in the market-place, one painted blue, one red, carrying the V-sign on their flanks; gaiety because there were laughter and clatter of feet on cobbles and pavements, there were sounds of country life and always the unexpected might appear down one of those very narrow streets —a great cart-horse drawing a load of corn, or a wagon of hay, or a pony-trap.

But Aylesbury, the county town of Buckinghamshire, should be seen at night, when there is room to move along the pavements, and the market is over, and the buses have departed with their last loads of shoppers to the outlying villages. Then, against the windy star-filled sky, the irregular roofs make an old pattern that has been there for centuries. The Great Bear hangs over the pointed gables of the little old houses in Church Street, and a shadow moves across a lighted casement window. The great church in the town's centre, although away from the bustle and noise of the market, stands serene and grand, proclaiming the eternal.

The narrow alleys by the King's Head and the little Dark Lantern, with houses leaning towards one another, and thin cats prowling on the stones, return to their Tudor life. The winding streets, running swiftly up and down, with crooked roofs huddled together and uneven jostling houses, squeezing one another so tightly that one seems to be pushed out of the row to run away and join the end of the line, all these make up the delightful and ancient town of Aylesbury.

In the daytime the colour comes back to the old houses, and how much colour there is! The ruddy tint of the roofs, the grey

215

walls, the pearly shimmer which often veils the town as one approaches the hill upon which it is built, a haze like that of a bonfire burning continually, sending out soft blue and grey mists, many shadows are in the walls and corners.

This old town is built on a hill, and the magnificent church is on the highest part of the rise, in the centre of a square of church-yard intersected with pathways along which everyone walks, to work or to play, dawdling or hurrying. Borough elections used to be held in the churchyard, and candidates addressed their constituents from an old tomb. It was a busy centre of life in the midst of death.

Near the church, leading directly to the gate and the tree-lined approach, is Church Street, a quiet street of real beauty. There are seventeenth-century houses, houses with projecting upper stories, the eighteenth-century Ceely House, and the old grammar school, now the museum. This county museum is a small, intimate and lovely place, with old country treasures displayed to perfection. The street curves round Parson's Fee to seventeenth-century cottages, almshouses called Hickman's Almshouses, endowed in 1695 but rebuilt, and, lower down the Prebendal House, once the home of John Wilkes on his marriage to Mary Meade.

Kingsbury, an open space, has an old inn, the Red Lion, part of which may go back to 1569. This square has been encroached upon in times past, by stalls or booths, and later by permanent dwellings erected there and obscuring other buildings.

In Bucks there are many examples of encroachments of houses in squares and broad streets. Perhaps a booth was raised by a market man, and this became a permanent structure, modified and added to, until it took complete possession. Aylesbury has shops built in the market square, backing on the fine buildings of the Bull's Head and the King's Head, and partly concealing these hostelries. A narrow alley between the buildings and the older hotels and shops is all that is left of the open space, and windows nearly meet across the way.

Kingsbury is the traditional site of the residence of Saxon and Norman kings, and the name of Castle Street shows there was once a fortress in the neighbourhood. There is a reference to

Henry II who granted a dwelling in Aylesbury to his otter hunter, for the service of supplying and providing him with three eels in winter, three green geese in summer, and straw for the King's chamber when he should visit Aylesbury.

The centre of Aylesbury is no longer Kingsbury but the big market square, on its sloping ground, with shops and inns around it and the County Hall at the foot. The County Hall was designed by Sir John Vanbrugh. The market square is the centre for county business as well as town affairs, for the Assizes are held at Aylesbury.

In the market square stands a clock tower which has replaced a small market house, pulled down in 1866, and this again replaced an "ancient dirty" market house built on oak pillars. Cock-fighting and badger-baiting used to take place here, and conjurers and fortune-tellers thronged the upper room.

It is a fine square, with its stone setts underfoot and its arresting statue of John Hampden with outstretched arm and sword in hand, at the top of the slope. Near is the statue of Lord Beaconsfield in his robes. At the foot of the square are two lions, with perhaps a small boy riding on the back of one and a woman resting against the plinth of the other. At this end of the square is the statue of Lord Chesham.

The county gaol was behind the present County Hall, and the debtors were allowed to parade in front of the County Hall, between boundary posts, to enjoy the "liberty of the stones." The White Hart Inn, which stood where now is an archway by the Town Hall, was next to the prison and it supplied beer for prisoners who could pay for the privilege.

As Aylesbury was a coaching and market town it had many fine inns, and the market square was surrounded by a goodly company, most of which have now gone. The splendid George Inn was pulled down in recent years, a great loss to the town.

The King's Head, which now belongs to the National Trust, was originally a monastery Guest House, and this beautiful old inn dates from before 1450. The lounge has a magnificent Tudor window, with small leaded panes and some of the original stained glass. It is oak mullioned and made in four divisions, with transoms. It is a marvel that the glass has remained intact in a market town that has had such warlike associations. There are figures of golden angels with spread wings holding shields with the arms of Henry VI and Margaret of Anjou. It is thought they were put there at their marriage in 1445. The window has too the arms of Edward, Prince of Wales, who was killed at the Battle of Tewkesbury. Five emblazoned shields were removed from this window a century ago, three of which are in the British Museum and two in Westminster Abbey.

This splendidly gay window once overlooked the market square, but now it looks on a narrow alley hidden by the encroaching shops. The room has wall-posts of oak, black with age and smoke, and the beams spring from them. Above the entrance to the courtyard, with its timbered archway and stable and coach-houses and steps leading to upper chambers, there is a modern oriel window. There is a seventeenth-century staircase with twisted balusters leading to the little upper room here.

The story above the oak-mullioned window overhangs, and is held by brackets. There are bright little window-boxes in summer, and always there is an air of well-being about the famous inn.

The King after whom the inn was named is Henry VIII, a constant visitor to the Guest House before his marriage to Anne Boleyn. Anne's father, the Earl of Wiltshire, was the Lord of the Manor of Aylesbury, and until her marriage Anne lived at the Manor House. When the monasteries were dissolved this Guest House was seized by Henry for the Crown, and the house given to the Earl of Wiltshire. Then it took Henry's name, and a painting of the King was on the hanging signboard until in recent years it was harmed by fire. In the seventeenth century the inn issued its own coinage, and some of these tokens can be seen in Aylesbury Museum.

The inn walls are made of wattle and daub, and there is a portion stripped from its covering of plaster and exhibited under glass in the lounge to show its interesting construction. One can see the foundation of wattle with the daub spread over it to form a thick strong wall. The meshes of the saplings are wide, and the skilful manner the walls were made is most striking.

Every inn has some kind of tale to tell, some legend of strange happenings, some memory of famous patrons, whether King or highwayman or soldier. In the Civil Wars the inns of Bucks were used by King and by Parliament as the battles surged and places changed hands. They were the headquarters of generals, and Oliver Cromwell's name is associated with several large inns. He made the King's Head, Aylesbury, his headquarters when the Parliament troops were stationed in the market town.

The old chair that was used by him is in one of the rooms. During recent renovations a hiding-place was discovered in the staircase, and there lay pieces of arms, a flintless horse pistol, and cavalry musket as used in Cromwell's army.

The Bull's Head is another old inn, situated in the market square, and hidden partly by later buildings. This good timbered inn was mentioned in 1481, but the older part of the present building is seventeenth-century. The lounge, which is the covered-in yard, has a gallery overlooking it, with bedrooms leading off, and one can lean over the oak beams to look at the life below, as in many old inns. Some of the bedrooms have timbered walls. A good deal of the Bull's Head has been skilfully rebuilt, using old material, and the long dining-room, with its black timbers and low ceiling and its baskets of beautiful flowers standing against the small-paned windows, is an attractive room. A little sitting-room has its own small staircase, and from its windows one can look to the busy market only a few yards away. The food at the inns in these days of austerity after the war is real market-town food—Aylesbury duck, green peas, and new potatoes. At Aylesbury there is no remoteness or greatness. It is as brisk and merry as a medieval town, with crooked ways and alleys and steps, and corners and surprises at every turn.

Twice a week, on Wednesdays and Saturdays, the market-place is filled with stalls laden with fruit and vegetables from farms and gardens. There are ribbon stalls and cloth stalls, china stalls and stalls of wooden spoons and tinware, the woodware made at Chesham. The flower stalls are heaped with every flower in season, larkspur and Iceland poppies in summer, primroses and polyanthus in spring, chrysanthemums in autumn, and holly at Christmas. The women pick flowers from their own gardens and make Victorian bouquets of charming variety, close-packed

219

with colour and only lacking the Victorian paper frill. Bachelors' buttons, pansies, carnations, and pinks, in a tight circle of colours, make these original bouquets which cost a shilling, and a better shillingsworth I have not seen. They are exactly right for Aylesbury market town.

The shifting crowd in and around the market stalls weaves like a shuttle through rows of green-shaded booths, with their varied colours of fruits and garments, their medley of pans and kettles. Among the stallkeepers is a white-haired colporteur with religious books which he carries from house to house in the villages during the week in a pack on his back.

It is noisy enough with the cries of the vendors, banging their wares together, the laughter of the people, the hooting of cars, and the rattle of cart wheels. There is something permanent about a country-town market; time seems unchanged, human nature, colour, noise, the chaffering are the same as in other days. The bawling of cheapjacks, the rattle of carts is the same, for many a humble little cart appears with a thin nag and a rough-coated driver at a market. At Aylesbury I saw a small four-wheeled cart, laden with vegetables, and the horse was caparisoned with scarlet and black harness, scarlet tabs on his back and scarlet reins, and the cart had colour on its bevelled sides.

Many of the towns in Buckinghamshire have market days once or twice a week, when produce is brought in by cart or old Ford car and sold in the streets or market-place. There is a continuity about these market days, they have been held for centuries, and the people cling to the privileges of the old charters which granted them the rights. The markets retain their old gaiety, but the cheapjack is less important and the quack and the preacher are not listened to with such reverence.

The control of the markets is in the hands of the Corporations, who often change their character with a loss of picturesque appearance but a gain in hygiene. No longer are cattle sold in the streets or horses paraded up and down, and one cannot walk among cows and stroke the noses of horses on a Monday morning.

Aylesbury cattle market is held in a square through the archway of the corn market. The great covered vans are brought there for the cattle to be exhibited in the pens on the slopes. Cows and bulls stand in the iron pens, sheep with startled eyes near them, and on the far side the calves and little pigs. The pigs are the only cheerful animals, resigned to their lot, and some of them sleep and some stand with alert little faces snuffling the straw. A cart drives up with a golden-haired child and a red bull calf. The little bull blorts sadly and struggles against its rope, and the child weeps.

In the round auction room the cattle are graded, five or six at a time, while people stand round the barriers. In one pen a great roan bull snorts, struggling wild-eyed, roaring at the crowd. In another six Herefordshire bullocks slide and push. Every animal gets near its fellow for companionship in that strange world of fear, away from the fields and gates and cowsheds of home.

The little shops of Aylesbury are fascinating in their variety, and they hold their own against the big stores which have come in recent years. A countryman, nearly ninety, told me that there were tallow chandlers at Aylesbury in his boyhood who made the thin long candles I remember we used for the Irish and farm boy's room. The tallow candles supplanted the rush lights which he used to make for his mother. Rush-lights were very cheap and they were made at home in bundles. A chandler, whose name was Kingham, kept a shop which the boys visited. Cotton made the wick and melted fat lay in a great bowl. The candles were dipped and lifted and dipped many times, till the layer of fat round the wick was big enough. They were tied by their wicks and hung up at the door of the shop.

When sheep were killed the mutton fat was sent to the tallow chandlers, who bought from all who had any to sell. The little boys ran down to the back premises of the chandlers' shops to watch the candle-dipping, which was one of the joys of life, like shoeing horses and killing pigs and tyring cart wheels. It was a malodorous place, which made it even more attractive.

Everywhere one goes in Aylesbury there is a glimpse of the beautiful cruciform church, which stands high with its tower soaring above the roofs. The tower is Early English, with Perpendicular battlements, and above them is a small lead clock-tower and spire, an incongruous addition of the time of Charles II. The church was built between 1200 and 1250, but it is thought that a church stood on this important site even as far back as the seventh century.

There is a Norman font, the "Aylesbury font," with a border of floral ornament and fluting below. The cup-shaped bowl rests on a square base, scalloped in high relief. It is the finest font in the county. During the dangers of the Civil War it was hidden away for safety.

At Aylesbury Church I enjoy most of all the alabaster monument, brought from deserted Quarrendon, of Lady Lee and her children, whom I go to see as if they were my friends. This Elizabethan family has lived through the centuries in the warmth of the lovely English marble, with a bunch of real flowers for their enjoyment and delectation. The roses are placed in a glass vase on the tiny altar before which the lady kneels, and it is said that ever since the day the tomb was set up fresh red flowers have been brought to adorn the place, at her request. I have seen geraniums, carnations, roses on the tomb, which is no tomb.

Lady Lee kneels on a cushion with tasselled corners in her full skirt and buttoned bodice, with little buttons on the high neck-band. Round her neck is a pleated ruff. She wears a bonnet with a veil hanging stiffly down. Her face is homely, kind, and sensible.

Behind her are the two tiny figures of her baby boys, Henry and John, small chubby infants, swaddled in bands, for they are Chrisom children. Their eyes are open, curls peep from their frilled lace-edged baby bonnets, as they lie on their cushions.

Behind them kneels their sister Mary, a young charming version of the mother. She has her dress buttoned to her neck, and she wears a ruff and a pretty diapered bonnet with a veil covering her hair. The date is 1584.

Part of the inscription runs:

A Knight haer feere Sir Henry Lee he hight,
To whom she bare three Impes which has to name
John, Henry, Mary, slayn by fortune's spight,
First two being yong which caused ther parents woe,

The third in flower and prime of all her yeares.
All three do rest wihin this marble stone.
By which the frailties of worldly joyes appear.
Goode frend, stick not to strew with crimson floures
This marble tombe wherin her cinders rest,
For sure her ghost lyves with the heavenly powers,
And guerdon hathe of virtuous life possest.

So people strew the crimson flowers at her tomb and she
kneels for ever among flowers of memory, with her three Imps,
at the market town of Aylesbury.

In the vestry there is an ancient piece of furniture, a heavy
oak cupboard which is the oldest vestment cupboard in the
country, and still used for the surplices of the choir.

The parish registers of Aylesbury Church date from 1564.
There are two quotations I should like to give, for they interest
me personally.

On 23 March 1734 Philip Thomas was executed for horse-
stealing. He confessed, and "he rode to the place of execution
in his shroud."

My father used to tell us of horse-stealing in his own youth
when the penalty was death. My grandfather's brood mare was
stolen one winter night. She was taken from the stable across
the yard and led away down the hills to the turnpike. There was
a hue and cry after the thief, who was tracked many miles by
the prints in the snow. The stage coach saw him but he got
away.

"He would have been hanged if they had caught him," said
they. For a horse was to a man part of his life, loved as a son.

There is an entry for November 1745. "The Parish was
sadly surprised through fear of an immediate visitt by the
Hyland Rebells from who Good Lord deliver us."

At Aylesbury the great white ducks famous throughout the
world are bred, and I went to see the duck farm where Mr
Weston, the breeder, keeps his birds. In an ordinary street
among the houses there is this delightful farm with its dozens
of snowy inhabitants. Water runs in little streams, and pools are
formed and islands, with ducks wandering about, and trees to

shade the company. The white ducks of this breed waddle in a regal manner with their heads held high and their intelligent eyes glancing boldly and proudly.

Mr Weston's great-grandfather was the original breeder of these special ducks, and for a hundred and fifty years the family have bred and reared and shown their ducks; they have exported them to all the countries of the world, to be the origins of more Aylesbury ducks, in China, in Africa, and Australia and India.

Before the war one could see about 2,000 ducks on this little farm, but only about 200 were there when I stood admiring them, for the food position made it very difficult to rear them. The great birds, with their long deep bodies and straight backs, walked with a certain pride, and none of the sudden jerky movements of ordinary little ducks. One pair of prize ducks weighed twenty-eight pounds, and even the young ducks at ten weeks old weigh six or seven pounds.

There was a flock of hens for hatching the ducks, and I was glad to see this motherly care instead of the hard-hearted step-mothering of the incubator. Beautiful things are ducks, clever things are ducks, and this duck farm is a place where I could lean over a gate for a few hours contemplating the family and hearing tales about them. It is an honour to be a county duck.

It must be very satisfying to be the breeder of a world-famous stock such as the Aylesbury ducks, and Mr Weston's father, who is over eighty, has the quick eye for seeing the possibilities of ducklings which appear alike to the ordinary person. He can point out a promising duckling who will make a winner at the show and perhaps carry off a gold medal.

At Aylesbury too, over a hundred years ago, dairy shorthorns were bred by Mr Fowler, whose prize shorthorns, Buttercup I, II, and III, were the famous mothers of shorthorns.

Aylesbury has the Chilton Cottage cheese factory, and a distributing and pasteurizing centre for milk to which the farmers send their supplies. Nestlé's vast milk centre is in the town, taking milk from the countryside. There is a light-engineering works too.

The most important works are the printing works of Hazell,

Ellesborough Church and the Vale of Aylesbury

Watson, and Viney. The great airy well-lighted rooms house machines which are a delight to watch. We saw the Linotype machine, with bars of lead lying near for making the type, and the compositor sitting with his manuscript, tapping out the letters which were made by the machine. Of all the various machines we saw in many rooms I think this was the most wonderful, but each piece of machinery acted with a kind of human intelligence, so that I could scarcely believe that when the people who tended them had gone away the machines were silent. Surely they go on with their work making strange books for themselves!

We saw the whole process of making a book, from the beginning when the galley proofs are printed, to the page proofs, printed from type set out in horizontal position, divided into pages, and printed on sheets of paper, to the cutting of the sheets and the stitching and binding.

Machines with hands lifted the sheets by suction, and machines folded the papers and dropped pages over each other to make a magazine. We saw the way magazines are made, with the colour printing of the pictures. There were school books being made in thousands, Shaw's plays, Lenin's works, John Wesley's hymns, Shakespeare's sonnets, *Debrett's Peerage*, and passport covers; piles of blue, maroon, and olive-green covers were waiting for the bindings, with strawboard and muslin. Girls stitched the backs together with machines which used great cream-coloured bobbins of thread.

Some of the work was done by hand, and a skilful woman arranged many pages for the beginnings of the books, with only a fraction of an inch between, so that they looked like a fine fan. She passed the paste over and fastened them in the books. Some illustrations have to be put in by hand.

The finished books, damp from the newly pasted bindings, were kept in clamps for the night to dry. Then they were wrapped in their jackets and packed for the publishers.

I decided that the best kind of factory is a printing works in the market town of Aylesbury, but when I asked a boy what book he was working upon he did not know or care, and he never stopped to glance at the tale.

From Cymbeline's Mount

We visited the recreation rooms for the workpeople, the reading-rooms, with comfortable chairs and an open fire, the games rooms for boys and girls, and dancing-room. Life is made very easy and pleasant in this world of books set in the county town near cornfields and farms and pastures.

Akeman Street, the Roman road, runs through Aylesbury, along the Vale, with few hamlets, to Waddesdon. It crosses the river Thame, near Quarrendon, the place of a lost church and manor house, and it passes through cornfields and meadowland to the wooded country and the hills at Waddesdon.

Waddesdon has all the golden-red warmth of other Buckinghamshire villages, but it has not the particular charm of the little collections of cottages one sees. It is a model village, up-to-date in many respects, a village built when Baron Ferdinand de Rothschild bought the estate in 1874. Yew trees, tall trimmed hedges, and neat gabled houses picturesquely designed give an air of solid comfort and prosperity to the place.

The church, massive and ancient, stands on a rise, with the village clustered around it. Great haystacks under the shade of two golden elms press close to the fence of the churchyard. Hay, corn, and church are very close to one another and the corn seems to keep the church warm.

It is a splendid building, and it was especially beautiful the first time I saw it. There had been a christening in the morning and the nave was banked with yellow and bronze chrysanthemums, and in every window stood a jar of flowers. Outside in the churchyard the chestnut trees were dropping their fans of yellow leaves, so that the ground was covered as if with a carpet. We stepped through the Norman doorway, out of the bright autumn sunshine, with the blue sky and the golden leaves, to the softer light of the church with all its chrysanthemums glowing there.

The air was scented with chestnuts and the pungent odour of the flowers, with wood smoke and wet moss, so that the church was warm and fragrant and alive. These things are remembered with nostalgic longing. We smell the tang of the autumn, the heart-stirring scent of chrysanthemums and moss, and we are carried back to other scenes and other days. So the church of

Waddesdon brought back a thousand distinct memories of villages and cottages and gardens.

There were Norman pillars in the nave with little buds carved round two or three of the arches and faces of men between them. The ancient font had footstools around it where godparents had been kneeling a short time before. Among the chrysanthemums' tangled yellow petals by the chancel arch lay a stone giant seven feet long. This knight in armour had his feet on a lion, and his hands clasped round a sword. He was decked out as if he had been a guest at the christening. Somebody had welcomed him with flowers on his head and in his hands.

The manor house of the Rothschilds, Waddesdon Manor, stands high on a far hill, with encircling woods. It is over 600 feet high, and it resembles a French château on the ridge. The woods are fir and oak, elm and ash, with box trees growing between as undergrowth.

We climbed the long steep hill towards the Winchendons, and went along the spine of the hill, with wonderful scenery on both sides, as the land drops away and rises again. Far away we could see the line of the Chilterns, and Ellesborough Church on its mound, and Whiteleaf Cross, and the pass which is the valley of Wycombe, and Coombe Hill near Wendover. The Quainton Hills were visible on the other side of the ridge. The great pile of the manor stood out among the trees, with a bowl of woods and fields below it. In the valley a fine herd of cattle was grazing, a pedigree herd.

A countryman of Waddesdon told us that the wooded hills across the near valley on the Rothschild estate were once fields and farmland with few trees. Full-grown trees were uprooted and planted to make those magnificent woods in the shortest possible time. Sometimes these trees were over forty feet high, and special carts were made to carry them. Percheron mares were brought over from France to draw these great loads. Many of the villagers still remember seeing the strange sights of those days. They say that most of the trees survived their transportation, and they continue their long lives on that hill slope and park where they were planted.

"He was very fond of trees and he moved them when he saw

those he liked, just as common people would carry off a flower," said one. The house was finished in 1883, with its woods and gardens. The village was rebuilt, old houses pulled down and new ones erected, but the spirit of the place remained the same, the traditions were remembered, for the rebuilding of a house does not destroy the continuity of time.

On the ridge, with its wide view of the manor and the countryside, is a model farm with an avenue of evenly spaced chestnut trees, also built by Baron de Rothschild. By the side of the road is a tiny chapel with tombstones, a Strict Baptist chapel.

The church of Over Winchendon is hidden in a fold of the hill, down a lane, with trees and the high wall of the little Jacobean house called The Wilderness near it. This house is the remnant of the manor house that was the home of the Whartons in the seventeenth century. It is one wing, and the foundations of the rest can be traced in the grass. Once it had Dutch gardens and an orangery. Now the orangery is a garage, and the windows are filled in. A long timbered barn covered with ivy backs to the churchyard, and there is pastureland with horses close to the church.

This is a most interesting and delightful little church, simple and charming, and the view from the churchyard is unsurpassed in beauty. A Norman doorway has pillars at each side, one twisted like barley sugar, the other carved, and through it we entered the tiny warm happy little building. This church has a very old pulpit, pre-Reformation, with three carved panels like windows of the Late Decorated period. Between nave and chancel there is a fifteenth-century oak screen, and on the high wall above the chancel arch is a helmet set above a stone unicorn's head.

The pulpit and the screen have been harmed by nails in the past as every generation has nailed up the decorations for the church festivals. The vicar told us that over six hundred old nails had recently been removed from the wood and many were taken out earlier. These are hand-made heavy old nails made by the smiths of centuries ago.

At the west end of the church are some sixteenth-century pews, grey as lichen, smooth as silk. This silky smoothness of

228

old wood, produced by hundreds of years of rubbing, is very fascinating to feel. There is the same silkiness in the wood of the old classroom at Eton College.

The font of this little church is Norman and over it is a carved lid which may be the sounding-board of a pulpit. There is an aumbry, with its original oak lining, in the chancel wall.

Outside the church, on the south wall of the chancel, are three mass dials, with their tiny centre holes in which a stick was placed. They are divided with twenty-four lines, and this would give the time of day. These mass clocks appear on the south walls of many of the churches in Bucks. They fell into disuse when clocks became general.

The three bells are each inscribed "Richard Chandler made me 1675." As we waited the old bellringer came in to ring one of the bells. He was perturbed over the damp which had penetrated the church in recent storms, and we all looked very solemnly at the streaks down the corner of the walls.

We went along the high ridge, enchanted by the views, recognizing hills far away and well-known landmarks, for this is quite the loveliest ridgeway in Buckinghamshire, we decided. There are many roads along the spines of the hills, but perhaps no other in the county has such a landscape spread out on either side as this.

Then we dipped down a precipitous lane to the thatched village of Nether Winchendon. This colourful village lies in a hollow, hidden away completely to itself. The walls of the cottages are washed with an orange colour which gives a sudden warmth and exotic richness to the little place among its trees. There are thatched roofs and dormer windows and flowery gardens, like a village in a folk-tale. One cottage had flaming marigolds growing against its orange walls. Another had snapdragons of tawny hue.

The Church of St Nicholas—surely this is an appropriate village for Father Christmas—is in the midst of the cottages, and it is gay with ivy berries and roses and green mounds and old grey walls. It is a lovely little church, with whitewashed walls and brass candelabras, and red brick floor, oak seats, and a tiny gallery. The floor of the tower has cobbles in the floor like a stable yard, and there is an ancient west door. The paving stones of the porch have a deep hollow worn in them by many feet through the centuries. It is one of the floors that have not been changed and it is moving to see the trace of generations of men who have passed there. Little openwork stone windows look out to the flowers in the churchyard, and there are stone seats in that restful porch.

Inside the church there are box pews like little rooms where people can sit round the walls in privacy. I regret the passing of box pews.

At the end is a gallery on two wooden pillars with the Royal arms in front and coats-of-arms painted in black lozenges on the walls. The little gilded organ is there, and a framed painted board with the following inscription of deep piety:

"This clock was given by the will of Jane Beresford, Widow, lady of this Manor, that it may remind all who hear it to spend their Time in an honest discharge of their Calling, and in the Worship of God that Repentance may come not too late. 1772."

A modern brass on an altar tomb is an engraved portrait of Francis Tyringham in uniform.

Outside the great elms, the cooing doves, and the little orange-coloured village, with its bucket and well, its marigolds and the tiny green with a pillar box in the centre, make as gentle an English picture as one could imagine.

We climbed upward and onward, until we reached the summit of Ashendon Hill. There by a gate under a great spreading elm we rested and stared across the country with a farm labourer who joined us. It was obviously one of those "gates with a view," and I think of the gate near Penn with its vista of the towers of Windsor, and the gate near Oving with its outlook to the Quainton Hills, and the gates I knew in childhood where we involuntarily rested and gazed over the hills. This was such a place, by the spreading elm of huge girth whose roots ran into the field like grey stone ribs. Although it was Sunday, our new acquaintance wore his working-clothes, for he was just returning from the harvest field. Men were down below on the hillside working at the elevator, struggling to catch the corn before the next storm broke across. Together we gazed at the Chilterns spread out in

a thin blue line, indigo and ultramarine, with Bledlow, Ellesborough, and the Oxford hills to the right of them.

Before us the fields dropped in ridges down to the cornland,
and some fields were brown, newly ploughed, and some were
green, where cattle grazed, and some had sheep and some had
shocks of corn, and some were pale gold with over-ripe barley
wet and waiting to be reaped, perhaps left to the weather. The
sheep had a restive uneasy look, and I inquired about them, to
the content of the farm man. He too was watching them, for
they had only just been bought and they were turned out to a
new land, tasting the sweet grass, exploring for the first time
their new pastures. I was glad I had noticed their disquiet and
not forgotten my early country lore.

From the opposite side of the vantage post we held there was
a continuation of the panorama, with Brill and Quainton.

"I reckon this is one of the best sights in Bucks," said our
new friend proudly. "It's said to be the third-highest place."

Just across the road was a very old red brick cottage, which
once may have been an inn. It had a water-butt, and a stable,
and a mighty pile of firewood, and this fine view from all its
windows. It was a little place with many memories, I could tell,
and not all of them happy ones either.

The small church of Ashendon is slightly below this highest
point, among the cottages and embowering trees. From the
churchyard one can get another view across the Vale, as if one
were on top of the world.

The Norman font has a carved lid, like a cage of intricate
wood, a Jacobean piece of work. The roof of the church is
medieval with strange faces below. In an archway is a thirteenth-
century knight, but I liked best a short epitaph to an Eagleton:

> Life's uncertain,
> Death is shuer,
> Sin is a wound,
> And Christ the cuer.
>   1661

Across the road from the church are cottages whose gardens
are so tightly filled with asters, mauve, blue, lavender, red, that

somebody must have spilled some packets of seeds there. They make a delicate rainbow mist of colours under the apple trees. The little boys, dressed in their Sunday suits, swing on a gate and wave shyly to me. I came away from Ashendon, leaving a bit of my heart behind.

CHAPTER XVI

HARDWICK AND WHITCHURCH

THE Buckingham road from Aylesbury passes over the river Thame, which is a very shallow stream here, flowing among flat meadows which could become like marshes after heavy floods. In these fields, near the Holman's Bridge, was the battle of Aylesbury in 1642. I always think of those lost men fighting so valiantly there in the marshy ground as I travel along that smooth highway. The discovery of this battlefield is a strange incident, for one would naturally think that such a momentous fight would have been talked about and remembered in every cottage home through the years and that after the battle the bodies would have been recovered.

It was not until 1818 that men digging for gravel in the meadow by Holman's Bridge discovered a large number of human bones. They were collected and buried in one common tomb at Hardwick churchyard, on the hill. No weapons were found, but it is known that they were so scarce in the Civil Wars the dead were searched after a battle and weapons used again.

There, under a great yew tree, by the south wall of the tower of Hardwick is a green-lichened stone chest with the following words engraved upon it, words which are particularly moving when one thinks of the wars during this century, and the hope each time that this is the last conflict.

"Within are deposited the bones of 247 persons which were discovered A.D. 1818, buried in a field adjoining to Holman's Bridge near Aylesbury.

"From the history and appearance of the place where they were found they were concluded to be the remains of those officers and men who perished in an engagement fought A.D. 1642 between troops of K. Charles I under the command of Prince Rupert, and the garrison who held Aylesbury for the Parliament.

"Enemies from their attachment to opposite leaders and to

233

opposite standards in the sanguinary conflict of that civil war, they were together united in its fury, united in one common slaughter, they were buried in one common grave, close to the spot where they had lately stood in arms against each other.

"After the lapse of more than a century and a half these bones were collected and deposited, together still, in consecrated ground.

"May the memory of brave men be respected, may our country never again be called to take part in a contest such as that which this tablet records."

North of Aylesbury the country changes, and the smell is different. It has the scent of richness, of farms, and flowers.

"I always notice a good smell in this region, like a warm country farmyard, with all the flowers a-blowing in the garden," said a Bucks countryman to me, sniffing the air.

Hardwick Church has this fragrance, like an old-fashioned parlour, where there is good furniture, and dried rose leaves, and the warmth of generations of fires and of people. The church, with its white tower and towerlet, seems to rise into the blue sky with happiness and joy.

There are cottages grouped round the churchyard and the flowers close to it add to the sweetness of the place. These cottages have little gables and overhanging stories, and many-shaped windows, cottages of thatch and brick and timber.

Close to the churchyard are haystacks, some of them half-cut, and great barns with red roofs. There are cattle standing in the farmyards, and once when we went the first lambs were bleating near the church. It is a little agricultural village, with a pump on the village green, and a good sound life of its own.

The Vale of Aylesbury, near Hardwick, has fossils in its Kimmeridge clay. They were found by ploughmen and others draining the land. The turnpike was lowered through a hill of clay, and the ammonites and bivalves discovered. The village people have many of them embedded in their houses, built into the walls of their homes. I like to see a fossil stone or a great shell ornamenting a cottage to give it individuality. In the north when people found these fossils they set them in little rockeries by their doors. The fertility of the Vale is due to this Kimmeridge Clay in the subsoil. At Hartwell the clay is covered with beds of limestone which produces good soil.

The road from Hardwick to Whitchurch is very broad with wide green margins which have their own paths. Many great elms grow by the roadside in the high hedges. One can almost say there is an avenue of elms the whole way from Aylesbury to Buckingham.

At the top of the hill as one enters the village of Whitchurch is the White Swan Inn, which is as pretty as any in Buckinghamshire. It is thatched and the old brick and timber walls have a red rose tree climbing up towards the roof. There are outhouses, barns, and penthouse, all thatched, and a box tree grows at the side. The painted sign, a white swan on blue water, is fresh and lovely in that windy spot. On the opposite side of the road there is a mellowed red brick wall round an old house, and along the outside of this wall there are so many rose trees in full bloom in summer that it seems as if you enter a garden when you come to this village.

All along the village street are diverse cottages, thatched and plain, with many varieties of roof and window, mixed with a few Victorian little villas, and through gaps and alleys one gets a view of glorious country stretching away for many miles, the Vale of Aylesbury, blue as chicory. Blue in the sign of the White Swan Inn is repeated in this landscape.

Raised a little above the road is the old courthouse, now a private house with a modern weathervane of horses and hounds on its gable. It has an overhanging upper story and original stone and brick chimney stack. There is another interesting old house which has been made into cottages at the corner of Church Lane. It too has the overhanging upper story. The old schoolhouse which is sixteenth-century has an oriel window. There are many thatched cottages, some with brand-new thatch, and all with little windows peeping through the eyebrows of straw. It is a delight to walk down this village street, to call at the saddler's, or to turn up the little lanes which go to the church. The sixteenth-century tower of this grand church has a sundial with 1828 carved upon its face. The shadow was pointing to 3.15 that sunny winter afternoon when I first saw it, and I looked at it with admiration for it was the largest and clearest sundial I had ever seen. Inside the church was cold and plain and severe, with little colour except the scarlet and blue light which fell through a richly coloured modern window, the only coloured glass in the church except a tiny bunch of flame in a high window.

This Church of St John the Evangelist is early thirteenth-century, but throughout the centuries there have been additions and changes. There is a wall painting of St Margaret fading away as are many of the wall paintings. In the chancel are poppy-head stalls. There is a beautiful west doorway, thirteenth-century work, with a pointed arch. Under the tower there is an ancient little door, bolted by a large wooden bolt. To draw the bolt there is a nail in the door which moves along a slot in an ingenious manner. The floor of this church is stone, unadorned and bare. There is much plain local stone about Whitchurch village, and the floor of the nave, worn and hollowed by countless feet, brought a feeling of strength and faith. Under the tower there is a seventeenth-century chest, with panel sides and front, and a drawer with three locks. We also saw a large oak cupboard, painted in delicate design and colour in a very modern manner with baskets of flowers and bright birds and roses; it is said to be Elizabethan.

In the chancel is a hand pointing to the earth where a lady lies buried. There is a similar device in North Marston Church.

There is a great memorial to a farmer, John Westcar, and carved on it are the farmer, a bullock, and three sheep. It is in memory of one who farmed on the famous Creslow pastures near, and although it may seem out of place in this ancient church I was glad it was there. John Westcar farmed at Creslow, the great pasture country near Whitchurch, from 1779 to 1825.

Bolebec Castle, a grass-covered mount and a bailey, is in a field in Whitchurch. There is a path up the great mound which is a natural hill with earthworks to make its defences. The bailey is separated from it by the road. The mount is defended by a drop of about twenty-one feet, with a broad ditch around it, beyond which is a second ridge. Everything has disappeared of the buildings of the castle, except the remains of a wall which show through the turf, and some of the foundations are still there.

This old castle belonged to Hugh de Bolebec, and it is thought that the earthworks were thrown up by him in King Stephen's reign. The land on the slope opposite is called Market Hill, for by tradition a market was supposed to have been held there when the great castle was flourishing. The terms, Lord's Garden and Lord's Strip, are still used for part of the land, which is now a market garden, from the Lord of the Manor's day. Now the castle is a grassy mound, with knapweed and harebells. At the edge of the moat in the field called Lord's Garden there is a spring, famous in the district for its water, which is called Fair Alice. Another spring near Oving is called Old Woman. Many of these clear, fresh springs in Buckinghamshire have their Christian names, for they were revered and honoured— as the spring at North Marston and one at Hartwell.

To the south of the church there is a fine Jacobean house standing in its gardens raised high above the road. This is Kempson's and at the farm a short distance away there is a pedigree herd of dairy shorthorns.

These gardens were brilliant with beds of flowers when we saw them, sweet williams and slender columbines in golden and tawny clumps, blue anchusa and red pinks with their colours floating in the air around the little green lawns. At the bottom of the grassy walk, overhanging the high bank of the garden, was a great chestnut tree, and at the top a walnut tree, the sign of a good farmhouse.

The lovely old house has an original stone gable and fine chimney stacks. We went into the field and saw the herd of thirty pedigree shorthorn milking cows, and then we went to the cowsheds with stalls and windows and water laid on, all very bright and clean. Each cow had her rations of chopped mangolds ready in her own bucket. Milking is done by hand here, which is a pleasure to find, for many of the farms—especially the very modern ones—use machinery. The milk goes to the village and the remainder to Nestlé's factory at Aylesbury.

We heard of the champion cow, Hestoe Barrington Duchess 37th, who gives eight gallons a day, and we went into the calf

place to stroke her small daughter, a red calf of good colour.
We saw the shorthorn bulls and the young two-year-old bull
and the little bull calf, each in a strawed chamber by itself. There
is a great thatched barn with timbers across its roof, a very fine
old place, in one part of which the cow calves are kept, but most
of the buildings are modern. We saw the dairy, with sterilizer
and the electrical milk-cooler and the long list of the cows with
their milk yield.

There are about thirty cattle in this attested pedigree herd,
and the farm is self-supporting, as barley and peas are grown for
feed and very little has to be bought.

Near Chetwode we saw a fine herd of Friesian cattle, my
favourite breed. I was told that dairy shorthorns are the most
favoured cows in Buckinghamshire, and next to them the
Friesians.

I went up a little alley between the houses into a wheelwright's yard to meet Mr Stephen Capp, wheelwright, musician,
undertaker, and village craftsman. The long workroom had
rows of tools, calipers, T-squares, mouldings, saws, gouges hanging on the wall over the carpenter's benches, where lay a brown
canvas carpenter's bag and divided boxes and nails. A ladder
went to the loft where timbers lay and a row of awls hung from
a beam. The ground was littered with shavings, thick curls of
which were deep on the floor. There was a good smell of wood
in this room. I saw a pair of yokes and chains for milking, such
as I remember farm men using, but against the wall were the
most interesting things, three 'cellos which Mr Capp was putting in order. Music is his hobby and playing the 'cello his
delight.

Mr Capp was working there, but he came out to the yard
where some carts waited for wheels. The tyring platform for
putting rims on wheels was in the ground of the yard. It has a
hole for the hub of the wheel to enter. Great care is needed in
putting on the tyre I was told, lest the felloes should be bent.
When the iron tyre is put around the wheel it is held by a
"tyring dog," a long handle with prongs to hold the tyre. If the
tyre is too tight the wheel gets a slight "camp" on it. A country
wheelwright is very proud of his own work, for he is a craftsman

above everything. Even the carts, in different parts of Buckinghamshire, have each their own kind of staple and tipping-bar,
so that a countryman can tell by looking at a heavy cart where
it has come from.

He sat in the parlour with us in his shirtsleeves, and he talked
to us, and the time flew past as his melodious voice went on. In
this little room was the good old furniture of other days, all
made in Buckinghamshire. An oak grandfather clock in the
corner, lovely old Windsor chairs, each with its own character,
one with a twisted rail across the back, another with a little boss
of brass inserted in its wheel, a third with a beautiful splat.
There was a hanging carved bookcase filled with books of Victorian days, the *Life of Gladstone*, etc. This bookcase was made
by Mr Capp in his spare time, every bit fitted and carved with
decorative acorns and leaves. The shelves over the fireplace
were his own early work, made as a present to his sweetheart.

On the walls hung the photograph of a cricketer in flannels
and, very modestly half-hidden, a small picture of Mr Capp
with his 'cello.

"Never a lot was spent on me," he told us. "I left school at
ten, and for years my mother kept a little slip of paper with
'This is to certify Stephen Capp has attained the proficiency of
4th Standard.' "

He told us of his musical days, when he played the 'cello,
"my brother Henry the violin, brother William the clarinet,
George Carter the cornet."

The country musicians used to go for miles to play and sing.
They would walk five miles there and five miles back, carrying
their instruments, including the 'cello, for rehearsals only, at night
after their work was done. They had walked hundreds of miles to
play their tunes. They went to Aylesbury, North Marston,
Winslow, and all the places round. The 'cello was an awkward
instrument to carry along the rough roads at night, and he made
a green baize bag for it. Most of his memories were of music,
for he had been a great player. He had had never a lesson and his
technique was all wrong for players nowadays, he told us sadly.
So he had given it up, but he was rarely interested in instruments.

He had seven 'cellos, which he was putting right, restoring them with loving care.

He told us some country tales, the kind of tale which I used to hear when I was a child, the country wit of the old people.

Two old men decided to live together at Stewkley. They were not related but they thought they could get on very well together. However they got so across one another as time went on that they had everything separate. Even the fire in the great inglenook was divided, and each had his own little fire in the corner of the fireplace, and sat in front of his own blaze.

One night one of the little fires went out, and the old man leaned across to the other to get a light.

"No, you don't," said the owner of the small blaze.

"All right, Will," said the other old man, taking out his steel and tinder-box, "all right. I can nick. I can nick."

And he proceeded to make a spark, by "nicking" his steel.

The sharp sound made by the flint on steel was called "nicking," and the saying "I can nick" came from this tale.

Mr Capp spoke of country expressions, and he told a tale which he heard from his grandfather relating to his great-grandfather, which brings the story to about 1780.

A well-to-do friend, Master Kimblett, came to see his great-grandfather, Master Capp, who was in money difficulties.

"How are you getting on, Master Capp?" he asked.

"I'm in trouble," replied Master Capp. "I want a little help."

"How's that?"

"Well, I've got a long ladder to rear up, and I can't raise it, and I want a little help to get it up."

This surely was the most delicate way of applying for a small loan, and I am glad to say the great-grandfather got what he wanted.

"It was the cunning way of putting it," added Mr Capp to me, and he used the word "cunning" in the old way, meaning clever—"Let my right hand forget its cunning" in the Bible.

The country cure used for a cut in the old days was a dried puff-ball gathered when it had the dark powder within.

Once his arm was badly cut by a chisel which slipped and

Aylesbury market. John Hampden's statue in foreground

went into the flesh so that a fountain of blood flew up from an open vein. The lady of the house bound it with Madonna lily leaves soaked in brandy, and this cured it.

For a small cut a cobweb was used as in Elizabethan days.

He took us to a small whitewashed room in an outbuilding where he had a little museum of things he loved. They hung round the walls and stood on a table among a litter of tools. Some day he would like to hang them properly and make a nice little place for them.

There was an "idle-back" which was used with a ratchet over a fire to tilt the kettle without taking it off the hook, as used in cottages and farmhouses. On a shelf were wooden bobbin-winders, pillow-lace bobbins, and patterns for making lace, all pricked ready by an old lace-maker of Buckinghamshire whom he knew.

Underneath was a shelf of old books bought at a sale of a man recently dead, whom they all loved—a Hebrew grammar and volumes of Milton. In a corner stood a great cart umbrella, with whalebone ribs, and a shepherd's crook belonging to a shepherd Mr Capp had known. This crook Mr Capp had used when he was the old Shepherd in the Nativity Play at the village church.

There were flints and steels and tinder-boxes. There was a delightful picture, a small portrait in oils, of a man with hooked nose and chin wearing the dress of a countryman of about 1700. In his round hat he wore a sprig of holly and he carried another spray. It was Old Jordan of Thame, who was perhaps a farrier or a horse doctor.

There was a swingel-and-flail for threshing, the staff of beech, the flail of blackthorn or crab or whitethorn, a wood that does not split easily. He had made it himself for threshing some beans lately.

A little wooden barrel, called a baver keg, bound in copper, with a cork in the bunghole and a tiny handle to carry it, was used by the harvesters in the hayfield, and made by local coopers. This cask held a quart, but another held only a pint. Each man had his own little barrel and he drank from the bunghole.

Another piece of Bucks craftsmen's work was a lading-can

Aylesbury font—late Norman work

of sycamore wood for testing home-brewed beer. The sweet-wort was the first drawings of the home-brew, and the man who helped to brew the ale used to sip from this wooden ladle, tasting and trying, till at last he rolled home tipsy. These lading-cans were made in Chesham.

Mr Capp showed us an ingenious example of the blacksmith's art. It was an iron matchbox with a bird perched on the side. When the bird was touched it dipped its sharp beak into a small orifice in the box and brought out a match. It was used at an inn to prevent men from carrying off the boxes of matches.

"It's a cunning bird," said Mr Capp. "It's dodgy, this is."

Stone beer-bottles with wickerwork around them for the harvesters stood there, such as I remember, and woven baskets large, and flat as hats, which were used for bread. These were made in the district. In my childhood we had two of these bread baskets in the dairy. They were lined with linen napkins and pieces of bread were placed within for the table. Their edges were formed of curving wicker, like torchon lace.

A fascinating device I saw was a long cylindrical green phial which women of two centuries ago filled with salt and small cut-out scraps of printed cotton, flowers or leaves or patterns, as an amusement for winter nights. With a long stick or pin they brought the coloured scraps next to the glass and held them there by salt. Slowly they made a pattern up the sides of the tube, keeping the materials fixed until the bottle was full. The appearance then was of a brilliantly painted bottle. It was hung over the fireplace by a string for the admiration of friends and neighbours. Even the green glass medicine phial was interesting.

Peck measures, made of oak with willow bottoms, were in this little country museum. I saw some of these recently in a seedsman's shop in Beaconsfield. They are going out of use now for most goods are sold by weight, and there was the chance of cheating by a sharp dealer. The measures were filled and stroked across with a stick called a strickle, hence the measure "a strike." These peck and bushel measures were made in Chesham as were also the butter-prints and other articles for use on farms.

At the foot of the hill that rises to Winslow, beyond Whit-church on the Buckingham road, the margin is even wider, for an old road curves across a stream where there are water-hens and forget-me-nots. Near the top of the hill there are two cottages raised on a bank above the road. One is rose-red with herringbone brick, the other is snow-white. Both are thatched and the patch of green in front is their garden for there is no division from the road. Roses and phlox and lilies grow there on the hillside.

Winslow has many cottages thatched and round-windowed, with green doors and flights of steps. The church has a fifteenth-century porch like a room, with a wonderful oak ceiling carved with angels and bosses, a porch where one wants to linger, and where one could almost live. Above the porch in a niche is St Laurence and there are grotesque faces with crooked mouths ogling the churchgoers.

In the chancel is a richly carved chair like a throne. The pulpit, which is the upper tier of a Jacobean three-decker pulpit, rests on the backs of four hawk-like birds, with their feathers all finely worked. In a glass case was a collection of Elizabethan books, locked up for safety so that we could only admire the bindings—a Bible of 1611, *Life and Works of Bishop Jewell*, of 1611, a *Book of Homilies* of 1762, and a black-letter *Commentary* of 1508.

Curfew has rung from the tower at Winslow since 1068, it is proudly said, although the tower was rebuilt in the fourteenth century.

All round the churchyard is a hedge of yew dividing the village of graves from the little old houses with their narrow paths. As one stands in the quiet church footsteps go pattering along the pathways outside the walls.

The seventeenth-century Bell Hotel stands squarely facing the long row of houses and shops, and near it is the George Hotel which has a long beautiful balcony of intricate ironwork. It is said this craftsman's work came from Claydon House. Cromwell's men were billeted here in the Civil War, and the Bell one of the old inns with legends of Dick Turpin, who perhaps visited this favourite house.

CHAPTER XVII

LONELY PLACES

ON low-lying ground near Aylesbury, by Akeman Street, is the tiny hamlet of Fleet Marston, "running marshland." This is a parish of three farms and some cottages and a very small church, with about 300 acres of land. We went across a field by a farm gate and a pond to reach the solitary little church in a clump of trees alone in the meadow. It looked like a barn belonging to one of the distant farms, I thought, as I threaded my way through the rough wet grass, keeping a wary eye on a great Friesian bull which was watching me with interest from the shadow of the church.

The little grey building with its old tombstones was almost lost in golden elms, whose leaves fluttered down continuously. A fence went round the churchyard, and I was glad to enter the wicket gate away from the bull, and I knew that if he came to the gate I should have to stay in church till the following Sunday.

I expected the barnlike church to be a ruin, but I was delighted to find a lovely ancient building, cared for, and loved, with fresh flowers on the altar, and clean carpets and furnishings. This is a twelfth-century church, restored in the fourteenth century, and again restored when it was falling to pieces in the last century. There is a splendid roof to the nave with great beams, and five queen-post trusses. This massive structure had been hidden for many years under a low flat ceiling until it was rediscovered. The arch of the chancel has half-open buds carved down it, like the buds of yellow water-lilies. The thirteenth-century font is plain and rough, and it seems fitting to have this strength in roof and font in a tiny church set in the fields. In the bellcote hangs a little lonely bell.

Through the plain glass of the window I could see my great bull staring solidly at the church, and I was uneasy until I was safely across the field away from his horns. Long afterwards I heard he would not hurt anyone.

Near Aylesbury there are villages that are depopulated,

haunted, lost villages, which give a sense of deep sadness. Quarrendon, only two miles from the busy county town, has gone. The church is a heap of ruins, stones hidden in elder bushes with a wire to keep cattle away. There is a field where the marks are left of the great Elizabethan mansion of Sir Henry Lee, Queen Elizabeth's Champion, which once stood in all its grandeur.

"It's all desecrated there. Don't go to see it," said a Bucks countryman to me. "Church stones have gone to make walls. Don't go, it's a haunted place."

We went through the field gates, across wet cornfields, to find it, but we were told by the farmer that it was impossible to struggle through the flooding brook which had made a morass of mud and water round the broken stones of the church, and I was glad not to go. Quarrendon consists of a farm or two and the great fields of pasture and corn in the rich Vale of Aylesbury.

It was a dark rainy day of early autumn after a wet summer, and German prisoners were working at the corn ricks, unloading sheaves of oats, struggling against the adverse conditions of rain-logged fields. The farmer spoke despairingly of his ruined wet crops and the losses incurred by many small farmers, some of whom were in even greater difficulties than he.

I thought of the drying-chambers the Romans had at Hambleden for their wet corn nearly two thousand years ago, and I thought of the farmers who have combines and drying-rooms to-day.

He had been a farmer all his life, and his father too—he belonged to generations of farmers who would not give in, but everything was against the small man. We stood in the rain, watching the men carrying the corn, under the black sky.

I remembered what I had read of Quarrendon in its prosperous days in Elizabethan times, when the great house stood and the Queen came to visit her knight.

"In the month of August, 1592, Sir Henry Lee was honoured by his royal Mistress's presence for two days at Quarenden in the Vale of Aylesbury."

A masque was performed in the grounds of the great house where now are fields and cornland.

Happie houre, happie daie,
That Eliza came this waie,
She with more than graces grace
Hath made proude this humble place,

they sang.

At the end of the masque there was a legacy bequeathed in fanciful terms to the Queen, which gives a picture of orchards, gardens, and wonders that were at Quarrendon.

"Woods, groves, Meddowes, Pastures, Arable Land, Riuers, Gardens, Orchards (stored with the best fruit, Queene apples, Pome Royalls and Souveraigne Peares), Fishing, Hawking, Hunting," and the like.

Dr Fuller says that in the eighteenth century one entire pasture, called Beryfield in the Manor of Quarrendon, was let yearly at £800, it was so rich.

There were troublous days too, for in a storm in 1570 Sir Henry Lee lost 3,000 sheep at Quarrendon besides other cattle.

Quarrendon is a sad place with this feeling of desertion, and we went along the field road that runs for some miles through many cornfields with wet sheaves in the Vale of Aylesbury. Ditch and wire bound the road, but no hedges. This is rich arable land, well-watered and flat, real country with no houses, until the road ends and the last gate is left behind. It is a lonely road, with a real loneliness in it.

If any fairies, ghosts, demons or goblins still dwell in England, then some of them haunt the woods and lanes of Buckinghamshire. It is their last refuge, except perhaps Dartmoor. Several times I have been told of lonely lanes, not solitary places, but roads where uncanny things have happened and might occur again. Countrymen and women have mentioned this to me of their own accord, for they do not speak carelessly of such things, nor say them to townsmen.

"That's a road I would not like to go along at night," says one. "It's terrible lonely, and you aren't alone, either."

A well-known writer of the county speaks of strange goblin spirits seen in a field by a countryman. I myself met someone who had a similar tale to tell of appearances she had actually witnessed in a garden near the Icknield Way. They were fairies, or sprites, about two feet high, golden-yellow, dancing in a ring. Their features were beautiful and from them came intense happiness and vitality so that the watcher was filled with joy too. Soundlessly they danced and then they were gone.

Here we went along the road between fields, stopping now and then to open a gate and shut it, and a horse clip-clopped in the distance along the hard road, and a tractor whirred in the field and partridges rose and flew overhead.

We could see the pretty village of Quainton amongst its trees, and the short range of hills called locally Conduit Hill (or Cundick), Woad Hill, Chalscombe, the Grove and Round Hill.

I liked Quainton with more than an ordinary liking when first I visited it, entering from the other side, and always I find it subtly exciting, although it is very quiet and remote. The lanes are tree-lined, and the little village stands on the slopes of the hill, with the windmill behind it and a round green hilltop above as a background.

There is a crooked village green with paths about it and across it, and sometimes cattle are grazing there and children playing and old men talking. The green slopes steeply, and at the head stands the stone cross. It is an old market cross of the fifteenth century, with three great worn steps where children have played for centuries, where proclamations have been read, and where the villagers have gathered in times of joy and also in times of war and trouble. The octagonal shaft is broken, and nobody knows its history, although it may have been harmed in the Civil Wars. It is part of the life of the village, and nobody has rudely restored or changed it. Near is a pond, rather choked and slimy, and behind the cottages the broken vanes of the windmill show.

The village is as charming as its name. There are Tudor cottages and a Queen Anne house, and seventeenth-century cottages. One has the date 1722 over the door and hollyhocks stand as high as the eaves. Some cottages have overhanging upper stories, some are gabled, and all have bright gardens of flowers.

Children are picking flowers, running races, flying kites, minding babies. It is a little village, full of life.

At a creeper-covered little house at the corner of the green was born in 1773 Thomas Lipscombe, the great historian of Bucks, who spent his life devotedly taking down the records of his beloved native county. The little house, with flower garden in front of it and white palings, is called The Magpie.

Thomas Lipscombe died as the book went to press, but he had fulfilled his desire and finished a fine piece of research work. He was baptized at the church here on 29 January 1773, and he died in poverty in London in 1846, "after devoting his energy and money to bringing out his great work, 'The History and Antiquities of the County of Buckingham' " says the memorial in the church. In 1946 there was a celebration of his centenary and his memory was honoured.

Down a lane, past the village shop which is thatched and has four ammonites embedded in its walls, past the cottages with low eaves and sunflowers growing tall, past the beautiful almshouses, is the churchyard with a row of crooked grey tombstones leaning forward like tired old men staring at the earth. Beyond the walls are the cornfields down in the great plain of Aylesbury, with its blue distances of faint hills.

A green woodpecker laughs, and doves coo in this quiet spot. There is a serenity about Quainton, and I am always happy to return to this village clustered round its sloping green.

The tower, with its embattled parapet, rises among the trees and on its face is a sundial cut with clear figures. In the fifteenth-century porch is a holy-water stoup, and small square-headed windows with three slits open to the air.

Inside the church one sees at once an arresting monument, one of those great pieces of sculpture which usually I pass by, but here I stop. A knight reclines there, with long curled wig, armour-clad. His hands are beautiful. The moulding of the long tapering fingers is excellent, his knuckles and bones and even his veins are in the marble, so that I hold up my own hand and compare the structure. His head is raised on a cushion, he lies as if asleep, poised ready to wake up. His wife behind leans forward, hands clasped, and forefingers touching as if she watches him and waits for him. She is alive, and he is only sleeping. It is Richard Winwood who died in 1688. His wife set up the monument by Thomas Stayner in 1689.

"Richard Winwood, one of ye deputy leivetenants of the County in the Reyne of King Charles ye second."

He built the row of almshouses near the church. He was Secretary of State to James I and he lived at the manor house at Quainton.

In a niche in the wall is a family in painted alabaster, all gathered together as if they were still alive in miniature. The husband and wife, dressed in black with white ruffs, kneel at a prayer-desk, facing one another, and a gold fringed cloth hangs down. Four prim little girls kneel near them. The memorial is to Richard Brett, rector of Quainton in 1595, and one of the translators of the Authorized Version of the Bible. This little memorial is intimate and cheerful, almost gay in its family life.

The font is fifteenth-century, and it has octagonal sides. There are some early brasses, one of a long-haired girl of the fourteenth century. The ring of five bells have inscriptions.

"Thinke no cost to much" is the Treble.
"That you bestow of all."
"To bring to pas."
"So good a thing."

Most of them were made in 1621.

There is a tale told about Quainton of a trial of faith at the time of the change of dates in the calendar, when eleven days were taken out, to the confusion of village people.

On Christmas Eve 1753 about two thousand people of the village and neighbourhood met at midnight in the rector's garden at Quainton with torch and lantern to watch for the budding of the thorn. It was said to be a true and veritable descendant of the famous Glastonbury thorn, which buds on December 24th each year, ready to be in full bloom on Christmas Day and to die off at night. They met to decide which was the real Christmas. As the thorn showed no sign of budding they decided it was not Christmas Day and nobody attended church or kept the day.

Near the churchyard are the almshouses, which were built in 1687. They are a charming row of six little cottages, with gabled roofs and windows that have original leaded lights. Over two of the doors are Richard Winwood's coat-of-arms, carved and painted. The chimneys are grouped together in fours. At the ends of the row are the coalhouses and outhouses with rounded gables placed symmetrically, so that the whole is a beautiful long building. In the front gardens are scarlet begonias, hollyhocks, and cabbages. At the back are apple trees and good vegetable gardens for the old people.

These almshouses were built by Richard Winwood for "three poor men, widowers to be called brothers, and three poor women, widows to be called sisters."

We met one of the old men who was hobbling home full of glee, in a dancing step, because he had just had a birthday, and he was seventy-eight. He was a cheerful, laughing soul, bright-eyed, fresh-complexioned, and his hair was still black.

"I used to work in yonder mill," said he. "I took corn to be grinded there, and I could carry two hundredweight up a ladder. Nowadays they can't carry half that."

He said he had worked in a coal and corn merchant's for many years, but, like most villagers, he had done everything, labouring and hedging and all. I often meet old men who have worked in their youth at carrying corn and coal, and they are always very proud and happy about it.

He lived by himself in one of the almshouses and he looked after himself, except that now and then a relation came to tidy up. He was disturbed because he had a tall apple tree in his garden and he could no longer climb very high. Frosts were coming and nobody gathered his fruit for him. There ought to be somebody to do these difficult jobs for the old, I thought. I saw his little house, which had one front room and a kitchen at the back and a good bedroom above, all very comfortable.

We climbed Quainton Hill one day to get the view across the country to Aylesbury and the Chilterns and the long line of misty blue hills. It was windy up there, for the ground rises steeply. Below were the thatched roofs of the village and the sails of the windmill, but in all the beauty spread around there was an ugliness, a great palisade of new corrugated iron around a garden on the slopes of this hill. Corrugated iron spoils some of the cottages at North Marston, where it has been used instead of thatch, but this fence was much worse.

An old road, which the country people call a Roman road, although it is probably an early British track, runs under Quainton Hill to Dedham's Lane, or Deadman's Lane. This is Carter's Lane, sometimes called Gipsy Lane, a way that is very lonely, a haunted road, as I have been told by people in different parts of the county who know it. It is gipsy land, where the gipsies have lived for generations. Now it is not so easy for them to stay anywhere, but the lane usually has a few of them. They alone know its secrets and they are secluded there. On one side are open fields, bounded by a ditch, and on the other a hedge of trees so rough and wild that until lately the lane was almost hidden and impenetrable. It has been cleared up and changed, but the loneliness remains.

In the ditch among the wild flowers and nettles there stands a large rough-hewn block of stone, fashioned like a monument, which is said by old tradition to be the gravestone of the King of the Gipsies, who was buried here centuries ago. Scratched deeply in its face is the date 1641. The figure 4 is reversed, in the way a child or illiterate person writes it.

This stone lay in the ditch for many years, known to the country people who always called it the Gipsy's Grave. Recently it has been set upright by the road. Even now it is difficult to find among the deep grasses and thick undergrowth of the tangled lane.

Others have told me of this haunted lane, along which they will not go at night. It was notoriously bad a hundred years ago, and dangerous on account of the lawless tribes who lived there.

There is a tradition about Cundick Hill, by Quainton. People say that at midnight a host of horses with headless riders gallops round the hill. This is well known, and some have actually seen them. A company of young men a few years ago were on the Quainton Hills at night when they heard a man on a horse approaching. They moved out of his way, for everyone heard the gallop of hooves. Then they saw the horse with the rider, who was headless, sweep past and disappear.

We turned aside from the rough lane to a branching road which ran between fields with wide margins of thick tousled grass, and tall elms and ash trees in the hedgerows, but no cottages or habitations. We were going to see Hogshaw, another lost village, depopulated and destroyed. We climbed over a fence to a field, with a cowhouse and stackyard, a moat and some willow trees. Our friend, a countryman who knows the place well, walked with us, and we lingered at this desolate spot. The cowhouse is built on the site of Hogshaw Church, but everything has gone, and only the memory remains to country people of this church which was finally pulled down in 1730.

A short distance away is Lower Hogshaw Farm, which is marked Fulbrook Farm on the maps now the village has gone. This good farm, with its haystacks and corn ricks all within old red brick walls, lichened and mossy, is the remnant of the once populous village. The font from Hogshaw Church is said to be there. The poppy heads from the stalls of the church are at Doddershall manor house on the staircase. Some carving from the church is on the walls there too.

The site of the village is close to the farmhouse, in a meadow called Ram Close. It is traditionally haunted, and the ghosts of the dead can be seen by certain people. There is a duck-pond in the field, which always has ducks on it according to an old tale. This is one of those odd little legends of bird-hauntings; either wild or tame ducks are there.

We went through this field, by the grassy track, along Steart Lane. This again is an ancient lane, part of the Roman road or British road, say the villagers, and it joins Deadman's Lane.

A countryman told us legends of this place, authentic tales handed down to him by old relations and villagers. His uncle worked for some years at Crandon Farm, and he saw strange happenings in the Hogshaw district. A bright light shone before him, several yards ahead, one pitch-black morning when never a star was out. This occurred in a field known as Dick Tarn. He saw this light on seven different occasions. Others had seen it, and they referred to it as the "Old Man with the Lantern," for the light had the clarity and flooding of lantern-light. Nobody was there, nor was any source of the light found.

This tale of lantern-light is akin to ghost tales in the north, and it has nothing to do with will-o'-the-wisp, which is a jack-o'-lantern moving and darting over marshy lands, a natural phenomenon of marsh gas.

This relation of his worked for a time at Hogshaw, and in the roadway of the field called Ram Close he was met by a very tall man who brushed past him, stepping silently. He said "How do?" in the usual way of greeting, and immediately turned his head. The man had vanished, and there was no cover, no hedge. This is an open field road. There was no sound and no sight of anyone, and he knew he had seen a ghost.

Another countryman related a story of Hogshaw Church which was traditional. King Charles lived in the upper vestry for some days when he was hiding from the troops. He was fed by a man named Ward, until it was safe for him to escape.

An old lady, who was eighty-five in 1935, remembered a cottage at Hogshaw. The house was all on one floor, but "inside you went up three steps and then one more." In the outhouse was a gravestone which was used as a table. The walls were built of rough stones, whitewashed over. There was a moat round the cottage and the garden led to the water. All around was unenclosed land, but the field was enclosed in 1778.

A lane which turns off the main Buckingham road between Winslow and Whitchurch leads to the ancient manor-house of Creslow. The traffic runs swiftly along the high-road. About two years ago all cars and lorries were held up by a large swarm of migrating rats which filled the road as they moved relentlessly forward, across into the fields towards Whitchurch.

A Beaconsfield countryman told me of a rat migration he had seen long ago at Jordans, Seer Green, in the steep lane which runs near the Meeting House. There was a rustle like corn shaking in the wind, or water rushing, and he climbed the bank to look over the field "to see what was doing."

It was an immense concourse of rats, close together, bodies pressed in a mob, with no space between them, coming along to the lane. He got quickly out of the way on his bicycle, for they would have gone over him and perhaps killed him if he had stayed in their path. They went over the bank, down into the lane and up the other side, straight across the fields in a dark mass of bodies towards Seer Green, probably to find corn ricks there.

The corn was thick in a large field by the side of the main Buckingham road, and very golden and rich it looked that sunny day, dipping down to the wood, on the field slope. This field has the name Heaven Low, which suits it to perfection, for with this ripe corn like pure gold it looked like heaven down below. It is one of Creslow's fields, for here, hidden away down the hillside, sheltered by the slopes, is a famous farmhouse, dating back to medieval times, but with all the modern business of a good farm.

Creslow pastures have long been famed as the fields where cattle were reared for the royal families of England, and these grazing grounds are still the finest in the county. The parish of Creslow is only 886 acres, and most of this was permanent grass until recently, when much has been ploughed. There is one vast field called Creslow Great Ground, supposed to be the largest grass field in England for it has 365 acres. It is a field known throughout the centuries. This grazing ground is in the centre of the county, and it was noted for the quality of its grass in Elizabethan days. The subsoil, which gives it its richness, is Kimmeridge clay.

In Tudor days the royal table was supplied with beef bred on Creslow Great Ground. The field used to carry 200 oxen, 300 ewes and their lambs all summer. Lately it had 20 shire mares and foals besides bullocks and sheep.

John Westcar, whose monument we saw at Winslow, farmed Creslow between 1779 and 1825. He was the greatest grazier in the Vale of Aylesbury.

The manor house of Creslow with its chapel was built about 1330, and there is a good deal of the original work left. The octagonal tower has walls six feet thick. The manor was given to the Knights Templars by Henry I, and after the dissolution it became a demesne of the Crown and the pastures were then used for the cattle of the King. A "steard" or keeper was put in charge, but in 1635 the lands were granted to Cornelius

254

Holland, "a miscreant upstart," who allowed the place to go to pieces, house, fences, and buildings. At the time of Charles II Creslow became royal property again.

It is the oldest dwelling-house in Bucks, and perhaps the most beautiful, with its grey limestone walls and its ancient strength, its gables, and tower, and mullioned windows, and the lovely roof of many angles. There are projections and wings and gable ends, and an outside chimney shaft. Although there have been many changes, rebuildings, and alterations, the essential manor house is the same, a never-to-be-forgotten sight. It is a picture in low tones, a soft-coloured shadowy place, with its great ash tree on the lawn throwing a pattern of blue-grey shadowy branches over the grey house front, and upon the smooth grass, the seventeenth-century garden wall and archway. A little carved face is inset in this wall, and other faces stare from odd places, carvings once brought from the chapel.

The great hall, a feature of medieval houses, had a floor inserted in it at an upper story, and a new staircase was added in the seventeenth century, but in all the alterations care was taken to use the old materials. Probably some of the stone came from the chapel and other buildings. It is known from the soot deposits on the arches which are now in attics that the hall was warmed by a fire in the centre of the floor.

The principal staircase of oak has turned balusters, square newel-posts with finials and pendants. There are fourteenth-century round windows of trefoiled lights, very charming on high in the walls, and some windows are seventeenth-century with mullions.

The east end has a gable, one side of which is stepped, the other side plain. In the angle at the apex is one of the little circular openings, quatrefoiled, of the fourteenth century. The west end also has stepped gables, very beautiful, and again in the apex a tiny round window looks out like a watchful eye seeking the lanes for a traveller.

An outside stairway of stone on the east side leads down to the most interesting room in this ancient house, for it is the crypt, under the drawing-room. It is a small circular room with triple ribs of stone in the roof, meeting at exquisite foliated

255

bosses, one in the middle of the roof and four others. A queer face looks from a tiny archway in the wall. Nowadays this crypt is used as a little outhouse or games room, for it is close to the lawn.

Some of the cellars in this old house have barrel roofs of brick, but the house is stone, quarried in the district. The chapel, which stands at the bottom of the lane at the entrance to the house, is now a great barn, with farm implements in it, and hay stored there. It is divided by partitions, but one can conjecture where the nave began and the chancel ended.

"The crypt is a cellar, the chapel a stable, the banquet hall a nursery," said someone of this old place.

There are two traceried windows in the side of this great chapel-barn, blocked up, and also a door which is blocked. We stood on the bank under the ancient walls gazing up at the carvings round windows and doors, thinking of the hands that had worked there centuries ago, imagining the hymns and prayers that had risen from that ancient building. At the gable end there are signs of another traceried window carved there on high, but a floor has been added to the chapel, and a flight of steps leads to the upper part at this end, as in many north-country barns and at my own home. Chapels and barns are much alike, in integrity and strength, and plenty of hymns were sung in the barns I knew. A box tree grows from the stone of the steps, rooted there.

Mr. R. J. Gee, noted breeder of Aberdeen Angus cattle, lives at Creslow and farms the land. The house stands half-hidden in the curve, sheltered by the low hill slope, so that it is invisible from the main road. Some of the stones in the lower parts of the house are very great blocks, making a grand foundation. There is no uniformity in shape or size. Like a mighty wall the house was built to endure for centuries, and for centuries it has stood there, remote, proud, careless of opinion, defiant, a farm-house and a treasure of which the county must be proud indeed.

There are two villages in the neighbourhood which interested me when I saw them in the company of a countryman who knows them well and loves them.

Hoggeston was once a stockaded village, and we could see the

Nether Winchendon Church

green ramparts of that circle enclosing the place. The church and two ponds lie within the ring of this earthwork. The church was originally built in the twelfth century, and there is a little bellcote turret of the fifteenth century. We saw the hassock made of roots of sedge grasses. It was the custom centuries ago to make footstools of this grass cut from the earth, and one remains here.

In a field close to the church was a cornfield quite gold, rich as the red gold of the dwarfs in the evening sunlight, half stooked and half uncut. It was a picture of fruitful earth.

We went on to see Dunton, a tiny village with a tiny church, whose box pews are high enough to conceal the worshippers during a weary sermon. It is very plain, with whitewashed walls, the simplest church I have seen in the county and almost unknown. The gallery at the west end has the names of the rectors of the eighteenth century painted on panels. Names I like are Sam Clutterbuck and Jeremy Preedy. There are oil lamps and candles, and on the wall is a mass dial with a hole for the peg.

The road from this hamlet back to the highway goes through fields of corn, with no hedges or fences, so that we drove among the sheaves. This is one of the charms of rural Bucks. There are many gated roads, through pastures, through cornland, through farmyards, with opening gates and shutting gates, the only direct route between outlying villages.

Doddershall Manor, near Quainton, is reached by a gated road, through fields where a herd of beautiful Friesian cattle graze. It is a sixteenth-century house of red brick, with great chimney stacks, with square-shafted chimneys, with gables and a porch of two stories with gabled ends. The lead rainwater pipes have ornamental heads and the initials T.L. and the date 1689. At the back of the house are carvings, the head of a king, a queen, and a lily, set in the walls. This house is moated with a good clear stream of water where ducks swim.

We went through the manor which has been in the family of Pigott for four hundred years, and we saw the lovely rooms with many treasures of paintings and furniture and carvings. In the cellar—an important place this—is a well. This well of sweet

Almshouses at Quainton

cool water is still used for drinking each day, and it has never gone dry during the centuries.

At the head of the steep little cellar stairway, off the hall, is the following advice of the seventeenth century painted on a board over the door.

> Welcome my friend, drinke with a noble heart,
> But yet before thou drinke too much, departe,
> For though good drinke will make a coward stout,
> Yet when too much is in, the witte is out.
>
> 1610

In the house there is the wall panelling from Quainton Church, and a frieze of tracery probably from Hogshaw Church. The newels of the fine staircase are surmounted with poppy-heads of the fifteenth century, cut in half, above the twisted balusters. These also came from deserted and lost Hogshaw.

Near Doddershall Manor is Doddershall Wood, which stretches to Grendon Underwood, linking up the great woods of this part of the county to the Shakespeare Woods.

CHAPTER XVIII

NORTH MARSTON AND OVING

I FIRST visited North Marston on a winter day, but I have often been to this most individual of Buckinghamshire villages, this unspoilt and unchanged little place, which is the epitome of all that one looks for, beauty, tradition, farms, country life, and that remoteness that will not accept a stranger easily.

We started off one January day, going through Penn and Tyler's Green where the little pond was ice-covered and very young skaters were trying the surface, first with stones and then with a tentative boot, past the cottage with a couple of yews trimmed like chessmen by the garden gate, and along the road on the hill crest looking over the valleys to Speen. It was a clear frosty morning with crystals on the hedges and the sky clear, cold ice-blue, like Gerda's Snow Queen sky.

We went down one of those valleys where houses line the sides of the roads, little narrow valleys in the Chilterns, which have been nearly spoiled. Then, suddenly, away from the houses, we swung up the road to Speen. At the cross-roads in this mixed village stands the post office in an old cottage. We dipped down a very steep zigzag road to the valley, and there, tucked away in a bend, was the picturesque little Plough Inn where Ishbel MacDonald lives. She opened the door to me, and in my mind I saw not the hostess in her coloured scarf but a girl called Ishbel whom I used to know long ago when I went shyly to supper with the Ramsay MacDonalds.

We went over the inn and admired its small cosy rooms and the whitewashed walls and dark beams. The fields rise steeply before it and I was told that nowadays the inn is run in conjunction with a farm. This is as it should be. I remember many farmhouses with inns where the new milk and eggs and vegetables of the farm add to the pleasures of the inn, and the inn helps the finances of the farm.

I heard too of the numbers of cottages at Speen where chair legs were turned on home lathes before the last war, but now the men go to factories at High Wycombe and work with machinery.

In the woods near Speen there were two or three bodgers at work, but we went on to Hampden Woods, where we saw some men with their little huts, their pole-lathes, their piles of trimmed pieces, and smoothly turned chair legs which fell in a heap from the lathe. On this ice-cold day they were outside cutting the newly felled trees into pieces ready for the lathe.

We dipped down the hills by Whiteleaf, leaving the high ridge of woods, with the splendid views across country, and down we went to Monks Risborough, to Kimble, and to Aylesbury.

Aylesbury looked gay and bright in the frosty sunshine and I waved to John Hampden in the market square, and I nodded to the little old houses, the Bear Inn by the roadside, the Bull's Head peeping through the enclosing houses, the noble King's Head, and all the gabled, higgledy-piggledy collection of little cottages and shops. We went by the roundabout where several roads diverge, for Aylesbury is an important traffic centre, and we took the Buckingham road. As we crossed a blue thread of ice-covered water, almost invisible, at Holman's Bridge, we went by the old battlefield of the Civil Wars. This is a haunted place, and I always imagine I see the men struggling in the marshy ground, fighting, dying, thinking of their Buckingham-shire homes as they fell. I said a prayer for their souls, and a flock of fieldfares flew across the meadows with flashing wings.

North Marston is a village famed for its church and for its wonder-working saint, Master John Schorne or Shorne. He was rector of North Marston from 1290 to 1314 but the tales told of him are spoken to-day and known to many. It is said that in a time of great drought he struck with his staff on the earth and a spring burst forth. The water from this spring had healing properties and thousands came to the village to use its waters. Houses were built for the pilgrims, and the village became a populous place of far-reaching fame. The spring is there now, feeding a well which is called Schorne's Well, or simply the Town Well.

The waters have been analysed and proved to be a chalybeate spring of clear sparkling water which contains ingredients that have medicinal properties. The healing powers of some spring waters are well known. We had a healing spring in our fields when I was a child, and women used to come to this chalybeate trough to carry away the water in bottles to drink for cures and to bathe their eyes. The water was icy cold, sparkling with imprisoned gas, but there was a strong taste of iron and the colour was pale gold. The spring was kept for the cattle to drink from although everyone tasted it.

The water of Sir John Schorne's spring was so strongly impregnated with iron that the taste was too strong for ordinary drinking, and after the days of miracles and pilgrimages were past, that is, after the Dissolution of the Monasteries, troughs were placed round it and the water kept for cattle.

After the year 1835 the spring was used for the town supply, and now the water is only slightly different from ordinary spring water. I drank at this village pump and enjoyed the familiar faint taste of the iron in the water. The people say it is beneficial to health, and there is a tradition of longevity and good health at North Marston.

The holy well, which arose so miraculously and which has never run dry through all the centuries, is a short distance from the church. It is walled with stone, and there are four steps down to it, but since a woman was drowned there the well has been completely covered in and a very ordinary pump stands over it. There are many wells and pumps in Bucks, at Latimer on the green where a little red roof covers the well, at Farnham Royal, at Chenies, but this venerable and famous well is unadorned.

The glorious Church of St Mary the Virgin stands high with battlements and carved pinnacles of great beauty, and gargoyles of wild cat and devilish beast stare down from the walls and tower. The stone for this church was quarried at Oving, I was told by an old villager, but the quarries are grass-covered now. The porch and ancient doorway with its carving date from about 1350, after the death of Sir John Schorne, when the church was enriched by the pilgrims who came to the shrine. The east window with five lights was rebuilt at this time, and it is said that an image stood in a niche which is there now, and the shrine was near the altar.

There is a wonderful old roof to the nave, where six carved wooden angels under the spandrels play musical instruments, among them a horn and a kind of concertina. The carved stone faces on the arches in this church are as alive and perhaps as malignant as any I have seen. They must once have lived, those characters staring down from the walls. One shows utter contempt, and another absolute cynicism, and a third is as proud as Lucifer, and a fourth bitter as Hell. I like these four hard men who look down on a more refined age.

There is always an air of alertness in North Marston Church, as if the angels really played up there, and the grotesque men talked, for whispering voices seem to chatter and murmur even as we enter, and only wait until we leave to continue their conversation. It is partly the fine carving, but there may be more in it than this. Anything might happen in this church of miracles.

The stone font has much-worn angels round the stem, carved five hundred years ago, in that golden age of craftsmanship. On the chancel wall is a finely incised brass portrait of Richard Saunders, an Elizabethan physician who died in 1602 at the age of sixty-seven. It is remarkable on account of the details of his dress, his ruff and doublet, his laced shoes, and he kneels on a tasselled cushion before his desk. The inscription is pleasing, and here it is:

> 'Tis as you see nought but the spoiles of Death,
> God's high controller and impartial taker,
> Free hold wee had of land but none of breath,
> All one day must resigne unto their maker.

> I was the world's acquaintance in my time,
> Acquainted and no more, so shouldst be ye,
> I had my part as thou perhaps hast thine,
> In wealth and frends such as were fite for me.
> I yielded up my reckening when I died,
> What wanted in the summe, Christ's blood supplied.

On the opposite wall is a tribute to his mother, in which he speaks of his unavailing skill to save her from the grave.

Near this is one of the most laconic and striking of epitaphs. A well-carved hand points down to the ground, with these words around it in large letters:

HE LIES DUST DOWN THARE.

It is a monument to Mr John Virgin, rector of North Marston, who died in 1694. This epitaph is often misquoted as "He Lies Just Down Thare," but the word is Dust, a more dramatic and forceful reminder.

There are many treasures in this church, one of which is a chained Bible of the sixteenth century with exquisite print and clear black lettering. It was open at the Apocrypha, and the words seemed eternal and very important as we read them in that magnificent old church where the pilgrims came in thousands to the shrine of Sir John Schorne.

The chancel and the vestry were built in the fifteenth century, with the offerings to the shrine. The stalls have poppy-heads and carved misereres, all fifteenth-century work. There are stone sedilia in the chancel with rich canopies over them.

The vestry is an important room with window, fireplace, and staircase to a room above. This upper room has also a fireplace and a narrow window overlooking the altar, and a little stair to a tower. The priest lived here and kept watch on the shrine and its wealth.

Master John Schorne is still very much alive in people's memories, and there are many references to him in the past. His second famous miracle was to catch the Devil and to keep him in a boot, where he could do no harm. There are pictures of him, on pilgrim tokens of pewter, brought from his shrine and made or sold in the vicinity as in French towns of the present day, and in Norfolk and Suffolk there are rood paintings of the miracle. He stands in the pulpit, holding a long boot, from which a little malicious devil peeps.

In a play by John Heywood his name occurs, when the Palmer, describing the journeys of his pilgrimages, mentions Maister John Schorne among other saints.

After his death he was raised to the dignity of a saint but not canonized. His remains were enshrined, and shrine and well were the object of the pilgrimages. Later, to get the offerings, the shrine was removed to St George's Chapel, Windsor, in 1478, after a Bull was obtained from Pope Sixtus V for its removal, but the bones were returned when the monks there were weary of the purchase, and it is probable that the pilgrims remained faithful to North Marston and the well, and the offerings at Windsor were small.

In Joan Ingram's will, dated 1519, a pound of wax was left for Master Schorne's light. Schorne was one of the most popular local saints in England until the Reformation, a Buckinghamshire saint.

North Marston has many village traditions. A small road known as the Pilgrims' Way is said by some of the oldest inhabitants to have existed on a site running from the well to the vicarage. Since the council houses were built they have found evidence of a road parallel to the new road, and these two link near the well.

The pilgrims sang a hymn to Schorne as they travelled the roads from Wycombe to Aylesbury, and on to Oving and North Marston Church. I have read this Latin hymn.

Another village tradition came from an old lady whose mother was christened in 1847 by the Rev. Richard Knight. He had in his keeping a manuscript book about Sir John Schorne. This said that attached to the well was a chained gold cup from which pilgrims who came from all parts of the country drank of the water. The money they paid for this was used to build the chancel of North Marston Church.

Another village memory came from one who remembers the traditions about Schorne passed down from one to another. They used the water for bathing their eyes, she said. She remembers some of the old people saying that a statue to Schorne blew down from over the east window to the churchyard, "but it was taken no care of" and it disappeared.

The references to the pilgrimages are numerous. Pilgrims went to Master John Schorne if they were sick of the ague, and the waters of the healing well cured the illness. There is a ballad which runs:

> To Maister John Shorne,
> That blessed man borne,
> For the ague to him we apply,
> Whiche jugeleth with a bote,
> I beshrowe his herte rote,
> That wyle truste him, and it be I.

As each pilgrim gave an offering to the saint, the annual amount was about £500, or about £5,000 of present-day money, but whether it went to Windsor or North Marston is not known

There was an image of him at North Marston which was moved to London at the time of the Dissolution. This image was of Sir John blessing the boot, or carrying a boot from which the head of the Devil appears. It stood in a niche near the altar.

A most ingenious suggestion has been made, which to me carries conviction, that the Victorian toy, the Jack-in-the-box, beloved by all children, wondered at by simple folk, sold at fairs and wakes, may have been a memory of the Devil in the boot of "Maister John Shorne." The bewhiskered face, grinning like an imp, popping up and then being forced down, is remarkably like the Devil popping out of the boot and being pushed back.

Mr Hastings Kelke, who has made a special study of the saint, thinks that the image which Dr London carried away held a boot out of which the Devil ascended or descended by some hidden spring, to the delight and amazement of the pilgrims who flocked to see it. Master John Schorne's boots were named in a mocking list of relics of the Reformers.

The traditional rhyme, sung by children, was once on the walls of the well:

> Sir John Shorn,
> Gentleman born,
> Conjured the Devil into a Horn.

It is thought that the village people kept up the traditional ceremony of well-dressing at North Marston at the holy well.

Well-dressing was a practice in the country districts of my childhood, attended by crowds of people who flocked to see the well
and wayside springs decorated with flowers, mottoes and wreaths,
when prayers were said and a procession was formed. There
were traditions that the wells never went dry, and people went
to thank God for the bountiful supply of water flowing from the
earth. Townspeople who have water from a tap in unlimited
quantities have no conception of the gratitude and the reverence
that country people feel to a spring that comes miraculously out
of the earth to fulfil their wants.

So a great number of houses were built for the pilgrims to the
well, and at Oving, where five roads meet, there is a road,
Puppet Lane, which is thought to be the way the pilgrims took
when they came to Sir John Schorne's well at North Marston.
This road, which disappears in the fields now, can be traced as a
track at the latter end of its journey. The name Puppet Lane has
been corrupted to Pulpit Lane and at North Marston this
becomes Featherbed Lane. Another lane is Ava Lane, which
may be a corruption of Ave Lane.

After this exciting time of pilgrimage, which lasted for centuries, the place became very quiet. The chancel was in a dilapidated condition and there was little money until it was restored
by Queen Victoria, to whom a fortune had been left by John
Camden Neild of North Marston.

James Neild, the father of John Camden Neild, was born
in 1744 at Knutsford, the Cheshire village later to become
famous in *Cranford*. He went to London, became a goldsmith,
and made a fortune. He obtained the lease of the tithes of North
Marston in 1798. Perhaps he was attracted by the similarity
between his native Knutsford and this Buckinghamshire village.
He made great exertions for the amelioration of the conditions
in prisons in Buckinghamshire.

His son, John Camden Neild, was reported to be a miser,
but the historian Lipscomb contradicts this and commends his
kindness to the poor. He may have lived in mean rooms and
worn old boots and shabby clothes, for that is the only way
that money can be held in hard times. I remember a farmer who
used to save every penny and live the most frugal life so that he

could make a little fortune to build a chapel. Neild died in
1852, and left nearly £250,000 to the Queen. She built Balmoral Castle and restored the church of North Marston to
much of its early beauty, with glowing stained glass in the east
window.

Neild's miserly ways are still remembered in the village, and
tales are told of his carefulness over every penny. He carried a
penny or twopence wrapped up in a bit of newspaper so that he
would never have to spend more, and he always wore very old
clothes.

An octogenarian friend of mine at North Marston tells a
true tale told to him by his grandfather. There had been a flood
at Winslow, and the brook had overflowed its banks and run
over the road near Granborough, where a bridge crosses the
low land. Neild was walking home from Winslow to save paying
for a conveyance. The brook at the bridge flooded the ground
on both sides and the way was impassable. A man carried
passengers over the water, charging sixpence a time. Neild bargained to be carried for threepence. He was hoisted on the
man's back and carried half-way to the little bridge. There he
was set down and refused passage until he paid the extra threepence to get across.

"He was hommocksing home across the dirty fields," said
they, using the Bucks word hommocksing, which means
trudging.

I talked to this bright-eyed, ruddy-cheeked man of eighty-
five, who was up in the apple trees gathering the crop of apples.
Never was such a hale and hearty octogenarian as he is and I
think it must be due to Schorne's well. He remembers people
coming in his youth from all over the place, with bottles for
this precious water. They even came from Oxford to carry
it back for their ailments. Sir John Schorne, he said, put his
staff down and the water sprang out of the earth in that old
miracle.

The spring has never failed in any drought. It is very clear,
pure, beautiful water and it deserves a better fate than an iron
pump and a cover of boards.

He spoke of the baker's oven where pies were baked at 1½d.

for anything that had meat in it, and 1d. for other kinds of pies. He was a baker himself. Churchwarden pipes were brought from the inns to the bakery to be cleaned. Sometimes thirty dirty old pipes would come, and they were put in the glowing ashes. They came out as white as when they were new. A bakehouse at North Marston still bakes pies for a penny or two, for those who want the convenience.

There were village stocks on the green, and a pound for stray animals. "It was a good strong pound which ought to have been left, but it was sold."

We spoke of other old customs, especially of firemen, for in 1705 there was a great fire at North Marston which destroyed most of the houses. The damage done was worth £3,456, a large sum for a village. Many old cottages and houses went, cottages with half-timbered walls and red roofs. The firemen about a hundred years ago were elected at the annual vestry. Surveyor, foremen, and constable were elected. The farmers looked after the roads, mending them with flints which came from Wendover; these were poured out roughly, and the farmers' cart-wheels did the rest.

When there was a fire, a trumpet or horn was blown to summon the men from their daily work. They all came running when they heard it. At Aylesbury this was the custom too, and at Wycombe. Some insurance companies had their own men and engines and they attended fires of their own insured customers. The sign of the Sun, emblem of the Sun Insurance, can still be seen hanging on the walls of cottages.

Some of the cottages at North Marston are thatched, and some are made of wattle and daub. Sticks of willow were woven and twisted and then plastered over with clay or a mixture of loams, and these filled the panels between the timbers. Walls so made one can see exposed at Aylesbury in the King's Head and at Amersham at the Malt House. It was one of the most permanent ways of old building. I went into one of these cottages, as cosy and pretty inside as out, and the village girl who lived there loved the little place with its herringbone brickwork and good stout walls. North Marston remains a country place with no fashionable influx of outsiders. It is unspoilt, but many of the old cottages have been pulled down and replaced by villas.

By the side of the steep hill dipping from Oving to North Marston there stand tiny cottages, like dolls' houses, with thatched roofs and pretty little windows and doors. These were built in the eighteenth century on the wide margin of the road, an encroachment. The old roadside can still be seen, with its tall row of elms. Roads, according to the Aylesbury records, had to be forty feet wide, and these cottages were built on the common land by the road.

The road rises steeply from North Marston to Oving, a pretty village on a hill with extensive and magnificent views. At Oving is the quinqueviam where five roads meet. The names of these roads are:

(1) Puppet Lane.

(2) Mid-Way.

(3) Pest House Lane. The old pest-house is still there, but now it is a cottage with no windows to the lane. The pest-house dates from the time of the Plague, and there are several cases of deaths from plague in the villages here mentioned in old records.

(4) The Baulk, which is the way to the British encampment whose mounds can be seen in a field by a farm.

(5) The Portway, which is the old Roman way.

Brown Willis says, at this meeting of five roads within living memory there stood a post with several hands pointing different ways, and one of them had written upon it, "This leads to Sir John Schorne."

Some of the houses at Oving are made of the local stone from the now deserted quarries. In these quarries coins have been found by a friend of mine, silver shillings of Elizabeth and Edward III.

Oving is a village of some charm. Perched on the edge of a hill, it stands with the country spread out before it and the hill drops suddenly to North Marston, with its church among the trees. There is a little green of smoothly shaven grass, like a series of small lawns in the centre of the place, with the church and the manor house and the bright little Black Boy Inn. The Black Boy is covered with creepers, and the red brickwork of the seventeenth century shines through the flowers, while roses and lilies fill the garden in front of it. It is all very small like the cottages and the church.

There is a warm scent of Buckinghamshire at Oving. It hangs in the air as sweet as honeysuckle, but more elusive, compounded of flowers and trees. As soon as I pass the boundary of Aylesbury and enter the Mid Bucks and North Bucks parts of the county this warm rich scent comes to me, but it varies with the place.

The little church of All Saints has a wooden gate like that of a cottage garden, opening on the green. The roof is Tudor, with carved bosses. The oak screen across the chancel is one of those simple country screens with no artifice or beauty except that innate in its thick rough style, so that I think it was made by the village carpenter or a craftsman monk.

On the wall hangs a list of rectors from 1241, when Geoffrey de Botteford was rector, to the present day. The patrons of this small church are interesting, for the church belonged to the Prior of the Hospital of St John of Jerusalem in England until 1566, when Queen Elizabeth was patron. Since then all the kings and queens of England have been patrons and the church belongs to the Crown.

There is an ogee arch in the wall, a lovely flowing shape with a tiny square window inset later of an angel with a trumpet. By the church is a farmyard, with the farm garden just under the wall, and cows feeding in the field close to the other wall. At the back of the church are four old pews with carved ends, and from them comes the same scent of old Buckinghamshire, as if the generations who sat there were still alive with their herbs and cowslip balls and pomatums. The church is filled with the sweet odour of those past days, and the fragrance comes even to the porch with its stone seats.

By the side of the road which drops steeply to North Marston between high hedges I saw some corn ricks, one of which carried a triumphal arch on the gable end. It was a ring with a cross within, made of corn and a tassel above it, proudly displayed as a challenge to a mechanical and time-for-nothing age. We saluted it, and it seemed the symbol of carefree happiness as it

270

stood there, high as a weathercock on a church tower, symbo-lizing man's thankfulness that the harvest was done. Bunches of wheat tied in a tassel ornamented many stacks in North Bucks, fastened at the gable ends like bunches of yellow flowers.

Chapter XIX

BRILL ON THE HILL

TOWARDS Brill the road has very broad margins with red campion growing in the ditches and meadow-sweet and Queen Anne's lace foaming over the borders. I have seldom found red campion in South Bucks, but in Mid Bucks it is not only very plentiful but the flowers are large and brilliantly coloured. I feared that this lovely flower was absent in the county until I found it here and at Chilton.

Brill stands on a hill about 600 feet high. It is a steep climb to this hilltop village or little town which is like a self-contained medieval place with a wide street of red brick houses and old doorways. It has two village greens, a church, and a manor house. From a distance it resembles a Provençal town in miniature set on the hill's summit.

There is a well-known rhyme about Brill:

> At Brill on the hill, the wind blows shrill,
> The cook no meat can dress.
> At Stow-on-the-Wold, the wind blows cold,
> I know no more than this.

Once when we went to Brill a fair had come to the village green by the church to stay for a week. The climb up for all the caravans must have been so difficult that they decided to remain when once they arrived. Little roundabouts and swing-boats and shooting booths all of diminutive size were there, with baby napkins hanging from the caravan washing-line, and the mother who owned the fair doing a good family wash for the winds of Brill to dry.

It was all very quiet in the daytime, she told us, but at night people came from afar to amuse themselves.

The twelfth-century parish church has a low tower of the fifteenth century, with a small lead spire and weathervane. The most interesting part of the church is the Jacobean roof of the chancel. It has arches resting on a tie-beam and the central arch

272

Creslow Manor House, fourteenth century

is shaped like part of a wheel with five pierced spokes tapering to meet a central boss. A carved pendant is the hub of this great beautiful wheel in the roof.

The grass is so deep in the churchyard that the old gravestones leaning this way and that are almost hidden. Beyond is a field which has great mounds whose origin is unknown. They may be earthworks made in the Civil Wars, or the site of the Palace of Brill. For Brill was a very famous place in medieval times.

Edward the Confessor had a palace or manor on this hill, and some of the Plantagenet kings stayed there, so it was evidently a very important royal residence. The parish of Brill lay within the great forest of Bernwood, which also enclosed Boarstall Castle. The wood from Bernwood Forest was used to repair the houses of the King's Manor at Brill, and there are records of the royal cellars being prepared for the King's visit. All trace of the Palace is gone, and even the site is conjectural.

In 1644 Brill was the winter quarters for the Parliamentary troops in the Civil War. Its splendid position made it almost impregnable. On one side of the hill below the town there are many mounds and ditches which were probably made at this time for trenches and earthworks. Now they are covered with blackberry bushes, but the ground is crumpled and creased with hillocks. Even the moles have had their field days here, for the place is humped with grassy molehills.

On the same side of the hill, looking towards Boarstall, there stands an old windmill which has worked for three hundred years, but now it is disabled. Its four sails, partly old and partly new, are a landmark for many miles. One beam is carved with figures and letters of the seventeenth century. It was a beautiful sight on the May Day I first saw it. Sheep and lambs lay under its shade, closely surrounding it. The sky was filled with great white cumulus clouds and the sun streamed down to throw light and blue shadow on this small plateau of the hill. In spite of the natural beauty of the position and the grandeur of the mill, standing there with its great timbers, the place was spoiled by tins and bottles and rubbish thrown about. Close to the mill was the village tip, a dump of old cans and kitchen gear, heaped

Seventeenth-century post mill at Brill

on this lovely hillside, on the soft green turf with its flowers and sheep and windmill, and the magnificent view across the country. This spot is so beautiful that it should be treasured as one of the gems of Buckinghamshire.

There was a mill at Brill in 1086, and two hundred years later a windmill was built from timbers of the Bernwood Forest. The ancient windmill may be a survival of one of those old mills.

Near the church across the green where one of the mounting roads enters the village, stands the Tudor manor house. It has red brick gateposts, and old chimney stacks and a surrounding wall. It is a timber-framed house and the date, 1757, upon one of the rainwater heads is the date of alterations.

Opposite the church is the Swan Inn, an old brick inn of the seventeenth century, with a wide fireplace and chimney-corner seat and some panelling in the parlour. The Red Lion Inn was built in the seventeenth century also. I liked a small cottage beyond the church with pocket-handkerchief garden of green lawn, purple stocks, and snow-white columbines growing in a row under the little windows.

In the middle of the nineteenth century it was suggested that Brill might become a fashionable spa. Down in the valley is a chalybeate spring, and it was proposed that Dorton and Brill should house the invalids who came to drink the healing waters. A pump house and bath was built on the edge of the hill overlooking the plain where the old red walls and chimneys of beautiful Dorton Hall rise among the trees. It is a grim building now, empty and falling to ruin, with windows broken when a flying bomb fell near, and great festoons of clinging ivy hanging from the walls like dark flags. This gloomy Victorian place has no affinity with the little old red cottages of Brill.

I asked why the proposed plan to have a spa had fallen through. I was told that it was "owing to Queen Victoria." A rival spa had been built at Leamington at that time and the Queen went there and started the fashion. Brill was neglected, the house stands forgotten on the hilltop.

Boarstall Tower lies a few miles away from Brill on the edge of Buckinghamshire, and we went down the steep hill to the long wooded valley and through gated fields to reach this ancient place. The Tower was the gateway of Boarstall House. This medieval fortified building is all that remains of the former greatness. It was, and still is, moated completely round, and in its days of strength it was a garrisoned stronghold like a small castle. The stone gateway has an embattled tower, of hexagonal shape, in each corner. It is entered across a bridge over the moat where the water runs deep. The gatehouse has grooves for the portcullis.

Boarstall has a romantic history and even its name has a legend attached to it. Edward the Confessor had a palace, probably the one at Brill. The great forest of Bernwood spread all over this part of Buckinghamshire. Remains of the forest are Wootton Park and King's Wood near Grendon Underwood. The forest was infested by a wild boar of great ferocity which eluded capture. A huntsman named Niel dug a pit, covered it with brushwood, and hid a sow within. The boar fell in and was killed by Niel. He cut off the head and sent it to the King at Brill. For this he was knighted and presented with a hide of arable land, a wood called Hulewood, and the custody of Bernwood Forest. This story is corroborated in 1266, when Henry III made a grant to the heir of the Fitzniels who were said to have held the land from the Conquest.

Connected with this story is the famous Boarstall Horn, which went with the Castle, a silver-mounted ancient horn which is still in existence. There was also a map of Boarstall in an old vellum book. They now belong to Sir Henry Aubrey-Fletcher.

Boarstall was an important stronghold in the Civil War. The King was at Oxford and the Parliamentary forces at Aylesbury, with Boarstall between them. The Royalists took possession first, but they relinquished it when concentrating their troops. At once they knew they had made a mistake, for the Parliamentary forces immediately entered it and the King's troops were harassed. It was retaken by the King and held against all odds. The little garrison held it bravely against continuous sieges for two years; when the King's forces were so weak the gallant little place at last was captured.

On Wednesday, 10 June 1644, the garrison surrendered. The

schoolboys at Thame were allowed by their masters a free holiday on this day and many of them went at eight or nine in the morning to see the Form of Surrender, and the strength of the garrison, and the soldiers of the two parties.

Sir John Aubrey possessed Boarstall at the end of the seventeenth century. His little son of five was poisoned by mistake here. Sir John left the place and pulled down the house. The gatehouse is all that remains of the fortified castle.

The little bridge with cobbled path and two arches of brick over the moat was built in 1735. Through the gatehouse there is now a lovely garden with smooth lawns which cover the site of the old house. There are magnificent trees growing by the edge of the moat, and vegetable gardens filled with strawberry beds and lettuces, for the soil here is very rich loam and an Italian gardener has looked after it for many years. Leaning over the moat near the house stand two great trees, a sycamore and a beech, and from the top of the roof we were level with the highest boughs. Twenty-five years ago Boarstall was in bad condition and unoccupied, but now a miracle has transformed it to a beautiful dwelling which seems to have come out of the "Sleeping Princess" ballet.

The central room is the dining-room with the four little round rooms at the corners under the towers made into bedrooms. We went up the stone spiral staircase to the long sitting-room with oriel windows at the end and the small round rooms at the corners. One of these was a tiny library, with narrow windows through which an arrow could fly. Another little room had a secret cupboard behind a panel, now made into a hanging cupboard and the floor boarded up. It originally had a staircase down to the depths of the earth, leading through a passage under the moat to the farmhouse near. The legend is that the young Princess Elizabeth was kept in the Boarstall stronghold and when Queen Mary sent for her she escaped by dressing as a dairymaid and going to the farm by the moat passage.

We went up the spiral staircase in the wall of the Tower through a door to the roof of the building. This roof is covered with lead and there from the battlements one gets a view of the country which cannot have been very different in the days when

Boarstall was besieged by the Cromwellians. Across the fields Muswell Hill, with its rounded top, must have been a constant menace to the Royalists, and away in the distance was Brill, with its army of Parliamentary troops to harass this little fort.

It was all very peaceful. Queen Anne's lace covered the banks of the moat with white flowers and ducks were swimming in the water. Across the moat was the farmhouse with mullioned windows and rosy brick walls. It was four o'clock and the cattle were coming home with swinging udders in a procession to be milked. Geese walked across the yard and hissed at an intruder. Five great stacks filled the stackyard and a new silo stood near.

I looked through the lovely stonework of the battlements, the stone balusters, delicately but strongly carved, and there over the doorway, so high it could only be seen from the roof, was a strip of most wonderful carving in the stone.

The old gatehouse is furnished with beautiful treasures, and the atmosphere is that of a beloved place. The village people had had a dance in the long room only the week before. The striped couches, the splendid hangings, the glowing colours, against the austerity of the grey stone walls brought back to life a former age.

Near Boarstall there are some old duck decoys in the ponds, but now they are out of use.

We left this historical part of the county to see Ludgershall. The irregular village is built round the large village green where children were playing, babies lay in perambulators, and mothers talked. There was plenty of room for safety from any cars that might come along. Akeman Street forms part of the boundary to the north of the green.

The Church of the Assumption of the Blessed Virgin stands in a churchyard like a garden of wild flowers, with tall buttercups and cow parsley, with archangel and bugle and ivy, all shimmering in the sunshine. Sometimes a churchyard looks neglected when the grass is uncut, but this one was like a beautiful field of flowers all ready for mowing.

There were many strange carvings on the gravestones of cherubs and angels, squinting and smiling, but I liked a plain stone which bore the name of John William Mole.

277

John Wyclif was the rector here from 1368 to 1374, when he went to Lutterworth.

Inside the church we were startled by the faces on the capitals of the pillars, some of the most strikingly alive and intent visages I have ever seen; men, hooded closely, with arms interlacing, grinned from the capital of one pillar. It is extraordinary carving, very bold and grotesque. The men wear capes with pointed hoods—liripipe hoods—like dwarfs. Others around the pillar had their elbows out and arms akimbo, and their keen faces were eagerly watching us, except one who was contemptuous of all people. A third capital had a ring of faces which apparently belonged to women. These were most expressive and brilliant in their execution. Some great craftsman of the thirteenth century carved these men and women out of stone, and one feels certain they were portraits.

There are fourteenth-century arcades which separate the nave from the aisles. There is a fifteenth-century roof with hammer beams and splendid carved pendants at the end of the beams. Angels carved in wood under the roof hold it up. There are two squints, long narrow peepholes, in the chancel arch. I liked the small old door to the bell tower, deep in the wall with steeply mounting stairs.

In the chancel, near the altar, is a tomb with Tudor brasses of three generations—the old grandmother, Anne Englishe, wife of Mihill Englishe, who died at the age of ninety-five, her daughter Anne Neele, and a child, all dressed in Tudor clothes. From the church door one can see a large farm with haystacks close to the little gate.

There is no manor house, but a moated site has the traditional name of King Lud's Hall. There are two seventeenth-century inns, the Five Bells and the White Hart.

Grendon Underwood is a place of rich traditions and legend. The stories come from John Aubrey. Tales go from one generation to another, passed by word of mouth, and Aubrey heard the tales from people who lived there in his time.

It is a village among the woods and it was on the forest footpaths which the gipsies and strolling players used. Shakespeare probably came this way. Aubrey says: "The humour of . . . the constable in *A Midsummer Night's Dream* he happened to take at Grendon, in Bucks . . . and there was living that constable about 1642 when I first came to Oxon."

Of course there is no constable in *A Midsummer Night's Dream* and Aubrey probably meant Dogberry in *Much Ado*. It is said that Shakespeare used to stay at the inn, the Ship Inn, on his journeys from Stratford-on-Avon to London. He got the inspiration for Dogberry and Verges from two characters he met on one occasion. So the tale is told, and some may hotly deny it and others firmly believe it. Two old women, who might easily have come out of *The Merry Wives of Windsor*, showed me the inn, now a private house called Shakespeare's Farm.

I had already seen the haystacks and long thatched barns of timber, and the fine old house, from the church. I stood in the garden of the churchyard, a wild garden, knee-deep in cow parsley, where rooks cawed in the elms and a cuckoo sang, and I saw this old farm.

I went inside the church and stayed a few minutes by the door where Shakespeare is said to have lain when the beadles roused him from drunken sleep.

In those days there was a porch, but this has been removed. The doorway is beautiful, with dog-tooth ornament cut on the arch and flowered capitals. There are marks here of the existence of a porch and within the doorway is a fifteenth-century holy-water stoup.

There is a hexagonal oak pulpit of Jacobean work, with good carving on it, and a cover for the font like a crown of wood, and under the tower is an Elizabethan chest. In the stair turret is a tiny door of oak with strap hinges, a fifteenth-century little door. I was glad, however, to come out to the cow parsley and the rooks and the sight of the farmhouse glowing down the road.

There are several mass-dials cut on the walls of this church, as in many of the churches in Buckinghamshire. I think perhaps anybody who liked could make a sundial when they wanted to know the time, and they carved it in the wall in the way people nowadays carve their initials.

There are three bells in Grendon Church, the treble made in 1621 by Robert Atton; the second and tenor made by Richard

Chandler in 1677 and 1664 at Chandler's Bell Foundry at Drayton Parslow, the little village to the east of Bucks looking on the pines of Wooburn Sands.

The sign of the original Ship Inn hangs in Aylesbury Museum. On one side of it is the painted picture of a Tudor ship with full sails, and on the opposite side is a different view of the ship. The white wooden frame and mouldings of this sign are very decorative. The colours are soft and faded by centuries of wind and rain, but the red cross on the sails and the blue water are very clear. Even now people go to Shakespeare Farm for a drink, thinking it is still an inn.

It is a lovely timber-framed house with brick filling, the bricks of rose pink and the roof of old red tiles with waves in it like water. When the roof was redone, owing to rain entering, the date 1545 was found cut in one of the timbers. The east part was the inn and the west half was a house, but now they are made one.

The east end is gabled and the windows are the original lattice windows, with oak mullions and some of the old leaded glass. The owners have had to put in double windows to keep the rain from seeping through the original panes. The attic has a small round window which may not be original, but one hopes it is, and that Shakespeare looked down the road from it, for this little room is the one where, by tradition, he slept.

The large room, the sitting-room of the house, has an open arched fireplace, and so has the room above. The staircase is original, in four flights, with flat balusters and octagonal newels with acorn finials at the half-landings. We went through the old house and saw the rooms with four-poster beds and furniture and hand-printed linen in keeping. Shakespeare's room is a tiny writing-room under the roof. This little attic has its own stair-way and it must have been an excellent private little room for the great dramatist. It is said that the inn could sleep forty people, and perhaps some of the rooms had partitions to make many of few.

This house, like many of the old houses, was in bad condition up to some years ago, but care has been bestowed upon it by the owners, Captain and Mrs Williams. The water in the cellars has been turned aside, for springs run under the foundations, and there have been settlements in the clay soil. Now it is restored to new beauty and strength. At the back is a round pond, and by the side are cowhouses, barns, and stables. A pedigree herd of Jersey cows is there, under the charge of an old labourer who is thatcher, herdsman, and everything else in these days of short labour. It is good to see a farmhouse, with dogs and horses and cattle, made from this old inn which must have been inn and farmhouse combined in Shakespeare's time.

The river Ray flows through the parish and forms the western border. There are many picturesque thatched cottages in the village, and cottages of timber with brick fillings. They are seventeenth-century, with the red brick chimney stacks and wide fireplaces of the period.

Chilton, in the same neighbourhood, is a village, homely, unspoilt and simple, and when I first saw it I lost my heart to it. It stands high with the hills of Brill near, and views across the long green plains to the Chilterns far away on the blue horizon. The cottages, some of them old red brick, others wattle and daub, with thick walls and bent strong sides leaning outwards, some of them thatched and some tiled, are all unique and complete little characters of a village. Like village people, each has its own life and individuality.

The lanes leading to Chilton prepare one for the loveliness, for they are bright with campion, archangel, silver weed, and bluebells.

Opposite the church is the wheelwright's yard, with cart-wheels, and a wagon painted primrose yellow waiting to be repaired. Timber is piled up and the sunk circle for tyring wheels is occupied.

Chilton has a delicious smell. An odour of flowers and something elusive and refreshing pervades the village, and in the church it is even stronger and more fragrant. Everywhere in the place it haunted me. North Bucks villages have their own rich scents, but East Bucks is more delicate and subtle.

The little church is built on a rise with cottages very close to it, and the manor house walls by the grass, with a doorway leading to lawns beyond. There old people were walking, enjoying the gardens.

The fourteenth-century tower has grotesque gargoyles which

281

are like devils locked out of a holy place. There is one in particular which is the head of an open-mouthed, grimacing giant
who is the bogey of fairy-tale days.

The roof of the nave is sixteenth-century oak with angels
there. Steps leading to the rood loft are built in the chancel
arch, but they are blocked. The red brick floor is scrubbed like
a cottage kitchen. There is something very warm and happy
about an old red brick floor in a church such as I have seen in
several of the small churches.

An oak screen with balusters divides the chancel from the
side chapel and within this, behind an iron railing, is the great
Jacobean tomb of the Croke family who lived at the manor. It
is indeed a family gathering, with Sir John in ruff and his wife
in a black dress. Eleven children kneel there, of various ages,
and they wear their best dresses and robes of state. There are
five men, two boys, three young women, and a baby. One of
the red-robed bearded sons is Sir John Croke, Speaker of the
House of Commons in Elizabeth's reign. The other is Sir
George Croke, who was an opponent of Ship Money and a
partisan of John Hampden.

A third son wears a robe with panels down the front of stiff
embroidery. His curled hair is bare, but the legal men wear little
black caps. One can see, from the breaking away of a cap, that
the hair with its curls was carved and the cap fitted upon it.
The older girls wear grand head-dresses with yellow beads
round their heads and panels back and front. In the middle of
this assembly is a little chrisom child looking lost among her rich
grand relations.

The churchyard is a perfect garden, set up above the village
with a steep daisied bank, and smooth sward, and a path to the
door, with tombstones making a guard of honour. Lilacs in full
bloom grow by the garden wall and a green woodpecker in all
his beauty of spring plumage walks among the graves. Cottages,
grey and blue or red and gold, stand in little gardens, and a man
walks home with a bundle of pea-sticks over his shoulder. Below
the church is a cottage whose small lawn is bounded by a grey
wall of wichert with a pointed roof of red tiles. Under this
wall grow orange and red primulas.

Chilton House, the home of the Croke family, is a large handsome place with a flight of steps at the front and fields and lawns running down the hillside. The view is very beautiful, of hills far away and green fields and woods near, and the great oval of a ploughed field in the middle distance, warm and golden. The house has been taken by the Bucks Old People's Welfare Society and now it is occupied by old men and women who live in the fine rooms and walk in the gardens. It is a happy thought to house them in this charming little village with the doorway in the wall to the church and the splendid vistas from the house front. Part of this house is sixteenth-century, and its mellowed red brick walls are very kindly and welcoming.

Near Chilton the roads are bordered with magnificent trees; an avenue of oak and beech of great size and beauty of growth follows the way on the rounded hill that runs down to Dorton. From the hill many miles of fields and woods, with clustered haystacks and farm buildings, can be seen in the plain below.

Dorton Hall, which was the seat of Sir Henry Aubrey-Fletcher until recently, stands in the valley, with the hill of Brill beyond. This great Jacobean hall is built round three sides of a courtyard, and its red clustered chimneys rise among many trees. It has two original oak staircases with moulded balusters and urn-shaped newels, and I read the date 1626 on one. The hall has the original plastered fireplace, and a great Jacobean oak screen, with very elaborate carving, divides it. In this beautiful hall walked a boy who went straight across, taking no notice of me, hands out to touch the door. He was blind. The house has been taken over by the Society for the Blind for educational purposes.

The Queen Elizabeth Room, a room lined with small moulded panels, is on the ground floor. Near it we saw a reception-room with long trestle tables, set with mugs and plates for the youngest children who live in this part of the house. It was all very well kept, and the little boys were full of high spirits.

On the first floor, up that beautiful staircase, we saw a very lovely room, oak-panelled with an elaborate plaster ceiling of great beauty. How I wished the boys could see it too! It was divided into geometrical panels with brilliant cartouches, with heads and grotesque faces. Pendants hung from the ceiling like stalactites of icy snow. The fireplace was carved with crests and panels and on the fireback was the figure of a horseman.

The long gallery, which was the ballroom, has a barrel ceiling. At one end was a lovely window with an intimate view of the little church of Dorton below, close to it. This room, which is 120 feet long, and a splendid dancing-room, was filled with little iron bedsteads, each covered with a scarlet blanket.

The drawing-room had more beds with sick boys and a blue-clad nurse looking after them. In one of the beds a boy sat up, his sightless eyes wide open, his hands held out. He was singing at the top of his voice a challenging exultant song, his own defiance to the world, with no regard to anyone. It was very moving to hear him and it brought tears to my eyes. All these young boys in the beauty of the ancient house and they cannot see it! Their fingers move over the carvings and panels, they touch the warm heavy wood.

In the entrance hall, with the carved screen and the elaborate stone fireplace with its crests and ornaments, the boys have a gymnasium. A vaulting-horse stands in a corner. A piano is there. A group of boys stood by the wireless set, listening to a talk. Others were playing football on the lawn with a young master leading them. I could not forget the singing boy with the rapt expression and he haunted me for many a day.

At Dorton Hall until recently was kept the Boarstall Horn, that symbol of office of the King's Forester in Bernwood Forest, and the cartulary, with the vellum charts of the manors, including Boarstall. There is a pictorial map of Boarstall in it. Now it has been removed for safety and I did not see it.

The little church, under the shadow of the great house and dwarfed by its magnificence, has Norman walls and a tiny turret. Two large posts hold the arches of the turret, which has weatherboarded sides and roof, very simple and plain. The font has the words "A gifte to Butyfie the house of God" upon its cover, dated 1631.

CHAPTER XX

STONE, DINTON, AND HARTWELL

WE drove from Great Kimble to Stone along a road which seemed uninteresting at first sight, but it was so tightly compounded of pictures I could walk up and down it for a month finding new pleasures. The cottages by the roadside had tiny gardens running to a triangle in a way some cottages "grow." I have seen them in Westmorland, in Yorkshire, Cheshire, and Derbyshire—the narrow triangular garden with the cottage at the base and a tree at the apex, and all the produce of vegetables and flowers packed within the cornucopia. It was December, but the gardens were beautiful in shape and promise, with tiny windows peeping down at a yew tree in one, a cherry in another, a thatched outhouse here, and a holly there. Then came a farm with straw ricks neatly thatched, and cattle and horses standing by the hedges, children playing and men working.

There is a great deal of fun and jollity in the shapes of these small houses in Buckinghamshire villages and towns. The people who built them must have enjoyed their individual work. Some of the dwellings seem to have been born for laughter, no matter that the windows are small and the internal arrangements are inconvenient by modern standards. People adapted themselves to their cottages because they lived in them all their lives, and they knew the ways of the rainwater tap which they had put in themselves, and they knew the doorsteps worn by their feet, and the bits of carving, the step up and the step down, the draught from a door, which they circumvented with a wooden screen fixed to the wall. So they and their house became part of each other. The pargeting on the front, the side window in the gable end with its secret view, the drip-stones on this cottage, and the ammonite embedded in the wall of that one, and the dormer added to another, all have memories and character for the country dweller. The steep roofs with stepped gables one sees in some villages are beauty raised up for all to admire from one generation to another, but the little windows and cupboards and stairways of the cottages are hidden amenities for the inhabitants themselves.

The village of Stone has a symmetry about it, for the cross-roads are bounded by stone walls, like a north-country village. The village pond is at the cross-roads, with ducks swimming, and a low wall to keep cars from driving into it. In one angle of the walls stands the fine old church with its yews on a slight rise. In another angle is the wheelwright and carpenter's shop, with the yard stretching down to its own gates. These walls have great fossils embedded in them, for at Hartwell Quarries these splendid encrinites were discovered and taken out to decorate cottages and walls. They are like carvings done by a prehistoric hand and I love to see them built into walls and houses as ornaments.

Old carts and drays and farm wagons were in the wheelwright's yard, and scarlet-painted wheels were reared against a wall. The tyring-platform for taking the wheels when iron rims are fitted was in the ground with the ashes of the fire near and some broken wheels. At the top of the sloping yard was the wheelwright's long shop, with timber and lathes and furnace, and next door to it was the blacksmith's shop and stalls for the waiting horses, now no longer used. The wheelwright, Mr Plestow, was busy in the orchard at the back working at the saw-pit. He showed me the kind of work done nowadays, for wheels are still needed and carts are still made. He did everything in wood that a customer might want. He was making gates, one of them a double gate for a house, and field gates. There was a pile of backs and fronts for blow-bellows ready for a craftsman over the way to finish off with leather and sell. There were squares of wood ready for electric lamps, and rungs for ladders, and seats for stools. This work filled the gaps between the larger and more important pieces of work.

His father had come there fifty years before, he told me, but in those days there was a lot of shoeing to be done for the many farms in the neighbourhood. We gazed sadly at the disused black-smith's forge and the empty stable.

Slowly I walked down the slope among the old carts, and in my thoughts I was far away, at a wheelwright's shop up a narrow valley where I waited with my father while a new cart was examined and the colours were chosen for body and wheels —bright red, glorious blue, warm buff, or rich dark green, but mostly red like a toy, picked out in fine lines in white, and our name in white curly letters at the sides. The carts in Bucks are often yellow with fine decoration, and I saw a splendid specimen in the fields near Boarstall Castle one day. Another of these great primrose-coloured wains was leading hay by the river and two of them stood in a farmyard and open cartshed.

Across the road, up the hill, was an antique shop made from a barn, next door to a cobbler's. Here an ex-airman was making chairs and blow-bellows, whose wooden bodies we saw at the wheelwright's. He showed us a model of a Tudor house. He had a fine collection of lace-bobbins gathered from the old lace-makers who no longer need their bobbins now lace is seldom made. He had found a countryman's smock-frock hanging behind the door of a barn, and this was displayed with a swingel-and-flail. The smock was well embroidered, buttoned down the front with smocking on both fronts, on the back, and on the sleeves. The old man who had worn it was long dead.

There was a lace-pillow here and a photograph of the old lady at her work, and a bobbin-winder and one of those simple machines which clever home workers devised for rolling straw-plait when straw was plaited for hatmaking. It was a small mill, like a tiny mangle, which was fixed to the back of a door and the plait was mangled in it.

There were old chairs, Windsor and other patterns, which had been made by local craftsmen. One little house-chair had a shell pattern carved in its back similar to the encrinites which adorn the walls over the road. So country people take their inspiration from homely simple things around them.

The village of Stone has thatched barns and cottages and the high walls have narrow red "roofs," to throw off the rain. It is a village where stone is present, in a county of chalk and flints.

On the little hill between the walls at the cross-roads stands the Norman church, with great yews guarding it at the gates. From the square tower, which is fourteenth-century, a row of faces look down, peering to the country. The south doorway has Norman zigzag carving and a king and a bishop.

The glory of the church is the strange, richly decorated font, a twelfth-century picture-book for those who could not read. The carvings round the bowl are clearly cut and full of imagination. A snake with a knot in its tail, fish swimming on stone, devils with tangled hair and wry mouths, a fawn, a fox, goose, dragons, goat, and lizard, all the odd beasts of fact and legend are woven into a pattern.

The chief figure of this intricate work is a naked man, with ribs deeply marked, his feet on a serpent, his arms outstretched. One hand holds a club over the head of a fearsome dragon with cloven tail, and the other hand is in the mouth of the second beast, whose tail is knotted. A fish, the emblem of Christianity, is on one side, a bird, the Holy Ghost, pecks at the beast on the right, and a smaller human being pierces it.

Between these decorative emblematical figures are wonderful loops and beaded chains woven in patterns, with faces of fox and devil, of goat and lizard peeping through the coils.

The allegory is explained in the *Records* of Bucks. "The Monster on the left is the Evil One with open mouth and unknotted tail, free to destroy and hinder the free course of the Fish, that is the Christian Faith. On the right is the same Evil Power, but a Hand is in its mouth and the tail is knotted: it is being subdued by the might of the Three Persons in the Holy Trinity, though it still holds in its claws a human head, whose expression is one of helplessness and terror."

This famous font originally belonged to Hampstead Norris, near Newbury, but it passed from one church to another until a hundred years ago it was brought to Stone.

One is apt to forget the deep interest and pleasure countrymen had in the decorations of their churches, in the faces looking down from high arches, in the wall paintings and font and screens. Perhaps some recognized faces they knew among that leering, squinting, mocking throng which inhabits the churches, who grin and sleep and yawn in their high places. No solemn saints are there, but ordinary knaves and beggars.

In the churchyard near the door is a great stone trough cut

288

Boarstall Tower Gatehouse, fourteenth century

from one huge block. There is a wall close to the church covered with ferns and little plants, ivy-leaved toad-flax and stonecrops, an unusual sight in a county where there is a scarcity of stone, and a pleasure to see.

By the side of the road, in a field, stands Dinton Castle, a mock ruin with four towers. It was built by Sir John Vanhattan to show off his fossils. It is an ivy-covered place lined with brick but with a stone exterior. Dozens of great ammonites are set in the stonework for ornament. People wander through the open doorways, exploring the little place in its group of fir trees. They are puzzled by it as they picnic under its walls. This Folly is a depressing sight, and I turned away to find a farmhouse with an avenue of chestnut trees, and many farm buildings, all thatched, so that with its corn ricks and haystacks it looks like a golden-roofed village.

Dinton is an unspoilt village with old farms, with flower gardens, beautiful church, and superb manor house, all close together. On the little lawn by the church gate are the village stocks, with sitting room for three pairs of legs, and also the whipping post.

Oliver Cromwell came riding to Dinton after the Battle of Naseby to visit Simon Mayne at the Hall. The great manor house of rose-red brick is separated from the churchyard by an ivy-covered wall and fine hedge of yew trees. The lovely group of Elizabethan chimneys rises above the shimmering grey-green lichen on the roofs. Eight gables are along one side of this old house. Oliver Cromwell's sword is preserved here. Simon Mayne, the regicide, was lodged in the Tower at the Restoration and he died there in 1661. He fought for Cromwell and signed the death warrant for Charles I.

John Bigg also lived at Dinton, and tradition says he was the actual executioner of Charles. He was stricken with remorse and he lived in a cave or hut as a hermit until he died in 1696.

The great house where these happenings took place looks very peaceful in the afternoon light, with its lawns and its many windows and weathered rosy walls.

In the lane is a medley of farm buildings, gabled, timbered, with red, golden-green lichened roofs, and walls surrounding

Capital in Ludgershall Church

them, mossy and ivied and roofed with red tiles. The barns and cowhouses and stables, with cattle and horses, give a feeling of prosperity and homeliness to Dinton. Stone walls bound the manor house, the gardens, and the churchyard, and the red sloping tiles roofing them make a little walled city of them. The colour of these walls and the church is a rich creamy gold which shines warmly in the sun.

The door of the church was wide open, and we could hear little children having their Sunday-school lesson and an earnest young man teaching them. Six serious little faces were gazing up at him. Outside a swarm of bees was clustering through a hole in the tower where the queen must have gone. The sound of them was like the roar of the sea as thousands beat against the stone walls trying to enter.

The south door is remarkable for its fine carving. There is a chain of little hearts winding down the doorway with their points outward. On the stone lintel is a dragon with a wide mouth into which a small St Michael is thrusting a cross like a battle-axe. This dragon has six great teeth and a long tongue, a real dragon. The tympanum above is carved in an elaborate and bold fashion with two dragons eating the fruit of the Tree of Life. Each one has a forked tail, erect, and jaws wide open.

Under the dragons and over the doorway is an inscription:

> Praemia pro meritis siquis desperet habenda
> Audiat hic praecepta sibi que sunt retinenda,

which has been roughly translated as

> He who despairs of guerdon for his pain,
> Should listen here what precepts to retain.

In the churchyard there is the shaft of an old cross, and near it, among the thick grass, grow many kinds of wild flowers, with the tiny lavender-blue mountain crane's-bill which I have also found near Beaconsfield. From this spot, over the red roofs, one can see the Chiltern Hills, Bledlow, and Brill afar, with green valleys between.

Women were walking around the church one Sunday when we were there. gazing at the view and enjoying the sweetness of the air. They looked like country women returned home after a long time away as they drank in the fragrance and loitered among the flowers. I spoke to them and they told me they were from the mental home, patients who were allowed out to walk on Sundays. They were absorbing the beauty to carry back with them to the block of buildings we had passed on the way.

Near the church is an old house with herringbone brick set in timber squares, a lovely house at which I always stand and stare with satisfaction. It was by this house I once talked to some village children, just out of school, when I asked some questions.

"It's one of the housen up there," they said, using the old plural of house as I have heard it used often in the north.

Between Stone and Aylesbury is Hartwell House, the great house famous as the one-time residence of the exiled King of France, Louis XVIII. This house of magnificence and beauty stands in a walled park, with stone outbuildings near. The entrance gates seem to lead to a fairy castle as one looks through to see the house within. To the left of the splendid entrance is a small dwelling-house, with red roof and grey walls, the bailiff's cottage. The bailiff stood in his garden among pansies and roses, rather forlorn in all the magnificence, as he told me of the past glories of Hartwell House. Now the great house is empty and in poor state within.

The magnificent staircase with the carved newels each supporting a historical or mythical figure had been removed to safety, but later it was replaced. These figures, which once rather frightened the French Queen in the candlelit house, are beautifully carved, and one can imagine the grotesque shadows cast by them on the walls.

The house has an entrance porch with carved pillars of stone and a carved doorway. Over it is a round oriel window, which rests on exquisite corbels of stone, cut as if to make lace. It is an embroidery of stone, and the window is glorious to see. Two more oriels are set in this front of the house.

A red rose climbs here, very small and frail and delicate against the great walls. There are fretted stone parapets and pedestals along the roof, and on them the French servants crowded together looking down from the high windows and galleries on a green foreign landscape a hundred years ago.

The stone of Hartwell House is local, the lovely creamy-gold stone which comes from a quarry near. The walls that surround the gardens are made of the same stone. In the garden in front of the main portion of the house, set in lawns like a small round mirror, is a diminutive pond with an island in the centre. The water holds deep red lilies and the island is filled with flowers. When I first saw it the gardens were wild with ragged robin and daisies, but now they are decked with orderly beds of gold and amber and crimson blossoms.

Four statues, half-faun, half-human, stand round the pond, in that disconsolate way of statues in our English climate, looking rather cold and unhappy.

When the King and Queen of France lived at Hartwell House, about 150 people stowed themselves into attics and rooms, so that the great house was packed to the utmost, and little wooden partitions were used to divide the chambers, to make more bedrooms. On the roof they had flowers along the parapets. They visited the cottages in Hartwell and danced and sang with the village people. How much one would enjoy talking to someone who had witnessed the gay French court in the little Buckinghamshire village!

The trees at Hartwell are magnificent, free-growing giants, with wide-spreading branches. Some of them have the marks of names carved by the Frenchmen on their trunks. A great beech in the grounds is the largest I have seen, and it grows there with thick trunks rising from the central body. Some box trees are cut in the shapes of a crown, a basket, and a dome.

The lake at Hartwell is one of the beauties of the grounds. It stretches beyond the lawns, and water feeds it from the springs in the lane near. Water-hens and chicks swim there, and one can watch them from the stone bridge which has an ornamental parapet, an arch of which came from Kew Bridge.

In a corner of the park is the little church of Hartwell. It was built in the eighteenth century by Sir William Lee—a copy of the octagonal chapter house of York Minster. An octagonal church can be a gay little place, and Hartwell church makes one

think of Christmas and Easter and festivities. There are two
little towers, one over the porch to hold the organ and little
else—it is so small—the other over the minute chancel. The roof
is fan-vaulted, with a pinnacle in the centre. Unfortunately when
I saw this church the lovely roof was falling, and the edifice was
labelled "Danger." Damp had entered, rain had loosened the
roof, and the thunder of guns had added to the damage, I was
told. Now they are waiting for it to be restored. So we stood
very gingerly by the door lest the roof should drop upon us.
We locked the door and retreated through the yew trees
and jungle of ferns and flowers, greater aconite, and wild
geranium.

The old rectory across the pathway outside the stone walls
has a beam dated 1552. We crossed the graveyard, which is
beyond the walls of Hartwell Park, and went down the road to
see the Egyptian springs, which run into the lake. The water
rises here, fresh from the earth, clear as glass, and falls into a
stone trough which reminded me of Derbyshire troughs by the
roadside. It is a lovely spot, this part of the road, with thickly
overhanging trees and running water and a curved stone seat
with an Egyptian figured inscription.

The cottages at Hartwell are thatched and some are timbered,
half-hidden in flowers and bushes. In the walls of Hartwell
are encrinites and ammonites which have been found in the
clay.

This is farming country, and at a large farm at Upper Hartwell I talked to the farmer who has a Friesian herd. Two of his
cows are champions. They give 2,000 gallons a year. I was
interested in the milking of these heavy-yielding cows, and I
was told that they are milked three times and sometimes four
times a day. The extra milking time is in the evening at 7.30.
They are all milked by hand, for I think it is a fact that the yield
is greater to a hand-milker. The farmer was the first breeder of
Friesian cattle in Bucks. For thirty years he had not bought
cattle but had bred his own herd. In Hartwell Park Aylesbury
Show is held, an agricultural show of perfection in this setting of
great trees and winding waters, and the house in the background.

At Thame, in Oxfordshire, there is a beautiful four-arched bridge over the river. This used to be called Crendon Bridge, for the village of Long Crendon is near. It is built on high ground with views across the blue distances. The narrow irregular streets with seventeenth-century cottages weave about like the needles which once were made at Long Crendon. Roses grow before the cottages, springing from the roadside, climbing the walls. There is something very delightful about this, an innocent and trustful air, as each little house adds to the beauty of the street. Even the butcher's shop is different at Long Crendon. A winged angel flies before one inn, and eight bells hang on the painted sign of another.

Long Crendon was famous for its needle-making. In 1558 Christopher Greening introduced this trade to the village and in the eighteenth century it flourished. The needles were made in cottage homes, but later factories sprang up in towns, especially in Redditch, and the needle-making at Long Crendon died away.

The Court House, which was once known as Old Staple Hall, stands near the west of the churchyard. It is a fifteenth-century house, long and low, timber framed, with the upper story hanging over the lower, and flowers close to the walls—bluebells, auriculas, and primulas—in the narrow strip of garden. The upper floor is divided into five bays, four of which make a large room with an open timber roof. These great beams, curved like the original tree-trunks, are very fine. From them now hang little swings for children for the room is a health centre, with toys and rocking-horse and little chairs. The east end of this building was originally one narrow lofty room reaching from the ground floor to the roof, but a separate apartment has been made by adding a floor. At this end of the house is the rectangular chimney stack. There is a large fireplace with a sixteenth-century wood lintel and a round brick oven.

The church at Long Crendon has a sixteenth-century oak roof to the nave. The doorway has plain carvings in the stonework of Tudor roses and one of the gargoyles is a fierce lion of grotesque imagery. Other beasts gaze down from the great roof to the country. The octagonal font of 1380 is surrounded by sturdy little lions, and small angels with outstretched wings are around its brim.

The Dormer tomb, behind painted railings with blue and gold spear-heads, holds Sir John Dormer and his wife. He is in complete armour, she in coif, ruff, and long dress. Their delicately moulded hands are upheld. The stone is painted and much of the colour is original. Blue and gold cushions support the lady's head, and tassels of blue and white hang there in rich decoration.

The church of Long Crendon has Bucks lace made by one of the lace-makers of the village. The edging of the Communion cloth was made by an old lady, and some napkins and cloths for the altar service are edged by her cobweb lace.

Down the nettle lane near the church I saw a sight more beautiful to me than anything in the church. It was a newly painted wagon, with a long yellow body and four red wheels, the wheels picked out in black and the back of the wagon picked out in red on the yellow. It was a splendid piece of workmanship, with its ladders and side rails or wraithes, as we called them, and pole. Two more wagons similar to this were in the yard, canary bodies and red wheels, dish wheels with twelve spokes at the back, ten at the front. They belonged to a farm lower in the valley, and there they stood in their Sunday sleep with the manor house close to them and the church beyond.

In the High Street of Long Crendon is a private house, once a farmhouse, with open gateway and a room which may have been the tithe barn, with its entry for wains. This barn is now part of the house, and the sloping yard has been made into a green lawn with flower beds. There grows a fine walnut tree, one of those bountiful trees which are harvest homes in themselves. Many of the Buckinghamshire farm gardens have a walnut tree, one of the happiest possessions. They are beautiful throughout the year, but in winter, when the boughs are bare and snow is on the ground, there is something exhilarating about them. Their shadows are blue and the trees come to intense life, with their lovely boughs and the shapes of the twigs spread out on the snow like reflections in a mirror.

There are two large houses at Long Crendon, the Manor House, south-east of the church, which is dated about 1680,

and Long Crendon Manor. This beautiful house has a courtyard and an early gatehouse with an archway. It is fifteenth-
century, with large central hall and wings.

Notley Abbey, now the home of Sir Laurence Olivier, is in
the parish. Part of it is thirteenth-century.

Chapter XXI

THE CLAYDONS

THIS corner of the county is the most interesting of all, for it gives an historical picture of Buckinghamshire people with a continued and unbroken tradition since the fifteenth century. The Claydon country is associated intimately with the name of Verney, and the four manors Middle Claydon, East, Bottle or Botolph, and Steeple Claydon form the Verney estate. Claydon House stands in its own park in the parish of Middle Claydon. The park is over 300 acres, and there are three stretches of water which were the fishponds for the house.

The original house was built about the time of Henry VII, but it was almost entirely rebuilt in a very magnificent manner in the middle of the eighteenth century by Ralph, the second Lord Verney. Part of his fine Adam building was pulled down later and now only the west front remains. However, there is a good deal of the earlier work within the house and the heart of the ancient house lives still.

Claydon House, alone in the park, has the little church of Middle Claydon close to it. This was the home chapel and the small priest's door is there now, with a flight of steps near the library window. To the east are the courtyard and stables and many of the old red brick outbuildings.

It must be remembered that a great house was self-contained, and the life of the country people was completely absorbed in its being. So here at Claydon House the family and servants brewed their own ale for drinking and baked their own bread, they churned their butter and ground the corn at their own mill. They bred their cows and sheep for meat, and had a flock of poultry and a pigeon house. They had their own smithy in the red brick buildings across the courtyard, and there they shod the horses and made hinges and bolts and bars, as in the estate yards of modern estates. They had carpenters to make gates and doors, to mend and keep in order the cottages and the great house with timber from their own woods.

297

Many of these buildings remain now and one can see the dairy with the churn which was turned by a horse, the great laundry house, the brewhouse for ale, the stalls for cattle, the stables, pigsties, and the rooms where grain was stored.

The life at Claydon House during the centuries is known through the Verney letters, those illuminating and simple documents which provide an insight into the everyday doings of this family. The story of the Verney letters is remarkable. When Sir Harry Verney came to live at Claydon he found a wainscoted gallery forty feet long at the top of the house full of boxes of letters and papers, parchment account books, and rent rolls. Some were gnawed by rats, but most were in good condition. Family portraits were pushed in cupboards and torn, and he had these beautiful pictures restored.

The letters concerned the Verneys who had owned Claydon for fourteen generations, and the most important were those letters written during the Civil Wars when Sir Edmund Verney was the Knight Marshal and his son Ralph was a Member of the Long Parliament. The letters are outstanding because Sir Ralph kept every scrap of paper, with bills, verses, notes, love letters, even patterns of silk for a baby's coat and embroidery silks for his sister, and songs and recipes and reminders.

The letters are vastly entertaining; they are written with such freedom, with no thought of future generations reading them, with pet names and jokes and mention of horses and dogs, of cures and illnesses, of troubles and joys, of games and cooking and shopping. They are so vivid in their continuity that those men and women of the seventeenth century live as clearly, nay, more clearly, than people of our own time. We feel we know them intimately, their weaknesses and difficulties, their loves and marriages and their little children and their clothes. Always through these earlier letters shines out the affection of Sir Ralph for his charming brave little wife, Mary, whom he called Mischief. Some letters discuss gardening, others speak at length about servants with sympathy and kindness and an equality that is missing even in these days.

Sir Edmund Verney was deeply attached to King Charles, whom he had served since boyhood. He went to Spain with Charles on that incredible adventure to woo the Infanta, and what an account he writes of the dirt there! His loyalty kept him on the King's side in the trouble with Parliament.

Ralph, his eldest son, supported Cromwell, but he refused to sign the Covenant and went into exile with his wife and two of the little children. Edmund, Ralph's brother, a delightful boy whose nickname was Mun, was the gallant cavalier. He was put to death in cold blood by Cromwell's men after Drogheda. Tom Verney was the scapegrace, the scamp of the family. He sponged upon all—the servants and anyone who would believe his specious tales. His letters are very amusing to us, although they must have been a trial to his relations. In one letter he naïvely asks for a quantity of beer for his servants and only a prayer book for himself.

The most poignant letters are from Ralph's wife Mary, who left her husband in France and returned to England to try to negotiate his safe return. Her thoughts are on Ralph and the children and she sends details of their shoes and stockings and food while she travels about the country meeting influential people.

Through these notes and bills and scraps of news one can construct a picture of surprising vividness and reality of Buckinghamshire in the time of the Stuarts—customs, roads, villages, the people, the trades, and food.

Sir Edmund Verney the elder married Margaret Denton, the daughter of Sir Thomas Denton of Hillesden, when he was twenty-two. The great house of Hillesden could be seen from rising ground at Claydon. Tradition says that two trumpeters used to sound reveille, answered by two trumpeters on the other hill a few miles away. Margaret and her young husband lived with the family of Denton at Hillesden for some years after their marriage to save money. It was here that eight of their twelve children were born. It was a beloved family house, where they romped and played with many young children—their own and the Dentons'.

Sir Edmund was away in London at the court a good deal of his time, and Margaret often stayed in London with him. While he was in Spain with Prince Charles his daughter Margaret was born at Hillesden.

When James I died and Charles became king, Sir Edmund

299

was made Knight Marshal of England. He lived in a house in Drury Lane and the children stayed at Claydon and at Hillesden. Both houses were their homes. Young Ralph, his eldest son, married Mary Blacknall, an heiress who was brought up with him, and he lived at Claydon, but young and old shared the two manor houses.

So it was with a feeling that we knew the Verney family who lived three hundred years ago that we drove along quiet lanes between overgrown hedges and across little trickles of brooks, to the village of Middle Claydon and down a road to the lodge gates. It was all very plain, as if we were going to a farmhouse, with cattle in the park and gates across the road to keep them within one portion.

The young family of Verney who live at Claydon now might be the family of that other century, even to their Christian names—Ralph, Edmund, Mary—and we felt they had just stepped through a curtain to greet us from past and present.

On the walls of the great house were the famous Verney pictures, portraits of brilliant life and vivid personality.

In the hall, over the mantelpiece, was the painting of Prince Henry, the eldest son of James I, clear-eyed, grave, regarding the household below him with a faint amusement and deep interest in all their affairs. I could not take my gaze off him; I waited to see him move his head and speak to us as this young generation of Verneys discussed the war and the jeeps and tanks and the engagements of the Gunners.

Tom Verney, the scamp, was in this room, excusing himself, careless of opinion and dress. There has been no brother Thomas since his day, I was told. He was in disgrace, but he didn't care a jot, and the young people had sympathy with his misdoings.

"That fellow is in danger of hanging in Paris, of pillory in London," wrote his uncle, Dr Denton, in one of his letters.

There is Edmund, the young cavalier, whom everyone loved, whose gay company the girls sought, who reduced them to tears of laughter when he came to Claydon on leave.

On the right of the fireplace is Margaret Verney, the mother. She wears a lace-edged white smock and sits with a wounded arm exposed so that all can see the deep scars. The cause of the wound is unknown, probably burns, and we can only guess at some brave deed known to them all.

The portrait of Sir Edmund Verney, the King's standard-bearer, by Van Dyck, is in the long picture gallery. He is bare-headed, wearing armour, with his helmet near him. His hand-some sensitive face is troubled by the turn of events. He seems to have foreknowledge of fatal results. He was slain at the Battle of Edgehill and his severed hand, still clasping the royal standard and wearing the ring Charles I had given him, was found. His body was not found. This ring is in the possession of the Verney family. His ghost walks along a passage at the top of the house as he seeks his hand, or perhaps because he died violently when his loyalties were torn between his son and his King.

Opposite the standard-bearer is the Van Dyck portrait of Charles I, bareheaded, wearing the star on his shoulder, a pic-ture given by the King to Sir Edmund.

As one enters the gallery there stands the forceful and magnifi-cent painting of Francis Verney, brother of Sir Edmund. He became a Barbary corsair, throwing off his allegiance to his country, sailing as a pirate. He died in poverty in a foreign land. He wears here the most beautiful clothes from Spain, and the suit is in the Victoria and Albert Museum. Tall, slender, hand-some, with trim little beard, he looks a typical Elizabethan gallant.

The bewitching young Mary Verney is here too, dressed in white satin with sky-blue sleeves and a string of pearls. Her demure charming face and sidelong glance are the spirit of Mischief, her pet name.

The great rooms, the hall, drawing-rooms, library, and pic-ture gallery have superb doorways and ceilings, long shuttered windows and fine fireplaces. The grand staircase is inlaid with ebony and ivory, and there is no apparent structure to uphold it, so that it seems to sweep upward on wings. The underpart of the staircase is also inlaid with squares of intricate pattern. The balusters are wrought with scrolls and ribbons and cornstalks of iron, with long delicately curling leaves of wheat and groups of ears which were once gilded. The wheat ears sway on their stalks, caught by the wind, as if they were living, and this is a marvel of wrought ironwork.

There are a Chinese room, a Gothic room, and best of all, a Tudor panelled room on the top floor. The muniment room is filled with manuscripts tucked away in pigeon-holes in the walls, waiting to be deciphered.

A suite of rooms is that occupied by Miss Florence Nightingale on the many occasions when she stayed with her sister at Claydon House. Parthenope and Florence Nightingale were the daughters of the Derbyshire squire, Peter Nightingale, who was our squire and friend in my grandfather's days. Parthenope married Sir Harry Verney. She was the brilliant writer and keen historian, and it is due to her diligent research and that of her daughter-in-law that the Verney letters were so wittily edited. Florence Nightingale loved Claydon House with its peaceful atmosphere, and the rooms she had there with their sunny outlook over the park seem to hold her personality within. There is a picture of Miss Florence, taken when she stayed at Claydon in the 'nineties, a smiling old lady of great power. The most delightful painting is a water-colour of Mrs Nightingale in a spring dress of muslin and ribbons flying, with her gay animated little daughters, Florence and Parthenope.

This house at Claydon must have had an influence on Florence Nightingale. It must have been present in her mind as a heaven far away when she was in the awful hospitals at Scutari.

We walked along the haunted passage and stayed at the spot where Sir Edmund appears, but I had no awareness of his presence. Near is the panelled room with Tudor woodwork and linenfold walls, a reminder of the ancient part of the house. In one of the great chimneys of Claydon a small chamber was discovered when the house was repaired. In this hidden room ten men could stand upright. The secret had been forgotten, for it was probably handed down from father to eldest son orally, with no written words, for safety. It must have had an entry from the muniment room at the top of the house. When enemies came the refugee could escape upstairs and then down the secret staircase and out by another door.

From the summit of the tower there is a magnificent panorama of Buckinghamshire, so that one feels one is gazing at the
whole of the green county. It looks very beautiful with its
hundreds of diverse fields, its bosky woods, but there is a sign
of industrialism, the tall chimneys of the brickworks. On the
horizon is Brill Hill; Hillesden Church can be seen near, and the
Chilterns stretch their blue backs against the sky.

In the park shine the three ponds, the fishponds of the old days
when fish was caught for the table. Cedars and cypresses grow
close to the house. These tall trees were grown from seeds Miss
Florence brought back from the Crimea.

Below are the old red buildings around three sides of a square,
but the courtyard in the middle across which servants and grooms
once hurried and dawdled, laughed and courted, is now an
orchard. The brewhouse is there, and the dairy next to it, the
laundry, stables, forge, workshops, and carpenter's shop, with
their ancient gear, their forgotten utensils, pans, and implements.

We looked down on a glass dome surrounded by the cluster
of gabled roofs of the house, little old roofs of many centuries,
sloping at acute angles, a labyrinth of attics with tiny windows
and lead guttering. There was the continuous murmur of bees
and a shimmering movement as the honey bees clouded the air.
They have made their hive in this domed roof for a century or
two, said Ralph Verney, and owing to the difficulty of climbing
to this place the honey can be taken only occasionally. A great
store was discovered the last time it was opened out, and every
bucket and bath in the place was filled.

We have seen honey bees entering holes in church walls,
making their hives in towers, and we wonder if they are ever
searched for the loads of honey that must lie within the great
stones.

Middle Claydon Church, with its fifteenth-century tower, is
across a little lawn. There is a flight of mossy steps with oak
handrail leading to the narrow door in the chancel, and we
entered this little church by the way the Verneys have gone for
centuries.

Inside, near this door, is a beautiful and delicate altar tomb
to Margaret Giffard, who died in 1539, a Verney ancestor. Her

303

dainty hands are lifted, her charming piquant face, carved in
alabaster, seems to be only sleeping. Her full skirt is pleated and
folded neatly, and her modish sleeves are puffed. A tiny dog
playfully pulls the skirt away from her little feet in their
ensible square-toed shoes. Two small angels hold the pillow
under her head. It is a delightful work of art with no reminder
of sorrow or death but of happiness and laughter at Claydon
House.

Close to the Verney door is a large brass of Roger and Mary
Giffard, and their twenty children done small underneath.

"On whose sowlis Jh'u have m'cy. 1543."

These were the Giffards who lived at Claydon on a hundred
years' lease from the Verneys. In 1620 Sir Edmund Verney
bought back the remainder of this lease and came to live at
Claydon.

The important monument I came to see was the famous
Verney memorial, erected after Sir Ralph's wife Mary, his
Mischief, had died at Blois. It was designed and wrought in
Rome in 1652. This monument of many-coloured marbles with
the Verney arms emblazoned on it and the phœnix at the top,
has portrait busts of the family. It is in memory of four Verneys,
Sir Edmund and his wife Margaret, Ralph their son and Mary.
Sir Edmund "killed at the memorable batayle of Edgehill,
father of 6 sonns and 6 daughters" is in armour, a grave soldier.
Sir Ralph, the conscientious letter-writer and adviser to his
family of sisters and brothers, relations, friends, and sundry, is
below, and Lady Mary, the charming girl whom he loved and
teased, is opposite.

The eulogy Ralph wrote is very moving and true.

". . . also to the perpetuelle honour and memory of that most
excellent and incomparable Person, Dame Mary."

We went softly from the church, down the Verney stairway
to the park, thinking of Mary and Ralph and their perfect
companionship.

There is a tale told by Lady Verney, the compiler of the
Memoirs, about this little church at Middle Claydon. The last
Lord Verney had the churchyard altered and the graves moved,

Norman tympanum in south porch at Dinton Church

and in the village the tradition exists that his ill-luck came from it, for he was ruined.

"He never prospered arter that, ye know. For why? He moved the dead. But they was all back again next marning safe in their graves."

"What? Someone carried them back, you mean?" asked the hearer.

"Nay, none knew how, but there they all was as afore," said the countryman firmly.

All country people know the respect for the last resting-place, and the misfortunes that are said to attend those who disturb the sleep of the dead.

East Claydon is a purely agricultural village, with soil of rich clay loam and several dairy farms. Pretty black and white cottages stand near the church and always I see milk churns waiting to be collected near the gate. Little green lanes wind through the village and tall elms grow in the hedgerows. The church has demon-faced angels on the chancel arch, and high on the inside of the tower is a woman's head craning forward.

An old Elizabethan house, the White House Farm, with a little lawn in front of it and a stone bay window with mullions, is by the road. It was lately the home of the historian Arthur Bryant. In the seventeenth century the sheriff, Mr Abel, kept horses here for the Assizes at Aylesbury. His daughter married young Edmund Verney, son of Sir Ralph, and here they lived. The wife went out of her mind and her poor ghost haunted the place for years, to the annoyance of Edmund who tried to lay the restless spirit.

The inn at East Claydon has the joint arms of Edmund and his wife and their initials over the door. Once the high-road to Buckingham and London passed through this village, but the road was diverted in the reign of Queen Anne. The old way is a track in the fields, probably not much changed, for Sir Ralph's coach stuck in the mud near Aylesbury and had to be dragged out by cart-horses.

Steeple Claydon is a village of wayside cottages and a church with a steeple, one of the few steeples in Bucks. Sir Thomas Chaloner, mentioned in Hakluyt's *Voyages*, lived at the manor.

x   305

Fifteenth-century Court House, Long Crendon

His son was tutor to Prince Henry, son of James I. He endowed a school here which still exists. This old school was restored by Sir Harry Verney last century. The Chaloner Library, one of the first free libraries, is housed in a little red brick gabled building.

From the churchyard one can see the house of the Verneys at Middle Claydon, for the villages are close together. There is a barn by the roadside where Cromwell's soldiers lay on their way to Hillesden. On the outer wall is a small tablet with the words:

THE CAMP BARN

Around this spot the Army of Parliament under the command of Cromwell was encamped March 1644, and on the 3rd of that month advanced from here to the attack on Hillesden House.

Now Margaret Verney's brother, Sir Alexander Denton, held the house of Hillesden against Cromwell. The story of Hillesden is both romantic and tragic.

Hillesden lay between Oxford where the King was and Newport Pagnell where the Parliamentary troops were stationed in communication with Aylesbury. Parliament forces had been quartered in the house earlier in the strife, and the inhabitants had suffered. Sir Alexander, Ralph's uncle, fortified the house and Colonel Smith took command. It was a brave venture, a mouse fighting a lion. He built barns and stabling for the cavalry and the country folk came to help the garrison. A thousand labourers and farm men from villages near made a mound of earth for the artillery, and they fashioned a wooden cannon from an elm tree hollowed out and hooped with iron. They obtained five pieces of ordnance from Oxford, and some ammunition which they stored in the church.

They were digging a trench, far too large, surrounding house and church, when the enemy secretly approached from Steeple Claydon from the above-mentioned camp barn. The church was carried, the old bullet-holes are in the door now. The army of Parliament poured through the defences, and the Royalists surrendered and were marched off to Padbury. The garrison of

263 men were treated with barbarity and thirty-one died. The house was set on fire and destroyed.

Pen Verney, Ralph's young sister, wrote to her brother in exile, "When it pleased God to lay the great affliction on my uncle, I was more consarned for him, but I did stand so great a loss in my own particular way that it had been a half undoing of me. We were not shamefully used in any way by the souldiers, but they took every thing, and I was not left scarce the clothes of my back."

Two love tales connected with Hillesden are told in the Verney letters. One of the attacking officers fell in love with Sir Alexander Denton's sister, Susan. It was a quick courtship during the fighting before the little group of distraught women walked across the fields to Claydon House. Captain Jaconiah Abercrombie married his Susan but he was killed next year by Royalists from Boarstall and buried at Hillesden.

Colonel Smith, the commander at Hillesden, fell in love with Margaret Denton, Sir Alexander's daughter, and after his imprisonment he married her. The valiant Sir Alexander died before gaining his liberty.

Claydon House was threatened, but happily it escaped. Hillesden was rebuilt, but it was burned down and now there are only mounds in the meadow by the lovely church.

This remote parish of Hillesden, with a few cottages, a parsonage, and the fine church, stands lonely in the fields with the road to it curving round through cornfields and meadows, through six gates, across a little bridge over the stream, ever approaching in a circling movement, so that one feels there is an enchantment over Hillesden that warns the traveller away. The rough track, the wide cornfields with no hedges or boundaries to the road, the cattle grazing in the paths, all keep it serene in its loveliness. For it is indeed a lovely spot, and the church is a gem worth travelling across England to see—a treasure in itself. The avenue of great trees which once led to the house is there still but the road is covered in deep grass, and it ends in open fields.

There, like a little palace on its slight hill, stands the most beautiful Perpendicular village church in Buckinghamshire. I stood in the churchyard, amazed at the delicacy and the charm of this fifteenth-century church. Its setting in this lonely spot adds to its beauty and brings a feeling of melancholy which is quickly dispersed as one enters the warm happy building which is bright with sunshine and flowers and colour. Ghosts may walk in the green field alongside the walls where the house stood, but the church has no such loneliness.

The walls are battlemented as if for that battle long ago, and an octagonal turret rises in a column of grace from them. It has tiny flying buttresses which meet to form a central shaft. It is like a crown of stonework, high in the blue air of a cold day of early spring. Eight pinnacles decorate the battlemented walls; little stone trees they are.

In the churchyard is the shaft of a fourteenth-century cross where men once preached to the people out of doors. Near it is the pit where the Royalists killed in the battle of Hillesden, 3 March 1644, were buried. This is the best churchyard cross in the county. Whatever was done before the cross was binding, and proclamations were read from its steps.

The north porch has a vaulted roof with fan-vaulting and a rose in the centre. The door is pierced by several bullet-holes. There are traces of carvings of sun, moon, and stars on the door. The handle too is a fine example of craftsmen's work, for it is made in the form of a ring with two snakes twisted together. The door latch has the simple crosses and lines as the smith made it.

The interior of this church is very light and gay. Angels are carved and painted on the chancel and at the east window. Some of these hold musical instruments, a guitar, an organ, a harp, a violin; others hold scrolls of music. At the east window they hold the emblems of the Passion.

The squire's large square pew, raised above floor level to give a good view of the congregation, is now a children's corner with tiny chairs and books.

The vestry has a room above it, and from this chamber the family at Hillesden could see the altar and share the service without being seen. A bridge originally joined this upper room to the big house which lay close to the church beyond the high red brick wall. The bridge was broken and the stairway blocked.

The sixteenth-century rood screen is extremely light and delicate, with linenfold panelling and tracery of leaves and gilded pomegranates. The church has some fifteenth-century glass, which miraculously escaped destruction when the Cromwellians sacked the place. One of the windows in the sanctuary shows St John, St George, St Christopher, and the Pope. The most interesting window has eight tales of St Nicholas, with Jews and robbers and murdered boy, with devil disguised as a pilgrim, with the ship, the famine at Myra, and finally the miracle of St Nicholas restoring the boy to life.

We walked through the gate with its red brick gateway to the meadow where Hillesden House once stood. Along the side of the church is an old red brick wall with lozenges of black brick, as in Tudor work. It is all that remains. By the gate grows a tall sycamore in full leaf very early in the year when other trees are only in bud. I am reminded of a country superstition that a sycamore which comes in leaf each year long before its kindred is a sign that human beings or animals were once buried near it. Perhaps some of the dead of battle were buried there. I know a sycamore in Cheshire with this tradition, a tree which has its leaves three weeks before others.

In that field of Hillesden it was very quiet, with a strange stillness. We looked over the country, all green where the house of the Dentons once stood, down to the group of elms by the fish pond and the avenue which leads nowhere, but except for the low hillocks and unevenness in the grass, nothing at all remains.

In 1648 a new little house was built where the old one stood, one of the Verneys sent the news, but this house in its turn was destroyed. "Sweete Hillesden" church stands solitary, a glorious memorial and a living church. There is always a good congregation of country people who walk a long way across footpaths to evensong, I was told by a village woman.

At the church gates were empty milk churns and a little post office and cottages. I went away filled with happiness in the existence of such a beautiful place.

We drove along many miles of winding narrow lanes to find Chetwode Priory, but the green way twisted and turned like a grass snake, and I thought there must be a spell cast over Chetwode as there was at Hillesden, hiding it from the searchers. All that remains of the thirteenth-century priory is the church and some walls which form part of the modern priory house close to it. The house stands in smooth lawns with yew hedges and a tiny lake with water-lilies, yellow and white, and a stream running swiftly through it. In the middle of the lawn is a well with good water which once supplied the priory.

Across the lawn, close to the kitchens, is the small priory church which has five splendid lancet windows in the chancel. They are like music, great chords for ever sounding. The church seemed filled with music, although only the birds sang. There was a lyrical beauty about its symmetry. In the triple lancet on one side of the chancel is the oldest stained glass in Buckinghamshire. This treasure had just been put back after its removal during the war. There is a picture of St John the Baptist and the Virgin with a crown in the pale golden-yellow and rich blue of glass made 700 years ago.

All around are fields, grazing horses, and country lanes, with few houses for miles. The peace and music of the country's depths are here on this borderland of the county.

Chapter XXII

BUCKINGHAM AND STOWE

THE cottages at Padbury, near Buckingham, have flowers growing under the house walls or outside the garden gates— roses and pansies and wallflowers—so that one walks among the little thatched cottages between open gardens. Padbury is one of the prettiest villages in Bucks, perhaps the best of all, and I think its charm comes partly from its flowers and partly from the quality and work of the thatch. For at Padbury lives a famous thatcher, Fred Gibbard, who belongs to a family who have thatched for generations. His designs for the work are as decorative as pieces of needlework spread out on the roofs. There are scallops and points, arcs and angles, laid out in golden straw like the edging of a Victorian white petticoat. Circles and triangles put together, triangles and arcs in conjunction, all are used to produce this effect. The edge of the thatch on a few cottages has a kind of stitchery like embroidery, and thatch is laid over thatch to form designs. One cottage has windows like eyes with eyebrows of thatch. Another is like a face peeping from a poke-bonnet of straw.

There is very good thatch too at Cuddington and at the village of Preston Bissett, some miles away down a much-winding lane. I saw the old inn, called the Old Hat, with a head-dress of golden straw, and every cottage there had an original covering.

The loveliest part of Padbury is on a little green by-way and here I found bergamot growing outside a cottage gate, with shaggy crimson flower and strongly scented leaf. I thought it was exactly right for the village. The seventeenth-century cottage next-door has original beams and chimney and twisty oak staircase.

The whitewashed inn, called the Blackbird, has a delicately painted sign of the bird singing on a silver spray with a white background. It hangs from a white wooden standard and two little green trees keep it company against the white wall of the

311

inn. Over the door is a canopy to keep off the raindrops. High on the wall a window is painted—a black window with white bars.

Orange marigolds grow close to the walls, and a grass plat drops down to the road. Many of the cottages and some of the inns in Bucks, especially in the north of the county, have these green aprons at their feet, with flowers growing there like embroidery on the apron border and spilling down the banks.

In this village most of the seventeenth-century houses have creamy-yellow walls and black timbers and thatched roofs, and some have the original chimney stacks. By the roadside in the hollow is a great tithe barn now used as a store for the grocer.

The baker at Padbury is Mr Middleton, whose ancestors are mentioned in the Verney Memoirs, for they baked bread for the Verneys at Claydon in Stuart times.

The village is remarkably well-kept and neat. Most of it belongs to All Souls College, Oxford. Through the fields runs Claydon Brook, a tributary of the Ouse. Kingfishers fly across and swans breed there.

Padbury saw much trouble in the Civil Wars for here in a battle with the Royalists eight Parliamentary men were slain and buried in the churchyard. The broken garrison from Hillesden was brought to the village with Sir Alexander Denton, after the fall of Hillesden House. It is not far from Buckingham and the forces must have swept through the deep road between the thatched cottages on their way to Steeple Claydon. Now a wandering workman asked me the way to the Claydons where he was going to work in the brickfields whose tall chimneys we could see in the distance.

The church of Padbury is hidden away, across the main road apart from the village. It is a thirteenth-century church, with some lovely little windows in the clerestory. There are piscinas, one of which has a wooden credence shelf said to be about 600 years old. The chancel roof has a carved head on one of the beams up high. The roof has king-posts dated about 1500. One Christmas Day I came here to the service and a fiddler sat by the chancel arch and accompanied the psalms and hymns.

The road from Padbury to Buckingham is lined with trees, grand ash trees and elms, which are fairly evenly spaced along the way. As we got near the town one winter's day, hedgers were busy trimming the hedgerows, twisting the saplings around the stakes they had driven in, and cutting away the lower part of the bushes. Hedges were left uncut throughout the war, and now men had started on the work of layering them. In North Bucks the hedges are more overgrown than in the south, for a vast quantity of ammunition was stored in the lonely places.

Other men were astride the road ditches clearing them out and making deep runnels for the water drainage. On both sides of the road stretched fields, some of them green with newly springing wheat, some freshly ploughed, others pasture land. Great stacks of hay stood close to the road. Giant ash trees, with black buds upturned, and elms with delicate lacy twigs against the sky kept us company. Trees fascinate me, and I remember their shapes and notice their individuality as if they were country people whom I had met on the way, and here was a fine company of woodland giants all going to Buckingham to market.

One piece of hedge was beautifully layered. It was such a pattern of upright stakes with the eddering along the top like a strip of well-woven basketwork, that I wanted to thank the old man who was working there for his craftsmanship. It was as good as any I had seen, and I longed to have a drawing of it. He must have taken a pride in his work and gone home to his wife saying, "I did a good bit of eddering to-day."

By the roadside, very near the town of Buckingham, I saw a white cock and his flock of hens busily feeding under the hedge with traffic rushing past. A few hours later, when I returned, they were still there scratching happily in the dust. I thought they were symbols of unconcern.

At Buckingham the road crosses the river Ouse, a blue, slow river, with reeds growing in its waters, and swans swimming and cattle standing on its low banks. It seemed in keeping with the quiet peaceful tranquillity of Buckingham that we saw sitting on a seat on the green bank above the road a friar in long brown robe and hood, with a twisted rope round his waist, just as if he had walked out of the Middle Ages.

My first impression of Buckingham that winter's day was of its quietness and its sleepiness, for nobody was about. The great market square was empty, a contrast to the busy square of Aylesbury. In this wide space, where on market days there are cattle in the pens and stalls with fruit and vegetables, there was nothing. I have never seen it so quiet since, but always there is a slowness and sedateness which is satisfying or not according to one's mood.

An embattled eighteenth-century building, which resembles a little castle tower, stands in the market square. It was once the gaol, but now it has even baser uses. A countrywoman told me that many wanted to have it pulled down. I wish it could be made into a little museum of crafts, for it is in a perfect place and it has an attractive air.

All round the square are old-fashioned shops and eighteenth-century houses, blending together in that harmony which comes from the influence of time. One of the houses, with massive timbers and gable, is sixteenth-century. Through a courtyard or alley one can see green fields which come down to the backs of the houses. It is a rural market square, with its fine eighteenth-century hotel, the White Hart, carrying the hart and a gold crown round its neck. The red brick town hall with a white swan, collared with a crown and gold chain, stands at the head of the square. The wind blows down the open space; it is always fresh and clean at Buckingham. At Christmas a lighted tree stands there under the stars in the silent square.

By chance we found the ancient wooden doorposts and tiny gate that lead to the little Norman chapel which was later a Latin school, a free school after the Dissolution. Dame Isabel Denton gave in her will about 1540 some money to a priest to teach the children there, and Edward VI gave a sum of £10 8s 0¾d a year out of the exchequer, and thus the chapel became a school. The Norman doorway has carved mouldings, and over a window two strange faces are cut in stone. The chapel belongs to the National Trust.

Next to the chapel is a charming little house covered with creepers which was the master's house in those old days. Now the caretaker lives in it.

We were taken to see a tall twisted chimney like a stick of barley sugar, an Elizabethan chimney in a plain little manor house. The Queen once dined in this rectory house. Queen Elizabeth came in progress to Buckingham in 1578 and went through the town "her sword royal and maces born and trumpets blown before her till she came to the mansion house of the Rectory," where she dined. It is a very small house to hold a queen and her followers.

The church stands on a high windy hill, with the chimneys of the town below in the hollow, so that little blue and grey banners of smoke always float past, and one can stand on the green lawns of the church and gaze down at them, and away to the woods. It is a thoroughfare with people walking on business bent or stopping to stare at the town spread out under its blue haze.

Buckingham Church once stood in the hollow among these houses, but it was destroyed by storms in the eighteenth century. The new church was built on this fine site. It has some carved bench-ends from the old church, one dated 1616, with shields and quarterings. Another is carved like a traceried window. There is a lovely modern east window, an altar cloth of green and gold, and angels on the reredos, all the gift of the Needle and Thread Society in 1890.

Down among the houses is the deserted churchyard, overgrown and forgotten, its tombs smothered in ivy and grass. There too is the old church cross. This Buckingham cross has had many adventures, for once it stood in the Horse Fair, then it became a sundial at a public-house, next it went to Preston Bissett, to Lillingstone Lovell, to Twyford, and finally to Buckingham again, to the churchyard.

The market town of Buckingham was partly destroyed by fire in 1725. The great conflagration broke out near the Unicorn Inn and 138 houses were destroyed, a third of the town. Lord Cobham of Stowe built cottages for the homeless, but later they were pulled down. There must have been great distress

315

and poverty at this time, and Browne Willis the historian thought the decay of Buckingham was due to it.

In 1644 Charles I entered the town with 9,000 foot and 3,000 horses, and there he stayed for a few days, seizing cart-loads of groceries and wines which were passing through to London. There is a house called Castle House still standing where Catherine of Aragon stayed, and later Charles I. He held a council of war here, and the room where he sat has a fireplace and carved mantelpiece with the date 1619.

The people say that after he left Cromwell came to the opposite side of the street. He came after the fight at Hillesden when he passed through Padbury. Pepys visited Buckingham and called it "A good old town." He gave the sexton's boy a shilling, a good tip, so he must have enjoyed himself there.

The summer assizes were held at Buckingham and in the winter they were held at Aylesbury. Buckingham had no gaol, and Lord Cobham built the little embattled place which stands in the market square. Although Buckingham was the county town its position in the north of the county was against it, and bad roads and ill communications made it unsuitable. Aylesbury, in the centre of the county, was much better placed. Buckingham was connected with the wool trade, but when it declined the town lost its importance and Aylesbury became the capital.

The name of Browne Willis the historian and antiquarian is inseparable from Buckingham. He had a passionate love for the town which he represented in Parliament for one session. He always called it the county town, and was insistent that others did the same. An odd figure, whose dress was so strange he was often taken for a beggar; he wore two or three coats with an old leather belt around them, and a blue cloak fell over all.

I always picture Browne Willis when I go to Buckingham, and he would be quite in keeping with the place if he walked down the market square to-day.

This country town has an impressive neighbour, whose character is totally different from anything else in this county of warm red cottages and farmhouses, of inns and thatched barns and simple things. We go up a side street out of the market square expecting to find perhaps the beginning of a suburb, but the town ends abruptly at a gateway leading to a straight avenue of great magnificence. This long approach, with wide verges on which grow double rows of elms and beeches with pathways between, culminates at a Corinthian arch spanning the road at the horizon.

The mighty arch with pillars and capitals, with swags of fruit and open stone balusters on the summit, is the frame for Stowe, the viewpoint only, for the road ends and between arch and house lies a lake. We looked through this archway at the symmetry of the scene laid out with superb artistry.

Suddenly I spied a little brown kettle on the handsome stone wall, and a doll's tea-party set out on the grand parapet. There were curtains at a window in the wall, and I was aware that the arch was inhabited. It was refreshing to see this homely note in the grandeur, this child's game of make-believe. Thus a little family might live inside Marble Arch.

To reach the house the drive swings round in great arcs, making a detour of more than a mile and approaching from the north-west. The park of 700 acres has small classical buildings here and there, and we passed between two of these, the Boycott Pavilions, designed by Vanbrugh.

One of these little pavilions is inhabited too. One is reminded of Grimm's fairy tales on seeing the temples and pavilions thus used, as if Rapunzel lived there or Hansel and Gretel.

An ornate little bridge spans the marshy ground in the hollow; stone pedestals adorn its parapet. The road runs up it to enter a queer enchanted land of kings, princes, and schoolboys.

Stowe House, the seat of the Dukes of Buckingham, the scene of unsurpassed splendour in the past, was made into a public school in 1923 under the headmaster, J. F. Roxburgh. The famous "J. F." built up a great tradition during his twenty-six years at Stowe. The house is magnificent as Versailles, splendid as a French château, but with more grandeur and less of the earthiness that the French always keep in their castles.

It is a unity, with symmetry that satisfies the senses, although it is at variance with the feeling of English life such as one experiences in the villages, where the manor houses are built up and added to through the centuries, with a wing here, a gable there, making a conglomeration of styles but one complete whole. Such perfect symmetry of design as exists at Stowe is unlike our English houses, but as a public school Stowe is achieving something for which it might have been originally designed. It is correct and satisfying as a great school.

Vanbrugh, who lived from 1663 to 1726, was the architect of vast houses and palaces which needed wide spaces for their fulfilment. The ordinary simple English landscape was too intimate and small, so cottages were swept away, gardens destroyed, and new landscapes laid out.

The manor of Stowe dates from Saxon times. In 1553 Peter Temple rented Stowe and rebuilt the medieval house as a square block with two wings. This house is the core of the succeeding houses rebuilt by generations of the Temple family.

Peter Temple was succeeded by John Temple, who bought the freehold, and Stowe descended from father to son. One of these, a Peter Temple, was a Parliamentarian and Member for Buckingham who was imprisoned for refusing to pay Ship Money, but he would not sit on the Commission to try Charles. Richard Temple was a Royalist in the Restoration Parliament. His son, afterwards Lord Cobham, succeeded in 1697, and he laid out the famous gardens by the help of Bridgman and Vanbrugh with the statues and fountains and parterres. Outside this formal garden were the wild gardens and park, which later Kent took over and transformed into the Grecian valley and Elysian fields. Vanbrugh invented the Rotunda and both he and Kent had a hand in designing the temples and pavilions which decorate the landscape.

In 1713 the village of Stowe was removed, but although Lord Cobham wished to make away with the church he was not allowed by the ecclesiastical authorities. So he planted trees to conceal it and the old church remains in the park. There too is an obelisk to the memory of General Wolfe. On the small hills are various temples, some of which are now put to good use in the service of the school.

The lovely Temple of Ancient Virtue was designed by Kent, and also the Temple of British Worthies with busts of famous men, an amphitheatre looking on to a glade of trees and water.

Kent's Temple of Concord is used to house a fine collection of birds, and another temple is the armoury. The Queen's Temple, which is used for music, has a Roman pavement of tessellated squares, which was given by Richard, Marquis of Chandos. This temple stands among trees on a rise. It has a flight of stone steps with balusters and pillars. The view from the doors is like one of those scenes tucked away in the corner of an early Italian picture. Fields, woods, a golden cornfield, and far blue hills are framed in arching trees to make a small clear miniature. Stowe has many of these exquisite vistas, set out with perfect art.

Capability Brown worked at the gardens of Stowe in Lord Temple's time, and he is mentioned by the poet Cowper who was living at Olney in Bucks. A world's wonder the place must have been, and one can imagine the village talk and astonishment and perhaps indignation as the changes were made. This is what Cowper says:

> Lo, he comes!
> The omnipotent magician, Brown, appears,
> Down falls the venerable pile, the abode
> Of our forefathers . . .
> He speaks—the lake in front becomes a lawn;
> Woods vanish, hills subside, and valleys rise.

Cowper disapproved of this grand gardening and he speaks of his own little garden and summerhouse.

"I write in a nook that I call my boudoir; it is a summer-house no bigger than a sedan chair, the door of it opens into the garden that is now crowded with pinks, roses, and honeysuckle, and the window into my neighbour's orchard."

Cobham built stately rooms, including a library which is now the boys' splendid library of books. Many famous guests came to Stowe, including Pope, Congreve, and Horace Walpole, and Frederick, Prince of Wales had his own state bedroom there.

Lord Cobham died childless, and he was succeeded by his sister Hester, wife of Richard Grenville. She had three famous children, Richard the first Earl Temple, Prime Minister Grenville, and her daughter who married the elder Pitt. Lord Temple was in two of Pitt's ministries. He made more alterations at Stowe, and it was he who included the wonderful marble hall with its processional frieze which is at the head of the flights of stone steps.

This great oval room has columns of coloured marble, pink and mulberry. Under the dome of the roof runs a frieze of many figures in high relief where sometimes a musical instrument or a waving arm is outstretched beyond the plane of the carvings. The pavement of this hall came from Bubb Dodington's place in Dorset. The common rooms for the boys are on either side of the circular hall, with reading-rooms and dining-halls. On the walls hang some fine pictures, including a Winterhalter portrait of Queen Victoria and Michael Dahl's portrait of Queen Anne, with its lovely colouring of grey and maroon. Ceilings are painted and tall shutters gilded.

The house itself has great colonnades on the north side and a flight of steps to a portico at the entrance front. An even grander flight of steps and portico guarded by lions is on the south side. This lovely south front was designed by Robert Adam for Earl Temple, and carries the date 1774 on the balustrading. The view from the steps of the formal landscape is very beautiful. The centre is the Corinthian arch against the sky, in the distance, and at each side trees stretch out their branches and two little matching temples nod to one another and the lake lies like a flowery mirror between in the valley.

New buildings have been added in recent years for the boys' houses. They are named after famous men of Stowe—Grenville, Cobham, and the rest. The names of the architects are commemorated in blocks of classrooms—Gibbs, Kent, Soane, Gibbons, Vanbrugh.

The "Gothic library," a room decorated in the Perpendicular Gothic style, was designed by Sir John Soane to house a collection of early Irish religious manuscripts, which since the great sale of 1848 have been in the British Museum. Now it is used as the headmaster's reception-room.

The most beautiful place to my mind is the chapel, which was designed by Sir Robert Lorimer who was the architect of the Scottish National War Memorial at Edinburgh. It is in keeping with the magnificence of Stowe, but it has its own beauty

320

Thatched cottages at Cuddington

and individuality. The great door has a relief of David and the Lion.

As soon as we enter the rich scent of cedar wood comes drifting from the panelled walls. The interior is extremely beautiful, with richly carved stalls down the sides, each with different design. The imagination of these modern craftsmen has been allowed the same freedom as in medieval times at Edlesborough. Animals abound, lions and monkeys, cats, foxes, and rabbits, each acting in some small intimate scene which should delight a boy. The stalls have the names of their donors and one with the Royal arms was given by Queen Mary. Some old work was brought from the private chapel of the house, but old and new are combined so skilfully it is difficult to distinguish between them. The brave coat-of-arms above the door is of the time of Charles II. High up, under the roof, are angels in painted stone, each head turned towards the altar, gazing at the miracle. The pulpit is by Grinling Gibbons, of inlaid wood, soft as silk, with hanging garlands of those delicate flowers of which he is a master—tiny roses and pinks and the peascod open to proclaim the author of their being.

In this great house, away in its parkland, among temples and lakes, woods and streams, flowers and thick grasses, 500 boys are being educated. There is so much space for those who love solitude, for those who wish to walk alone, that it should produce poets and thinkers as well as practical men. I talked to a boy who was leaving after some years at Stowe. He said he had been so happy he wanted to walk through all the old familiar places to say good-bye to them, and he went into the woods alone.

Turret, Hillesden Church

CHAPTER XXIII

BIERTON, WING, AND STEWKLEY

BIERTON, a village near Aylesbury, has thatched cottages and little old red houses, some with clumps of golden stonecrop on their roofs. Doors open directly on to the village street from a row of these small dwellings.

Lime trees border the churchyard where, on a knoll, stands a fine church with gargoyles and faces staring down. This is a large and lovely old church with high arches in the nave, very light and graceful fourteenth-century work. The grand central tower is thirteenth-century, and it has a little lead spire. The tower is carried by four wonderful clustered pillars and the arches between them soar high to the fifteenth-century nave roof.

Underneath are some little dark red and yellow tiles, with animals and tracery, set in the floor. The floor of Bierton is a patchwork of stone, of red bricks and some tiles, and medieval gravestones. It is an old country church floor, with pitchers of flowers standing at the foot of the arches. The tall chancel windows are filled with pale gold glass which sheds a soft light in the grey building.

On the chancel wall is a memorial of slate and alabaster. Samuel Bosse, who died in 1621, kneels there facing his wife, four sons behind him, three daughters behind her, and below them six babes on white cushions with white coverlets tucked snugly around them. The faces of this family are delicately coloured and their hair is golden. The girls wear black bonnets and they all kneel on red and white cushions.

In the chancel is a carved chair, said to be Tudor work. The pulpit is modern, with a canopy, and it compares with the best craftsmanship of the past. This fine church, austere and grey, lighted by the golden glass and by the jugs of many-coloured phlox, is like a small cathedral church standing in the quiet small village.

A black and white farm stands close to the road, and next to it is a thatched farm with great barns. Some cows were grazing

322

on the green verges of the high-road in the thick grass which is common land, and a man lay there keeping an eye on them that sunny afternoon lest they should stray on the road. It was a pastoral scene, reminiscent of France. But there are many delightful little rural pictures on the roadsides. The roads have wide margins, with heavy crops of grass and footpaths through them for the traveller on foot. There stroll the lovers, the tramps, the leisured loitering along. There I pick meadowsweet and dog-roses and honeysuckle and butter-and-eggs. I like these broad grassy tracks where one can walk safely, where the cows graze and children play.

The way from Bierton to Wing goes through rolling country with superb views across to the Dunstable hills, where the white lion is carved in the chalk. The sky always seems lovelier here, the clouds have more room, the sun, the stars, the rain, all take on an added glory. Every time I have been here I have felt the same exhilaration of space and wind and movement.

The road runs through fields of wheat and fields of barley, past the thatched Red Lion Inn, with its dancing little lion hanging out before the white walls, and the malthouse with its steep red roof like a Flemish picture, and between hedges of pink wild roses and snow-white roses. Meadowsweet fills the ditches with creamy abundance, and bitter-sweet and bryony clamber over the nut bushes. Low red brick bridges, very small, span the trickles of water, which call themselves brooks.

Wing is a village which is the proud possessor of the finest Saxon church in Bucks, and perhaps the most perfect in the country. This old church, with its apse and crypt and its strong plain walls, was built about the middle of the tenth century, soon after the first introduction of wall-pilasters and windows with mid-wall shafts to England.

From the outside we can see the seven-sided apse, which has these narrow pilasters and arcading. The three arches of the crypt are low in the tangle of grass, and through them we discover the central room which once contained the relics of a saint. The walls of the crypt are very thick and built of flint.

The outer door of the church is superb, with its beautifully wrought iron hinges and two animals guarding the arch. Inside one is amazed at the strength and simplicity of the wide chancel arch, with its Saxon windows above and the little baluster shaft down the middle of the window.

The Saxon church was restored about five hundred years ago. The splendid roof of the nave was made with large carved angels, figures of men and saints on the ends of the beams, and strange figures on the bosses, and angels with odd wings. The round-headed windows down the church are beautiful. In one of them is some old glass, with Adam and Eve and a little green tree between them. There is a feeling of strength and endurance in this church as if all who had ever knelt there had left a store of courage for future generations to discover and draw upon.

On the wall of the north aisle there is an Italian-style altar tomb of Sir Robert Dormer, the Lord of the Manor of Wing in 1515. He died in 1552. The elaborate and graceful tomb has heads of oxen, eyeless, with curling horns and beards. Over the tomb is Sir Robert's helmet of iron and a little dove.

An ancient wooden chest is near this tomb, with straps of iron around it and across the sides. There is usually an old wooden coffer in a church where once the vestments were kept, and the ironwork of locks and bars and bands is very strong.

In the chancel is a richly painted tomb of Sir Robert Dormer, another member of the family, Master of the King's Hawkes. He kneels, wearing armour. His wife has a stiff farthingale, a scarf round her neck, and a gold flower band round her hat. Two roses fasten her shoulder cape. Below them kneel the sons and daughters, two of the boys in buttoned jackets and square-toed shoes, with good thick soles, and girls like their mother with farthingales and bonnets with roses. I am always intrigued by the pretty clothes and button-holes these young people wear, and their gay attire instead of the mournful gloom of later centuries. They are as happy as children at a party in their best garments. Opposite this fine painted tomb is another Dormer monument, very bright with colour, and this one, carved in alabaster, is Sir William Dormer and his wife, at his feet a bird, at hers a cat or spotted leopard. The date is 1590, the age of adventure. Three daughters kneel there in frilled bonnets and ruffs, and the full sleeves of their gowns have an elaborate pattern of cross-cut lattice work such as I have not seen before. The son wears painted armour and there are three babies.

Beautiful as these painted and carved figures are there is a little brass tablet in the south aisle I like even more. An engraving shows a Jacobean porter, Thomas Cotes, who died in 1648. He kneels in the full cloak of a countryman. His high hat, his great key, and his staff lie near him, and his hands are raised in an appealing gesture. He was the porter at Ascott Hall, the home of the Dormers.

The inscription says:

> Honest old Thomas Cotes
> that sometime was porter at
> Ascott-Hall hath now, (alas)
> left his key, lodg, fyre, friends
> and all to have a roome in
> heaven, this is that good
> man's grave. Reader prepare
> for thine for none can
> tell but that you two
> may meete to night, farewell

> He dyed the 20th of November 1648.
> Set up at the apoyntment and charge
> of his friend George Houghton.

As I stood one day in this Saxon church, revisiting it, a strange crooked little man came softly in, slipping silently through the ancient door, leering and ogling me, and beckoning with crooked fingers. In broken words he told me of this brass to the porter of Ascott, and he hobbled to the chancel, swiftly moving, with crooked arms waving and bright wild eyes flashing. He ran with a strangely rapid pace up the aisle, glancing behind to see if I were following, and then he pointed to the Dormer monuments. He could not speak articulately, but he had a wealth of gesture. Like the spirit of a Saxon serf he hovered about, dressed in a loose leather jacket and scarf, with tousled hair and bent back. He rattled his long finger nails like castanets to make an uncanny accompaniment to his mouthings as he sped through his well-loved haunts. Away he rushed again to the far end of the church,

BUCKINGHAMSHIRE

beckoning me to Honest Thomas Cotes. He peered up close into my face to see if I appreciated the marvel and beauty of the church. Then he disappeared behind the organ, silent as a mouse, and I thought perhaps I had really seen a goblin-sprite, one of those stone figures come to life.

At Wing there are almshouses with gables and dormer windows for the very old and a modern hostel with "Ablution Room" and bunks for the young Land Army. The Cock Inn, by the roadside, has a splendid figure of a great cock, with head uplifted, beak open, as he crows to the sky, against which he is silhouetted. With golden-green feathers and fine green sweeping tail, he calls from the red-tiled roof of the old inn. A long gable dips nearly to the ground, and there is herringbone brickwork in the side of the house. Inside the neat little rooms with their sloping floors are cheerful and bright.

The yard of this inn has barns and stables falling to decay; a pitiful sight it is to see these good farm buildings with broken roofs, for here again the inn was once combined with a farm.

Near Wing is the village of Stewkley, even more famous for its magnificent church. It is an enchantment in stone, with a wealth of carving in doorways and on arches and around the windows and along the walls. This Norman church of marvellous workmanship was built in 1150 in a little village of small cottages with manor house and farms close to the side of the road. For the first time we saw strangers peering round, admiring the church, for this is renowned and visited and sketched by artists and students of architecture.

The great central tower has pinnacles and large gargoyles leaning out very far, a creature with wide-open mouth leers down, one hand to his mouth as if he is shouting to the world some obscenity, and there are a lion and a bird up there. There are interlacing fishes and zigzag carving in the walls of this beautiful tower.

The chief glory of the outside is the west doorway which has three arches and spiral ornament round the capitals. The central arch contains the door, and over this is a tympanum carved with dragons. The outer arches are carved in chevron design with animals and birds.

326

The two great arches under the central tower are most intricately and minutely carved with animals and figures in an astonishing display of genius. There are over forty different creatures on one arch. These two arches are of different depths, with chevron carvings on the outer and these figures of imagination on the lower part.

In the chancel, above the altar, a deeply splayed window with the same chevron design is set. The chancel roof is painted in an interlacing pattern in deep rich red, with ribs of stone between. All around the church the carving runs, and each of the lovely windows is framed in the chevrons.

There is an exquisite treasure in Stewkley Church, a broken alabaster picture or monument, quite small, of a Virgin crowned with a gold crown and two angels with her. Her long slender hands, her delicate face, resemble a Botticelli Madonna. St Joseph stands near with a satchel.

At Granborough Church, near North Marston, I saw a little alabaster panel of the Crucifixion which had been found in a farmhouse gable. At Upton Church there is a tiny alabaster scene of the Crucifixion.

Stewkley Church is the home of many martins, which were flying round the eaves, curving in lovely flight, to dart under the edge and feed their young. The air was filled with their shrill cries and with the flash of their wings and tails as they moved in circular motion. I stayed a long time watching them, and some seemed to weave circles, of which the church walls were the tangents, and some swept round without stopping, while others again stayed a moment to give their young food and then continued in the same aerial movement. All round the church the birds flew, for the nests were on every side.

Under one wall the grass was shaven and standard rose trees grew, with heads of red and white flowers. There was a humming as if bees had taken up their abode in the church, as at Dinton Church, but it was probably from hives near. A cedar tree grew in the trim churchyard, and at the foot of the great beautiful tower was a clump of tall white foxgloves.

I went to see a craftsman at Stewkley whose work interested me, for he makes and mends violins. William Capp lives in a little thatched cottage with a paved yard in front of it, and the buildings where woodwork and carpentry was done in former days. Like his brother, Stephen Capp of Whitchurch, he has a collection of old tools and implements which were in use only a few years ago. These hang round the wide fireplace in the cottage. The roof of this cottage was being rethatched, and I watched the thatcher finishing off for the day. On the left of the roof lay the weight for keeping the straw in place. The edges of the thatch were clipped and finished off with a design in willow strips. A great heap of straw lay in the yard ready for the remainder of the roof, a surprising amount I thought, but it would not be sufficient I was told. There has been much thatching of cottages since the war, and I visited my friends in different parts of the county to find them with dust sheets over the gardens and the thatchers up long ladders.

In a small workroom, off the living-room, I saw thirteen violins hanging on a line and more on a table, with bows and pegs. William Capp lengthens the handles of violins which have the old short length of handle. He splices them with sycamore, so accurately the join is scarcely discernible. Violins are made of pine wood, with sycamore backs and edges. Very finely grained wood is chosen for the back and the polishing takes a long time.

William Capp showed me a violin he had made himself, with back and sides of sycamore. He had actually cut down the tree whose wood he had used. It was a beautiful piece of work. He has made many violins, one of which was played at a London symphony concert by the leader of the orchestra.

He mends bows in an ingenious manner. The ivory tip of a bow, with its little curve, is often snapped. He uses box wood which is like ivory when it is worked, very hard and white, and this can be carved into the requisite shape. He showed me a box-wood handle to a walking-stick he had made. The box trees for this work are grown locally, and of course there are many on the Chiltern slopes. We talked some time about making violins, the shaping, the traditional form of the instruments. I saw the very fine and delicate inlay which he puts round the edge of the violin, following the outline, with two strips of ebony and a strip

328

of pale creamy lime between, so thin it looks as though drawn by a pen. This violin-making in Buckinghamshire at High Wycombe and Stewkley is an intricate craft, needing delicacy and carving of a high order.

I admired the flowers in the cottage window, a blue campanula which was a cloud of azure bells, and another with clusters of white flowers. The name for these flowers in Buckinghamshire is "Benny."

In the yard was the little sawmill and workroom, and opposite the house, within the small enclosure, was the smallest thatched cottage I have ever seen. There is one room down and one upstairs, but the whole is so compact and so well made it would serve as a model for a tiny dwelling. William Capp's son lived there when he was first married.

Stewkley, Wing, and Soulbury make a triangle, and we went across the gated road through Liscombe Park, which is about 400 acres, to the little village of Soulbury. The house is the home of the Lovetts. The church is at the edge of the park, and within is a monument to a Lady Lovett. The lady wears a black farthingale and kneels facing her husband with two daughters. A pink-faced cherub with blue eyes and red lips and gold wings floats there with animals and more cherubs, very bright and gay, to give delight to the young.

This church has clear glass, and the whole building is very light and fresh and airy. The priest's door was wide open and flowers grew even by the doorstep, so that they seemed to be entering the little church of Soulbury.

An epitaph bears this eulogy of a lady:

If Wisdome, true repentance, and religion,
Birth, beautie, worth, youth, wealthe, friends,
    prayers, or praise
Could have praeserved a body from corruption
The Lady might have lived yet endless dayes.

The village of Soulbury has some fine old houses, and among them I noticed an old red brick house of fine proportion with many windows. It was once the village school, but now it has been made into two houses and the children are sent away. A woman who had been educated there was grieved over this as she talked to me about it.

"Are they going to take away all the village children and bring them up in towns?" she asked. "They will forget all their country life and get new ways."

This question has been asked in several villages where the little school is now empty, especially in South Bucks.

One of the houses at Soulbury was tiled on one side of the roof and thatched on the other side, with the thatch going over the ridge. In the middle of the road was a great stone.

"It has been here since the Ice Age," said a village woman proudly as we watched the cars move on either side of it.

There are some lovely villages in this part of Buckinghamshire, away from the hills, in flatter country—Drayton Parslow, with its unique font, with sunk panels and figures carved within, Swanbourne, with its little manor house, and Mursley.

Mursley has a wide street and many thatched cottages. Queen Elizabeth came here to see Sir John Fortescue of Salden, who was her tutor and cousin. He built Salden and lived there in great state. James I and his children visited him. The house was pulled down in the eighteenth century. In the church is a brightly coloured monument to Sir John and his wife. He is in black and gold armour and he wears red hose. She has a black Elizabethan gown and cloak with white ruff and cuffs, and her dress is similar to the one we associate with Mary, Queen of Scots. Her face is very expressive, and I feel this is a portrait of a charming lady. On the altar tomb below this pair is a fine brass of Sir John's first wife who has a richly embroidered front to her Elizabethan dress.

On the opposite side of the chancel is an equally gay and decorated monument to Sir John's son, Sir Francis Fortescue, his wife, and children. They kneel at a desk with open books. Below them are their children, six boys in red on one side, four girls in blue on the other.

On the top of this monument are perched a little peacock and a small brown bear. Two fat cherubs with rosy faces and gold wings adorn the sides. One can imagine children from the villages gazing entranced at this painted scene, set up for the enjoyment of posterity.

By the roadside at Mursley there is a little pond, its green water thick with rushes and reeds. The old red cottages beyond the pond are so close to it they seem to grow in the reeds, and their reflections lie in the water.

Sir John Fortescue built a house for his daughter and this little Tudor manor house stands in its garden near Swanbourne Church. The church at the cross-roads has a fine thirteenth-century tower, and cut in its face is a little stone clock, resembling a large pocket-watch. The door of the church is fourteenth-century and it is nailed with great square nails and banded with iron bands which have a simple design of criss-cross cuttings.

In this church at the west end is a little modern archway room with open screen and steps to the tower for the bellringers, a memorial room. On it is a painted coat-of-arms of George V. The pulpit is carved Jacobean, one of the best of all the Jacobean work in the churches of Bucks.

The manor house, a plain Tudor little house of great charm, was the first hostel to be opened by the Bucks Old People's Welfare Committee, and it supplies a great need for a home for those who are past work and require extra care and companion-ship. I went through the house, into those small Elizabethan rooms, much altered a few years ago. The bedrooms had three or four beds in each, with patchwork quilts and chairs and tables. In the hall sat an old man mending a rug for the household. In the sitting-room the old people were resting after dinner in easy-chairs, some reading the paper, others softly sleeping, others quietly talking together.

It is a communal hostel where all live together, staff and resi-dents, and there is plenty of freedom for the old people to do as they like. They pay something towards their keep and the remainder comes from subscriptions.

A gardener was working in the large kitchen garden, and close to the house were little lawns and flower gardens with fields beyond, a quiet and beautiful countryside.

CHAPTER XXIV

OLNEY AND GAYHURST

OLNEY, a little market town of grey stone in the north of Buckinghamshire, was the home of the poet William Cowper. He lived as paying guest with his friend Mrs Unwin, who took charge of him. He had already suffered from an attack of insanity, but he seemed to be cured when he removed from Huntingdon to the fresh clear air of the town. There in a gaunt red brick house by the market square he kept his tame hares, which gave him intense pleasure, and there he wrote his poems and his hymns.

Once upon a time I was seeking among the old books in an attic and I found an ancient crinkled-leaved little volume, bound in grey boards. I turned the dark pages and scanned the small print for something of interest. Then I came across the account of those hares and their gambols and vicissitudes. It was the *Letters of Cowper* which I had discovered. I did not connect them with *John Gilpin*, whose adventures I knew very well, for my mother declaimed them to us as we sat round the bedroom fire. I had no notion of the author, for I was only eight years old, but I was much interested in the hares Bess, Puss, and Tiny.

So Olney was a place of pilgrimage one cold day in December. This little market town is grey as a north-country village. I thought I was in Yorkshire as I stood in the quiet market-place and felt the cold wind blow through me. The river Ouse is slow-moving and tranquil as it gently flows by the town. Rushes and reeds fringe its banks, and the long flat wooden bridge which crosses it at the entrance to the town is very near the surface of the water. Willows grow there, and water weeds, and swans float in the shallows. It is a river for reflections, and its mirror held the tall slender spire of Olney Church across the meadow as I stood on the bridge loitering and gazing at the water. I liked the river better than anything, for it has kept its beauty in spite of works on its banks and houses close to it.

The church has a pinnacled spire, which rises from the tower

332

in four tiers, each with a narrow spire-light, like a four-storied house, and grotesque heads look down. In this church preached John Newton, the curate whose influence on Cowper was so profound. Newton had spent his early years on board an African slave-ship and the memory of those wild scenes inflamed his sermons and his religious ardour. He was a great friend of Cowper and together they wrote hymns. Cowper wrote sixty-eight, including "God moves in a mysterious way," for the collection Newton was making.

In 1772 Cowper had another attack of mania, and Mrs Unwin nursed him. It was when he was recovering that his friends collected animals to amuse him, and the three hares came to live with him. The hole through which the hares, Tiny, Bess, and Puss, entered the parlour from the kitchen is still there, a little doorway made in the thickness of the wall. Puss, the first hare he possessed, nearly died, but Cowper nursed it himself and gave the little creature herbs and grasses as medicine. When the hare was well enough to take a short walk it carefully licked its master's hand, the front, the back, and then between each finger. These hares spent the evening in the parlour, where they would leap over each other and see which could spring the farthest, to the amusement of the poet and his friends.

In 1779 the Olney hymns were published, and Cowper began to write with ease and fluency for the first time. *John Gilpin* was published in 1785. The rooms of the house are now called after the poems. Cowper's bedroom is called John Gilpin's room, because he wrote that celebrated poem there after he had heard the tale from his friend Lady Austen. There are many editions and illustrations displayed in glass cases round the walls.

In Mary Unwin's room are her workbox and lace bobbins, and a wooden bobbin-winder such as all lace-makers used. Cowper's chair and his day-bed and many simple possessions are in the house, but I felt that something vital to a good museum was lacking. The tall ugly house is depressing, and the spirit that wrote *John Gilpin*, the laughter and merriment in the story, the tinkle of teaspoons when the friends had tea, seemed to be subdued by grief and sadness, either from the cold grey daylight which fell on the square outside the windows or from the icy chill of the rooms and the haunting feeling of Cowper's madness. There should have been a fire burning in Cowper's grate and a chair drawn up for his ghost.

The garden was much more cheerful, with its apple trees and little lawn and the summer-house where Cowper wrote. Unfortunately this summer-house is filled with the pew in which the poet sat in church.

Cowper used the garden and the arbour continually, for like many poets he found "the sound of the wind in the trees and the singing of the birds" were much more agreeable to his ears than "the incessant barking of dogs and screaming of children."

The square was quiet enough that December day, and every time I have been there Olney has a remoteness as if it is asleep, waiting to be wakened to a new life. I wanted to see a busy market in the great empty square, a horse fair, with stallions and mares and little wild-eyed foals, or a wakes-week fair with gipsies and merry-go-rounds, or a sheep fair, when the grey sheep would match the grey walls around them. I wanted to hear bells ringing and carol-singing. These would be right for Olney.

At five o'clock the hooters sounded and men with tawny-red leather aprons and overalls came racing to their homes for tea. One of the men stopped at a little window and tapped on the glass, calling to a collie who was looking out for him, and dog and man gazed at each other with an understanding love.

He was a tanner in a works where two hundred men are employed. No longer do they use stripped oak bark for tanning as in the old days, when the oaks in the woods near Beaconsfield and Wycombe were stripped for Chesham and Wycombe tanneries.

We chatted for a time about Olney and its manufactures. They make boots and shoes, for Olney has long been famous for the excellence of its leather, and also they manufacture plugs for cars in one of the factories we could see by the river over the reeds. Then the tanner went indoors, smiling and alert, to greet that watching collie and to have his tea.

The hooters and the chattering men and the tinkle of bicycle bells dispelled the silence for a short time, and then Olney settled down to its mists and quietude. "Ooney" the people call it, and the name has the music of the river and the softness of the mists.

When Cowper was fifty-five he and Mrs Unwin moved from the tall grim house at Olney to Weston Underwood, a pretty village about two miles away where they must often have walked in an evening. It was a happier habitation for the poet, for the village is beautiful and peaceful with the serenity one feels at once.

The entrance is romantic, for one goes through a stone gateway of 1700, part of Weston Manor. The village displays all its charms of thatched cottage and barns as if it were part of the manor.

On an autumn day the street was like a poem of Cowper's for along the lane, towards the thatched cottages, came a boy with a yoke on his shoulder and a couple of shining milk pails hanging from the chains. Four white ducks waddled solemnly along in single file down the middle of the road, gazing to right and left with deep content. At the door of the thatched post office sat a ginger cat, and in the elm trees which line the village the birds were singing. Cowper's Oak, the village inn, has a painted sign hanging over the street from its raised position on a bank, and opposite are some old cottages.

Cowper's house, a two-storied house in the street, with dormers and bright windows, looks much more pleasant than the house at Olney. In this house once lived the curate, and the rent he paid was a basket of pears from an old pear tree, so the name of the house became Pear Tree House. Other places in the county have had delicate rents—for a mill the rent was a wild rose, and for a manor house part of the payment was a clove gilly flower. Here the poet lived for a few happy years until insanity struck him again. The death of William Unwin, Mrs Unwin's son, affected him deeply but he recovered, only to see his friend slowly become paralysed. Then he nursed her, and tried to repay the devotion she had showered on him. They moved again, to Swaffham and East Dereham, where Mrs Unwin died, and in 1800 Cowper died too.

The church at Weston Underwood has a little flight of steps to enter the churchyard, and from this raised place there is a

335

view down the long valleys with Olney spire in the distance, a view Cowper must often have seen.

Near Olney along a quiet road through fields we came to the village of Clifton Reynes. It was here that Lady Austen lived. She had a great influence on Cowper's writings. As well as the story of John Gilpin which brought forth his famous poem, she suggested other work—"The Loss of the Royal George," and "The Task."

In the church at Clifton Reynes are four oak figures, wooden effigies of knights and their ladies, unique in the county. They were carved in the fourteenth century.

Another quiet village among the water-meadows is Milton Keynes, a little place of thatch and farmhouse, with a fourteenth-century church. The country vicar was busy cutting the grass in the graveyard.

"I always put the churchyard before my own garden," he explained, as he came to us in his shirt sleeves. "My garden gets neglected but I manage to keep the churchyard grass cut."

We went through the beautiful church together, and with pardonable pride he showed us the shields he had painted, the heraldry of the rectors associated with the place. They were Lewis Atterbury, the Jacobite rector, William Wotton, and Chancellor Finch.

In the churchyard was a memorial of wood with fine lettering, to the men who died in the 1914–18 war. Inside the church was another memorial, a great door to the tower. The tower is on the north instead of in the usual position at the west end. There is a chained Bible in this church, and a fourteenth-century font, rescued from the churchyard.

At Hanslope there is the tallest steeple in the county, rising from a beautiful church. Hanslope has a market square with thatched houses surrounding it, whose windows have very tiny panes of glass. The High Street has little old houses, many of which are built of stone like the Cotswold villages. It was a noted lace-making village one hundred years ago.

Gargoyles of strange aspect stare from the church walls, and there is a bear with ragged staff among them. The same emblem, in a wall painting, is within the church on the chancel wall.

Cottages at Padbury

The fifteenth-century tower with its spire is 186 feet high. It has little crockets projecting from its sides and flying buttresses and pinnacles.

We heard an old tale of Hanslope. The tower had to be repaired and a famous steeplejack, Robert Cadman, came to do the work. He refused a ladder and climbed to the top by the crockets. On his back he carried a little drum which he played when he arrived. He hung the drum on the weathervane while he made his repairs. Then he descended and spent the evening at the village inn. When he had drunk deeply he discovered he had forgotten the drum. He insisted that he must climb up to recover his treasured instrument. Luckily the villagers persuaded him to wait till the morning when he would have got over his drinking. So next day he climbed the steeple again, took down the drum, and returned safely to earth.

It is said that he repaired many of the high steeples of England about a hundred and fifty years ago, always refusing ladders and always playing a tattoo on his drum, but at last he fell and was killed.

Inside Hanslope tower hang two twenty-foot fire-hooks, with double hooks at the ends, which were formerly used for taking burning thatch from cottage roofs. They are fitted in a well-designed iron holder high on the wall. There is a fire-hook of a different pattern on the wall outside the church of Edlesborough near Ivinghoe Beacon. These fire-hooks are very heavy and strong and they look as if three or four men would be needed to wield them.

The great airy light church has interior walls of rough stone and this plainness adds to the beauty of the building. The floor is of old red brick, and there is a simplicity and at the same time a splendour about the place. There are Norman arches and a Norman door and a fifteenth-century roof to the nave. There is a gallery with twisted balusters and a little organ. There are box pews and three stone seats for the priests, and a piscina with arches and carved shafts. The chancel arch is Norman, and it has five pillars with capitals, all different, moulded together. Near the church gate is a farmhouse built of stone at Tathall End, and there are many good buildings and barns. A stream

z 337

Stowe

runs gaily by the roadside. People have forgotten to spoil Hanslope and it remains as it was, a lovely village.

We were going to Gayhurst but we were caught by Stoke Goldington and Ravenstone on the way, of which we had heard from country people who love these places.

At Stoke Goldington there are a church and farm alone in the fields with plough land around them away from the little village. It is like a north-country place with its stone walls and wild blue geranium.

At Ravenstone there are grey stone farms and great haystacks and corn ricks close to the church wall. I counted ten haystacks in a row, with farm buildings of stone and an open barn with six strong pillars supporting the roof under which carts and farm implements were kept in shelter. For shelter was needed that day of storm. It was sad to see men hurrying to drag the huge stack-cloths over the corn in a downpour of heavy rain. Several ricks had no protection because there were no cloths for them.

Some of the cottages had low stone walls and their roofs were thatched. By the side of the road was a little thatched post office with roses climbing over it and near it was the village green, very small, with chestnut trees and a seat for the old people.

Inside the church, which was on a rise among fir trees and farmhouses, there is a pulpit with sounding-board of the seventeenth century, and a chapel holding the grand tomb of Lord Chancellor Finch. I was more interested in the straw hassocks, good stout country hassocks, a memory of early childhood. One could kneel upon them and stare about or crouch low and sit upon them, hidden from all eyes, for they were comfortable seats for the young.

The important thing at Ravenstone was the almshouses which were founded by Finch. We opened the gate at the far end of the churchyard and stood in the rain gazing at the charming little houses. They looked very warm and comfortable with firelight glowing in the rooms, very secret and gay. Even the dahlias in the gardens glittered in the tumbling rain and the green bushes had a radiant air about them. There are twelve little old red brick cottages, six a side, facing one another across a green grass-plat as if they were dancing a set figure. Six old men live on one side and six old ladies on the other. In front of each tiny house is a patch of flower garden and at the back a good-sized vegetable garden. The whole domain is enclosed by a low wall. Lovely country spreads around them and the farms and haystacks and fields are close to their walls. They were certainly worth a long journey in the rain.

From Ravenstone we went to the beautiful and romantic house of Gayhurst with which I had already been captivated a month or two earlier.

It was a perfect summer's day when I first saw Gayhurst. Gayhurst! Gayhurst!—the name came ringing to me, calling me, although I had no idea what I should find, and I stopped at the little thatched post office in the tiny hamlet at the park gate to ask if I might enter. The post office stood in a garden of flowers and the kind postmistress assured me that I could go through the gates to find the church and house of Gayhurst, and I should be made welcome. She smiled benignly at me as she peeped from behind the kitchen door to see who was the stranger.

The postmistresses of the Buckinghamshire villages have diminutive houses where they sell their stamps and bake their cakes and tend their flower gardens. I remember with pleasure the post office at Dorney, and one at Chenies and the little thatched house at Claydon, and many another.

We went through the park gates and had lunch by the side of the lake where we watched a pair of swans and seven cygnets swimming in single file among the reeds. It was very quiet, except for the talk of the water-hens and the plop of a vole. In the distance we could see the tower and little cupola of the Wren church of Gayhurst, but when we turned the corner of the drive we were startled by the sheer beauty of the house, standing proudly there in its green lawns. Gayhurst is a jewel of the country, an Elizabethan E-shaped stone house, serene after its eventful history, cool and elegant with its mullioned and transomed windows and its pinnacles.

I walked through a gateway to ancient grey stone stables and coach-houses, cottages and workrooms with red-tiled roofs, the many buildings of an Elizabethan manor house built round the cobbled courtyard. I found the gardener who had the key of the little church. It was incongruous and startling to hear a wireless playing a jazz tune when one expected to hear a servant man singing "Greensleeves." The key was enormous, and I carried it back over the lawns feeling like the gaoler in the *Beggar's Opera* to unlock the door of the charming church among the yews.

There were box pews and a two-decker pulpit with a star-inlay ceiling to the canopy which was carved with crowns and foliage. Little schoolboys sit in the box pews down one side of the church on Sundays, for the house of Gayhurst is now shared between its owner, Sir Walter Carlile, and a preparatory school. The Royal arms, carved in stone, gilded and painted, are at the east end of the church and the Wrighte arms, dated 1827, at the west end.

On the wall is a great Roubilliac statue of Sir Nathan Wrighte, Lord Keeper of the Privy Seal, in his legal robes, and of his son, a monument too large for the delicate church, I thought. He bought Gayhurst in the early eighteenth century. Over the altar the Commandments are written, and the first has the emphatic double negative: "Thou shalt not have none other gods but Me."

We left the church and sauntered down through yew hedges to see the fishponds, now made into ornamental waters. Red and white water-lilies floated there and a water-hen swam across very busily. This water garden with its hedges and flowers and little green paths round the ponds is very small, compact, and charming.

We were taken over the great house by Lady Carlile and we heard the tale of secret plots and tragedy. The Elizabethan house of Gayhurst was given by Queen Elizabeth to Sir Francis Drake as a reward for his voyage round the world. He sold the house the next day to William Mulsoe. Mary Mulsoe, the heiress, married Sir Everard Digby, who became involved in the Gunpowder Plot.

In the house hang the legal documents of these transactions—parchments with the exquisite writing and elaborate initial letters of the Elizabethan age. One deed, relating to the gift of the

340

house to Drake by Queen Elizabeth, has a fine engraving of the Queen in the corner and her signature at the bottom, with others. The sale of the house by Drake to Mulsoe bears the strong romantic signature of Francis Drake. There is also a deed of sale of some lands signed by Everard Digby. These lands were said to have been sold to provide money towards the cost of the Gunpowder Plot.

Mary Mulsoe and her husband were converted to Roman Catholicism by Father Roger Lee, and their house became the centre of plots. A movable ceiling was constructed by a Jesuit, Nicholas Owen, and this false ceiling hid a little room with secret exits. We saw the marks of this ceiling in the Digby room, and the fireplace which led to the secret chamber. There was an escape up a chimney and in another part of the house a hide-hole and a long passage which had steep steps in it to the roof and to the cellars. Those great airy cellars held a labyrinth of secret ways. The house must have been honeycombed with escapes, but many of them have been blocked up. At Gayhurst one realizes the way in which men could be hidden and fed and kept in privacy until the time was ready for their final escape.

There is a legend at Gayhurst that the secret room made by this movable ceiling was discovered in a dramatic manner. The men who searched the house had found nothing, and at last they commanded that candles should be lighted in every room and a survey made from the outside. One window had no candle burning, and this was the blocked room whose window had been left for symmetry.

In another wing there is a false window, painted black so skilfully that it appears from below to have glass. The oratory, used by Digby at the top of the house, has no outside lights, its windows being cleverly concealed behind a gable.

In 1605 a pilgrimage to St Winifred's Well at Holywell was undertaken, and this began and ended at Gayhurst. The Digbys took part in it and Guy Fawkes stayed at the house. Sir Everard is said to have been repelled at first by the plot, but later he agreed to be one of the conspirators. At this time he was an ardent young man of twenty-five. He arranged to have a hunting match on November 5th at a house in Worcestershire, and when the King and Parliament were blown up he was to seize the King's daughter, Princess Elizabeth, at Combe Abbey.

The plot was betrayed by one of the conspirators who wished to save his brother-in-law's life. Digby attempted to escape, but he was caught, tried at Westminster Hall, dragged on a hurdle to St Paul's, and on 30 January 1606 he was hanged. He confessed before hanging and gallantly took all the blame.

His wife and two baby boys were allowed to stay at Gayhurst, and one of these boys was Sir Kenelm Digby, who married the beautiful Venetia Stanley. He became famous as an astrologer, admiral and court favourite. There is a delightful little tradition about the snails in the woods at Gayhurst. Sir Kenelm brought edible snails from the south of France for Venetia, who was consumptive. The descendants of these snails are there now, carrying their white shells tinged with red, the *Helix pomatia*.

This legend reminds me of a more remote story of snails on Cymbeline's Mount and Beacon Hill at Ellesborough, told to me by a learned countryman. There is supposed to be a distinct variety of snail there, the descendant of snails brought over by the Romans.

The deep impression of the Gunpowder Plot remained very strong in Bucks and later there was a wild rumour started by a mole-catcher's boy of another plot, and Gayhurst was suspected of storing arms for a Papist rising. It is said that at High Wycombe there were always great festivities for Guy Fawkes day, with rival bonfires in the four wards and fireworks and a feast for the mayor and aldermen.

Among the important rooms at Gayhurst, beside the Digby room and the oratory, are the ballroom, the Burleigh room, the Drake room, the Prince's room (where Edward VII stayed after his illness), and the Medici room.

The Medici room, called after the famous room at Blois, has panels covering the walls, but instead of the arabesques which decorate the little panels and secret cupboard in the palace at Blois, here each long narrow panel is painted with a British wild flower or fruit. Foxgloves, primroses, wild roses, loosestrife, red campion, ladysmock, bee orchis, and rock-rose, all the galaxy of the fields are there, with only two or three duplicates when the

342

French artists became so enamoured with their work they painted pansies or mullein again. The panels are a delight to the eye with their decorative treatment and fresh colours, and the secret cupboard is only a place for a book or two instead of the poisons Catherine kept in her boudoir. There is a very ornate and gilded fireplace in this room which accords with the gaiety of the walls, although it is overwhelming for a private house.

Another room has a Chinese hand-painted wall-paper, put up in Tudor times, brilliant with trees, birds, and flowers in great variety, painted in clear colours as if the work had been done the other day.

Under the windows there is a tiny formal garden of box hedges, miniature green hedges which form two mazes with a pattern of circles and squares. There are about twenty-five little enclosures in each complete square which make a labyrinth for a Lilliputian to walk within. From the rooms above it is like a couple of pieces of green embroidery laid out on the grass.

We went down the Digby Walk, a haunted walk where the ghost of Digby is supposed to wander. It was one of the ways of escape. It goes across the edge of the lawn between hedges of cut yew which widen as the wood is reached and the yews grow tall. The path leads about a mile to the bath house which is reached by a hidden passage under the road. Here is a reservoir of spring water, a chalybeate spring, famous from Roman days, whose character has changed in recent years for the iron has left it. In this bath, or reservoir, Digby hid when a search was made for him.

The great kitchen at Gayhurst has a look-out window like an oriel in one of the walls where the housekeeper sat and watched the kitchen wenches below. There is a vast fireplace and the food used to be sent to the dining-room on a kind of little railway which has lines in the corridors.

The old laundry rooms with their devices for drying clothes on wet days and the primitive machines for pressing and ironing still remain.

We stayed a few minutes at the door of the house looking out across the lawns to the yew hedge and the little church. Some old initials are scratched on the doorposts, initials of the Digby family. Among them is a memory of the execution of Charles I.

1649
X C.

We left this fine old house with its memories. Soon the new school term would begin and young boys would fill the rooms with laughter and gaiety. The house is kept with loving care and consideration for all its beauties and traditions.

344

CHAPTER XXV

LACE-MAKING AND
SOME NORTH BUCKS VILLAGES

BUCKINGHAMSHIRE has long been famous for its lace-making, an art and an industry which has almost died out. There is a tradition that the making of lace started with Catherine of Aragon who had several manors in the county. A manor was at Claydon, which has a long history of lace-making, for Steeple Claydon was given to Catherine by Henry VIII and St Katern's Day was kept as a festival until Victorian times by the lace-makers.

Bone-lace is mentioned in 1577 and about that time the Flemish weavers and lace-makers fled to England, bringing their crafts. Some of these settled at Olney and Newport Pagnell, and this part of the county, with Hanslope and Stony Stratford, was the strongest centre for lace-making.

The lace was called bone-lace, which is the original name for pillow-lace, because the bobbins were made of bone, although wood bobbins were used later. An old Bucks countryman carved for me in a few minutes a wood bobbin such as his mother used. He told me that when he was born, eighty years ago, his mother made him little shirts edged with Buckinghamshire lace which she had made on her lace-pillow. His sons wore the shirts and then his grandsons and the lace was as good as the linen.

In 1626 a school was founded at Great Marlow by Sir Henry Borlase for boys and girls, the girls to knit, spin, and make bone-lace. Since then many small schools for lace-making were started, often in cottages where the children learned to use the bobbins when they were very little.

A countrywoman told me that her mother went at the age of eight to the lace school at Lane End, and very proud was this little child of the honour. The children had lessons first and then they spent several hours learning to make lace. At Beaconsfield there was a lace school where the mother of Jack Norris learned to make lace, and his sister and cousins were lace-makers. At

Coleshill an old lady made lace until recently, and the mothers and grandmothers of many of the countrywomen were all clever-fingered with the bobbins and threads. At North Marston Mr Cheshire told me of his lace-making family. His mother learned to make lace when she was only four years old, but all the family learned and most of the village. Some lace-makers are still left there, and at Radnage and Prestwood lace is made.

Mr Cheshire's mother made black worsted lace for which she got £1 a week, which was a good wage in those days when farm labourers only received 10s and had their families to keep. His grandmother made lace by the light of a rushlight and a bowl of water. This round glass bowl was placed between the light and the lace and a soft glow was focused on the work. They used farthing rushlights in those days, not candles. They made these themselves from the piths of rushes, stripping off the green rind as we used to strip them for the farm labourers to weave roses of ivory. They could buy farthing rushlights, but it was more economical to make them and they made great bundles very cheaply, using mutton fat for the tallow.

"I could show you three lace-makers all sitting at their doors around here on a summer's day," said a friend in a Bucks village in the north of the county. "The lace-machine destroyed the market, but a few old ladies who make it are left."

At Long Crendon there are one or two lace-makers working. Some of the lace is on the altar cloths in the church of Long Crendon and most exquisite work it is.

In the seventeenth and eighteenth centuries most of the women, not only in the cottages but in the manor houses, could make lace. In the *Memoirs of the Verney Family* Sir Edmund Verney of Claydon says that one of the men had given him some very good lace made by his daughter, to be used for a cravat.

At High Wycombe lace-making was done on a large scale, one of the employers being Ferdinand Shrimpton who lived at Penn. He was eight times Mayor of Chepping Wycombe and he had hundreds of women working for him in their own homes. The lace was taken to London every week, generally on Mondays, and sold at the lace-markets. One such market was at the George Inn, Aldersgate Street.

Newport Pagnell was the chief lace-making town, and a market was held every Wednesday. Olney and Hanslope had their patterns from there and sent their lace to the market. Hanslope had 800 lace-makers out of a population of 1,275 at the beginning of the nineteenth century. The lace made there fetched from sixpence to two guineas a yard.

Aylesbury too was a great lace-making town. No women worked in the fields, for the wages from lace were much higher, and the work more delicate and suitable for their fingers and their artistic taste. Some workers at Aylesbury got 25s a week, and married women who did their own housework as well earned £1 a week, a considerable sum in those days. In the elections no candidate could hope for success unless he promised to help the home industry and defy the machine-made lace. Nottingham lace was already starting to destroy the art of the lace-makers for handwork could not compete against the machine.

In 1897 the North Bucks Lace Association was formed to encourage lace-making, to revive old patterns, and to get good wages for the workers. I was able to buy some yards of Bucks lace recently at a village.

There are many varieties of Buckinghamshire lace, and one of the best is known as pillow-point or half-stitch. There are examples of the graceful and exquisite patterns in the Aylesbury Museum. Some are made with the needle stitched on net, a needle-run lace.

The names of the kinds of lace have a delight in them. "Bean and Pea," which has a resemblance to these homely vegetables; "Shamrock," with its little trefoil leaf; "Running Water," with its ripples; and "Strawberry," with its conventional heart design, are some of the best known of the narrow lace edging.

At Lacey Green beadwork took the place of lace-making in recent years and the work was sent to London. Beadwork was also a cottage industry in Beaconsfield, where it was made in the cottages close to the churchyard. Many village women earn extra money by tambour work now.

At Aylesbury each year a lace queen was chosen from among

347

the lace-makers. She was carried on a platform with her pillow, and one can imagine that her dress was beautiful and the lace which hung around was an advertisement for her wares.

Women sat at their doorways with the thick pillow either on their knees or on a spider-like stand. The pillow is a hard round cushion stuffed with straw, very firm to the touch, and beaten to make it compact. It is covered with "pillow-cloth," a closely woven material. The design is pricked on a strip of stiff paper or card and it is laid on the pillow, passed round it and pinned in place. Very fine linen thread is used for the lace. Once there was a difficulty in getting the fine thread and silk was used instead. Amersham and Great Marlow used to make black silk lace. Some was made in Beaconsfield too.

The thread was wound on the lace-bobbins by means of a little wooden spindle called a bobbin-winder, a machine of simple construction. The bobbins which were made of wood or bone were often elaborately carved with mottoes and the name of the sweetheart, husband, or friend. Here was a chance for the individuality of the lace-maker. I have some in my collection with Bob, Job, and Robert, with Mary and Susan pricked upon the bone, and marked in scarlet or black. Some have copper wire wound about the ends as ornament, and some have spots of metal inserted.

At Olney, in Cowper's house, there are many lace-bobbins which have posies and mottoes pricked or cut on their handles: "My Love for Thee will never fail"; "Fear God."

At High Wycombe there is a good collection of lace-bobbins and in many a cottage a little store is put away. A lace-maker gave me two beauties of carved wood from her bobbin box. At the ends of the bobbins are coloured beads threaded on wire, strung through a small hole in the wood, to weight the bobbin.

Some lace-bobbins are very old indeed and they have been handed down from one generation to another. In cottages in Bucks there are the pricked-paper designs for the lace and bits of unfinished work left as the old hands that made the lace have dropped them for ever. Many bobbins are needed for one piece of lace, and they hang down over the lace-pillow in a bunch of many-coloured beads. Some very fine and elaborate lace needed

as many as 200 bobbins. The ends of the threads are attached
to pins firmly inserted in the pillow on the pattern and the lace-
maker starts to twist her threads, fixing the lace-pins in the
pricked design, tossing the bobbins across as she moves the pins.

For warmth in the winter an earthenware pot, called a
dick pot, filled with glowing charcoal was once put under the
chairs of the workers, similar to those one sees in the seventeenth-
century Flemish pictures of country life.

I met my first lace-maker by chance in the village of Thornborough near Buckingham, where I went originally to find the
medieval bridge over the Claydon Brook, a tributary of the
Ouse. This is the only ancient bridge in Bucks. It is about 165
feet long and twelve feet wide, but it has little embrasures, angles
on one side, a square on the other, where one can stand in safety
from any passing car and gaze down at the water. For the river
is beautiful at this place, with shining reeds and water forget-me-
nots close to the old grey stones of the bridge. Two swans and a
cygnet were swimming among the rushes, watching us with
beady eyes and waiting for us to move. Then swiftly they
glided under the barrier of thick reeds to the blue water. It is a
very low simple bridge, with little buttresses and six small arches,
all close to the surface of the water. On the bridge is the boundary stone between Buckingham and Thornborough.

We loitered at this quiet place, and indeed whenever I see the
Ouse or its brooks I want to stay for hours, to watch the swans,
the ripples, the gentle motion. At last we went on, past the Lone
Tree Inn, by itself at the cross-roads, to the village.

Near the roadside between Buckingham and Thornborough
are two large barrows, grass covered, twenty-five feet high. One
of these was opened in 1839. Inside there were many ornaments
of bronze, including a lamp so perfect that the wick remained in
it. There were elegant jugs, a dish, a bowl, and an ornament of
pure gold with a figure of Cupid chased upon it.

There is a stream running through Thornborough spanned
by three tiny bridges, with ducks swimming and children
playing. The Manor House looks like a medieval house, too,
with its stone walls, cream-coloured topped by dark red tiling,
its tithe barn, its farm and cattle. The house was once part of a

monastery and a barn was perhaps a dormitory, but there has been much restoration. Smooth lawns and walnut trees, a little garden filled with many-hued snapdragons, a high wall smothered in crimson roses, and the stream running by make a picture.

At the far side of the village green there is a little thatched cottage in a small garden packed with cabbages and roses, phlox and beans, and there lives Miss Palmer, who makes lace. She is a little woman with a sweet face and charming manners. Her sudden shy glances, her smiles, and her bright eyes are the mirror of eternal youth. She is slim and quick-moving as a brown wren. She was just going leasing in the cornfields to get corn for her sister's hens when I called to see her.

She told me about gleaning in her childhood. All the family went out together for the day, and there was a particular way of gathering the corn. Each small fist must hold the wheat ears below the head of corn till the hand was filled and the long straw hung evenly down. The bunches were put in a big cloth with the cornheads touching, north, south, east, and west, and the cornstalks hung out of the four corners. This corn was taken home, and carried to the barn to be threshed with the flail, then to the miller, and the flour was made into bread.

"We children always liked a bite of real white bread better than our gleaning bread," she added, ruefully. "It didn't rise! Perhaps my aunt wasn't a good baker."

This manner of placing the corn is similar to the method in South Bucks, when the little bunch was called a "dolly" by the young gleaners.

She fetched her lace-pillow on its stand from the little side room and brought it to the light of the open door. This dumpy pillow belonged to Miss Palmer's grandmother, and we calculated its age by a complicated process, for she was very old when Miss Palmer was a tiny child. The pillow must be about 130 years old now, we guessed, and we thought of the yards and yards of exquisite lace that had been made upon it—lace for weddings, for babies, for fine ladies, lace that was a work of art as surely as a picture painted or a panel carved. The "lacing" was removed to disclose the snowy lace pinned to the pillow. This "lacing" is a piece of cotton material, pink print in this case, which covers the lace, with a strip across the pillow and a hanging piece. Large brass pins, about two inches long, held a square of thin card which lay under the bobbins. A strip of cloth was drawn tightly across under the heads of the bobbins where they were wound with lace-thread.

We watched Miss Palmer place her small brass pins, used because they never rust, in the paper pattern pricked out with the design. A very small pincushion was fastened to the pillow. It had the brass pins and also pins with sealing-wax heads which are used for the bottom or foot of the lace. The red-headed pins were placed at the foot of the fine piece of lace to hold it firm. Then the threads were twisted and the bobbins began to fly with such speed that I was amazed. It looked like an exciting game or the playing of a musical instrument; the pretty bobbins were tossed rapidly and the pins were moved. Four of these bobbins were always in use, the centre core of the lace, but some had a rest between the movements.

We saw the little buds and ferns, the curves and whorls created, as those nimble old fingers sped over the pillow. It was so fascinating I found I was always staring at the flying bobbins with their jingling beads instead of watching the growing lace, which was visibly increasing.

There were about thirty bobbins hanging there, each with gay beads on the wires. When the hole for threading the beads is worn away the bobbin is discarded. Some of these bobbins had ornaments of metal inserted, some were of carved bone or wood. Some had names of old friends carved in the sides slantwise and coloured to show up on the white bone. One of them belonged to Miss Palmer's father, and his name and the date of carving were pricked out. The lace-makers were deeply interested in their bobbins, each of which had its own characteristic charm, and they were proud of the workmanship in them.

When Miss Palmer was a child her aunt made her do two rounds of the pillow each day before she went out to play. She hated the sight of the pillow, naturally, and vowed she would never make any more lace, but when she was older she returned to it with interest.

Her aunt lived by making lace, which she sold at Bucking-

351

ham. She used to walk there, over the long stone bridge and through the lanes to the market town where she sold her lovely lace at a very low price to a middleman. Sometimes he gave her a different pattern and he varied the price according to the intricacy of the work.

Miss Palmer went as a young cook to London, and she was brought to the drawing-room to show her ladies how she made lace. She was so nervous as they watched her that she muddled all the bobbins up and made many mistakes, for her hands were trembling. Happily the ladies didn't know the difference and they were filled with admiration for the web she made. When she got back to the comfort and homeliness of her kitchen she soon put it right!

One day a lady admired Miss Palmer's lace so much and the way the bobbins flew she gave her three semi-precious stones to be used for jingles. They were threaded on the wire and they hung down, amber, cornelian, and topaz. Everybody looked at this precious bobbin which had pride of place on the lace-pillow. Alas for human cupidity! A fellow-servant who had been dismissed cut off some of the bobbins, including this one with the jewels, and carried them away.

"But I don't bear her any grudge, although I was upset at the time," said Miss Palmer, smiling.

I sat in the pretty cottage, with its wheel-back chairs, its lustre jug on a shelf, its kitchen fire, and I looked through the open door down the flower garden to Thornborough Green with its pond close to the walls of the manor house, its church tower, its farm buildings, and haystacks.

Another time when we visited Thornborough we crossed the river by a small bridge near the village of Thornton and went along a road that is often impassable. The river moves slowly through the fields which have no deep banks and the water easily overflows. There are bulrushes and water-lilies in this quiet reach of the Ouse and its brooks. A small wooden path, raised high on a bank, runs alongside the road, and people walk along this when the way is flooded.

The roadman cutting the grass and opening out the ditches told us of the great flooded tracts in winter when people come to

352

Stewkley Church, Norman doorway

skate. There is duck-breeding and a decoy pond out there in the fields.

About a mile from Buckingham is the village with the pleasing name of Maids Moreton. There are many seventeenth-century cottages with timber frames and brick fillings in the traditional manner. The place is noted for its fifteenth-century church of St Edmund. This church had the good fortune to be entirely rebuilt in 1450 at a time when English architecture was at a period of perfection. Two maiden ladies, the daughters of Thomas Pever, were the origins of this noble work, and they are the Maids of Moreton. A slab in the nave marks their grave and set in the stone is a modern pair of brasses with the maids wearing chaplets of flowers on their long hair.

The church and rectory stand at the entrance to the village among many trees. From the churchyard one can see a great distance across the Buckingham countryside. A cobbled path among the tombstones, almost hidden in the canopies of ivy, leads to the porch of the church.

The magnificent tower, with a flying key as a weathervane, has gargoyles like birds in the corners, and winged birds with the faces of men crouch on the north porch. The west front has a porch with fan-vaulting in the roof and a window above it. The north porch has an embattled parapet and fan-vaulted roof. Its doors are richly carved, and the inner door has a great lock 500 years old set in a solid block of wood which spans the door.

The church is extremely beautiful and the roofs of nave and chancel are the original work, with bosses of angels and shields, and in the centre a boss of Christ with His hand raised. There are sedilia, with canopies of traceried stone elaborate as lace-work. The font has cockle-shell ornament and the screen is very fine, with angels at the sides.

In the tower the six bell-ropes hang from the fan-vaulted roof, and there is a painted notice commemorating famous peals rung there, which always interests me.

"On Feb 21, 1914, in 2 hours 40 minutes, a Peal of Bob Minor with 5,040 changes was rung.

"On April 20, 1914, in 2 hours 46 minutes, a Peal of Grand-sire Doubles with 5,040 changes was rung."

2A

Olney Church

Another tower notice reads:

"This year ye Parish Bells wch were but three in number were cast into five at ye parish charge. They weigh thirty three hundred and a half and fourteen pounds. They wrang ye 22nd June, 1717."

There is an interesting extract from the parish register fastened to a great oak door that hangs on the wall of the tower. The door is pierced with many bullet-holes, and a gap is torn in the structure. The damage was done in 1642.

"This yeare the worst of Parliaments wickedly rebelling against ye best of princes, King Charles the First," begins the dramatic indictment.

"In the church of Moreton the windows were broken, a costly deske in ye form of a spread eagle guilt, on wch we used to lay Bpp Jewells Works, hewed to pieces as an abominable idoll, the cross (wch with itts fall had like to have beate out his braines yt did itt), cut off ye steeple—by ye souldiers and att ye command of one called Colonell P— of Warwickshire. We conveyed away what we could and among other things ye Register was hid."

A wooden basket or receptacle for loaves of bread in the church is a reminder of an ancient charity, and the Norman font was left by the Maids from the original church.

The road onward to Lillingstone Dayrell passes through lonely and beautiful country, along lanes bordered by masses of wild flowers growing for some unknown reason in clumps of colour such as a herbaceous garden might envy. Here a bank of scarlet poppies, sown thickly, and there a mass of blue tufted vetch, rich dark blue flowers covering the ground and climbing on the bushes, with scabious in a drift of lavender blue, hundreds of flowers, yellow bird's-foot, a golden bank, and then creamy meadowsweet. I noticed the same effect in a long lane near Hawridge where the flowers grew in their kinds.

The country in this North Bucks region has changed, for we are near the Northamptonshire border and there is stone in the cottages, although the thatch remains.

The park of Stowe school is near the village, and the country

354

is agricultural and wide. The royal forest of Whittlewood was partly in this parish, and a member of the Dayrell family was a ranger of the forest with certain hunting rights. They owned a horn called the Purlieu Horn which bore the date 1692.

The few houses of the village are near the old turnpike road to Buckingham, now a lonely road. The church stands in the fields, with sheep and cattle near it and only a rough road bumping through the long grass, so that I expected to find the small building locked and deserted. We closed the field gate carefully lest the cattle should stray, and went through the herds.

The tiny church was bright and fresh and beautiful, lighted by candles, decked with flowers. One has many surprises in Buckinghamshire and not the least is the gaiety and charm of very small churches hidden away in fields. This church was remarkable for the round little arches, one in the tower, another in the chancel, which made frames for the pictures within them. The tower and chancel arch are Norman, untouched and simple in their beauty. In the centre of the chancel is an altar tomb, with the figures of Paul Dayrell and his wife lying there. She wears an elaborate dress with puffed sleeves, and her shoes have stout soles as if she still walked through the fields in muddy places. Her grim old face is that of a woman who has worked very hard all her life. I like old Dorothy Dayrell. A red velvet banner embroidered in gold and white hangs from the wall, with the Dayrell motto and the date 1659.

In this church there is another altar tomb with most delightful brass portraits of Paul Dayrell, buried in 1491, and Margaret, his wife. He is a handsome boy, with a dog, and she is pretty and young. A sardonic stone face, a marvellous character carving, looked down from one of the walls.

Close to the church, alone in this parkland, is a group of red-roofed old stables and outhouses, and a couple of little cottages, rather lost and lonely in the fields. We looked round for the manor house or some large dwelling, but there was nothing. The old man in one of the cottages told us he had worked on the estate all his life and now he and his wife are retired. Next-door lives an old lady also retired from work.

The manor house was pulled down "a long time ago," before

355

he was born, said he, and the stones had been taken to build a house across the fields. This really happened in 1767, but the memory of the happening had remained and the stories of that time. The foundations of the manor house had been left, and under the field where we stood those great cellars still existed. Now they were the haunt of foxes and badgers. He had actually been down when they were digging the earth and seen the cavernous rooms underground.

The buildings belonged to the farm and the two cottages had been made out of a stable. They were attractive and comfortable, covered with roses, and in front of them little strips of flowery gardens.

Close to the church and cottages is a small lake closely patterned with water-lilies. The white lilies grew in hundreds, with their flat shining green leaves concealing the water. Some were tilted to show their rosy undersides, some were curled like sea-shells, but the snowy lilies were a vision to remember. We could hear the water-hens and coots, but there was no room for the birds to swim. On a small island a great willow dipped its slender branches down to the flowers, and water reeds fringed the edge of this entrancing lily-pool. Beyond were cornfields and Old Tile Farm with its stacks.

We went along narrow roads to Leckhampstead, and at some of the farms on the way we saw tassels of wheat decorating the gables of the corn ricks in most attractive bunches. It was a pleasure to know that thatchers even in these days of austerity, bad harvests, and short labour, had that old sense of doing something extra, making something beautiful, and challenging a dull world with a little flag of hope. These wheat sprays were well made and very ornamental.

A stream runs through the village of Leckhampstead, and ducks were swimming on it, which is always a homely sight. This stream, the river Leck, winds past the church, and a tiny three-arched low bridge by the churchyard leads to a farmhouse. Another farm stands across the road, for this small village is pastoral, with horses, barns, stables, and church together.

Menacing figures with wings lean far out from the thirteenth-century tower in this ancient place of great interest. The doorway of the church is one of the best in the county, hidden away in this remote little village. Three supercilious and enigmatic faces gaze down from the stonework of one door with such sardonic expressions of contempt that one feels disconcerted. I should get to know these stone faces very well if I lived at Leckhampstead, for they appear to be very much alive. There is rich carving on this Norman doorway and the two capitals are different. The door has wrought hinges of good design and workmanship.

Swallows had made their nests along this side of the church, and the birds were flying to their little mud homes, flashing their wings and dipping low.

The south door is one of the famous doors of Buckinghamshire. It is dated about 1120, and it has been kept safe from the weathering of years by an added porch. Over it is a stone tympanum with two dragons fighting for a little long-eared man smiling between them. Above the scaly column on the left of the door is a winged figure, and the right column has a kind of feather moulding, and a face upturned. A diaper of cross-stitch is carved below the tympanum, as if the stonemasons had thoroughly enjoyed themselves experimenting in design and ornament. Even the wings and tails of the dragons have beading to fill the spaces.

A tiny door, only big enough for us to enter stooping, led into the church. Inside there are most original and strange stone heads on the walls above the Norman arches. One of them is a man with great square open mouth and tiny hands to his eyes, as if in mockery of weeping. Another is the head of a lion, with huge tongue lolling out, and traces that it had once been painted red. A third is a man with a large nose and great eyes, from whose mouth leaves are projecting as if he is tasting them. What strange symbolism is here! Or perhaps it is no symbolism, only gargantuan humour.

The beautiful font is early fourteenth-century with carving to make a picture gallery for the people of Leckhampstead. It is octagonal, and in the panels are St Catherine holding a wheel in her hand, while a fireworks wheel spins near her. A second panel has Mary and the Child under a sculptured arch, a third

357

BUCKINGHAMSHIRE

the Crucifixion, a fourth four Tudor roses, a fifth a tree and wild boar, and a sixth a figure with a crosier.

There is an altar tomb of a Crusader, with sword and shield, his feet on a lion whose hairy-ended tail curls round.

We left this little village filled with wonder and admiration for the craftsmen of old who had worked there. The splendid carvings in some of these small churches show goodness and wit, and caricature and poetry in the individual workmanship. It was because God was living for those craftsmen. He and the devils and angels were near all the time, and the masons and wood-workers carved them as they imagined them. Nowadays so few believe in devils and angels, that the life has gone out of them. At Leckhampstead they live in the stonework of the exquisite little church.

358

CHAPTER XXVI

IVINGHOE AND PITSTONE

By the side of the road there were beds of wild thyme, deep purple, and stretches of wild marjoram, whose colour varied from rose-red to magenta and then to pink. There were bushes of musk mallow, and bright gold lady's slippers in long cushions on the banks. Each species of flower was distinct and aloof from the others, so that we passed a succession of flower-beds set out for the delight of the honey bees and the butterflies. This road to Hawridge and Cholesbury is enchanting with its flowery borders. On the common, high on the ridge where one looks down to a green valley, there are masses of yellow bedstraw, most delicately scented. I do not know whether all bedstraw is the same, but on Hawridge Common the air is fragrant and rich with the flowers which grow in abundance. This is a lovely and simple place, with the scattered houses on one side and grassy border to the quiet road, and the common beyond so that each child can run out and play among furze and flowers and bushes of thorn.

A windmill stood behind some cottages, its sails unmoving, although a strong wind was blowing. Like other windmills it was not in use. The ridge here is nearly 600 feet up, with falling fields below, and an exhilarating air about the place. I liked the Full Moon Inn, with its good painted sign. There are earth-works in these parts, one at Hawridge Court Farm which is built on the edge of the "fort" and has a rampart which is sixteen feet high in places.

Further on this ridge, which has neither hedge nor ditch to make a boundary, is Cholesbury, where the great British earth-work enclosing about fifteen acres contains the little church and the vicarage just within its borders. The double rampart and ditch are clearly defined, and the sides of the rampart are steep. It is crowned with beech trees, whose roots are laid bare as they run down to the deep ditch. The field enclosed by this prehistoric ring has two old ponds called Bury Pond and Holly Pond, with crab-apple trees and hazels, and bloody cranesbill grows there, which seems an appropriate flower. There is a tradition that converts were baptized in one of these ponds in the early days of the church.

We dropped down a steep hill through a wood where there was an outdoor timber-yard—trees cut, sawn, and split into pieces for chairmaking under the spreading boughs. It is always interesting to see the woodmen working on the spot instead of in factories, and we stayed a few minutes to watch them in the bright sunshine.

Four months earlier we went along this road and onward to Ivinghoe and Pitstone, and at that time, in a wintry March, the Chilterns were white with snow, and snow was piled high like a hedge on each side of the road. It was a wonderful sight to see these snowclad hills as a background for the elms which were already plum-coloured with little blossoms. The trees along the Icknield Way grow to beautiful shapes, each one distinct and perfect. The great camp at Halton and the hospital stand in the fir woods, with beech higher up the slopes of the hills. Snow-sprinkled dark boughs and the white steep hills behind gave an impression of a miniature Switzerland on that bleak March day. Even the people, hooded in scarlet and blue, seemed too gay for our country. The contrasts were startling under the dazzling sky, with the Ivinghoe Beacon covered with snow. People climbing the sides looked very small and their black shapes were silhouetted against the sky at the summit as if they were on a mountain. The Chilterns were transformed to the Alps by the wizardry of snow and sun and clear air and blue shadows. Perhaps the old Icknield Way had something to do with the enchantment, for the ancient road must carry with it some memory of the long past and the travellers it has known.

We climbed the Beacon on a summer's day when it had lost its remote majesty and the immense strength it seemed to possess under the snow that early March. It was now a steep hill with the chalk showing through the turf in places, and little flowers growing close to the earth. Small tufted bell-flower, that denizen of the Chilterns, azure harebells, wild thyme, rock-roses, and clustered wild marjoram, all were there, but among the little

360

flowers we found pink bushes of thorny restharrow, growing high and stiffly beautiful. This plant grows to a good size near Whitchurch on the hills, where the long spiny trusses of blooms are like rose-coloured gorse.

From the summit of Ivinghoe Beacon we looked down at the Quainton Hills, the long line of the Chilterns, the Lion at Whipsnade; Dunstable Beacon and the fields of many colours lay in the foreground, strips of barley, oats, and wheat, each clearly defined, the wheat tawny-gold, the barley amber, the oats pale as flaxen hair, and the harsh yellow of charlock and the purple of willow-herb on the hills.

Suddenly there was a roar, and up the long spine of the Beacon came a troop of Army motor-cyclists, bucking and jerking on their machines. So this secluded peaceful place was invaded by explosion and smell as if to remind us that nowhere is safe from man's endeavour. Like a noisy company of trippers they rushed about and then, uncomfortably clinging to their handlebars, they jerked away, probably as thankful to escape as we to see them go.

The windmill at Ivinghoe stands solitary in a field, a national monument, with no vanes left. Ivinghoe village rests on a lower spur of the hills, and the Upper and Lower Icknield Way meet near it as they go on to Dunstable and leave the county of Buckinghamshire.

The fine old inn, the King's Head, in the main street of Ivinghoe opposite the green, has rows of windows looking out to the wide views below. It is a fifteenth-century house, rebuilt in the seventeenth century, but keeping its oak beams and wide fireplaces. As we sat in the room cows and horses passed close to the windows, going to the farms near.

Ivinghoe, which is a purely agricultural village, is surrounded by pasture and cornland. The name was taken by Sir Walter Scott for his romantic novel, *Ivanhoe*, and I had half-expected to find a wild Scottish town instead of a farming village.

There is an old rhyme connected with the place:

> Tring, Wing, and Ivinghoe,
> Hampden of Hampden did forgo,
> For striking the Black Prince a blow,
> And glad was he to escape so.

Although this seems to refer to a legend that an ancestor of John Hampden struck the Black Prince in a game of tennis and lost his manors in consequence, the tale is discredited, as these were not his manors.

Another rhyme says:

> Tring, Wing, and Ivinghoe,
> Three churches all in a row.

The names make such a jingle of bells no wonder the rhymers played with them.

The church of Ivinghoe, which stands on a projecting ridge, dominates the village by its grandeur. It is a cruciform church of the thirteenth century, and it is important enough for a much larger place. It stands boldly on its ledge with the old houses opposite, the King's Head with barns, stables, and open courtyard, and all the wide country falling away. Everything here seems unchanged throughout the centuries, but much alive.

The roof of the church is its glory, for it is decorated with angels whose golden feathered wings, outstretched in flight, seem to be supporting the timbers. I gazed entranced at these angels, while below in the church little groups of Sunday-school children sat in corners with their teachers having their lessons. There are many interesting features for the archæologists: the capitals of the pillars with their wreaths of foliage, the lancet windows—but for me the angels were the attraction. Beasts and men also were in the company of the angels on the roof. Carved wooden figures of the Apostles at the ends of the beams had their feet on stone corbels, shaped like grotesque and frightful beasts' heads. Some animals rested their paws on the stone, others with huge grinning mouths and enlarged eyes stared down, controlled by the Apostles, the holy men above them, and the cohort of angels. Near the chancel is an even more wonderful roof, with roses and leaves carved upon it, as well as the figures of angels.

Down below were thirty-eight bench-ends which at first sight appeared to have ordinary carved poppy-heads, with flowing lines in the conventional manner, but I might have guessed that the irrepressible medieval craftsmen would not have allowed such an opportunity for amusement and sarcasm, for impudence and wit, to escape them. When I peered more closely at these wooden ends of the benches I saw faces leering at me, half-concealed in the way that Rackham's gnomes and goblins lurk in the trees. I thought it was my distorted imagination, for the light was dim and mouths grinned where no faces should be. Then I found that most, if not all, of the poppy-heads held faces concealed in the carvings and many had two, one at each side, so that those in the pews could be as well entertained as those outside.

How I wish I had gone to church and sat among goblins like these in my childhood! What a treat for every child at Ivinghoe to sit among this fairy-tale company and to listen to a sermon and dream of whatever might be murmuring near with reedy soft voice in the carved wood!

I was left with the goblins to discover who and what was concealed there. I saw a dragon, with queer, squinting, leering eyes and long hair; I saw dwarfs and gnomes, little faces and large ones, some of them all mouth and eyes, others with small neat faces, more inimical than the others, because they were ready to spring from the wood, and in one bench-end there was a walking man with frills at his wrist, and pointed boots, and curled head, stepping out. In every case the conventional shape of the poppy-head served to make the tall hat, or the piled-up hair, and the sweeping ears made the side-hair. One had a Tudor rose, perhaps carved by a gardener who disapproved of the antics of his fellow craftsmen.

I like to think of generations of children and men at Ivinghoe enjoying the picture gallery, the exhibition of fine sculpture in the church, and then going off to Edlesborough a short distance away to find even more carvings. There must have been some good craftsmen in this region, brilliant and alive men, who were full of humour mixed with a spark of malice, as they tried to outdo one another in fantasy.

The pulpit is Jacobean, with carvings of grapes climbing up it and fierce hounds, or werewolves, chasing in and out of the wood. The plain lectern is Elizabethan, very beautiful and restful after all the wizardry of the church. A sounding-board hangs over the pulpit, and at the back of the pulpit are figures carved in such high relief that they have been partly broken. Jesus Christ is there with a Cross in His hand, stepping from His coffin, and two Roman soldiers stand near.

On the wall outside the western gate of the church was a great iron hook with massive wooden staff bound in iron. This was one of the implements used for dragging burning thatch from a house on fire. There was a man-trap also on this wall, a reminder of the fate of robbers, when man-traps and spring-guns warned away the thief in garden and farmyard and wood.

Children were standing round a lorry near the church, laughing and pushing each other in excitement, one day when I was at Ivinghoe. They held tightly to bags and sacks. On the lorry stood a man with a weighing-machine. He took each sack and weighed it and emptied the contents on a pile of green leaves which lay there. I thought at first they were vegetables from the cottage gardens, but the children had been collecting herbs for Dunstable. This week they had gathered elder leaves. One girl had picked ninety pounds, and for this she had just received the payment of 7s 6d. She was a very proud little girl. Another had managed to get nine shillingsworth of elder leaves. They were not told the name of the herb until two days before it was required. Then they rushed off and the leaves were freshly gathered.

One week it was poppy petals. For this delicate flower they got a shilling a pound. The payment varied according to the scarcity of the plant. They had gathered red nettle, and they had tried to find ground-ivy. The ground-ivy week was a failure, for there was not enough to pick, and they had no money. Lime might come later, they thought. We were standing under lime trees with their little fruits hanging down, all ready for the pot. I was glad to see this herb-gathering by all the eager little country children.

It was windy at Ivinghoe even on that summer's day, but in winter when I have been there the wind blows fiercely, sweeping down the Chilterns to the little street, cutting to the bone. Even on a winter's day Ivinghoe is not bleak, for there is always colour and warmth absorbed in the land, concealed and brought forth for winter's cheerfulness. That is one of the delights of the Chilterns—the richness stored away, the secret hoard of treasure.

Below the road level, towards Edlesborough, there is a deep hollow where two slopes meet to form a bowl, cut off by a third crest. It is a curious formation, like a trap in which cattle might be driven with no escape except up the steep hillside. The name of this grassy hollow is Coombe Hole, but none of the country people knew its origin.

By Pitstone Hill we turned to see the hamlet of Pitstone and the little grey Norman church with its tower rising from the midst of cornland. The road to Ivinghoe goes along the shoulder of Pitstone Hill and the two churches are visible at once, as well as the tall chimney of a cement works blossoming with a tuft of white smoke.

The name Pitstone has an interesting derivation. An early spelling was Piglesthorne, and another was Pightlesthorne, which is thought to be a combination of a personal name and the Old English "thyrne," a thorn bush.

Ripe red-gold wheat grew breast high around the low wall of the churchyard, and the sound of the wind in the corn of that elevated place in the Chilterns was like shrill organ music, sweeping over the little old tombstones. Pitstone Hill stands above, and the Beacon looms against the sky.

This is a most beautiful tiny church, homely and happy as a thatched cottage with a family of children within. It is a short distance from the village, and its path goes through the fields to the gate, but there is no sense of remoteness about the church. Perhaps the corn makes good company with its lively motion, and in winter the ploughfields have their birds.

There is a Norman font with carving of flowers and fluted arches and the cable roll which one sees in some of the Bucks churches. The piscina is carved with a sun god with flaming hair, or so he seems to me. Around this arch is delicate work, and at the base two little faces—one of sorrow and one of joy.

On a wall is a brass, which was dug up in the churchyard in 1933, of a woman with long folded dress, very clear and fresh.

"We refused £40 from a London gentleman for that. He badly wanted her," said an old man to me.

In the wall there are the remains of the rood stairway with complete steps. Some pews are sixteenth-century, with carved beading on the back, and there are two box pews. The pulpit is

365

Jacobean, elaborately carved with a canopy and a standard with scrolls.

We went into the vestry to see the treasured old chest of the thirteenth century, well known as the Pitstone Chest. It has hinges and bands of wrought iron and great nails. The iron bands hold the timbers together, and a long Y-shaped band down the centre, forked like a sycamore twig, is both ornament and extra strength. It is always a pleasure to see these old pieces of furniture kept in churches instead of in museums. Some hold altar cloths and some the vestments. The lid of a great oak chest was lifted for me in one church and I saw a pile of linen with Bucks lace edging, carefully preserved there.

There was no mortising in these very old chests, and the ends slide into grooves cut into the back and front. In this chest the wood is two inches thick, and the iron bands hold the pieces together. The Y-piece has a lock or fastening between the forks and the straight tail is nailed down the centre of the chest.

The chest, which is a sturdy and strong box, had been locked for many years, and nobody could open it. When at last it was undone some old vestments were found within. There is a record of a cupboard hidden in the vestry wall which nobody has yet discovered.

When I think of Pitstone Church I think of the flowers decorating it; many-coloured larkspur, light as air, and love-in-a-mist, and pink and blue annual lupins, all arranged with an eye to beauty, flowers from the cornfields, flowers everywhere, and the fields of wheat and barley and sainfoin pressing round, as if all were one.

From Pitstone we returned to the road and dipped down to Edlesborough.

The church is on an eminence, high above the valley, and below is Church Farm with its beautiful long tithe barn of the sixteenth century, of red brick, timber-framed, with mossy roof and wooden steps leading to an upper chamber. The bays are about sixteen feet long and the whole building is about 180 feet in length. Great beams cross the roof and the upright pillars stand on low walls of stone. There are two threshing-floors, one with the doors of the barns opening into it and a winnowing door. In the farmyard under the shadow of this magnificent barn many little Berkshire pigs were feeding and playing, racing away and peering round like children. I could scarcely drag myself away from them.

The barns of the Buckinghamshire farms are noble buildings, small churches, where birds sing in the high beams. Some were built more than three centuries ago by the village carpenter and mason, and the thatcher came to roof them. These great barns stand in many villages, often close to the church. They are built on a foundation of a low wall, of brick or of stone, rough hewn. The great timbers holding up the roof are sometimes built on pillars of brick, standing out from the walls. They make divisions of the roof-trusses, called bays, and these hold the corn. The floor was the threshing-floor when the work was done by hand, and there was usually a winnowing door or window. Edlesborough barn is Tudor, and it has five bays.

Some of these long barns have black weatherboarding sides and brick and flint gable ends. There is a fine old barn of the sixteenth century at Addington. One day when we were driving to Winslow and Buckingham we went through the gates into the great park of Addington, where sheep graze and many birds live. By the manor house and church are the village stocks. The barn of the old manor house is one of the finest in the county. There are five bays, each about twelve feet long. The shape is that of a cross and there are wide doors in the gable. The rafters continue downwards to form "outshuts" for chaff or for calves or carts. Bledlow has a good barn, and also Holtspur Bottom Farm, Beaconsfield, but Buckinghamshire is rich in these great beautiful barns.

Edlesborough Church is like a look-out post, a fort on the spur of the hill. The mound on which it stands is probably an ancient barrow as in several of the Buckinghamshire sites, pagan and then Christian church taking up the same position. It is dedicated to the Virgin Mary. The way is steep and on a wild day with stinging snow crystals in the air, as when I first saw it, it seemed to be exposed to all the winds with no shelter at all. Away in the distance the line of Dunstable Beacon stretches, and Ivinghoe Beacon looks down from the back.

367

This is a church famous for its carvings, perhaps the most renowned of all in Buckinghamshire.

We had come to see the carved woodwork and at first we were disappointed, for the doors of the chancel screen and the vestry were locked. The chancel screen was gay and decorative, painted in reds and greens and golds in the 'sixties. I like this brightness and lightness in a church. The screen was delicately carved in 1450, so that it looked like a fine lace canopy of wood across the stone arch. A frieze of gold oak leaves spreads across the top, and at the chancel side there was a glimpse of fan-vaulting in pale golden wood, a wonderful and tantalizing sight as we tried to peer through the circular frame of scarlet and gold. When an old lady came with the key we entered that beautiful chancel, and saw the carved pictures made for long-dead generations who surely must still be hovering near to see these treasures. I know one church in the Chilterns where the ghost of the rector actually came to his church—he loved it so much, and this church perhaps has its invisible company.

The stalls in the chancel have perfect carving of animals and men—a harpy, a monkey, an angel, and a bishop.

The misereres are a marvel of intricate work and imagination. There is first a mermaid, scaled and lovely, with her tail curved round, and a beast suckling at her breast. On two curving "strings" are sun faces, shining to her at the bottom of her sea. In another miserere is a dragon, with tail and scales, and frogs on the curves around it. There is a fine figure of a wide-eyed owl, and on another an eagle with two eaglets. A beast with claws and a bat complete this strange and exciting menagerie, which must have given delight to villagers and priests for centuries.

The wineglass-shaped pulpit of 1450 has an elaborately carved canopy with a pinnacle and finials of extreme beauty. The pulpit must once have had figures carved round the sides on the little pedestals which are now empty. By the pulpit once hung the hour-glass in a simple iron bracket, ready for the priest to turn and let the sands run as he preached. I once had one of these "hour-glasses" which took only half an hour to run through.

Medieval bridge at Thornborough

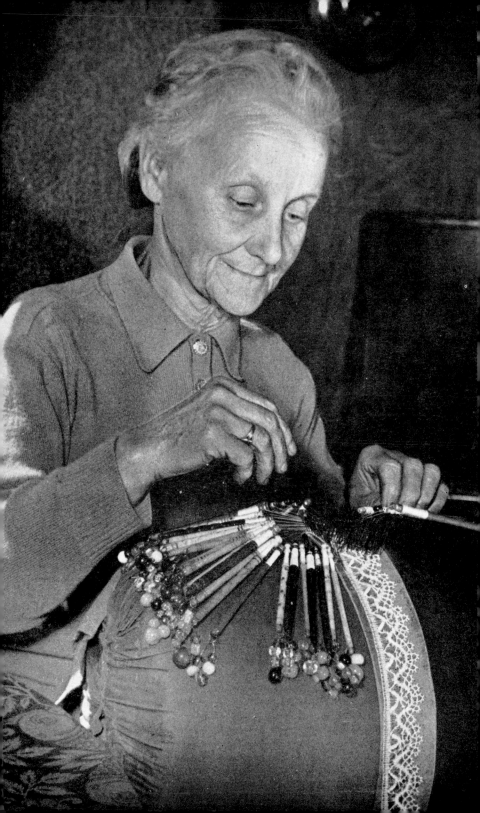

"No need for me to have an hour-glass or even a watch," said a Buckinghamshire vicar to me. "My gravedigger always reminds me when he thinks it is time for me to stop my sermon. After I have been preaching ten minutes he gets up and noisily and ostentatiously walks down the church to blow the organ ready for the hymn. Sometimes I want to call out 'Just a little longer, Harry. I'm not quite ready,' but it would be no use. He decides when my sermon is to end and I abide by his decision."

Under strips of carpet in the aisle are brasses which are clear-cut and plain to read. The famous "Rose brass" is there, a Tudor rose with "Ecce" in the centre. Its four petals with four pointed sepals are incised with four pregnant lines:

> Quod sapendi habui.
> Quod donavi habeo.
> Quod negavi punivi [not clear].
> Quod servavi perdo.

which my companion roughly translated as:

> What I've spent I've had.
> What I gave I have.
> What I refused I am being punished for.
> What I kept I lose.

In this church of many treasures there is a little stained-glass window of outstanding beauty. It is fifteenth-century glass, only a few inches long, set in a deep embrasure so that one looks down the tunnel of the whitewashed thick wall to see this glowing jewel at the end. It is a pilgrim, carrying a Bible and a forked staff, wearing a bright red cloak and a gay yellow hat with a cockle shell in the front.

We went to the vestry with the old lady, who did not wish us to miss the carved stone figures on the walls. A dragon, a skull with a crown over it, a broken chalice, and two portly angels were there. We saw the oak chest, dated 1689, with iron latchets. I liked better than these a brass of John Rufford in plate armour, and his three young and attractive wives. The brasses show fur-edged gowns and petticoats of quilting, ruffs, and slippers like our bedroom slippers, all very clearly defined.

2B 369

A Buckinghamshire lacemaker at Thornborough

This fine church on its high mound in a grove of sycamore trees is a landmark for many miles.

The churches of Buckinghamshire, especially those of Edlesborough and Ivinghoe, show great variety of simple and fantastic little carvings. The wood is sculptured into merry shapes of beasts and men, with scowling faces and puckered mouths and squinting eyes, and often the laughter of some wide-mouthed men. The animals carved there are fantastic beasts—dragons eating their own tails, monkeys at play, owls, mice, foxes.

We dog-loving people have forgotten the pets of earlier days, the monkeys and squirrels and hares which were the companions of the people, and it is remarkable how often these were carved while the dog is omitted, unless it is a fierce beast like the one at Dinton eating the Tree of Knowledge. Sometimes there are dogs on monuments—I think especially of the little dog on the Claydon tomb of Margaret Giffard. In the Middle Ages, with all the squalor, there was an intense love of beauty in ordinary things, an awareness that it is there, always present, for the imagination was young and vivid. We are humorous in caricature, which must have a caption to explain it. They could not read and they carved their wit and made a thing of beauty to last a thousand years.

CHAPTER XXVII

LITTLE HORWOOD, WHADDON CHASE, AND STONY STRATFORD

NEAR Aylesbury the blue wild geranium grows by the side of the road. Oak trees are evenly spaced in the hedgerows as if they had been planted there, and then oaks change to elms, for we are approaching the elm part of the country. Here is a haystack partly made, with a red and yellow elevator beside it just over the hedge, there a field of wheat turning gold, and then a field of barley. The hedges are untrimmed and very high, for labour is scarce.

Hardwick, the charming little village, with farmyards and stacks, and the church tower with a towerlet on the top, comes into sight. Swallows are flying low. Hedges, tall as houses, have ash and elm and sycamore in them. We pass the White Swan, outside Whitchurch, with its thatched roofs and painted picture of the swan on blue waters, and go through Whitchurch with a glimpse of a round-windowed shop and the cottages I know so well. Near Winslow the wide verges of the road are mown and lie in swathes. The hedges have been cut and labourers have been at work. A cottage roof has yellow stonecrop growing thickly on the old worn thatch.

At Great Horwood four roads meet in a circle of grass with the village pump. There is a farmstead with red walls around it. Little girls are skipping in the lychgate of the church and we go through to look at the tower which has gargoyles staring down with wide-open mouths in an interested way as if they are watching the life down below. I have noticed this in many churches, for these are no disinterested stone figures, but real watchers. There is a fair on the green, merry-go-rounds and washing. This is an old-time fair of tradition.

The village of Little Horwood has thatched roofs on its cottages, crooked chimneys, and bulging walls, little windows, and a good life within. On the wall of a small shop I read the words, painted on a board: "Licensed to sell patent medicines, tobacco,

371

and snuff." There are quite a number of snuff-takers in Bucks, and little snuff-boxes are offered in a friendly way for a pinch.

Near the wicket gate to the high churchyard is the Shoulder of Mutton Inn. This L-shaped small thatched inn, whitewashed and trim as a buttonhole of daisies, has a gay flower garden at the back and farm buildings close to it. It was built probably in the sixteenth century, and it has the original timber framing with braces in both stories at the north end. The south end has a half-hipped gable, and an original chimney stack with a little modern arch holding the two shafts together. There is a shining white-ness to the walls, and an air of well-being. The taproom has still its large open fireplace, although a modern fire is now there. There is a settle across the corner of the fireplace in this little inn with its uneven stone floors. A tiny steep staircase opens into a parlour. It is one of those homely inns which abound in the county, where men have no feelings of superiority, where there is no modern glitter.

Over the inn door a local signwriter had printed the name of the inn, the date 1600, and the name of the innkeeper. It was well done, with good lettering, and the panel was attractive, although the landlady thought an earlier date should have been written there. The barns and stables had old beams and mangers and stalls, for the inn is still partly a farmhouse.

The small church, which matches the inn for both comfort and homeliness, stands on a rise above the road. It is dedicated to St Nicholas, the Father Christmas of childhood, and when I went inside there was a congregation of tiny boys and girls sit-ting in the pews of this thirteenth-century church.

On the walls are striking remains of paintings, rather confused in their detail as a sixteenth-century artist has worked on the surface of a thirteenth-century picture.

The early painting is of St Nicholas rescuing children who had been slain, but the chief figure, added later, is that of a man representing Pride. He stands boldly there, naked and arrogant, and the picture is full of life and vigour. He is part of the alle-gorical painting of the Seven Deadly Sins.

"The deadliest sin of all is Pride," said the Sunday-school teacher, impressively wagging a finger to her little flock, and I wondered what strange impression they were receiving as they all turned their small vivid faces to the wall painting where the man stood. They might have been children of the sixteenth century learning about the church pictures.

Near the village is Little Horwood Manor Farm, a large modern farm which was built by Mr Gee, senior, and now is farmed by Mr Dewar. There were notices warning of cattle crossing, and I stood watching the familiar sight, for the cows were coming to the milking from the fields beyond the road.

They walked very slowly, proudly, gazing about as they stepped delicately across the road, as if the world were theirs. It was a pedigree herd of Ayrshire cattle. They were such beautiful creatures I asked the cowman to be taken over the farm buildings to see more of them. He was as proud of them as if they had been his own, and we stopped a few minutes watching them as they slowly ambled down the field to the red brick buildings, with two land girls in attendance.

We went into the cowhouses after the herd and saw them fastened in their modern stalls in the cleanest, brightest cowhouse I have ever visited. The whitewashed walls, glittering in the sunshine, the clean windows, the beautiful red and white cattle with their long horns curling upward, made a picture. Eight cows were milked at once with the milking machine. There was a washing-place, through which they passed, with rubber brushes and a flow of water, to spray them. Their udders were washed by hand with cloths. The cows, waiting there so quietly, looked ready for the Royal Show. There are seventy cows in milk and a herd of 200 on this large farm.

We went to the "maternity ward," where cows and new-born calves stood together in several stalls, warm and comfortable, the calves gazing serenely about, the mothers alarmed and on the alert for any danger. There were young calves in pairs, with a little cat for company, for calves love to have a cat with them.

In another building we saw several cow calves which were a few weeks old, nuzzling and pushing and trying to attract our attention as we leaned over and scratched their heads.

Then we saw the young bull, a splendid animal named Minsden Marston. He was tame and gentle and he nuzzled the

373

cowman and shook his head playfully. In a building to himself was the great bull, Nethercraig Duplicate, from Ayrshire. Sullen, fierce, and magnificent, he stood in his stall and I kept away. He was fastened to a sliding wire for exercise in his airy chamber.

We went into many buildings to see the crushers which grind the corn, beans, peas, and oats, and to watch the drying-machines for making hay powder. Grass is cut when it is only about six inches high and it is dried by this process. Three crops can be taken off and dried in a season. There were many bags of hay powder in one large barn, and I held a little in my hand. It was green as grass, with no loss of colour, and soft as flour. It was a product which the cows love when it is fed to them in winter. The scent of it was like a hayfield in the midst of a summer day, with honeysuckle and wild roses. It was worth £26 a ton, I was told, and they made so much they had more than they could use themselves, although with the increasing difficulties of farm feeding stuffs there would be less to sell. I thought of all the little farms, struggling along, without these driers and machines, and I wished they had the opportunity of using Government drying-chambers for corn and for this dried grass.

There was the cooler for the milk, and I was glad it was a cooler I knew, such as we used. The milk passed along pipes to the cooler and ran into churns. The night's milk was kept in a refrigerating room, ice-cold.

"Ah, we kept ours standing in the cold-water troughs," said I. "It stood deep in the spring water which was nearly as cold as your refrigerator."

The churns were sterilized by machinery, and I remembered the scalding, and the copper pan of boiling water, and the carrying of this water to wash and then to scald the milk cans and churns, the scyes and measures. Now one man could sterilize many churns at once, and men are employed in the factories making the machines to be used. This is a transfer from country life to town.

I saw the big yard where the cattle are turned as they wait to enter. They were patiently standing there, with their great horns and silky bodies shining with health. They are kept indoors all winter, I was told, and I was glad of that, for in South Bucks the cattle often stay out in snow and frost all night, and I feel unhappy about them. They stand the winter quite well, but they give much more milk when they are kept warm and comfortable in the cowsheds, said the cowman.

It was very interesting to see this herd of Ayrshires after seeing so many shorthorns and Friesian cattle in Bucks. The only drawback of the Ayrshires, as far as I know, is their long horns. I kept away from the sharp tips which could rip up a cow's side in a moment if there was a fight. I was told the cattle might be dehorned if more were kept, and then they would stay in covered yards for the winter.

This farm grows all its own food, except a little cow-cake. It is self-sufficient and draws on its own land to feed the cattle winter and summer. There is only a small staff, but the farm is highly mechanized. Only one old horse is there!

I was sorry to leave this really delightful place which was so well kept and so happy. The cowman was deeply interested in his charges, and proud of them and kind to them. Of course each cow has her own name—Angela and every girl's name through the alphabet—and, as all country people realize, each cow has her own character, her likes and aversions, known very well to the cowman. I longed to show these cattle to my father and many farmers whom I once knew, for they would have had the greatest admiration for them.

We drove away out of the gates and along the road, past fields where more Ayrshires grazed (a bunch of young stirks), and we thought we had seen one of the finest sights in Bucks that day.

Hayfields, haycocks, stacks, elevators—all were busy, for it was July and haymaking was in progress after a wet early summer.

We drove through this rich undulating country of Mid Bucks to Whaddon Chase, up the long hill where in the grassy verges grew cushions of tufted vetch, shading soft lavender, blue and purple, where pink thorny restharrow and meadowsweet and bugloss blossomed.

Whaddon stands on a plateau, about 450 feet high, with views of a misty blue country stretching for many miles. I thought it was the finest panorama I had seen as I stood in the elevated churchyard among the tall grasses and yellow bedstraw, although Ashendon and Bow Brickhill are perhaps as beautiful. The tower of this church is visible for many miles in North Bucks, rising from the bower of woods around it.

I pushed open the door and I was enchanted as I looked within. The sweet scent which filled the air came from earthenware jugs of lilies which stood on the floor, and the floor itself was made of old red bricks, warm and welcoming as a houseplace.

I am always aware of the feeling of church floors; indeed of all floors from moss in a beech wood to the stone of a stable and the wood of a threshing-barn. The shining tiles which pave some churches give me discomfort and misery as I tread upon them, whilst red brick floors and stone always seem to be in keeping with the church walls.

In this church there are four Norman pillars with capitals carved with flowers and dragons, rich ornaments in a plain old church. By the chancel arch are the remains of the rood stairs, and two little square windows high up light the arch. A small gilded organ is tucked away so that the church is left free.

The church was so well kept, so comely and simple, we explored it with delight. The old side chapel has an original roof, and some good modern chairs with the names of the donors carved on the backs. The reredos is modern wood-carving of Christ and two angels, and the hands are very expressive. The altar rails are seventeenth-century, sturdy and simple.

There are two interesting memorials, one to Lord Grey de Wilton who served in France at the age of twenty in Queen Mary's time and had an adventurous career in Scotland and in Ireland until he died at Whaddon. The other had an elaborately carved canopy, crowned with fleur-de-lis. Under this little roof were brasses of Thomas Pygott, Serjeant at Law, who died in 1519, and his wives and children in clear-cut clothes and headdresses.

The most vivid brass in the church, which is polished so that one can see the detail clearly, is that of an Elizabethan lady, Margret Myssenden, who died in 1612. She kneels praying in

376

her nice full dress, with every fold and every pleat clear, her ruff freshly starched, her high hat similar to some modern hats one sees in London. On her left is the brass of a small skeleton, engraved with such a sense of rhythm and with such art that one can but stand and admire the work and praise the craftsman who made it. Above this brass are some bits of fourteenth-century glass set in the window tracery.

There is a record of a clock given to the church. "Amy Emerton, the wife of John Emerton, gave a clock to the Parish church in Whaddon in the yeare 1673." Scratched on this brass record in the curly ornamental style of the period is the name of Anthony Chandler, 1673, the maker of bells.

This old church has many small treasures, such as oak chests, and two wooden alms-shovels with the date 1643 carved on them, and a dog's head carved on the end of a beam over the font. This dog's-head beam has a pulley which was a device for lifting the lid of the font. It is fifteenth-century work, and a good example, I think, of a village craftsman's amusing fancy. "Mine own cur," said somebody about five hundred years ago.

Below the church are the woods which are all that remains of the forests of Whaddon Chase, but the Chase country covers several miles. At Whaddon are the kennels of the Whaddon Chase Hunt. The Grafton also hunt in North Bucks but their kennels are outside the county. At Great Linford are the kennels of the North Bucks Otter Hounds, one of the four chief packs in the country.

"Oh yes, they still hunt the little red fox," said an Irish labourer. He was working at the farms along with fifty Irishmen who came over to find work in England.

Whaddon Hall, until lately the seat of Mr Selby-Lowndes, can be seen on its own high land, shining in its background of woods. Queen Elizabeth visited the Hall when Lord Grey de Wilton lived there. He had altered the old house a good deal and brought water through pipes into the quadrangle. In 1698 the Hall was bought by Thomas Willis, the father of the antiquary, and Browne Willis partly rebuilt the house and lived here for fifty-six years until he died in 1760. His library was left to Oxford University.

Willis cherished an ancient oak in the garden which was said to be the one under which Spenser wrote his *Faerie Queene*.

The Lowndes Arms stands at the roadside below the church, and there are several seventeenth-century cottages in the village. Some of the field names of Whaddon are Ladymead, Water Furrowes, Candlers, and Wood End Field. The lower part of the village is Wood End, and near there is a chalybeate spring, Bretch Well.

At Whaddon there is a row of tiny white bungalows, the prettiest I have seen in the county. Nobody could object to these charming dwellings, crouched low like white mice, hiding among a wealth of roses and tall lilies.

Stony Stratford, named after a stone causeway which crossed the Ouse in ancient time, is an old market town and borough on Watling Street. The Roman Watling Street is here the High Street, very busy with traffic which sweeps across the bridge into the county of Northamptonshire. This bridge, built in 1835 to replace a dilapidated bridge which had been harmed in the Civil Wars, has three stone arches and a long raised causeway running through water meadows to raise the road above flood level. I leaned over to look at the water and I saw the lovely river with yellow water-lilies below me, with green flags and reeds, with tossing brown plumes, with water-hens and swans and all the gay array of country river life. I should not have been surprised to see an otter peering up to watch with curiosity the lorries rushing along that bridge. Willows dipped down and a man was gathering hay on to a loaded cart close to the water's edge. In the centre of the bridge was a stone marking the boundary between Buckinghamshire and Northamptonshire. Near the bridge is a corn mill, standing on the site of an old mill.

This pleasant little town has had an eventful and tragic history. It was twice swept by fires, in 1736 when fifty-three houses were destroyed, and six years later when another fire burnt down 113 houses and the church of St Mary Magdalen, with damage assessed at £10,000. Fires were a great danger, and Buckingham and North Marston also suffered badly in the eighteenth century. The church tower was left standing, but the church was not rebuilt.

378

On a house is a sundial set up as a memorial of that first terrible fire, and these words are inscribed on the wall:

Tempus et ignis omnia perdunt
April 17. 1739

Near it is a house with the sign of a currier, and another is a saddler's, with a chamber stacked with leather, cured ready for work, and the pleasant smell coming from it to the road. The town has good old shops and new traditions, and in an ancient little house with a courtyard and old buildings at the back one can buy hot waffles for tea.

In the High Street are two inns, the Cock and the Bull, each with a splendid sign hanging out in a frame of intricate and beautiful ironwork. When I first saw them the sun was shining and the black shadows of the iron on the wall, together with the wrought iron, made a wonderful design. The brilliant cock and the great bull are said to have given rise to the phrase "cock and bull stories." The Cock Inn has a doorway with richly carved posts and lintel. This inn was mentioned in records of 1500.

In the market square there are cottages with shutters at their windows, and some have the old-fashioned double door. Two silver-birch trees wave their graceful boughs in the highway before the cottages, giving delight to all who pass. The church of St Giles, built in 1776, stands here among the houses, with no rail and no churchyard but little greens and pathways, so that it is a part of the community, undivided from everyday life.

Near the market square is Horse Fair Green, and close to this green with its surrounding ring of houses is a Baptist chapel built on the site of one founded in 1656. In it there are oak candlesticks treasured from that early chapel.

Stony Stratford was a place of distinction in days long past, with its bridge over the Ouse and its Watling Street. Here rested the body of Queen Eleanor, and a cross was erected. It was destroyed in the Civil Wars. The town was close to Salcey Forest and it was a hunting centre in the thirteenth century. The most interesting and tragic story is that of the young Prince Edward V and his half-brother, Lord Richard Grey,

379

who slept here on their journey to London in 1483, when Richard was taken prisoner by the Duke of Gloucester. The inn where they lay is the King's Head which stands in the market square.

Shakespeare refers to this incident in *Richard III*: "Last night I heard they lay at Stony Stratford."

In 1516 Margaret of Scotland wrote to her brother, Henry VIII, from here, and he sent letters from Stony Stratford in 1525. He stayed at the town in 1540, probably at the Swan. Stony Stratford was a baiting station, and there were many inns in the sixteenth and seventeenth centuries.

The great industrial town of Wolverton stretches out almost to meet Stony Stratford. There are vast railway repair works here, which employ thousands of men. Also there is the printing works of Messrs McCorquodale, where some of the finest books and magazines and every kind of printing and bookbinding are done.

CHAPTER XXVIII

THE BRICKHILLS

THE three villages collectively called the Brickhills lie on the extreme east of the county on high wooded sandy soil, a region which differs in many ways from the rest of Buckinghamshire. The country is as beautiful as anywhere, with the dark pine woods and the rich red sand. The woods stretch for many miles, with heaths and copses of beech and oak and fir, and wide spaces of rough land.

The river Ousel divides this luxuriously wooded country from the more pastoral land around Wing, Stewkley, and Soulbury, but the great railway centre of Bletchley and the town of Fenny Stratford stretch out their suburbs so that one keeps to the little roads through the woods and the quiet ways by the river.

The giant teazel flowers in the hollows of the river bank near one of the small bridges, and meadowsweet grows thickly in the ditches by the road. There are swans and waterfowl and many birds in the quiet backwaters. For a time the peacefulness of Buckinghamshire is broken by traffic along the main roads, but there is always a by-way, for of all the counties of England this must surely have the greatest number of good little roads, pathways, and lanes.

Near Stoke Hammond there are three locks over the canal which accompanied us from Marsworth. This is the Grand Union Canal, a branch of which passes to Aylesbury. I have a great liking for a canal, and this one is as picturesque as any, with gaily painted canal boats, low white bridges, and locks, and men standing on the banks fishing. There is a traffic of goods carried along this waterway.

The country round Great Brickhill is pastoral land, partly sand and partly clay, with a subsoil of lower greensand, and on the rising ground are pine woods which give it a distinctive quality. The little village green with its three fine sycamore

381

trees has a few cottages and an inn, but the main part of the village is on the hill summit. The cottages are seventeenth-century, with timber and brick walls and roofs of thatch and good little gardens. Slate is coming here to take the place of thatch in some cases.

The thirteenth-century church, which lies at the end of the village, has a central tower with a ring of six bells. The windows are clear glass, and the place is light as air, with trees waving outside. There is a real country atmosphere about this church, which is dedicated to the Nativity of the Blessed Virgin. The south aisle and chapel were built in 1460. There is an original piscina here.

It was neither monument nor brass that attracted me as much as a corn dolly which hung in the vestry. It was wonderfully plaited from many cornstalks, and it shone like polished gold brought from the cornfields to the House of God. The wheat ears made a tassel with twelve heads, and the stalks were plaited in an intricate spiral design of ridges, almost like the furrows of a ploughed field, closely woven together, tapering to a loop by which the emblem of the fruitful earth was suspended. Sometimes this loop is curved stiffly like the end of a shepherd's crook, but this one was tied with straw. The beautiful piece of hand-work was about eighteen inches long.

Every year in this little village a corn dolly is made from the best wheat gathered at a farm, and the dolly is brought to the church for the harvest festival. It is laid near the altar as an offering, a reminder of the Bread of Life. Then it is taken down, its work done. This was the custom in many churches in the old days, but Great Brickhill is the only church where I found this tradition still kept. In Wiltshire and Gloucestershire they are made and hung in the churches.

In many of the Buckinghamshire village churches they have small neat sheaves of corn, a sheaf of barley on one side of the altar, a sheaf of wheat on the other, and a loaf of bread between. The loaf is made in a traditional shape for the village. The wheat is grown locally, threshed and ground at the farm, and made into bread for the church.

There is a small piece of land here called "Bell Rope Piece" which is let yearly, and the rent is divided between ringers and new bell-ropes.

Little Brickhill lies between Great Brickhill on the west and Bow Brickhill on the north. It is perilously situated on Watling Street, the ancient highway which is now a main road with such a weight of traffic that Belisha beacons stand in the village to allow one to cross from one cottage to another. After the quiet of the country lanes around it is almost terrifying to get into this rush of lorries, especially as the village keeps its little old houses and its simplicity.

The Roman station, Magiovintum, was in this parish, and in the eighteenth century this village of Little Brickhill was an important posting station. The assizes were held here, too. It is said that thirty coaches passed through daily. There were many inns, but only one of these old inns has survived. Even their names bring visions of the former bustle and gaiety of this little place; the Hartishorne, the Bear, the Lion, the Black Bull, and the Green Tree are mentioned in many old records. There was a Thursday market with the royal grant of a fair.

The chief industry of Little Brickhill was providing food for the travellers and post-horses for the coaches. Now, alas, all the old glory has gone and the posting town is a village again.

The stone cottages in the long steep street have slate roofs and they have not the charm of many Bucks homes, but the gardens are full of flowers and the fir trees growing on the sandy soil make a beauty of their own.

The twelfth-century church is situated on a rise above the traffic which sweeps below it. There is a finely carved doorway and the chancel is fourteenth-century. There are several great woods stretching almost to Woburn Sands, woods which have been here since the Norman Conquest. Back Wood and Broom-hill's Wood are two of these, with Lady Hills, a tract of moor, and Goose Acre. There were many enclosures of common and waste land in this district in the eighteenth century and earlier. Timothies Close, Turfe Close, and Teggs Close were made into fertile land.

Bow Brickhill is the prettiest of the three villages, and the Wheatsheaf Inn, in the valley by a grassy road, is a little Tudor house with thatched roofs standing under a group of trees.

The main village of whitewashed cottages climbs the steep hill which leads to the church, about 100 feet higher than the houses. We walked up the slopes into the fir woods where the soil is rich golden-red sand lying in soft drifts under one's feet. Rhododendrons, great fir trees, beeches, and oaks grow there in dense green shade. People were having picnics with their children, who had brought buckets and spades as if they were at the seaside. It was indeed like the sea, and one could imagine a great blue ocean lay below in the valley. It was very blue down there and the view from this height was magnificent, but it was the cerulean blue of distance. It all seemed very remote from the rest of Buckinghamshire.

In the woods above the church there is a prehistoric encampment and ditch, and the church is said to be built on the site of an ancient look-out post. It certainly is in a superb position for looking over the country for enemies on foot or in the air.

The church, partly built in the twelfth century, is modernized. Browne Willis, the antiquarian who did so much for the decrepit churches of Bucks, restored the church of Bow Brickhill in 1756 and rebuilt a wall. There are an octagonal font of the fifteenth century with angels around it and a pulpit about the same date. The four bells which ring down the deep valley are old.

Several aged people were struggling up the long hill with flowers for the graves, walking very slowly, stopping to take breath, and I thought it must be very difficult for them to climb to church in wintry weather.

The village of Wavendon, near Bow Brickhill, has a famous pulpit which I went to see. The cottages here are thatched and they are grouped round a green with a pond. The church itself, which has a fifteenth-century tower, has an ancient hollow elm of great size by its gate where one could shelter from a storm. Three iron chains bind the vast body of the tree, and many branches rise from the broken trunk.

The pulpit, which is said to be by Grinling Gibbons, is rich with carved fruit and flowers which hang there in a wealth of beauty. Fir cones and apples, pears and pomegranates, make a

Maids Moreton Church

permanent harvest festival, with little cherubs among them. One babe has wings and wears a bib under his chin. The other has tiny curls and lips open to speak. All the flowers and fruits are different in this work by the greatest of wood craftsmen. The pulpit was carved originally for St Dunstan's, Fleet Street, and many famous men have preached from it.

From the quiet little villages in the fir woods we went to Bletchley and Fenny Stratford, two towns which have joined up in one great district of houses and shops and works. Bletchley has railway works, and it is an important junction which every traveller to Cambridge knows. It was with surprise and delight that I turned out of the streets and traffic to find a bit of a country town left, with orchards and a red-roofed farm and the old church of Bletchley among cottages and fields.

The church, which was built in 1400, has a splendid tower rising above the green churchyard, where are many poplars and a fine avenue of old yew trees. There is a Norman doorway of great beauty of carving, with "beak heads" around it. Each face is different, and it is fascinating to discover the features of these creatures put in the doorway in the enchantment of stone. They have big goblin eyes and long beaked noses. In the centre is the head of a king. Circular carving surrounds them in lovely arcs. Little faces are without it, one of sorrow with downcast eyes and sad mouth, another of joy with round eyes and laughing mouth.

The capitals of the pillars have carved flowers upon them. There is an altar tomb with an alabaster figure of Lord Grey of Wilton. He lies there, his hands a marvel, his finger-nails and rings all perfectly chiselled, his gloves lying by his side, his head resting on a helmet over long-stalked flowers, his feet on a lion with sweeping tail.

Near this monument is a picture in brass, a portrait of Dr Thomas Sparke, rector of this parish in 1616, engraved with much interesting detail. He kneels with his family, and behind the group are the church towers. Opposite stand his congregation of Elizabethan days, a crowd of people in cloaks and hats and full-skirted dresses, all listening to him. Above them are Death with a spade and an angel blowing a trumpet.

2C   385

Ivinghoe Beacon

The choicest of the treasures in this church of good things is the Charles I Bible. It is a great book bound in red velvet and cornered and adorned with silver, engraved with tiny faces, and clasped by two silver hasps. It belonged to the King, whose portrait is within. At the end is the famous engraving of Charles praying, with a crown of thorns, his earthly crowns on the ground. This book was printed in 1638 and presented to the church by Browne Willis in 1710. The print is very clear and very black, and the Bible has the Book of Common Prayer, the Psalms and music, all in one.

The chancel has a painted ceiling of the twelve apostles. Stone corbels hold up the timbers of the high medieval roof of the nave. One is a bearded man and others are queer figures with tiny legs and large open mouths. There is a poor box, mounted on an oak pillar, banded with iron. The words carved upon it are "1637. Remember the Pore."

The windows of this fine church were open wide and the sound of the rustling poplars filled the air with their music. It was fresh and lovely with splendid roofs and doors. One door had a gigantic key. I was sorry to leave this place with its atmosphere of peace and beauty, and I stood for a long time looking at the great tower against the white cumulus clouds in an intensely blue sky. A queer gargoyle like a large pig leaned down and grinned from the grey stones. Bletchley is a surprising mixture of old and new, a modern town round the railway, and this little village with its rectory cottages, its farms, and Bletchley Park.

Fenny Stratford, its busy neighbour, is on Watling Street. At the cross-roads of Watling Street and Aylesbury Street stands an eighteenth-century red brick church where Browne Willis the antiquary was buried. A sermon is preached here every St Martin's Day, when two little cannon, "Fenny Poppers," are fired in memory of Browne Willis's grandfather, a surgeon who lived in St Martin's Lane, London. Browne Willis owned estates at Bletchley, but through his many charities and church rebuilding he lost most of his fortune. He rebuilt this church of St Martin's as a memorial to his grandfather.

The long bridge over the Ousel at Fenny Stratford was built on the site of former bridges, for this has always been an important place between London and the north-west. It is a fine bridge with three arches and a long causeway. Fairs and markets were granted to the town even in the thirteenth century and revised at later dates. Now there is a cattle market every fortnight, and fairs are held twice a year.

Fenny Stratford suffered much in the Civil Wars, when troops were quartered in the town in 1644. Later it was visited by the plague and so many died the road was closed and traffic diverted. There was a centre here for lace-making and straw-plaiting, but these crafts have died out through the introduction of machinery and imported straw. Now the prosperity of the town is renewed by the railway works at Bletchley and by several factories. Brushes are made at Fenny Stratford and there are timber works.

Near the church I saw a lorry laden with brand-new wheelbarrows made in Fenny Stratford down by the river, so, as I love a wheelbarrow, I went to see this good factory belonging to Messrs Rowland Brothers. There in the wooden buildings we saw great trees sliced in longitudinal sections, the trunks moving slowly along as the machinery cut into them. We watched these long slices cut again by different machines to make the parts needed for gates and handcarts and the different kinds of wheelbarrows needed by navvies, by builders, roadmen, farmers, as well as the gardener.

Wheels were made, some of them with iron spindles which came from a foundry and some with wooden felloes which men were fashioning. I stayed to look at the wheelbarrows being assembled and strongly built. There was a yard with piles of timber seasoning, and many whole trees lay there. English oak, ash, elm, wych-elm are used for this work, but there was some imported timber.

I liked the great elm beetles which we could hardly lift, and the "dobbin carts" of oak and ash framing and sturdy bodies of elm. Ladders are made here and wood is turned for many purposes. They were working at a big contract for a kind of fencing needed on modern housing estates, and other work was held up till this was finished.

At Messrs Rowland's works the sawdust is used for fuel and

made into gas fuel, so that they are self-supporting and independent of the vagaries of supply.

I was interested in the strange articles found in the interiors of trees, embedded deep in the wood. There was a horseshoe which was found in the heart of a great oak tree, a shoe that was perhaps hung up on a young tree centuries ago. Many stones are found and great nails and hooks of another age, all of them objects which once dangled on the tree while the bark grew around them and they gradually entered the tree's body. There was a museum of these things which have been discovered. Unfortunately they often break the saw which cuts the trunk in slices. We went into a room kept for mending the long band saws which have been harmed in this way.

At Newport Pagnell there is the large motor works of Tickford Ltd., who are motor-car body builders. This firm were builders of coaches in the old coaching days, and now they have switched over to modern coachwork. Many of the men of the district are employed here.

The road from Fenny Stratford to Newport Pagnell follows the line of canal and river, sometimes running between them, so that we looked to right and to left at these waterways with their own particular life. We visited the village of Simpson with its church at the roadside, and then Woughton-on-the-Green with its large green like a field, with cattle grazing there and a farm beyond and gates enclosing it. Willen Church, a dark-red brick building which was built by Busby, the headmaster of Winchester, in the seventeenth century, holds up its little tower in the trees, and the unfortunate vicarage, which had just been burned out, stands at the side of the road.

Newport Pagnell is an ancient town mentioned in the Domesday Book as Newport, and Pagnell is the name of the owners of the manor in the twelfth century. The two rivers, the Ouse and the Lovat, flow past and the Lovat divides the town.

The High Street, which is very wide, is intersected by St John's Street which crosses the Lovat at Tickford Bridge and now becomes Tickford Street. The Northampton road crosses the Ouse by the North Bridge, built of stone. There were bridges over the rivers at these places in the early years of the town's history, and the cost of their repair was a heavy burden on the town.

The broad High Street was the market-place and the monks of Tickford Abbey could buy and sell there, free from toll. Stalls were erected in front of the houses and shops on market days and fair days for centuries, and gloves, poultry, and meat were sold. There were many inns, as the town was a thorough-fare with its two bridges crossing the rivers. The Swan, which has a seventeenth-century staircase, is mentioned in 1543.

Near Tickford Bridge there was once the Hospital of St John the Baptist, founded in 1240, and built again as Queen Anne's Hospital in 1650. The Queen Anne is Anne of Denmark, wife of James I. In the present building, rebuilt 1891, is a beam with the following words painted on it, a relic of the 1650 structure:

"Alyou good Chrystianes that heere dooe pas by give soome thynge to thes poore people that in St John's Hospital doeth ly. Anno 1615."

There is a house in St John's Street with an inscription out-side saying, "This house belongeth to Queen Ann's Hospital and was rebuilt by Madam Tasker, a citizen of St Giles, Cripplegate, London, Anno Dom. 1690."

The church is a magnificent building with embattled and pinnacled tower and large churchyard which looks over the river Lovat to the country. It stands in the centre of the town near the busy road junction with houses close to it. The porch of the fourteenth century has a vaulted roof and a priest's room above it. The second porch has its roof resting on corbels.

By the chancel arch, on the narrow turret doorway, is nailed a large brass portrait of a man of 1440. I was interested in a little man who was gazing at it. He shuffled rapidly round the church, his bright eyes shining with excitement as if he saw invisible things. He danced from one thing to another, looking upon them with the deepest affection and joy. Together we searched for parts of Bunyan's pulpit which was supposed to be there, and he told me he knew every church for many miles. All his spare time he cycled alone exploring and discovering for himself. Newport Pagnell Church was his well-loved home and he knew intimately all its history. He loved the county of Buckinghamshire with a deep love, a fanatical love, which pleased me.

CHAPTER XXIX

BUCKINGHAMSHIRE WORDS
AND SAYINGS

BEACONSFIELD Cattle Fair was held on February 14th or
15th. There was a local saying in connection with this fair:
"If the sun shines before twelve o'clock on Fair Day, the
winter's not half over."

February 14th was Candlemas Day, old style, and there is
a well-known country rhyme for that day which seems to be
the source of the above saying:

> If Candlemas Day be fair and bright,
> Winter will have another flight,
> But if Candlemas Day be clouds and rain,
> Winter is gone and will not come again.
>
> If Candlemas Day be mild and gay,
> Go saddle your horses and buy them hay.
> If Candlemas Day be stormy and black,
> It carries the winter away on its back.

Another Bucks rhyme used by countrymen is:

> If the calends of Februar' be smiling and gay,
> You'll have wintry weather till the calends of May.

It is interesting to notice the use of the word calends.

The fourth Sunday in Lent is Mothering Sunday. It was the
day when scattered children, away in service or married, returned
to visit the lonely mother with a small gift. The children of the
present day in some villages give their mothers flowers, or they
prick with a pin the following rhyme on paper:

> Mothering Sunday's come again
> We go a-mothering down the lane,
> The sweetest flower of all the spring,
> Mother dear, to thee we bring.

A child at Forty Green, Beaconsfield, pricked this for her
390

mother and gave it with a bunch of wild flowers, primroses and the first violets, set in a paper-cut frill.

Jack Norris always warns me in May of the number of frosts that will come.

"As many mistises in March,
So many frostises in May,"

says he. All through March he counts the misty days and notes them in his pocket-book. He says the days of frosts in May correspond with the dates of these mists.

"There'll be fourteen frostises this May, so you'd best be careful and put some newspaper on your apple blossom," he warns me, as he stands by my gate.

"When will they come?" I ask, as if he had private information from heaven itself.

He tells me, and adds "especially bad on the 14th, the 16th, 20th, 22nd, and 24th."

It was true, we had frosts on all those dates and I covered my tender plants with cloches and put newspapers on my little trees.

The blacksmith at Terrick, Ellesborough, gave this rhyme for weather to the Rev. C. White:

March will search,
And April will try,
And May will tell whether you live or die.

Another Ellesborough man says, "There are twelve cold days in May." This accords with the old saying, "Expect no summer before the 13th of May."

The Bucks superstitions about the moon are those which are current throughout England in all country places.

The moon lying on her back is the sign of dirty weather, a well-recognized portent.

Children's hair was cut at the new moon and never cut when the moon was on the wane, for everything grows with the moon. As soon as the moon began to increase a mother said, "It's time you had your hair cut. The moon's new."

In Bucks they speak of the moon being on the waste when

the moon is waning. They never say waxing moon, but the growing moon. A new moon first seen on the right hand brings good fortune. When it is on the left hand there will be "ups and downs" that month.

That it is unlucky to see the new moon through glass is a very common belief in all parts of the country.

A farmer in South Bucks complained to me about a cornfield which was full of thistles and the crops had failed. It had been taken over from him and sown at the wrong time, against his judgment.

"Sow dry and plant wet," said he. "They went and sowed in soggy wet land."

He spoke of a record crop he had had, in the year 1945, when farmers rejoiced over the crops.

"The most wonderful corn crop we've had for thirty years, and we knew it was coming. For why? Because we had snow, thunder, lightning, and hail in January. That's the sure sign of a big crop of corn," said he. "My father before me said the same. Thunder and lightning in January, and grand crops of corn to follow."

Some villages are the sources of humour. Haddenham has many jokes told about it. It is a long straggling village with three village greens, a lovely place with little roofs to its cream wichert walls. A Haddenham woman tells me she is always teased when people hear where she comes from. They say the pond has a thatched wall to keep the ducks dry at Haddenham. They say Haddenham people put a foot out of the window to see if it is raining. It is good-humoured joking and real country wit.

Hedgerley too has a few local jokes, one of which about the treacle-well I have given elsewhere.

"Where are you going?" asks a too inquisitive person.

"Down to Hedgerley to see the boat race," is the answer from one who does not wish to give a direct reply.

In the north I have heard a more abrupt reply to the curious: "Where art thou going?" "To follow my nose," is the answer.

An old Bucks man sang this short and expressive song to me. a song which has a deep philosophy in it, and a joke.

392

BUCKINGHAMSHIRE

Here we suffer grief and pain,
Near the hills they do the same.
So they do next-door.

I heard the following song in both North and South Bucks,
sung to a plaintive and lovely air which ought to be preserved.
It was sung by an old man to E. Lambourne of North Marston,
and Jack Norris of Beaconsfield told me it was what they sang
when they "went mummering." It has a Shakespearian melancholy.

We will wear the weeping willow,
For a twelvemonth and a day.
And if anyone should ask
The reason why I wear it,
Tell them my true love
Is gone far away.

The famous "Prickly-lie Bush" was sung at North Marston
by an old man lately and recorded by E. Lambourne, who also
heard it at a jovial meeting in another village. This is a delightful
song, with a good chorus which all the old men know.

THE PRICKLY-LIE BUSH

CHORUS: Oh, the Prickly-lie Bush, the Prickly-lie Bush,
It grieves my heart full sore,
And if ever I get out of the Prickly-lie Bush
I'll never get in any more.

YOUTH: Oh father, dear father,
Have you any gold or silver in your pocket,
Or any bright money to set me free?

FATHER: I have no gold for thee,
Nor any bright money to set thee free,
To save thy body from the cold clay grave,
And thy neck from the high gallows-tree.

CHORUS: Oh, the Prickly-lie Bush, the Prickly-lie Bush,
It grieves my heart full sore,
And if ever I get out of the Prickly-lie Bush,
I'll never get in any more.

393

YOUTH: Oh mother, dear mother,
        Have you any gold or silver in your pocket,
        Or any bright money to set me free?

MOTHER: I have no gold for thee,
        Nor any bright money to set thee free,
        To save thy body from the cold clay grave,
        And thy neck from the high gallows-tree.

CHORUS: Oh, the Prickly-lie Bush, the Prickly-lie Bush,
        etc.

YOUTH: Oh brother, dear brother,
        Have you any gold or silver in your pocket,
        Or any bright money to set me free?

BROTHER: I have no gold for thee,
        Nor any bright money to set thee free.
        To save thy body from the cold clay grave,
        And thy neck from the high gallows-tree.

CHORUS: Oh, the Prickly-lie Bush, the Prickly-lie Bush,
        etc.

YOUTH: Oh sister, dear sister,
        Have you any gold or silver in your pocket,
        Or any bright money to set me free?

SISTER: I have no gold for thee,
        Nor any bright money to set thee free,
        To save thy body from the cold clay grave,
        And thy neck from the high gallows-tree.

CHORUS: Oh, the Prickly-lie Bush, the Prickly-lie Bush,
        etc.

YOUTH: Oh sweetheart, dear sweetheart,
        Have you any gold or silver in your pocket,
        Or any bright money to set me free?

SWEETHEART: I have some gold for thee,
        And some bright money to set thee free,
        To save thy body from the cold clay grave,
        And thy neck from the high gallows-tree.

CHORUS: Oh, the Prickly-lie Bush, the Prickly-lie Bush,
        It grieves my heart full sore,
        And when I get out of the Prickly-lie Bush,
        I'll never get in any more.

An Ellesborough man told of the following "rough music" which was sung by all who took part in the act of primitive justice in a village in 1885.

The Town Crier rang his bell and proclaimed:

Oh yez! Oh yez! Oh yez!
This is to give notice
There is a man all in this place,
He's done a thing which is disgrace.
He's whacked his wife both black and blue,
And that's the cause of this hulloo.
Although we wish this man no harm,
The people say we must alarm,
To let him know for the time to come,
To do with one big band and drum.

All taking part walked to and fro in front of the house where the offender lived, beating cans and tins for three nights. The third night they burned the effigy which had been carried round the village.

I was told of another case of "rough music" by an old man who once took part in it. This was no case of wife-beating or infidelity, but a sense of injustice which roused the villagers to take the law into their own hands. The rector used to go to the cottages at dinner-time, it was said, to look at the tables set for the meals. The prodigality of the village people shocked him, and he complained that the poor lived too well. This incensed the people and many left the church and went to chapel.

One summer the squire proposed to give a treat to all the children. The rector called on him and demurred.

"I hear your lordship is going to give a treat to all the children in the town," said the rector. "The chapel children have had a treat already, and I want you to give it only to the church."

The news spread like wildfire, and the irate villagers cried, "We'll rough music him. We'll give him rough music."

They collected their musical instruments and serenaded the rector. My informant, who was a young man at the time, carried a tin can with two big stones inside which he rattled.

395

They had tin trays and drums and whistles. They marched up and down the road by the rectory gates playing their uncouth music, as rough as music could be, to show their displeasure. The town crier, Bob, rang his bell and called, "Oh yez! Oh yez! Oh yez! This is to give notice," and the "proclamation" was made.

The two policemen marched up and down but they could do nothing, for the crowd of a hundred people with their music also marched up and down to be within the law, continually moving.

Then the squire drove up in his carriage and pair, but the horses shied and refused to pass. He called the police but they had no control.

"Is there nobody who can make them move away?" he asked

"There's one man they will listen to," returned the police, and straightway they fetched the minister, who consulted with the squire. He held up his hand and spoke to them, and the old man remembered his words very clearly.

"Please! Please! All you good people," he cried. "I've just heard from the squire that if you go quietly home the feast will be given to all the children, whoever they are."

So they cheered and went away home.

"As for the rector," said the old man, "he left soon after, and the people gave him no present, but they gave the curate a grand present, just to show the difference."

A lovely little song which an old man of North Bucks used to sing in his youth was given by Mr Jesse Flitney of Chalkshire, Ellesborough:

The lark in the morning when it rises from its nest
It mounts in the air with the dew upon its breast.
Around the jolly ploughman it whistles and it sings
And at night it returns to its old nest again.

"Do you know that a lark faces the wind when it rises?" said a countryman to me the other day. "It always runs to its nest. It never drops by it, lest folk should see."

I hear quite a lot of animal and bird folk-lore which is current in Bucks among the country people.

"A bird often goes with the cuckoo and sometimes he feeds it," said an old friend. "We call it the 'cuckoo's mate.' It's about the size of a thrush. You can see it flying after the cuckoo, and it warns it and is its friend. I've seen it many a time."

I could not discover this mate of the cuckoo, although I heard of it from other Bucks countrymen as well as from Irishmen. Then I came across a reference to it in an old book of folk-lore. It is the wryneck (*Junx torquilla*), which is called in some parts the "cuckoo's maiden."

Tales of foxes and their cunning I heard, and rats and weasels, all from close observation.

Mr Becket of Ellesborough gave these calls of the ploughman which he used when he was a ploughboy.

"Gee up" is go forward.

"Come hither" is turn to the left.

"Gee wut" is turn to the right.

The word "woot," or "wut," is spoken to the last horse when turning.

It is interesting to compare these calls with those used in Derbyshire when ploughing.

"Gee up" or "Gee hup" is go forward, for great exertion when a horse is heaving a heavy load up a steep hill.

"Arve" or "Orve" is turn to the left, a long-drawn-out word which I have often heard rolling through the air like a song.

"Gee back" is turn to the right.

The song for November 5th, as sung by a North Bucks countryman, goes like this:

> Remember, remember the fifth of November.
> Gunpowder treason and plot.
> I don't see no reason why gunpowder treason
> Should ever be forgot.
> A stick and a stake for King George's sake.
> If you don't give me one I'll take two.
> To rickety racket your door will go.

As Gayhurst in North Bucks was intimately connected with the plot this rhyme probably had significance.

A song sung at North Marston a hundred years ago by the

hawkers selling brooms in the villages and remembered by a very old woman is this:

Come all you fair ladies,
Come buy a broom.
A large one for a lady,
A small one for a baby,
So come my good lady,
Come buy a broom.

I believe these broom-sellers came from Holland and Flanders, mostly women neatly dressed in bonnets and dark dresses with aprons.

I have always been interested in country words and many of those used in Buckinghamshire are those I heard in my own north-country childhood. This is natural enough, for they are the language of the country people throughout England, and many are the old original words of ancient lineage, while the words used by more polite society are the upstarts. It is difficult to separate words into their counties and the same expression may be used in Buckinghamshire, Yorkshire, and Dorset.

In thatching, for instance, the worker who draws the straw into bundles ready for the thatcher on the stack is "yelming" it. The bundles are called "yelms" or "yellums," and the evenness of the yelms determines the smoothness and perfection of the work. In seventeenth-century records of Bucks a "yellmer" got 2d a day with meat and drink.

In the cornfields the sheaves are put into shocks, whereas we use stooks in the north. Men go "shocking" in Buckinghamshire.

In hedge-layering the upright stakes knocked into the ground are bound by twisting the branches through them like weaving. Willow and ash shoots are the most supple, and when woven they make an impenetrable fence. The work is finished off by twining in the top briars and willow to edge it. This is called "eddering" or "heathering." The hedges look like a piece of embroidery binding the hems of the fields.

"She is going a-flowering" is a lovely expression for gathering flowers.

A flower has a masculine gender. "I don't rightly know his name, but I've seen him before," said a woman when I showed her an uncommon flower. Likewise a tree is masculine. "Cut him down," they say.

The lesser striped convolvulus, whose candy stripes of pink and white bells shine in the wayside grass, is called the bell-wind.

The greater knapweed is called a paint-brush.

The greater stitchwort is shirt-buttons.

For wood-sorrel the name cuckoo-flower is used; in other counties allelulia, and I remember the name wood-sour too.

The lady's-smock is called milkmaids.

The toad-flax is known as wild snapdragon.

The dog-daisy, or marguerite, is called horse-daisy.

For goose-grass the name is sweethearts, a name we gave to briars.

Bladder-campion is cow-rattle, for the seed-box is like a rattle.

Herb Robert is soldier's-button.

Quaking grass or trembling grass is wag-wanton, another delightful name.

Marsh marigolds are butter-clocks.

All these names were given to me by a country child who used them regularly.

Blow is used for bloom, especially apple-blow.

The hornbeam is called the ay-beech.

Lattermuth is the second growth of a crop.

Lattern fruit is late fruit—a late variety of apples, for example. I often hear this expression.

"We'll soon be seeing the brown, madam. The two loveliest times of the year are the bud and the brown," said a Bucks woodman to me one September.

The green woodpecker, which is common in Bucks so that I often have three or four on my lawn close to the windows, is called the wetile.

"That's an old wetile. It's going to rain," say the country people when they hear the green woodpecker laughing or calling. It is the rain bird, and I have noticed it usually rains when the wetile laughs.

399

The word "stail," used for the long handle of a besom or hayrake, fork or hoe, is general throughout England. This old English word supplies a want, and ought not to be lost.

To "bunt" is to attack with the head as a ram attacks. This also is a well-known word and not purely local.

"Okkard" means obstinate, a meaning in use for centuries in country England. A cow who will not go into her stall for milking is "okkard." A woman who won't see reason is "okkard." "As okkard as a little pig."

"Accle" means to fit, or to work in correctly. A woman making a dress might say in despair "It won't accle," meaning the parts will not fit. It is a word used mainly in connection with mending, making, or repairing.

"Aggle" means to be vexed or irritated. "The children came in, the house was upset, and I was fair aggled."

"Dilling" is the smallest pig in a litter, the Anthony as it is called in some parts.

"It's a funny thing, but the dilling always does the best. It pushes its way in somewhere," said a countryman to me.

"Garm" is to besmear or to clog. "Shoes all garmed up" they say.

"Over-right" is opposite. "He's bound to be over-right that hedge."

"Pimmocky" is dainty over food, picking at it, and the word is used for animals as well as human beings.

To "shut in" is to put the horse in the cart ready for a journey or for work.

To "shut out" is to unharness.

The "mullin" is the bridle of a cart-horse.

The "backbun" is the strap over a horse's back to hold the chains.

"Slummacky" is untidy.

"Unkid" is uncouth, strange, and solitary. A wood can be unkid, meaning a place of fear.

A "pitch" is a slope, as distinct from a hill. "Going up the little pitch" they say of an incline.

A snail is an "oddy-doddy." The hod is a basket, a shell, or a case. Doddy is a rhyming addition, also meaning a snail—dodman.

"I saw a lot of oddy-doddies in the garden," said a woman to me.

"A dish of tea" is often used for a cup of tea. Men always drank from a basin, brightly coloured or striped blue and white, and never from a cup which would not hold enough. Each man had his own and no other, and they were all different. We had these many-coloured basins for men's use in the fields and in the house.

"This bit long" means a certain length.

On the subject of a new mackintosh an old man told me that he had seen one in a shop, and, "I said to myself, that's just my nib. That's just my stamp." So he bought it.

A child who ate well was called "a little trencher."

"Nowadays all they think about is besting one another," said my old friendly sadly, comparing present time to past.

"Leasing" is gleaning.

"Routed" means to stir about or move by force.

"Wichert" is white earth, used when mixed with straw for making houses. Haddenham wichert is supposed to be the best for this purpose.

"To farm out" is to clear out or to tidy. "It's time we farmed out the pond" means to remove the rubbish from the pond.

"You must farm out my chest of drawers," means to tidy it.

"Scummerous" is abashed.

"Shambles" go round the sides of carts, and at back and front are the "ladders," "tail ladder" and "fore ladder," where we used "wraithes," "frontboard," and "tailboard."

An expression I like is "It's a cunning piece of work" for a clever piece of craftsmanship, used in admiration.

"Have a longer tarry with us" is another felicitous expression which always pleases me.

"Housen" is still used in Bucks even by little children in a modern village school.

An expression of surprise is "Lawks-a-mussy-ay-do."

Another portmanteau word is "insiderouter." "You've got your frock on insiderouter," said an old man to his daughter.

Often the country word is the same but the pronunciation is broader.

Ewes are called "yowes," but it is the same word.

Sheep are "ship"—compare the pun on Shipwash at Hambleden.

"Disannul" means to be put about, worried.

"Dra'ter" is a contraction of drawer-towel, the cloth used by lace-makers to draw over the lace when the pillow is put away.

"Mawkin" is a mop for cleaning the long bread oven.

A "bist" is a screw of paper or a tiny parcel. A bist of pepper or tea is the small twisted paper of these things which workmen carry with them.

"Stoan and pindle." A man at Oving described his cottage as "built of stoan and pindle." Pindle means the smaller stones collected from the stone-pits.

An "emmet" is an ant, as in Shakespeare.

"Hommocksing" means trudging, walking slowly. "He was hommocksing over the fields."

"Nackered" means "done up." "I was nackered when I got home."

"Brevet," another word meaning worried. "He's breveting about something," or "He's on the brevet to get back." Words used in North Marston.

"I'm sick and sated" is a good expression which also I heard at North Marston, the home of many dialect words because it has changed so little.

"Athirt" is used for athwart. "It's athirt the garden."

"Athirt overender" is an expression for "over there."

This word was used recently by the old sexton to the vicar as they stood together in the graveyard. The old man said he used to dig graves at Monks Risborough and he came across bodies or skeletons "athirt t'others."

While this sexton was digging a grave a few weeks ago he pointed to a vacant space with his shovel and said, "Old Ted wawnts t' come 'ere."

Then he continued, pointing to the next grave, "Tha's 'is missus. 'E wawnts t' come nigh 'er."

"Will there be room?" asked the vicar.

"Aw ah!" he replied. "We can get 'im in there somehow, 'cos 'e ain't very tall."

Old Ted is in the best of health and much younger than the gravedigger, but the ancient sexton is eternal.

"A mound" is a fence or rail and this word is very old. "Shall I come and mend your mound?" said a labourer to a friend of mine, referring to his garden fence.

In the parish registers of Ellesborough the word is used.

"1829. Paid for the churchyard mound. £1-2-6.
1835. Oak posts for churchyard mound. 6-0."

This word mound, well known among country people, was supposed by the educated to refer to a tumulus, or to a mound no longer in existence, until the real meaning was remembered.

How intimate are these old church registers! The personal descriptions of the people are entered—a wheelwright, a yeoman, a widow, a goodwife.

In the churchwardens' accounts for Ellesborough Church in 1723 a bricklayer and another head workman received 2s 3d a day each, while a labourer was paid 1s 2d. In 1821 a bricklayer received 3s a day, and the labourer 1s 8d. In 1826 a hundredweight of coal cost 1s 11d and four years later it was 2s 6d. The carriage was 3s, which made the price very high.

I like the names of some of the country people of those days:

1674. Dammaris Gomme (both mother and daughter).
1683. Anastase Wade.
1690. Rabbina Neighbor.
1704. Packington Neighbor, yeoman.
1693. Avice Reynolds.
1711. Keren-happuch, daughter of Robert Rance of Wendover.
1721. Pleasant Bruce.
1789. Zilpha Hollan.

There are two interesting entries in the baptismal register:

"1724. A tawny youth from the Indies, baptiz'd Benjamin, first by me examined and desired of me Christian baptism, his syrname is Sinolary.

"1788. Plato, son of Anne Hearne, a travelling gypsie; born at Buskey Lees,—illegitimate."

Chapter XXX

THE MUMMING PLAY

I met Jack Norris one winter's day and we stood by the eighteenth-century houses in the broad Beaconsfield street talking of this and that. His fingers were bent over the handle of his walking-stick, he leaned towards me with his rosy old face wreathed in smiles.

"D'ye see that cottage over yonder? Just by it, up the entry, there used to be a little school where I learned my lessons. They taught lace-making there in those days."

I looked across at the tiny old red brick cottage where he and the village children went to school with a dame to teach them.

I asked if he had ever acted in a mumming play, and his face lighted up with the remembrance of it. Indeed he had! He had been dressed up with a lot of others and they had gone all round the public-houses in many a village, singing and acting their play. They began about ten days before Christmas and gave performances every night. They walked miles to give the mumming play.

> "In comes I,
> As light as a Fly.
> I've got no money,
> And what cares I?"

he chanted, and then he laughed with glee at the memory. We stood there, on the pavement, with the cars rushing past and the Army lorries swinging round the green circle, and shoppers hurrying to the grocer's and the fish shop and the bow-windowed chemist's, and he told me of other days, evoking the past so that I felt that these people around us were phantoms of the future.

"There's one as went a-mumming with me," he cried, pointing with his stick across the wide street. Up the road, under the shadow of the black and white timbered Saracen's Head, came a bent old man wearing a greatcoat, stumbling along with his staff. He might have been brought from another era of time, he

404

looked like Father Time himself as he moved along, unconscious of our gaze. We stood and watched him as he rounded the corner with the painted Saracen above him, as he walked with tottering steps past the courtyard entrance, past many windows, towards the little cottages.

"And there's another as went with us," cried my companion, and we saw a second figure come up the long road and wander past the Saracen's Head. I felt we were conjuring up something from the deep past; I felt that in another moment snow would fall and a coach and four would clatter up the Wycombe End from Oxford, and cloaked and hooded figures would descend at the door of the famous hostelry. The ostler would run out, the stable doors would open, fresh horses would be led into the yard, and the heavily cloaked coachman would perhaps wind his long horn. I thought that the band of mummers would come round the corner of the Saracen's Head, dressed in their motley, with ribbons fluttering and drums beating and pipe playing, and children running after.

"I'll come and act the play for you, ma'am, if you like," said the old man. "I remembers it all." So it was agreed.

Every year the mummers went round the villages at Christmas time, acting their play. In many counties there were different versions of the mumming play, but probably each parish varied the play to suit the actors. The simple plot of the play, which was the same throughout the whole of England, showed that it had a common origin. There was a fight between two characters, one of whom was a soldier. A man was "slain," and the doctor was called in. The slain man was miraculously cured with a bottle or a pill. I remember a version we acted in our home when we were children, where the doctor held out a black bottle to the fallen St George, saying:

> "Take a little out of my bottle,
> And pour it down thy throttle,
> Then rise up, Bold Slasher,
> And fight again,"

and we draped antimacassars around our heads and fought again.

All the characters vary. Sometimes there is St George, or the

Duke of Cumberland, or King George. There are soldiers and odd strange people to give a part to many. A man dressed up as a woman was an integral part of this mumming play. All the faces were blacked for disguise. The costumes were of the simplest kind: a top hat, a soldier's helmet, cut paper frills and streamers pinned to jackets and waistcoats, dangling ribbons of bright colours. The swords borne by the fighters were wooden laths with cross-pieces or walking-sticks, and sometimes a real sword.

The characters were announced by one of the actors who entered first. So Jack Norris acted the play for me, and I wrote down his words as he declaimed them and sang them, and laughed over them. He came knocking at my door, and I opened it as if I lived at the inn. He hobbled in and did his part most valiantly.

This is the version of the play which was acted at Beaconsfield and Wooburn and neighbouring villages. Many hamlets were visited, and they finished up at Wooburn Green.

The mummers stood outside the door of the inn and one character, Hi Down Derry, knocked loudly and pushed the door open and called:

"Please remember the mummers!"

This warned the company that a performance was about to take place, and the people at the inn prepared for the mummers.

Hi Down Derry now enters with a broom in his hand, with which he sweeps the people back and makes an open space while he chants:

"Room, room, for me and my broom,
Hi Down Derry! Hi Down Derry! Hi Down Derry!
I come round this Christmas time
To make you merry."

[*He sweeps vigorously at the legs of the people, and then goes to the door and beckons to* FLY.]

Come in, Jack Fly.

[*Enter* FLY.]

FLY: In comes I,
    As light as a Fly;

406

Got no money
And what cares I? [*Dances round the room.*]

HI DOWN DERRY [*calling at the door*]: Come in, King George.

[*Enter* KING GEORGE, *wearing soldier's red coat, wooden sword in hand and helmet on head. He walks up and down with martial step.*]

KING GEORGE: In comes King George with noble eye,
    With his broad sword in his hand.
    Where is the man that bids me stand?
    I'll knock him down with my gracious hand.
    Mince-pies hot, mince-pies cold,
    Bound to lay him down before he's three days
     old.
    Send him to the cookhouse for all untold.

HI DOWN DERRY [*calling at the door*]: Come in, jolly valiant soldier.

[*Enter* SOLDIER.]

SOLDIER: In comes this jolly valiant soldier.
    Where is the man that bids me stand
    And knock me down with his gracious hand?
    I'm your man! I'm your man!
    A battle! A battle! Betwixt you and I
    To see which on the ground shall lie.
    If I should happen to gain the day
    On the ground you first shall lay.
    So mind your head, and guard your blows,
    Or else you'll get a tap on the nose.

[*They fight a hard battle and the* KING *falls to the ground.* HI DOWN DERRY *now calls for the* DOCTOR, *who is outside.*]

HI DOWN DERRY: Five pounds would I give for a doctor,
    If a doctor was but here.

DOCTOR [*from without*]: The doctor won't come for five pounds.

HI DOWN DERRY: Ten pounds would I give for a doctor,
    If a doctor was but here.

DOCTOR [*from without*]: No! The doctor won't come for ten pounds.

HI DOWN DERRY [*shouting*]: Fifteen pounds.

DOCTOR: No. The doctor won't come for fifteen pounds.

HI DOWN DERRY [*bawling*]: Twenty pounds I give.

DOCTOR [*without*]: The doctor will come for twenty pounds.

HI DOWN DERRY: Come in this noble valiant doctor,
Come in for twenty pounds.

[DOCTOR *enters, wearing a black coat and carrying a little black bag. He walks about, tapping loudly with his stick.*]

DOCTOR: In comes the noble and jolly doctor!
I'm doctor here, I'm doctor there,
I'm doctor everywhere!
I don't go about like you shim-sham doctors,
I go about to cure, not to kill.

HI DOWN DERRY: Cure this man, doctor.

DOCTOR: I will if he isn't quite dead.

HI DOWN DERRY: What can you cure?

DOCTOR: The hipsy, pipsy, palsy, and the gout,
Pains within and pains without.
Bring me an old woman that's been dead ten years,
In her coffin twenty, and buried thirty.
If she has a sound hollow tooth in her head
I'm bound to fetch her round.
George, George, you have been to France, I've been
to Spain,
Take one of these pills, and rise and fight again.

[*He rattles some peas in a box, gives one to* KING GEORGE. *He feels him over, and the* KING *kicks and wriggles, with great laughter from the onlookers, and rises.*]

SOLDIER: We've had a ring, we've had a right,
And now we'll have a jolly good fight.

[*They fight, and this time the* SOLDIER *falls. The* DOCTOR *goes out while they are fighting.*]

HI DOWN DERRY [*calling at door*]: Come in, Jack Finny!

[*Enter* JACK FINNY, *who is really the* DOCTOR.]

JACK FINNY: How dare you call me Jack Finny?
My name is Mr Finny, otherwise John Finny.
I can do more than you or any other man.

HI DOWN DERRY: What can you do?

JACK FINNY: Cure a magpie of the toothache,
And a jackdaw of the headache.

HI DOWN DERRY: How do you do that?

JACK FINNY: Wring off his head and throw his body in the
ditch.

HI DOWN DERRY: Cure this man.

JACK FINNY: I can cure this man if he is not quite dead.
He is dead and stiff, by the spring of his legs.

[*Touches him and the leg jerks up.*]

But this is a case I've seen before.
Take one of these pills, and rise and fight no more.
Take one of these pills,
It'll work you through and through.
Body, soul, and stomach too.
Rise up, this jolly valiant soldier,
And fight this man no more.

[SOLDIER *rises.*]

HI DOWN DERRY [*calling*]: Come in, Big Head.

[BIG HEAD *enters, his head enlarged by a great hat or some
device.*]

BIG HEAD: In comes I, as ain't been yet,
With my big head and little wit.
My head's so big, my wit so small,
But I'll sing you a song that will please you all.

He sings a popular song, and other songs follow for the rest
of the evening.

We will wear the weeping willow
For a twelvemonth and a day.
And if anyone should ask
The reason why I wear it,
Tell them my true love
Is gone far away.

REFERENCE BOOKS

A History of the County of Buckingham (Victoria County History). Vols. 1, 3 and 4.

Royal Commission on Historical Monuments in Buckinghamshire. Vols. 1 and 2.

The County of Buckingham (Lipscombe). Four volumes.

Memoirs of the Verney Family during the Civil War, Frances Parthenope Verney.

The Penn Country and the Chilterns, R. Richardson and Charles Bathurst.

The Buckinghamshire Miscellany, R. Gibbs.

The Progressions and Public Processions of Queen Elizabeth, John Nichols. Four volumes, 1788-1821.

Transactions of the Buckinghamshire Archæological Society.

INDEX

INDEX